The politics of economic decline

*Economic management and
political behaviour in Britain since 1964*

The politics of economic decline

Economic management and political behaviour in Britain since 1964

JAMES E. ALT

*Associate Professor of Political Science,
Washington University, St Louis*

CAMBRIDGE UNIVERSITY PRESS

CAMBRIDGE

LONDON · NEW YORK · MELBOURNE

Published by the Syndics of the Cambridge University Press
The Pitt Building, Trumpington Street, Cambridge CB2 1RP
Bentley House, 200 Euston Road, London NW1 2DB
32 East 57th Street, New York, NY 10022, USA
296 Beaconsfield Parade, Middle Park, Melbourne 3206, Australia

First published 1979

Printed in Great Britain at the University Press, Cambridge

Library of Congress Cataloguing in Publication Data

Alt, James E
The politics of economic decline

Includes bibliographical references and index.
1. Great Britain – Economic policy – 1945–
2. Great Britain – Economic conditions – 1945–
3. Political psychology. I. Title.
HC256.6.A68   301.5'1   78-67295
ISBN 0 521 22327 X

Table of contents

For Elaine, Rachel, and Adam

Preface

Over the decade I have spent in Britain, I have come to be struck by the similarities between the British economy and British weather. Neither one seems to perform as well as most people would like, people talk about both almost incessantly, and, of course, no one ever seems to do anything about either. The last is not for want of trying: during the last ten years the British economy has been unprecedentedly managed, or tinkered with, by successive governments. The result has not been a breakthrough into rapid economic growth, but rather a protracted period (with brief exceptions) of increasing unemployment, high rates of inflation, and continuing uncertainty about the balance of payments and the value of the currency. A decade like the one through which Britain has just passed, with its political obsession with economic management on the one hand and economic failure or decline on the other, is an uncommon opportunity to look at the connection between economics and political behaviour.

There are two sides to that connection. One side deals with the behaviour of governments in economic management, and the other with the behaviour of the public as it is affected by, and reacts to, economic change. This volume has more to say about the second, on which in general less research has been done. Essentially, it charts the interconnections between economic policies and developments, popular perceptions and expectations of these economic trends, popular preferences among conflicting economic goals and policies, and a range of electoral considerations like partisanship, support for the political system, and social and political attitudes. In this way it should be of assistance both to economists formulating models which actually involve the perceptions and expectations of individuals and to electoral analysts concerned with the role of the economy in election outcomes. Themes which recur include the importance people attach to economic problems, the realism of popular economic expectations, the absence of a partisan connection in many economic attitudes, and the tendency for economic decline to undercut generous social and economic policy attitudes. This covers a lot of ground, and readers will doubtless notice that some of the themes are better supported than others. I have tried to provide a warning wherever interpretation and speculation take over from analysis, but at the same time tried to present any evidence that might be relevant.

This volume deals with Britain. Three books, Tufte (1978), Rose and Peters (1978), and Hirsch and Goldthorpe (1978), which will appear before this one, provide a comparative context for many of its conclusions, and can well be read in conjunction with it. The importance to this book of the work of Butler and Stokes (1969) – and of their assistance in supplying and permitting free analysis of their election studies – should not be forgotten, despite occasional criticisms of their analyses. I myself will be quite pleased if this book stimulates someone else to continue the study of politics and the economy as much as theirs did me. The support of the Social Science Research Council for all the election surveys – and the cooperation of everyone involved in carrying them out – on which much of this book is based should also be acknowledged. I also acknowledge the support of the Social Science Research Council for my position as Chief Research Officer for the surveys of the 1974 elections, and my gratitude to the Directors of those studies, Bo Särlvik and Ivor Crewe, for the unfettered access I have enjoyed to the data resulting from those surveys. I also appreciate the permission to reproduce and analyse large amounts of data appearing in the *Gallup Political Index*. Some of the data were supplied by the Inter-University Consortium for Political Research. The use of the statistical packages SPSS, TSP, and FAKAD is acknowledged.

For helpful suggestions and encouragement I would like to thank, among others, Michael Parkin, Douglas Hibbs, Ian Budge, and Richard Rose. The intellectual debt I owe to Brian Barry is evident at a number of places. My doctoral examiners, Peter Pulzer of Oxford and William Miller of Strathclyde, scrutinised an earlier version of this book and raised many awkward questions, in spite of which I am very grateful to them. Many thanks also to Anthony King, who read a later version with meticulous care. Two friends in the Economics Department at the University of Essex, Mike Wickens and Alec Chrystal, put up with many of my questions, and read and commented on large portions of the manuscript. I would also like to thank the referees, and the editorial staff of the Cambridge University Press for all their assistance. I appreciate their help enormously, and absolve them, and all the others, from any responsibility for such errors as remain. The manuscript was typed and retyped by Jacqueline Bayes and Desne Harrington, to whom I am abjectly grateful. For reading the manuscript, criticising it, and shouldering the burden of the effects of having done so, I give my humblest thanks to my wife Elaine.

J.E.A.

Wivenhoe, Essex
May 1978

PART I

Introduction

1

Politics and the economy in Britain

> Inflation, as we all know, is socially disruptive. It transforms an ordered
> society into an undisciplined mob. This is what happened in Germany
> in the 1920s and in many countries in Europe after the 1939–45 war.
> *Raymond Fletcher, MP, in Robbins et al., 1972*

Even if that passage appears to be something of an overstatement – and it is
noteworthy that, when it was written, the annual inflation rate in Britain was one
third what it was to be just two years further on – there is no doubt that economic conditions are widely considered to be important determinants of other
political and social phenomena. People have sought in economic states the roots
of such diverse things as enduring party cleavages and allegiances, authoritarian
values, and governmental popularity. And indeed it has been argued that the
simplest way to break up an existing social order is to debase its currency.

Nevertheless, the precise relationship between economics and politics has
always proved a little difficult to pin down. In part this may be due to impre-
cision of measurements, and in part because people have gone looking in some of
the wrong places. Unquestionably, Britain has recently gone through a difficult
economic experience. Successive governments have tried – and failed – to provide promised quicker rates of economic growth. In fact, growth in Britain has
been slower than in most other Western countries, and its slow growth has been
accompanied by high rates of inflation and unemployment, by both domestic
and international standards. If economic change, or indeed the concept of personal economic well-being or security, is ever to obtain political significance (in
the sense of being related to political attitudes and behaviour), it should happen
in modern Britain, through this experience of economic difficulty coupled with
the importance people attach to economic affairs as an issue. Similarly, the centrality of economic affairs produced by the shock of unprecedentedly high post-
war inflation and unemployment rates should produce – if anything could – a
high degree of awareness among the public of the states of the economy and the
issues involved in economic management. All this is at the heart of this study of
empirical political economy.

Government economic policy and the electorate

Britain more than ever before has an economy managed by the government. The share of national income appropriated by government in one form of taxation or another is well over 30 per cent and over a quarter of the workforce is now employed in the public sector. The government has an ever-increasing share in British industry, either through public ownership or through loans and grants to assist individual firms. Moreover, the economy is constantly in the news; various newspapers run their own versions of a retail price index to monitor inflation, and trends in relatively remote indicators can be front-page news. Nevertheless, even though it may be widely believed that no government can survive without making something of a success of its economic policies, there appears to be very little understanding of how the public perceive government policy and its effects, nor indeed how these perceptions are linked to actual political behaviour.

Indeed, only recently has it been acknowledged that there might be such a thing as a 'politics of inflation'. Parkin (1975) put forward a 'framework for posing questions about the politics of inflation'. In his view, a government has economic targets, and economic instruments. It manipulates those instruments in order to optimise some blend of economic targets, subject to a variety of con-straints. These targets are aspects of 'the economy', namely the inflation rate, the unemployment rate, and the growth rate of real income. Government policy is then composed of actions taken with respect to a number of instruments, which fall in the areas of *monetary* policy (policy with respect to money supply, credit, interest rate, and exchange rate), *fiscal* policy (expenditure, taxation, transfer payments and subsidies), direct *controls* (incomes policies, currency export limits), and finally moral *suasion* ('voluntary' policies like the Social Con-tract, as well as exhortations to buy British, work harder, and so on). Govern-mental economic policy at any time consists of actively manipulating one or more of these instruments to achieve some target, or state of some aspect of the economy.

Policy operates subject to a variety of constraints. One constraint which should not be overlooked is that some targets are incompatible with others, and that policy may thus have to achieve some optimal blend of targets because of tradeoffs between them rather than maximising some aggregate return across the economy. An internationally open economy like Britain's is subject to a variety of shocks from the rest of the world, including movements in world commodity prices, the general level of international economic activity, and of course the effects of domestic economic and related policies within the economies of Britain's major trading partners. The other factors on which Parkin comments include the desire of politicians to gain re-election, the ideological beliefs of pol-iticians, and the particular interests they are prepared to foster, and the climate of opinion about economic policy, not just in universities, but in the major sources of advice to governments. In addition to these beliefs and interests of politicians, there are also broader constraints relating to the general degree of social unrest and divisiveness such as feelings of frustration with real income growth and prospects, feelings of unfairness about the distribution of income and the strength of trade unions.

Parkin then goes on to say

Developments in the economy as well as other social political [*sic*] factors also may be presumed to have an effect upon voters' choices which, in turn, may be presumed to have some influence upon government policy, if not directly, at least by way of the government's beliefs about how their actions will affect subsequent voting behaviour.

And that is all that he has to say about social and political factors, voters' choices, and the economy. That is by no means his fault, for in fact there is little written on these matters, and certainly there has been virtually nothing written since the beginning of the rapid inflation of the mid 1970s.[1] Nevertheless, it would appear to be the responsibility of the political scientist to increase the understanding of the links between politics and the economic perceptions, attitudes and preferences of the public.

The making of economic policy is constrained politically by the preferences and voting decisions of the electorate, either because economic policy is formulated with one eye on the next election or because the actual voting results in the selection of a government which itself affects the nature of economic policy. Insofar as an evaluation of economic policy is involved in the electoral decision, this evaluation will rest on a number of components, including perceptions of economic developments, expectations about future developments, and preferences with respect to alternative policies. All these are likely to be closely related to each other. What an elector would prefer to see done may depend on what he sees happening. Preferences and expectations may depend on knowledge about economic possibilities, which includes not just accurate perception of economic trends but also realistic assessment of the possible effects of different economic policies. All these will mix together — with different blends in different cases — to colour the assessment the elector makes of which party is the one to back economically, which will in turn have larger or smaller effects on the ultimate voting decision. Moreover, economic changes can affect wider aspects of the ideological competition between parties, and thus affect people's attachment to both the party system and the broader political system.

Strategies for the study of economics and politics

Even if there has been little written about the impact of recent economic developments in Britain on political attitudes and behaviour, it is nevertheless the case

[1] One review, reflecting interest in Marxian political economy, is Axford and Brier (1976). Another point of view is Brittan (1976), and yet another is Burton (1978). There are also the various pieces reviewed below in passing, but little systematic effort to deal with politics in a society where economic management was constantly in the news.

that political science has long been concerned with the relationship between management and development of the economy on the one hand and political attitudes and behaviour of the electorate on the other. This interest is a reflection not only of a common belief that economic variables are of critical importance in determining political attitudes and behaviour but also of an apparently widespread belief (at least among politicians) that successful management of the economy is a critical test of the success of a government and of its ability to continue in office. The fact that both these beliefs have proved difficult to substantiate empirically does not lessen their importance. Rather, it accentuates the need to search for clearer conceptualisations of the problems involved. In order to study the relationship between economic considerations and political behaviour, two choices must be made. Each choice is essentially dichotomous, and all four combinations of the two choices are possible. Table 1.1 summarises these alternatives.

Table 1.1. *Strategic questions*

	Whose economic conditions?	
How measured?	Country's	Own
Objective	I	II
Subjective	III	IV

The first choice is summarised in the distinction 'objective–subjective'. Let us say that one wishes to show that economic conditions have an effect on political behaviour. In order to show this, one must first decide whether only the *subject*'s own perceptions of economic conditions are admissible as evidence, or whether to admit as well one's own judgements (as *observer*) of the subject's economic conditions. This is similar to, though not quite the same as, the distinction made by the authors of *The American Voter* (Campbell et al., 1960) between 'external' and 'personal' conditions. In their case, what constitutes the difference is whether or not the subject is aware of the condition being used in the explanation. In this case, the distinction rests on whose standards are used to measure the relevant condition. Take, for example, the case of income as an explanatory variable, and argue that some piece of behaviour is explained by having a high income. The objective–subjective distinction rests on whether, in allocating an individual to the category 'high income', one used an observer's view of his income, or used instead the subject's view of it. Doing the latter does presuppose awareness on the part of the subject. Doing the former, however, does not in principle assume anything about level of awareness.

The other choice, 'country's–own' well-being, regardless of whether the measure of economic conditions is the observer's or the subject's (or indeed both, should they happen to coincide) is whose economic condition is the relevant explanatory variable. If the behaviour of an individual is to be explained, then his own economic condition is clearly a candidate for explanatory status: the question is whether any other conditions might be. Let us say (again, for example) that an explanation is sought of why an individual endorses some particular form of political action. That the action was in his own economic interest is certainly the sort of thing which most people would accept as an explanation (though there might be considerable argument about what counts as evidence for the proposition). Would the economic interest of anyone else be acceptable as an explanation? Country and class are obvious candidates. In the case of country, one can certainly visualise a proposition of the form 'subject acted in such a way because it was for the economic betterment of the country rather than for himself' though the explanatory power of such a statement looks very weak unless either (*a*) it pertains only to the short term, and it is implied that in the long term what benefits the country will benefit the individual, or (*b*) the country's condition which improves does not cause the individual any deprivation while improving someone else's lot or indeed benefits the individual in some way of which he is not aware. In any other case — that is, of individuals accepting deprivation in the name of the country's economic improvement for extended periods of time — the explanation appears to rest on appeals to 'nationalism', 'altruism', or long-term hope rather than the usual kind of economic reasoning.

On the other hand, accepting an asymmetry between personal economic interest and class interests is much more difficult. It doesn't appear absurd to say that an individual endorsed some action which benefited members of his class but not himself, at least given the sort of proviso made in the case of country. On the other hand, no good examples of such explanations spring to mind, and furthermore, such an explanation is inconsistent with the tradition of seeing class solidarity as an *expression* of self-interest. These two dichotomous choices thus exhaust the strategic alternatives available to someone wishing to investigate the relationship between economic conditions and political behaviour.

A literature exists in the tradition of each quadrant. Quadrant I includes studies like those of Lipset (1960), Cutright (1963) and others, who attempt to estimate the extent to which a pattern of political institutions or values (generally, democracy) requires certain levels of economic development as preconditions. Here are also those studies which see aspects of individual behaviour (generally forms of partisanship) rooted in the current economic state of the country, including such diverse studies as Converse's (1958) demonstration that the correlation between class and party choice increases in 'hard times' and the long literature predicting either governmental or presidential popularity in opinion polls or indeed mid-term congressional election results from data relating to inflation and unemployment rates or other indicators. Quadrant II, relating to objective measures of personal economic condition, incorporates an enormous literature, as long as objective measures of social class are taken to reflect economic well-being. If only income or wealth are considered to be objective individual economic criteria, the relevant literature becomes much thinner. The work of Goldthorpe et al. (1968) and Butler and Stokes (1969) provides examples.

The literature on subjective economic perceptions and political attitudes and behaviour is distinctly thin. One example of a Quadrant III study is in Almond and Verba (1965), where they consider the linkage between Germans' political participation and national pride, observing that in Germany the source of national pride is typically rooted in national economic achievement rather than in political institutions. Another study is contained in Chapter 14 of *The American Voter* where voting is linked to perceptions of recession or feelings about general business conditions and the outlook for the economy. Part of this last study crosses the line into Quadrant IV, since it deals with perceptions of the impact of the recession on the subjects themselves. In the case of Britain, Butler and Stokes' *Political Change in Britain* contains rich analyses of the impact of perceptions of economic management and individual well-being on support for the political parties. It does not, however, extend the discussion into the area of the linkage between sense of personal well-being and other political attitudes, nor does it have much to say about the politico-social determinants of economic outlook.

The economy as a political issue

The work of Butler and Stokes provides a convenient point to begin this study. Not only is their study the most thorough investigation of the electoral consequences of economic management in Britain, but it also suggests that subjective measures of economic well-being can be shown to have political consequences. Paradoxically, their own work may be partly responsible for the absence of serious research into the consequences of the economic decline of the 1960s and 1970s in Britain, for the model of economic effects Butler and Stokes endorse, a 'valence' model, discourages rather than encourages detailed scrutiny of the links between the state of the economy, popular perceptions of the economy, subjective personal feelings of well-being, and economic policy preferences. By a valence model, Butler and Stokes suggest that where economic issues are concerned, there is broad consensus at the levels of both mass public and policy-makers over not only the ends of economic policy but also the means whereby these ends are to be achieved.[2] The link between economic management and electoral behaviour is one in which the government of the day is rewarded for producing the desired economic ends — generally, increased prosperity — and punished for failing to produce them. Because there is consensus on both ends and means, insofar as the quality of economic management bears on partisan electoral choice, it does so only as a matter of the elector's relative confidence in the political parties as economic producers.

It is important to note that Butler and Stokes are making both an empirical

---

[2] The consensus does not extend to the level of rhetoric in inter-party political arguments. The consensus argument states that both parties share a common economic analytical framework, or would actually do the same things in the same economic situation, or both, but not that leaders of both parties would ever go so far as to say the same things at the same time.

and a theoretical claim for their model. The empirical claim is that they have shown it to be valid, in the sense of conforming to available evidence and giving an account of the role of the economy in electoral politics. The theoretical claim is that their model is superior to any other: not only is it a valid model, but it is the only valid model of the electoral consequences of the economy. Claims like these deserve careful scrutiny. In fact there are reasons for believing that neither claim holds up all that well. Even if the validity − not superiority − of a valence model is admitted, the evidence they provide for theirs is less than convincing. Moreover, the theoretical superiority of the valence model of economic effects rests on a misunderstanding of the nature of issues.

Political analysts have for some time been at pains to point out that not all political argument consists of positional disputes about concrete policies, but that rather what may be at issue is the relative competence of the parties at achieving something both sides want, or indeed something relating more to style or ideals than immediate wants of members of the public. Reacting against Downs' (1957) spatial market theory of party competition, Stokes (1966) argues that there are indeed 'position' issues which 'involve advocacy of government actions from a set of alternatives over which a distribution of voter preferences is defined'. Then there are 'valence' issues which 'merely involve the linking of the parties with some condition that is positively or negatively valued by the electorate'. The argument between the parties hinges, if the condition already exists, on who deserves credit or blame for bringing it about. If the condition is in the future, the argument rests on which party is more likely to bring it about. Many of the central themes of post-war electoral politics are of this sort: these include corruption and economic recovery and prosperity. Finally, Stokes argues that 'whether a given problem poses a position- or valence-issue is a matter to be settled empirically and not on a priori logical grounds'. This contention is both vitally important and correct, but not in quite the way Stokes suggests.

Stokes argues that prosperity is an archetypal valence issue. The issue of prosperity − since every party and elector wants it − hinges only on which party is more likely to bring it about. It is conceivable, he says, that parties might take up positions over amounts of prosperity, thus turning prosperity into a position-issue, but that 'it is *not* such an issue in our politics is due solely to the . . . overwhelming consensus as to the goal of government action'. The point that is missed here is that consensus on ends does not imply consensus on means: that everyone wants prosperity does not imply that everyone is agreed on how to achieve it. However, the counter-argument that if parties are unequally likely to achieve prosperity, they *must* propose to achieve it by different means, is equally invalid. As Downs points out, parties can have and be seen to have identical policies (ends and means) and still be differentiated with respect to perceived competence or sincerity based on past performance in office.

It is worth remembering that behind valence issues may lie differing positions, some of which are capable of sensible unidimensional representation. Robertson (1975) points out that underlying the consensual issue of corruption (everyone is against it) lies a continuum of how far one is prepared to go to fight it. Similarly, underlying the question of prosperity might be the question of how far one is prepared to see the government intervene in the economy to achieve it. The point of this is, however, not that every issue is *really* a position issue, but that every issue has, or can have, both valence and position aspects. Better put, on every issue there may be at any time either consensus or dissensus between the parties with respect to *either* the *ends or* the *means* to those ends. Furthermore, whether there is consensus on means or ends is an empirical matter, as Stokes suggests. Indeed, it is contingent on both historical circumstance and party political strategy. To speak of issues as if they were in some way compelled always to be valence- or position-issues is indeed to confound an empirical matter with an *a priori* classification. Empirically, there are two questions to deal with: 'what makes an issue position-like?' and 'why is it that at some times an issue is more position-like and at others more valence-like?'

In the first place, every issue involves considerations which range from the short term and concrete to the highest-level abstractions of political argument. To members of the Labour Party, nationalisation of industry has often been a matter either of denying industrialists the benefits of owning profitable concerns and/or of guaranteeing workers better conditions. Nevertheless, people commonly argued for nationalisation also on the grounds of middle-order economic interests: full employment, rational planning of industry, economic growth, efficiency, and promotion of competitive prices. Moreover, even at the mass level, the issue of nationalisation is bound up with concerns ranging from the short range and economic to the long term and moral, as these unprompted comments from respondents to the British Election Study October 1974 cross-section survey (all opposed to further nationalisation) show:

> 'they will have to spend too much on compensation, money they haven't got';
> 'nationalised industries don't pay their way — never have done';
> 'in the past it's been a case of overemployment';
> 'industries will be nationalised and will function much less efficiently';
> 'they will cripple the small businessman and all initiative, and then he will work for some nationalised industry, where he can take as much sick leave and time off as he wants, and a vicious circle starts';
> 'policy of nationalising industry doesn't give enough incentive for making any effort. The people who work there will not lose [their] jobs so they don't care'.

The Labour Party does of course not see itself as in favour of laziness or waste. The point is that as higher-order abstractions are brought into political discourse, they may well be of a sort which all people agree are good things. This will particularly be true when these higher-order principles are of the sort Brian Barry (1965) calls aggregative, where they do not involve taking away from some people to give to others. Efficiency is probably consensually sought for, at least as long as no one suffers in connection with it, while equality — the other half of what Okun (1975) calls 'the big trade-off' — is far more controversial, particularly when people feel that 'levelling down' is likely to be involved.

This brings us to the other distinctions that underlie the 'valence-ness' of some issues. Issues may involve notions which are more or less consensual, as Stokes and many others point out. Moreover, some issues turn on ends or goals, while others turn on means to ends. The ends of political activity may be taken to be justified in themselves, or they may be justified by reference to higher-order ends. The justification is characteristically in terms of some benefit to be provided, or opportunity for securing some benefit to be increased, in a way which outweighs any costs involved. Justification of a policy which is really a means to other ends (e.g., nationalisation) is more complicated, since the justification of a means to something else requires not just an argument for the desirability of that end, but also showing (i) either that the means are indispensible to the achievement of the end or if not indispensable, that no other means to the same end exist with lower costs, and in either case (ii) that any costs associated with these means are outweighed by benefits associated with the end. It is this complication which produces the room for all the arguments relating to nationalisation cited above, for all the ends cited — industry, efficiency, growth — are consensual enough, and what is at issue is either whether nationalisation is indeed a means to them, or whether its benefits, if any, outweigh attendant costs.

Issues, therefore, do not become position-like simply because of absence of consensus on ends, or valence-like because of consensus on ends. There may be consensus or dissensus on means and consensus or dissensus on ends. The four combinations of these two pairs of possibilities are all logically distinct and empirically possible, as Table 1.2 suggests. What the valence-position distinction really reflects is a continuum running from the upper left-hand corner to the lower right-hand corner of Table 1.2, with the most valence-like issues located in the lower right-hand corner. The examples in Table 1.2 all relate to economic management of one form or another. At the most fundamental level, there may be disagreement on the extent of government intervention (1) with a market economy, where disagreement covers both means to achieve ends and the ends themselves, which in this case might relate to whether one seeks efficiency or equality as paramount economic goals. One can at other times see consensus on

Table 1.2. *The economy as a political issue*

Ends	Means	
	Dissensus	Consensus
Dissensus	(1) Economic intervention	(2) Income supplements
Consensus	(3) Control of inflation	(4) 'Butskellism'

means emerging on some issues, even while there may be dissensus on the ends which these means are serving. For instance, it is possible to endorse forms of direct cash payments (2) to individuals as income supplements, either to promote equality or to stimulate the economy. Similarly, one can support incomes policies as a means either to control inflation or to promote social justice (Jones, 1973). Issues where there is consensus on what there is to be achieved but dissensus on how to achieve it are common: the question of inflation control in recent years is of this sort, with all parties agreed on the desirability of controlling inflation (3) but a measure of disagreement among them on whether the way to go about it is through reducing expenditure, increasing unemployment, controlling wages and prices, and so on. The most valence-like cases of consensus on both means and ends, when political argument is restricted to questions of competence, include economic management in Britain in the 1950s. There the label 'Butskellism' (4) emerged to describe a case of bipartisan consensus not only over goals (stable economic growth, low unemployment and slow inflation) but also over means of achieving them (control of aggregate demand through fiscal measures). Even in such a case the consensus between parties can be exaggerated, though more pernicious is that the brief experience of such consensus in the 1950s appears to have misled analysts into believing that economic management is always such a consensual policy. What is more to the point is to realise that something like 'the economy as a political issue' is a broad concern that contains more and less valence-like aspects at different times. If the position-like aspects are at any time trivial, they can safely be ignored. But the fact that they are trivial at one time does not guarantee that they will remain so, and reasons exist that the same issue is at one time more and another time less consensual or valence-like.

Economic decline and the emergence of issue positions

Harder economic times present a set of circumstances in which not only are competitive parties more likely to take up competing positions with respect to economic management but individuals are also more likely to have an incentive to pay attention to these competing claims, and to adhere to positions or preferences with regard to economic policy. A political issue need not be the same thing at the level of political leaders and followers. Assume that, where issue opinions are concerned, the masses respond rather than lead. Therefore, a first answer to the question of when issue positions emerge among members of the mass electorate is, when they have emerged among political leaders. Among leaders, consensus rests on historical and economic circumstances, and, in response to these circumstances, it rests on the competitive advantage of the competing political parties.

There is evidence (Robertson, 1975) that over the last half century, the Conservative and Labour parties have become more moderate and consensual with respect to economic intervention during 'good times' or conditions of economic recovery or boom, and have moved apart ideologically during hard times. The reason for this is that good times are universally valued and therefore both parties find it expedient, during good times, to be identified with this value. Since their respective ideologies involve altering the status quo, they avoid stressing them, which is a reasonable procedure, at least as long as their respective supporters are sufficiently risk-averse not to believe in getting more of a good thing by altering the status quo. It is the case that the ostensibly most consensual period of economic management in Britain — the 1950s — corresponded to a period of recovery. It is a mistake to assume that therefore either there is a tendency toward consensus in economic management which is irreversible or that such management has always been consensual. In the U.S. in and after 1932, what divided Republicans and Democrats was not only some abstracted notion of 'competence', but also a set of proposals — the New Deal — for achieving recovery and prosperity. It is oversimplifying greatly to say that between McKinley and Roosevelt Americans simply 'changed their minds' about who was more likely to achieve it. Of course they changed their minds, but in the presence of competing claims about different *means* to achieve prosperity.

More generally, the consensuality of economic management rests on historical and economic circumstances, because politicians are at any time the creatures of prevailing economic theories, whether because they are trained in economics themselves, or because they depend on academic advisors and trained civil servants for advice on policy and its execution. Enduring positional disputes such as free trade versus protection may simply disappear because it appears that only one position is acceptable owing to changed circumstances or because one position becomes intellectually unfashionable. The emergence of the welfare state and collectivist politics enshrined the consumer with the right to be represented (Beer, 1965), and made the cost of living and wage levels almost consensually the responsibility of government. In part, then, the positions which politicians might represent rest on current intellectual and social developments.

Economic decline may also incline individuals to hold economic policy positions. One determinant of attitude formation is often taken to be want-satisfaction, which means that individuals form an attitude toward some object when it is seen as relevant to satisfying some want of theirs through direct gratification or through a perceptible increase in the opportunity for future gratification. Attitudes do not develop where the objects of these attitudes are irrelevant to an individual's opportunity for want-satisfaction. When alternative political–economic strategies are not seen as relevant to one's material position — perhaps, when most wants are being satisfied through the present state of the economy — there is no incentive to invest in information about economic alternatives. On the other hand, those who are pessimistic about their own prospects — which comes to include a greater proportion of the population in harder and more uncertain times — will be more likely to adhere to positions with respect to economic change. Moreover, holding an attitude is more likely in the presence of a greater information flow, or through greater centrality to the individual simply through thinking more about it (Converse, 1970). It is only possible to interest oneself in an information flow when there is such a flow and that will be, as before, when the parties create one. So in both senses of centrality — perceptible relevance to want-satisfaction and visibility in public debate — harder times appear to be a precondition for electors' adhering to economic positions.

The Butler–Stokes analysis

In terms of the valence model provided by Butler and Stokes, the previous discussion exaggerates the ability of the electorate to inform themselves about the stands of the parties and to assimilate the requisite information about economic theories to hold consistent and meaningful opinions about something like economic management. Therefore, regardless of what is going on at the level of leaders, economic management for the masses will be a matter of tying recognisable political symbols (parties and candidates) to valued ends (full employment, prosperity) as an extension of partisan loyalties. Of course, prolonged incompetence at economic management may shift individuals away from their preferred party, particularly when it has failed while in office. Beyond this, the details of alternative strategies of economic management do not really penetrate, or do so only ephemerally.

Such a view is probably correct at times, and probably was correct during the relative affluence of the 1950s, when it was developed. Certainly if the parties do not create alternative positions, the public will not, if in matters of opinion the public responds rather than leads. Because of the absence of survey evidence, it is unknown whether, in such a period as the 1930s when there were clear policy differences between the parties, many more electors did adhere to meaningful and stable opinions about economic policy. That the evaluations of government performance which they describe are made by electors is beyond dispute, and that such evaluations are of considerable importance in the electoral process, or at least were of considerable importance in the period they discuss, is similarly not open to doubt. On the other hand, the recommendation that such a model contains all that can usefully be said about the connection between economic management and electoral behaviour is by no means obviously to be accepted. The validity of this claim depends on the evidence for the acceptability of the valence model, which they present as four separate arguments (Butler and Stokes, 1975, Chapter 18).

The first argument deals with the *correlation between perceptions of personal economic well-being and changes in support for the government.* A positive correlation between the two is always present: support for the Conservatives increased between 1959 and 1964 by seven per cent among those reporting themselves better off both in 1963 and 1964; Conservative support in the same period declined by eight per cent among those reporting themselves consistently worse off. Similarly, support for Labour between 1964 and 1966 increased most among those who felt that they had become worse off in the last years of the Conservative administration and better off under Labour. Moreover, class support for the parties is affected by perceptions of personal well-being. For instance, Conservative support in the working class in 1963 was greater among those who felt they had become better off in the previous three or four years than among those who felt they had become worse off.

The second argument deals with the *correlation between voting intention and satisfaction with the government's handling of the economy*. Evidence for this rests on the correlation between two series derived from monthly Gallup polls between 1959 and 1964. One series displays Labour's lead over the Conservatives in mass voting intentions: the other reveals Labour's lead over the Conservatives in electors' satisfaction with the parties' 'handling of the economy'. The close correlation between these two series is taken to be evidence that satisfaction with a party's handling of the economy is a principal determinant of voting intention. Aware of the counter-argument that economic satisfaction could be the consequence as well as the cause of voting intention, they adduce two further supporting arguments: one to show that there is no similar correlation between voting intention and assessment of such other policy areas as international affairs or health and the other to the effect that, in terms of fluctuations of the series, it appears to be the government's rather than the opposition's economic competence which is most salient to the electorate.[3]

The third argument extends the second. Not only is popularity — as reflected by voting intention — linked to perceptions of economic management, but it is also a *reflection of perceived macroeconomic trends*. Through displays of correlated series, Butler and Stokes argue that unemployment was the most visible indicator of government success or failure in the 1959—64 Parliament, but that between 1966 and 1970 it was replaced by the current balance of international payments as the indicator most visible to the public. Butler and Stokes argue that only the balance of payments in this role meets three necessary criteria. First, that the balance of payments was such a visible indicator is consistent with the finding that in 1970 more of the electorate approved than disapproved of Labour's handling of the economy. Second, it is consistent with Labour's success in maintaining the belief that it had inherited its economic difficulties from its Conservative predecessors. Finally, this role of the balance of payments is consistent with the idea of a late swing to the Conservatives during the 1970 campaign, since even though the balance of payments figures in June 1970 reflected considerable improvement over those for 1964, the last set of monthly figures before the election showed a considerable deficit.

The final argument deals with the question of *personal and national economic*

[3] The evidence they give for this argument is incorrect. The argument arises out of Figure 18.14 (Butler and Stokes, 1975) which is said to be the difference between the two series plotted in Figure 18.15. In fact, the two figures cannot be related to each other. (Since the two lines in Figure 18.15 cross, there must be a zero point in Figure 18.14 in 1963. There isn't.) Their argument may nevertheless be correct, but as it stands, it is not corroborated in the figures.

effects. Butler and Stokes show that perceptions of personal economic well-being fluctuated much less during the 1966–70 Parliament than did satisfaction with Labour's handling of the economy during the same period. Between 1966 and 1970, the difference between proportions of the electorate feeling that they were becoming better off and feeling they were becoming worse off stays at about one or two per cent. On the other hand, the difference between proportions feeling satisfied and dissatisfied with Labour's handling of the economy drops from a net of +28 per cent (excess of satisfied over dissatisfied) in 1966 to −36 per cent in 1969 but rises back to +16 per cent in 1970. Since a series reflecting feelings about whether or not Labour had made respondents better off hardly swung 'across a period that included moments both of hope and despair for Labour's economic policies' the authors conclude that 'we should pay the closest heed to the links the electorate draws between the parties and the economic health of the country as a whole'.

The first two arguments, that changes of voting are linked to changes of personal well-being, and that vote intention correlates with satisfaction with the government's handling of the economy, are largely unexceptionable, but do not in themselves establish either the validity or superiority of a valence model of economic effects. The other two arguments are critical to the valence model, and these are considered below in some detail.

Macroeconomic indicators, the balance of payments, and vote intention

Much rests on their claim that monthly trends in the balance of payments predict vote intention, for if something as remote and complicated as the balance of payments is really a good guide to government popularity and voting, the valence model has a strong empirical grounding. It is hard to imagine the public desiring anything other than a surplus on current account or having any familiarity with alternative methods of achieving a surplus. If monthly announcements of the balance of payments really were linked to vote intention or voting, one would have to interpret the announcements as symbols of good times or bad, for which the government received credit or blame.

However, the literature they cite in support of the argument for macroeconomic determination of vote intention is by no means unambiguous in support of such an argument, and many of the more recent efforts have tended to argue *against*, rather than for, the direct connection between macroeconomic indicators and vote intention (see below, Chapter 6). Moreover, they present no real supporting evidence for the correlation between monthly series, since the only statistical measure of goodness of fit which they present does not relate to the *independent* contribution of the balance of payments toward predicting vote intention.[4] In fact, even on inspection of the two series, the balance of payments

[4] Butler and Stokes give an R^2 of 0.7 for an equation including lagged popularity and the balance of payments, but present neither regression coefficients nor estimates of the standard deviations of these coefficients. In the time period 1966 to 1970, popularity one month explained about 70 per cent of the variance in popularity the following month, implying that the balance of payments has no additional independent effect.

probably has rather little effect, since the most protracted period of Labour's unpopularity in 1968–9 is one in which the balance of payments by and large continued to improve. Of course, even if there is no particular independent correlation between the balance of payments and vote intention, it could still be the case that the balance of payments was a sort of summary criterion used by the electorate to judge Labour's economic performance. (Indeed, this was the judgement the Labour Party asked them to make at the end of their term in office.) This would still support a valence model through the remoteness of such a standard from everyday life, in the sense of the preceding arguments. Though not a theory of the determination of monthly voting intention, there is still a valence model of economic electoral effects, at least if satisfaction with the government's economic record must be shown to correlate closely with the government's handling of the balance of payments.

To buttress the claim that the balance of payments was the basic indicator used to judge Labour's economic performance, satisfaction with the one must reflect satisfaction with the other. However, satisfaction with the government's record was by no means the same thing as satisfaction with the government's handling of the balance of payments. There are no time series data for 1964–70 from which to obtain correlational support for this contention. However, in November 1969, 47 per cent of the electorate indicated satisfaction with Labour's handling of the balance of payments, and only 32 per cent indicated dissatisfaction (NOP data). At this time, the vast majority of those who felt that the balance of payments had improved also felt that the government deserved the credit for the improvement. Nevertheless, in the same month, a clear plurality of 48 per cent 'disapproved of the Government's record to date', while only 35 per cent approved of it. Four months later, in March 1970, a plurality of 44 per cent disapproved of the 'Government's handling of the Economy' while 38 per cent approved; the plurality four months earlier would have been even more heavily against the government. Finally, voting intention in the November 1969 poll stood at 33.5 per cent for Labour and 38 per cent for the Conservatives. While voting intention *may* reflect approval of the government's record, and more importantly, approval of the government's economic record, satisfaction with the handling of the balance of payments does *not* imply satisfaction with the government's economic record.

Nevertheless, there would still be considerable force in Butler and Stokes's argument about the crucial role of the balance of payments in the electorate's assessment of Labour's economic record if it could be shown that the public themselves regarded the balance of payments as critical to their electoral choice. The last pre-election poll in May 1970 indicates that, in response to questioning about the 'most urgent problems' of the day, while 57 per cent of respondents mentioned economic affairs, 35 per cent referred to prices or the cost of living, nine per cent to unemployment and only 11 per cent to all other economic matters, including the balance of payments (*Gallup Political Index*). Unfortunately, earlier reports do not disaggregate 'economic' responses, so it cannot be said whether earlier in Labour's tenure of office the balance of payments loomed larger in the public mind, as by 1970, the balance of payments was greatly improved.

Evidence of a more direct kind is given in Table 1.3, concerning the reasons people gave in 1970 for liking or disliking the parties. In fact, no one mentions the balance of payments in connection with the Conservative Party, but this is consistent with the expectation that it is a standard used to judge the performance of the government. One cannot fail to be struck by the damage done in Table 1.3 to any claim that the use of the balance of payments to judge the government emerged *during* the 1966—70 Parliament: references connecting the balance of payments with the Labour Party in the summer of 1969 are practically non-existent (0.3 per cent, regardless of party affiliation of the respondent) and far less frequent than references to any other economic policies. The balance of payments enjoyed more currency as a topic *after* the 1970 election, when it rises from last to next-last among the six economic themes mentioned in connection with the Labour Party. Then it is mentioned by 4.1 per cent of the electorate, about half the proportions mentioning any of prices, taxation and rates, or nationalisation, and slightly more than the 3.4 per cent mentioning financial or budgetary affairs. Moreover, in 1970 the party of the respondent is important: while only 1.7 per cent of Conservative voters mention the balance of payments in connection with the Labour Party, 6.8 per cent of Labour voters do so (overwhelmingly as a reason for liking the Labour Party) and indeed it is the single most common *economic* response among reasons given by Labour voters for liking the Labour Party.[5] Even so, it is mentioned about one third as often as social policies of one sort or another, and less than one quarter as often as the general idea of class-related benefits. It appears to be the case that rather

Table 1.3. *Economic themes in Labour imagery 1969—70*

Proportions of voters mentioning:	Year	
	1969	1970
Prosperity and employment	3.3	4.9
Balance of payments	0.3	4.1
Prices, cost of living	6.9	7.5
Finance, the Budget	3.9	3.4
Taxation or rates	11.6	8.8
Nationalisation	6.1	9.7

Source: Data are from the Butler—Stokes 1969 and 1970 cross-sections.
Responses include both favourable and unfavourable to the Labour Party.

[5] These data are coded from unstructured responses to the questions 'Is there anything you (like) (don't like) about the (Conservative) (Labour) Party?' Among Labour electors in 1970, when giving reasons for liking Labour, 6.8 per cent mentioned the party's handling of the balance of payments, while virtually none mentioned taxes or prices, and 6.3 per cent mentioned employment and/or general prosperity. Eighteen per cent mentioned items dealing with social policy.

than being a standard by which Labour was judged, the balance of payments represented the one kind thing its supporters could say about the economic record of the Labour Party in 1970. Indeed, about the same proportion of *Labour* voters (6.6 per cent) mentioned taxation as a reason for *disliking* Labour as mentioned the balance of payments as a reason for liking it.

Butler and Stokes also claim that an important feature of the balance of payments was that Labour could blame their problems with it on their predecessors, and claim to be doing no worse than had the Conservatives. However, this could be said of other economic targets, notably inflation, as for most of their term Labour could argue that the inflation rate was no worse than the one they had inherited. But inflation is not a remote indicator of economic management, untranslatable into direct personal experience for most of the electorate. If prices were the basis of electors' evaluation of Labour's economic record, then it no longer follows that the economy must be a valence issue, for inflation involves political questions of both means and ends. Insofar as Labour did no worse than their predecessors at dealing with inflation – and the balance of payments – the claims for the valence model are weakened accordingly.

Personal and national economic evaluation

What Butler and Stokes claim lies behind the evaluation of the government's economic performance is a simple linking of one or another of the parties with 'good' or 'bad' times, where these relate to *national* economic goals. Two comments can be made about this claim. The first is that part of the evidence for it lies in showing that net satisfaction with Labour's handling of the economy 1966–70 swung more sharply than did perceived impact on personal well-being. This need only show, however, that satisfaction with the government's handling of the economy is a more volatile, but not more meaningful, indicator. Furthermore, it must also be remembered that Labour *lost* the 1970 election, at a time when Butler and Stokes's survey showed that 16 per cent *more* of the electorate were satisfied with their handling of the economy than were dissatisfied. This could in turn be taken to suggest that it is easier to satisfy people with your handling of the national economy than to get their votes, particularly if in the short term you satisfy them with the national economy without at the same time making them feel better off. If this is so, then the claim that it is to perceptions of national economic management that we should pay most attention is over-stated.

Another weakness of the notion that people are reacting to trends in management of the national economy is that it suggests that perceptions or evaluations of economic management are not differentiated with respect to different economic indicators. Table 1.4 presents some relevant evidence suggesting that evaluation of the parties relates to specific economic indicators. Gallup have asked repeated samples 'Which party do you think can best handle the problem of (maintaining prosperity?) (prices and the cost of living?) (unemployment?)'. The table presents the results of taking the net Conservative lead over Labour

Table 1.4. *Relationships among partisan evaluations of economic competence*

Period	Observations	R-squared	Equation
April 1971 to October 1975	14	0.42	$U = -6.89 + 0.588P$
September 1959 to October 1975	20	0.67	$U = -6.35 + 0.649P$
October 1970 to October 1975	14	0.64	$P = -8.8 + 1.26Pr$
September 1964 to October 1975	20	0.58	$P = -6.6 + 1.15Pr$
September 1971 to October 1975	13	0.41	$U = -11.85 + 1.04Pr$
November 1957 to October 1975	19	0.67	$U = -12.57 + 0.87Pr$

Notes: Symbols are U = Unemployment, P = Prices, Pr = Prosperity. Observations are net per cent Conservative minus per cent Labour in response to 'Which party do you think can best handle the problem of (unemployment?) (maintaining prosperity?) (prices and the cost of living?)
Source: Gallup Political Index, various.

with respect to each of these indicators, and regressing each on the others. The results suggest two things. First is that the average net Conservative rating for handling prosperity is six points better than for prices, and 12 points better than for unemployment. This in turn suggests that each of the parties is not seen as equally competent in all areas of economic management. Second, the correlations between the series, while strong, are not particularly high for time series of a few points, and particularly for series which are expected to measure the *same* thing. The unemployment series in recent years seems particularly independent of the other series, which may reflect the lessening importance attributed to unemployment in British national politics in the early 1970s. In any case, there is ample reason to believe that the electorate's assessment of the competence of the two parties in the area of price management has not been always the same as its assessment of their relative abilities at maintaining prosperity.

This again would not matter if Butler and Stokes were borne out in their claim that prosperity is the key to evaluation of economic management. (One can take this to be their argument, since 'competence at maintaining prosperity' or 'handling the current economic situation' is as close as one can get to an assessment linking the parties with good times or bad.) In September 1964, in the last poll before the 1964 election, the *Conservatives* were 13 points ahead of Labour with regard to maintaining prosperity. In June 1970, *Labour* was held to be better at maintaining prosperity by three percentage points. In February 1974, the *Conservatives* held a three-point lead with respect to maintaining prosperity. Each time the leading party was swept from office. In October 1974

Labour retained office while leading in the last pre-election poll in terms of ability to maintain prosperity. On that occasion, moreover, as on all the previous ones, the party which won had a much larger lead with respect to ability to manage prices. This should not be interpreted as a fluke, or as evidence that opinion polls produce nonsense. Rather, it shows that voting has been tied more closely to management of prices than to management of the general economic situation, and that, contrary to the advice of Butler and Stokes, in analysing the electoral consequences of economic management, one should pay closest attention to those things which are closest to the electorate, and which have the most immediate impact upon them. Furthermore, if what is at issue is not something as remote as the balance of payments or as diffuse as good times, it will also make sense to inquire more closely into the attitudes on which people base their evaluations of governmental competence in economic management.

This point is reinforced if one considers actual voting behaviour. Table 1.5 shows proportions voting Labour in 1970 (when they were the incumbents), divided by social class and further by perceptions of whether people felt themselves personally better off or not under Labour and by satisfaction with the Labour Government's economic record. At first sight, the table simply shows that it was easier to resist voting Labour if one was satisfied with their economic record than if one felt personally better off under Labour: thus, 76 per cent of the working class who felt better off voted Labour, but only 62 per cent of the working class who felt satisfied with their economic record voted Labour. This may make too much of the data: it is clear that the proportion of the working class who felt satisfied with Labour's economic record is much larger than the proportion feeling better off. Among the small group (181 in all) in the working

Table 1.5. *Voting effects of personal and national economic evaluations in 1970*

	Per cent voting Labour in 1970, by economic evaluation					
	Personal Felt under Labour Government			*National* Felt about Labour's economic record		
Middle class	Better off	54%	(68)	Very/fairly satisfied	46%	(257)
	No difference	28%	(339)	Neutral	14%	(79)
	Worse off	5%	(254)	Very/fairly dissatisfied	5%	(291)
Working class	Better off	76%	(220)	Very/fairly satisfied	62%	(576)
	No difference	47%	(555)	Neutral	34%	(141)
	Worse off	15%	(261)	Very/fairly dissatisfied	13%	(246)

Note: Data are from the Butler–Stokes 1970 cross-section sample, total number interviewed = 1,843. Numbers in brackets are the base for calculating proportion in a group voting Labour. The personal question is 'Did the Labour Government make you better off or worse off, or didn't it make much difference?' and the national question is 'Speaking more generally, how satisfied were you with the Labour Government's handling of Britain's economic affairs?'

class who felt 'very' satisfied with Labour, 79 per cent voted Labour. (But this group is now smaller than the group feeling better off.)[6] Even if there is *no* difference in the underlying ability of personal and national economic perceptions to predict voting, this would still show several things of interest.

One is that the assessment of economic record contained no vote-predicting information other than that contained in personal perceptions of well-being. More important, the frequencies in Table 1.5 show that it is *easier* to get people to say that they are satisfied (even if only fairly) with the government's economic record than to say they felt better off under a particular government. In other words, there is no contradiction – and indeed it appears to be a common response – to say 'all in all, I suppose their economic record was all right, but I didn't feel better off with them'. And people apparently do not feel under any compulsion to vote for a government about which they feel that way. While a majority (though slight) of those satisfied with Labour's economic record did vote for them, a much clearer majority of those feeling better off with Labour voted for them. While it is easier to make people generally satisfied than to make them feel better off, this satisfaction does not seem to have the same voting payoff for the government – not, at least, until people are very satisfied with their government's economic record. Thus the wide swings in satisfaction recorded by Butler and Stokes – like the large majority satisfied with Labour's economic record – may prove to be a poor rather than a good guide to ultimate voting behaviour. Moreover, while no one would deny that the ultimate evaluation of economic management described by a valence model does take place, the closer the performance of the economy comes to people's daily lives, the more important it becomes to include in the analysis popular economic perceptions, expectations, and policy preferences. While there remains a great deal of value in Butler and Stokes' pathbreaking analysis, it should be clear that there is a great deal more to be said about the economy as a political issue.

[6] More formally, both personal and national evaluations may define incumbent-voting probability functions which are *identical*, starting at 1.0 among the most positive and falling to 0.0 among the most negative. In that case, if the two evaluations could be tapped so as to produce categories of *equal* frequency (which the Butler–Stokes questions do not), one might find the two indistinguishable in their effect. Indeed, this is exactly what the 79 per cent Labour vote among the very satisfied working class and 76 per cent Labour vote among the better off working class suggest: no difference in the probability of voting Labour among groups each of which contains about an equal section of evaluative opinion.

2

The British economy in the 1970s

The state of the economy, and what could be done about it, dominated British politics in the 1960s and 1970s. There were of course many achievements in other areas of public policy. The Labour Government of 1964 to 1970 is likely to be remembered for a variety of social reforms, including particularly legislation dealing with abortion, sexual offences, and divorce. Provisions of the 1965 Rent Act, the introduction of supplementary benefits in 1966, the Race Relations Act of 1968 and especially the reform of the education system begun in 1965 may still be having repercussions when the Labour Government's failure to achieve its economic growth targets has long been forgotten. Similarly, many actions of the Heath Government − joining the EEC, the reform of local government, the introduction of the principle of regular reviews of pensions, and even decimalisation − were of great importance. The Industrial Relations Act of 1971 − like the previous government's failure to introduce industrial relations legislation − may have produced long-lasting effects on the relationship between government and unions. The continuing confrontation between the Heath Government and organised labour may well make it impossible for any Conservative Government in the near future to achieve much in the way of voluntary cooperation from the unions, and may have reintroduced the question of the rights of organised labour as a principal point of cleavage between the two main political parties.

Despite these developments, the problem of Britain's economy was never solved, and was never very far from the heart of day-to-day politics. Indeed, most of the actions listed above were affected by economic policy. Comprehensive education was never backed by a suitably large capital construction program because of repeated cuts in expenditure in this area in the late 1960s. Thus the introduction of comprehensive education frequently took the form of simple mergers of existing schools with few attendant benefits. Had the policy been backed by expansion of facilities comprehensivisation might not have retained a lingering air of unpopularity − but such expansion was impossible in the economic climate of the times. The same could be said of the raising of the school leaving age to sixteen, for again the reform took place without suitable accompanying expansion of facilities. Recurrent sterling crises − or, perhaps better put, a decision to put maintenance of the exchange rate before other policies − lay at the heart of the Labour Government's failure to achieve many of its grander social reforms. The downward float of the pound after mid-1972 avoided a balance of payments crisis arising from the excessive outflow of capital created by monetary reforms the previous year. The float may have contributed to the inflation in the British economy resulting from the rising costs of imported goods. The extra price inflation made maintaining an incomes policy even more difficult and contributed to the resulting confrontation between government and unions.

This chapter looks at economic policies and developments in Britain between 1964 and 1974, using the distinction raised in the Introduction between targets and instruments. It will describe trends in a number of major target areas: growth rate, inflation, unemployment, and balance of payments. It will look also at the principal instruments available to the government, in the form of monetary policies, fiscal policies, and incomes policies, and consider both the legal—institutional base of these instruments and wherever possible illustrate the application of these instruments by following relevant trends. This chapter is not, however, an exercise in economic theory, nor does it become involved in an attempt to analyse the *causes* of Britain's economic problems, which is a job for economists. What it does is to describe the trends in major areas of economic policy which everyone would agree were important, and it does this to provide a context in which to set the discussion which follows. This chapter provides a picture of economic deterioration and the failure of economic management in Britain between 1964 and 1974. The chapters which follow discuss the public's reaction to this failure, and its consequences for politics in Britain.

Economic policy 1964—74

'There is wide agreement about the major goals of economic policy: high employment, stable prices, and rapid growth. There is less agreement that these goals are mutually compatible, or among those who regard them as incompatible, about the terms at which they can and should be substituted for one another' (Friedman, 1968). In a way, the history of British economic policy from 1964 to 1974 was a matter of first coming to terms with the fact that these targets looked increasingly likely to be incompatible, and then trying to devise ways of substituting among them. The end result of these years was that Britain had not only high unemployment, but also slow growth and unprecedentedly unstable prices. (Strictly, the inflation rate is only a target with floating exchange rates, and then the target is domestic relative to world inflation.) Two other major targets of government economic policy are often taken to be the balance of payments and the distribution of income. The question of the balance of payments (or more strictly, foreign exchange reserves) is central in an open economy like Britain's, highly dependent on imported materials for production as well as personal consumption and therefore dependent on exports to finance the required imports. The question of the distribution of income, on the other hand, is much broader, including questions of redistribution of wealth and income among individuals as well as maintenance of balanced employment opportunities among the various regions of the country. The balance of payments was a recurrent problem between 1964 and 1974: the country began the period with a large deficit and, in spite of repeated government efforts to improve it, ended with a much larger one. On the other hand, it is very difficult to summarise trends in the distribution of income, though probably the safest conclusion is that, despite major regional policies, tax reforms, and alterations in a variety of benefits, not a great deal of change in actual distribution took place.

The Labour Government came to power in 1964 with a manifesto promising sustained economic growth without the cyclical 'stop–go' policies of its predecessor. Their view of Conservative economic policies of 1951–64 was one of alternatively stimulating demand (through relaxing credit restrictions and lowering taxation) in order to promote economic investment and employment and then depressing demand (by fiscal measures in the opposite direction) when stock and/or labour shortages promoted inflation and increased demand brought the balance of payments and the pound's exchange rate under pressure. Demand restriction in turn promoted unemployment and restrained economic growth.

The Labour plan was to promote economic growth through (i) coordinated economic planning, reflected in the creation of a Department of Economic Affairs with responsibility for preparing a National Plan for Britain's economic growth; (ii) selective intervention, through limited nationalisation, and rather more through grants and loans, particularly managed by the Industrial Reorganisation Corporation; and (iii) control of inflation, through an effective prices and incomes policy. The organisation around the National Plan was in fact a means of collecting and exchanging information among industries with a view to increasing investors' confidence: as such it was largely an extension of the (retained) National Economic Development Council created in 1962. The first (and only) National Plan (Cmnd 1764), published in September 1965, contained estimates of a growth rate of about 4 per cent per annum, making 25 per cent or so by 1970.

Labour came to power intending to use a voluntary incomes policy to avoid the need for intermittent demand expansion and restriction. In the past there had been several attempts at 'pay pauses' of one sort or another, but nothing approaching the tripartite consultative National Board of Prices and Incomes which was announced in early 1965 and the arrangement for referral of wage claims to a Trades Union Congress committee reached in September of that year. In November 1965, however, referral of pay claims of 'economic significance' was made mandatory, and the remaining voluntarism of the agreement disappeared in the pay standstill and restraint announced in July 1966. For the next four years the Government set wage increase guidelines and retained the power to delay wage increases.

The first year of the Labour Government saw a range of increases in taxation, largely to finance extension of social welfare benefits. Expenditures were then reduced to avoid a run on sterling in July 1965, and one year later, in July 1966, to meet further pressure on the exchange rate, a severe deflationary package of a wage freeze, hire purchase controls, tax increases and spending cuts was announced. While this eventually proved inadequate to retain the $2.80 exchange rate – the pound was devalued to $2.40 in November 1967 – it did mark the end of Labour's concern with expansionary economic policies. The Budgets of Spring 1968 and 1969 were both deflationary (to divert resources into export industries), containing a variety of tax increases and restraints on borrowing, and it was not until the Conservatives' first Budget of 1971 that the promotion of expansion was again considered possible.

The Conservative intention was to restore the importance of market forces in the economy, and in particular to avoid the use of government compulsion in determining wage bargains. Fiscal and monetary measures were to be the principal means of government intervention. Both the Budgets of 1971 and 1972 were expansionary: income tax was simplified and cut, allowances were increased, and Selective Employment Tax was reduced. The pound, which had been realigned against other major currencies in December 1971, came under pressure in 1972 and was floated in June. The Budget of 1973 was also expansionary in its net effect, though its principal changes were the replacement of SET and purchase tax by value-added tax, in line with EEC policy. Two months later, in May 1973, when inflation and a looming balance of payments deficit began to be seen as more serious problems than stagnation, public expenditure was cut, and an emergency program of expenditure cuts was announced in December of that year, following severe international inflationary pressures in many commodities, of which the most visible was reflected in the oil crisis. For the second time in a decade, the expansionary intentions of a government ended in hitherto unprecedented levels of restraint.

Up to the middle of 1972, the Conservatives had pegged their hopes for wage control on the high level of unemployment left over from the restraint of 1969–70, and on enforcing limited wage settlements in the public sector. However, as expansion got under way, so did inflation, and in November 1972 the Conservatives were forced to introduce a 90-day freeze on pay and some prices, followed in April 1973 by the introduction of a statutory limit on wage increases. In November 1973 the limits were altered to allow for further rises, particularly for 'unsocial hours' and where changes in differentials had occurred. Threshold increases to keep up with changes in the cost of living were also introduced. How the policy might have continued is not known, since the government was defeated in the election of February 1974. Further details are available in Beckerman (1972), Livingstone (1974), Stewart (1977), and Blackaby (1978).[1]

[1] For completeness, the Labour Government elected in February (and re-elected with a Parliamentary majority in October) 1974 was committed to avoiding statutory incomes policies, largely through proposed voluntary co-operation from the unions. In June 1975 the voluntary incomes policy was abandoned, and various forms of statutory controls on income increases were maintained over the next three years. A novel feature of prices policy in 1974 was subsidies on a range of commodities, but much of the economic policy of 1974–7, including international loans with fixed DCE targets, expenditure cuts, and high interest rates to counter a declining exchange rate, was relatively familiar.

Targets of economic policy 1964–74

How did Britain fare in this decade? Not very well, almost regardless of which indicator is chosen. The major targets – growth rate, inflation rate, unemployment rate, and the balance of payments[2] – are not independent of each other in practice, and the purpose of economic policy is to find some outcome which reflects an optimal balance among them. Where possible, comparative figures for other Western industrial countries are presented to suggest the range of possibilities surrounding the actual British trends.

Growth rate

Growth is difficult to measure, since definitions vary widely. It is most common to measure economic growth by considering the *real* value of Gross Domestic Product or Gross National Product, each of which principally measures output of goods and services. Britain's real growth rate – about 2.3 per cent per annum – was more or less the same in the 1960s as it had been over the previous decade (Denison, 1967). The same average growth rate is reflected in the behaviour of *real* earnings shown in Figure 2.1. While growth rates throughout the industrial Western world were lower in the 1960s than in the 1950s, what was important in the British case was how much lower the sustained growth rate was than in other countries. Even the moderate success of the government in boosting the growth rate to over 3 per cent in 1964–7 meant that Britain was being outstripped, and not just by the familiar booming economies of countries like Germany, but also by less likely countries such as Italy, Greece, and Spain. Indeed, the predominant growth rate of about 2.3 per cent per annum means that real income would grow by 25 per cent in more like ten years rather than the five forecast in the National Plan, and would double in over 30 years, rather than in 17 years as it would at the (moderate) French annual growth rate of 4.4 per cent. Moreover, not only did Britain's growth rate remain low, but the 1950s and 1960s also saw Britain overtaken by her neighbours France, Germany and the Netherlands in terms of gross national product per capita. In 1960, Britain's GNP per capita had been 40 per cent higher than that of the Netherlands; by 1972, it was 20 per cent lower.

The same conclusions emerge if one considers growth in terms of industrial production rather than GNP. (Industrial production reflects the real value of output in all industries, but *excludes* services, distributive trades, transport, communications, and agriculture.) Partly because the British labour force has not

---

[2] The question of distribution of income is omitted from this discussion. Two good sources for information on this question are M. Stewart, 'The Distribution of Income', in Beckerman (1972) and Atkinson (1975). Stewart provides some evidence that in the years 1964–70 the net effects of taxation and cash benefits moved in a direction indicating benefit to the worst off. Atkinson's data (at pp. 50–4) suggest a redistribution of income between the top 10 per cent and middle half of the population taking place in the 1950s and 1960s, which is possibly attributable to lower rates of unemployment and increased employment opportunities for women. Problems of measurement, and particularly the enormous assumptions that have to be made about the distribution of non-cash benefits, bedevil any analysis, and make further summaries of findings in the present discussion of little value.

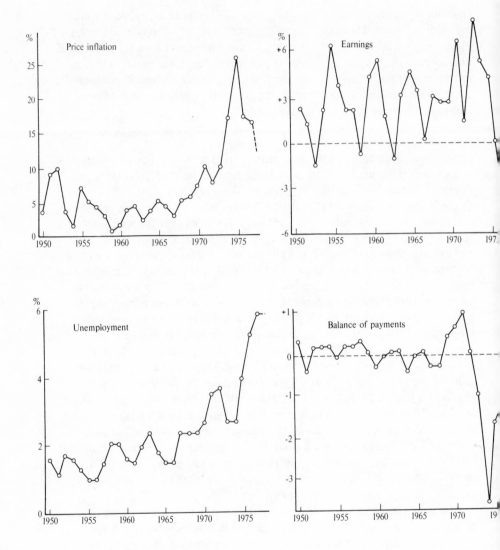

Figure 2.1. Average annual rate of increase in retail prices, average annual rate of unemployment (Great Britain, excluding school-leavers), average annual increase in weekly earnings (all industries, adjusted to constant prices), and current balance of payments (current prices, £'000 millions)
Data from *Economic Trends*, various, and *British Labour Statistics 1868–1968*.

grown, the contrasts are even sharper. The average annual rate of growth of industrial production in Britain between 1965 and 1974 was about 2.1 per cent, half that of the United States (with an expanding labour force) and one third that of France or Italy. By any measure the conclusion is unavoidable that in these years Britain failed to achieve sustained rapid economic growth. Moreover, the ambitious plans of 1965 and 1971 apparently did not succeed in boosting the growth rate any more than the stop—go policies of the decade before. Various reasons for slow growth have been introduced, including the absence of an agricultural work force to mobilise into manufacturing (Denison, 1967), the growth of the public sector (Bacon and Eltis, 1976), and low investment levels.

Inflation rate

Not only were growth targets missed, but the chronic British problem of inflation also became worse. Money wages multiplied almost tenfold between 1948 and 1975 but retail prices multiplied almost fivefold. The resulting 100 per cent growth of 'real' incomes is consistent with the growth rates of the previous section. In fact, largely due to the hyper-inflation (as it then seemed) of the early Korean War years, the average rate of inflation in the 1950s was slightly higher than in the 1960s, though of course nothing at all like the rate of inflation in the 1970s. On the other hand, what may be most important about the British history of inflation is its character of *gradual* growth. The 'shock' of 15—20 per cent inflation in the mid 1970s is cushioned by the experience of (nearly) ten per cent inflation in the early 1970s, which in turn is cushioned by the 6—7 per cent inflation of the late 1960s. Even this is not at all new: long periods of inflation at annual rates of nearly 5 per cent were common in the late 1950s and early 1960s. Insofar as the British people are currently experiencing rapid inflation, they have had a long time to get ready for it.

Moreover, throughout the last 15 to 20 years, Britain's inflation rate has persistently been among the highest in the industrial Western world. As Figure 2.2 shows, Britain's price level relative to that in 1959 has, subsequently, almost always been higher than that of the United States, Canada and West Germany. For a long time it was similar to that of France, but has become higher, and is similar to that of Italy and Japan. Indeed, over the five or six years to 1975, no other country shown in Figure 2.2 had an inflation rate as high as Britain, except for very short periods. (Note that this comparison ignores any differences attributable to construction of the individual country price indices.)

Unemployment rate

All would still not be lost if stability in prices had, say, been sacrificed to maintain full employment, as many recommended it should be. Nevertheless, as Figure 2.1 shows, unemployment as well as inflation increased rapidly through this period, to a point where the *average* rate of unemployment for 1971—5 (and it is currently much higher than this average) is over two and a half times the rate of the early 1950s, and indeed nearly double that of the early 1960s. The clearest

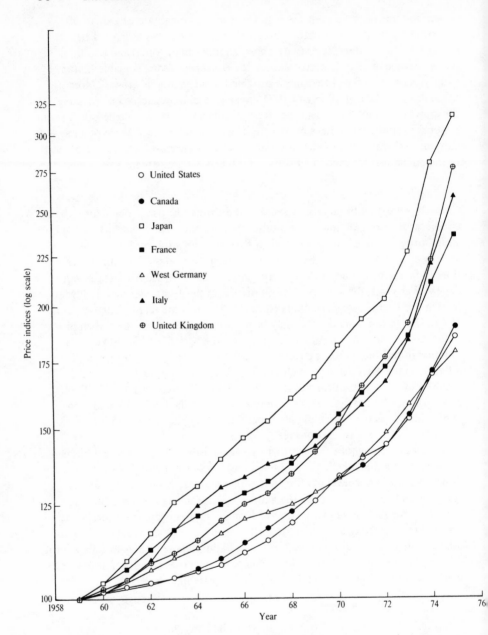

Figure 2.2. Consumer prices in seven countries 1959–75
Source: *National Institute Economic Review*, **54** (November 1970),
p. 74 and **78** (November 1976), p. 81. Adjusted to 1959 = 100 from
published figures.

indication of Britain's increased unemployment is that in every year after 1970 unemployment was higher than it had been in any year up to 1970: the earlier cyclical peaks of unemployment are two per cent in 1952, 2.2 per cent in 1959, and 2.5 per cent in 1963. The unemployment rate does not fall below 2.3 per cent (for the whole year) in any year after 1966.

Moreover, not only did unemployment in Britain increase sharply, but it increased by more than in many other countries. It is hard to compare unemployment between countries because of different methods of counting, and definitions of, unemployment, but the best estimates we can find provide a picture as follows. Compared to other countries, and in particular to the United States, the British definition of unemployment is narrow, and yields a lower estimate of the unemployment rate than would be the case if other systems were used. As Table 2.1 shows, the American method of counting would substantially increase the 'official' level of unemployment in Britain. Indeed, under the American method of counting, the British unemployment rate in 1975 would have been over six per cent, rather than the published 4.3 per cent. Not only does British unemployment appear to be higher, but it is also higher relative to some other countries than the officially published figures indicate.[3] British unemployment in recent years has always been higher than that in West Germany: put on a comparable basis, unemployment in Britain appears to be much higher than in France, rather than as high, and British unemployment appears to be as high as that of Italy, rather than a great deal lower. Some estimates suggest that

Table 2.1. *Unemployment rates in Britain and selected other countries, published and adjusted*

Period	Official British unemployment rate	Adjusted to American concepts: unemployment rate in				
		Britain	France	West Germany	Italy	USA
1951–5	1.4					
1956–60	1.7					
1961–5	1.8	2.8	1.8	0.4	3.3	5.5
1966–70	2.2	3.5	2.2	0.8	3.8	3.9
1971–5	3.3	3.8	3.4	1.8	3.6	6.1

Sources: Official British figures from the sources cited in Figure 2.1. Adjusted figures are from: C. Sorrentino, 'Unemployment in Nine Industrialized Countries', *Monthly Labor Review*, 95, June 1972, 29–33 and R. Myers 'International Comparisons of Unemployment', *The Banker*, 1975, 1257–62.

[3] The British practice in counting the unemployed is quite restrictive, as it includes only those who have paid social security contributions at the full rate, are registered at employment exchanges as unemployed, and are actively seeking work. This results in the exclusion of a number of different groups of workers, notably women, who are excluded from the count in Britain but would be included in other countries. The interested can refer to a long series of articles by Myers and Chandler, and Sorrentino and Moy in the *Monthly Labor Review* between 1962 and 1975. The most recent, which also suggests that earlier work had exaggerated British 'undercounting', is Myers (1975).

in the 1960s Britain moved from having one of the lowest unemployment rates of Western countries to having one of the highest, though subsequent figures suggest that these studies may have overestimated the correction to the official rate. There is no doubt, however, that unemployment in Britain increased greatly over the last decade, and that the British unemployment rate is now, by Western standards, at least fairly high.

Increased unemployment has not been borne equally by the regions, however. The period has seen a transfer of resources from the heart of England to the periphery. In particular Scotland and Wales have fared *relatively* better than the rest of the country, with the biggest losers being the Midlands and the South West. Unemployment in Britain roughly doubles between 1950–2 and 1973–5 (chosen only for convenient reference): in this period in Wales unemployment increases by only a third, and in Scotland by half. By comparison, it more than triples in the West Midlands and nearly triples in Yorkshire, Humberside and the East Midlands, and increases by more than the average in the South West. Thus, East Anglia and the South East have become the areas of lowest unemployment, replacing the Midlands, and the North and North West have become areas of high unemployment, on a level with Scotland and Wales, simply by having average rates of increase in unemployment over the last quarter century. Nevertheless — and even though those northern Labour MPs who resented the apparent favouritism shown to Scotland and Wales in the Devolution Bill of 1976–7 clearly had some basis in fact for these feelings — the strongest trend is the upward movement of unemployment felt everywhere in the country, which dwarfs the smaller changes in the position of the regions.

Balance of payments

The balance of payments can be measured in several ways. It is conventionally measured in two parts: *visible* trade, in which the balance reflects the different amounts of money spent on bringing imports into the country and earned by selling exports outside the country, and *invisible* trade, in which the balance concerns the net flows involved in capital earnings, as well as other items like earnings in shipping and other transport. One can also distinguish between the current and capital accounts, each of which contains visible and invisible balances. The course of Britain's current balance (in annual terms) is also given in Figure 2.1.

Throughout this period Britain carried a deficit on visible trade. That is to say, more was consistently spent on imported goods than was earned on exported goods, with the exception of a very brief period in 1970–1, when the two were very close. Similarly, Britain has always in this period had a surplus on invisible trade, largely through earnings on capital invested abroad. The question hanging over the balance of payments has always been whether the surplus on invisibles would finance the visible deficit. For much of the 1950s and a few years in the early 1960s it did, but Britain's position deteriorated in the 1960s. In 1964 a surge in imports stimulated by expansionary government policies drove the current balance into the red. Briefly in the black in 1966, large balance of payments deficits were encountered before and after devaluation in 1967. The improvement which followed (peaking in 1971) gave a surplus in each year up to 1972. Expansion in 1972 plus an increase in imports in 1973 led to a deficit, which, largely through the increased price of oil, was of unprecedented size.

In the long term – say from 1950 through 1972 – the balance of payments does roughly balance. That is, allowing something for the devaluation of the pound in the later part of the period, most overseas debts could be repaid, and the total of surpluses and deficits over these years roughly cancel. Even the smaller deficits of the years before 1974 had consequences in other areas of economic policy. Repeated international borrowing to protect the currency reserves while repurchasing sterling from overseas led both to expansion of the money supply (through government borrowing) in the 1960s and to restrictions on domestic credit and demand (through other monetary and fiscal policies) as the price of obtaining further international support. Even the floating of the pound did not really alter this, as the official discount rate was frequently raised in the 1970s in order to attract foreign currency into Britain and maintain the exchange rate.

However, this is moving across the line from targets into the area of instruments. In summary, up to the external shocks at the end of the decade to 1974, the balance of payments was the one area in which the British government succeeded in reaching its targets. The devaluation of the pound does not single out Britain as a failure, for the currencies of (among others) France and the United States were both devalued as well in this period. Moreover, as recently as 1972 Britain's international financial position was as strong as it had ever been since 1960. On the other hand, the central targets of government economic policy are rapid growth, stable prices, and high employment, and all recent British governments have adopted these goals. It appears that in Britain, not just have some of these goals been sacrificed for the achievement of others, but indeed all three goals have been missed, and simultaneously. In the years after 1974, unemployment was higher than in the recent past, and high by international standards; inflation was unprecedentedly high for peacetime Britain, and the rapid growth that preoccupied the last few governments proved as elusive as it did in the 1950s.

Instruments of economic policy

Instruments are means to ends, but, as is so often the case, they frequently appear as ends in themselves. For instance, an expansion of credit may in the short term give the illusion of an increase in real income – to those who make purchases with the increased credit – and in the long term it is associated with expansionary policies intended to expand real national income. There may also be inter-party differences in preferences among instruments which achieve the same end. In fiscal matters, it could be argued that Labour politicians prefer to manipulate expenditure and Conservatives taxation (Livingstone, 1974). Thus instruments as well as targets may become the source of political debate, and the subject of public preferences. The next few pages describe the instruments commonly available to the British government in managing the economy, and the uses made of these instruments in the decade up to 1974, under the headings monetary policy, fiscal policy, and incomes policy. (Exchange rate policy will be considered as a part of monetary policy.)

Monetary policy

Monetary policy is principally concerned with controlling the supply of money, though for a long time it could have been said to be about control of interest rates. There are a variety of definitions of money, which depend largely on whether one is concerned with it as a means of payment and exchange or whether the concern is more with total available deposits of money as a store of value. Indeed, sometimes the focus of monetary policy has been on some aggregate measure of domestic liquidity[4] rather than on the stock of currency. There is also a related area of monetary policy concerned with the external trading value of the currency.

In the years up to 1971, there were seven principal powers involved in monetary policy. These included (1) open-market operations in government securities; (2) minimum cash and liquid asset ratios (in terms of total deposits) for the London clearing banks; (3) bank rate, the minimum rate of interest charged by the Bank of England for advances to the discount market; (4) a special deposit scheme, whereby some banks could be required to deposit extra money with the Bank of England, affecting their liquidity and ability to lend; (5) requests to the clearing banks to alter either the amount or character of their lending, made frequently in the late 1950s; (6) actual ceilings on bank loans to the private sector, used commonly after 1965 by the Bank of England in consultation with the government; (7) controls on hire purchase terms (amount of deposit and length of repayment period), which was in fact a power of the Board of Trade (Bain, 1970). Asset ratios were not commonly altered, and therefore were not an instrument used to achieve particular targets; similarly, open-market operations, though constant, are used more for internal money-market purposes than to give overall direction to the money supply. Moreover, open-market operations were constrained by the need to sell government debt. Thus interest rates were often a target of policy – to stimulate capital flows and stabilise markets – rather than a means of controlling the supply of money.

[4] The two conventional definitions of the British money supply are M_1, which includes currency in circulation plus all forms of private sight or demand accounts in sterling, and M_3, which includes M_1 as well as public sector bank deposits, all time deposit accounts, private non-sterling accounts of UK residents, and deposits with the discount houses. Deposits of one bank with another are excluded, and deductions are made for transit items (that is, to reflect the time lag between entering a credit in one account and entering the corresponding debit in another). The Labour Government accepted publicly in 1969 a target for the growth of domestic credit, which reflects that part of the money supply M_3 not affected by movements in the balance of payments or reserves. Domestic Credit Expansion (DCE) targets have also been used as conditions of subsequent international advances to Britain.

The major reform policy of September 1971, 'Competition and Credit Control', was intended to restore the influence of market forces. In particular, deposit banks were freed from their agreement to pay a common interest rate on small deposits, and all banks became subject to a minimum ratio of 12½ per cent between reserve assets and liabilities (Bain, 1976). By manipulating the market in qualifying reserve assets, the Bank of England continued to control interest rates; its power to call for special deposits was nevertheless also retained. In October 1972, the traditional bank rate was replaced by a Minimum Lending Rate linked to the market rate for Treasury bills, switching the target of policy from interest rates to money stock. Institutionally, some of the changes have been more apparent than real: the Bank of England called for special deposits in 1972 and 1973; in November 1973 the authorities independently raised the Minimum Lending Rate irrespective of the prevailing Treasury bill rate; the growth of individual bank liabilities has been restrained by request, directive, and even threat of taxation, and at one point the banks were made to keep the interest rate on small deposits to 9½ per cent to protect the building societies. On the other hand, policy-makers clearly thought the changes real, and the measures of 1972–3 reflect a policy turnabout designed to cope with difficulties in money supply control engendered by 'Competition and Credit Control'.

Figure 2.3 displays trends in the area of interest rates and the supply of

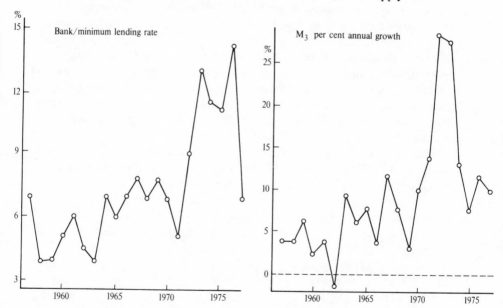

Figure 2.3. Bank rate / minimum lending rate and per cent annual growth of M_3 money supply at end of each year 1957–77
Source: *International Financial Statistics*, various issues. Money supply is 'money' plus 'quasi-money', or 'time savings, and foreign currency deposits'. Money supply data before 1963 are estimated.

money. A change not shown in the figure is that Minimum Lending Rate results in more frequent but smaller alterations. There is no very pronounced trend in rates before 1971: bank rate was as high as seven per cent in 1957 and 1961, and eight per cent in 1967 and 1969, but by the end of 1971 stood again at five per cent. Between the end of 1971 and 1973, it rose from five per cent to 13 per cent (because of inflation, the rise in real interest rates is smaller), and did not slip below 11 per cent until 1975, at the end of which it stood again at 12 per cent. The great increase was caused by desperate attempts to control a rapidly growing money supply, which grew by 83 per cent between 1970 and late 1973, an average annual rate of growth in excess of 22 per cent. In 1972 and 1973 in fact the rate of growth of M_3 was approximately 27 per cent per annum. (In only three years in this period, 1966, 1969, and 1971, was the rate of growth of the money supply smaller than the current rate of increase in retail prices.) Particularly after 1972, much of the increase in money has covered an unprecedentedly large public sector borrowing requirement.

A related area of monetary policy deals with exchange rate policy — the means whereby the external trading value of the pound is set. Before November 1967, the pound had stood at $2.80 for nearly 20 years; Figure 2.4 begins just before devaluation and displays the value of the pound in dollars since then. Working with fixed exchange rates in the 1960s, the principal means of attempting to maintain the exchange rate lay in placing surcharges on imports (done in 1964, requiring deposits on imports (done in 1968), and restricting the amount of currency which could be taken abroad by travellers (done in 1966). The first two were intended to correct the visible balance of payments by reducing imports, and thus reduce the number of pounds leaving the country; the third was a direct control on the latter. When these were insufficient to counteract selling of pounds, loans from other countries and international organisations were obtained to protect currency reserves. There were also capital account restrictions on overseas investment.

Following the 1967 devaluation there was a devaluation of the franc and a revaluation of the deutschmark. Repeated exchange crises, particularly surrounding a weak dollar, led to a widening of exchange rate margins in August 1971 (really a limited float) when the dollar was devalued, a major realignment of currencies in December 1971, and the floating of the pound, followed by other EEC currencies, in June 1972. The dollar value of the floating pound fluctuated considerably in the period up to the middle of 1975, and then began a precipitous decline into 1977, though against the dollar some ground was made up by early 1978. Floating exchange rates are now effects rather than instruments of policy, moving in response to policy setting the rate of domestic credit expansion (Dornbusch, 1976) — but this, like the general economic-theoretical problems of floating exchange rates, is beyond the scope of this volume.

Fiscal policy

Fiscal policy includes the areas of taxation and expenditure. The control of expenditure belongs to the Treasury through a variety of rules, though expendi-

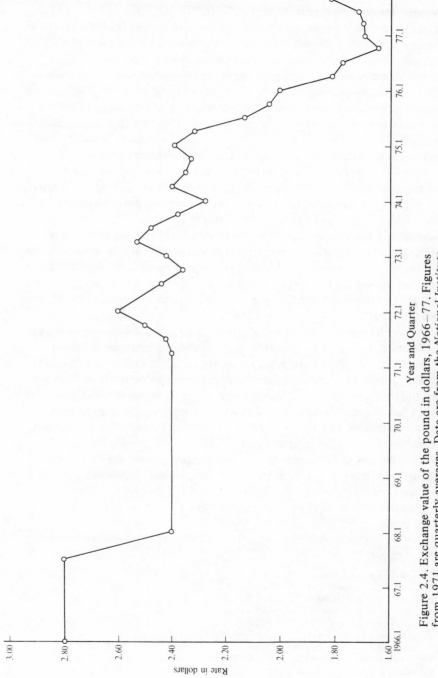

Figure 2.4. Exchange value of the pound in dollars, 1966–77. Figures from 1971 are quarterly averages. Data are from the *National Institute Economic Review*, various.

ture is also subject to review by parliamentary committees (Brittan, 1971). Detailed, long-term forecasting of expenditure was much discussed in the 1960s, and in December 1969 the Government published in the first (Cmnd 4234) of an annual series of White Papers giving five-year expenditure and more limited revenue estimates. Government expenditure can directly stimulate or depress activity or employment in particular sectors of the economy (notably construction); for this reason expenditure cuts have been a frequent means of economic regulation. Announcements relating to cuts in expenditure – outside the normal process of announcing estimates – were made on at least half a dozen occasions between 1964 and 1973: the cuts of £1,200 millions announced as an emergency measure in December 1973 were at the time the largest ever made.

Even before 1969, the Government had begun announcing long-term targets for aggregate *real* expenditure: the Labour Government announced in February 1965 that spending would rise by at most 4½ per cent per annum between 1964–5 and 1969–70, and subsequently revised this figure down to three per cent. Nevertheless, expenditures are difficult to control, and Figure 2.5 shows that expenditure (including transfers) between 1964 and 1969 grew at a rate close to five per cent per annum in real terms (9 per cent in money terms). Similarly, the expenditure forecast for 1974–5 in the 1969 White Paper had grown by 2.6 per cent in real value even *after* the massive expenditure cuts of October 1970 and December 1973.[5]

Part of the root of ever-increasing public expenditure has been the increase in public sector employment, identified in one analysis as the cause of Britain's economic decline (Bacon and Eltis, 1976). Figure 2.5 also includes a series reflecting the proportion of the workforce employed in the public sector, including central and local government and public corporations. If one takes the extreme case (1961 to 1973) there is a growth of 31 per cent in public sector employment, but the slightly extended series 1959–74 suggests that this exaggerates the true growth, which is on the order of about 20 per cent over the whole period. The bulk of this growth takes place in local government employment, but, as the figure shows, it is small in comparison with the growth in public sector spending and borrowing.

Between 1959 and 1974 public sector expenditure grows from just under

---

[5] Jay (1973) makes a series of adjustments for price changes and extrapolations based on continuing growth targets, which provide the following estimates for expenditure in 1974–5 (index values, projected 1969–70 expenditure = 100):

Cmnd 4234 December 1969	115.1
Cmnd 4578 January 1971	110.5
Cmnd 4829 November 1971	112.8
Cmnd 5178 December 1972	120.5
Cmnd 5519 December 1973	122.7
(after the emergency cuts announced 17 December 1973)	118.2

Even after deflating for the effects of price increases, forecast expenditure, though cut in the plans of late 1970, had nevertheless substantially increased over the long-range target of 1969 even as early as 1972.

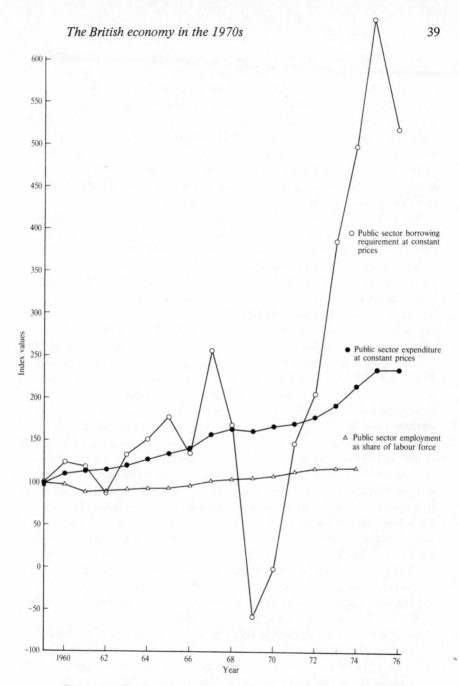

Figure 2.5. Public sector expenditure and employment 1959 = 100
Public sector expenditure data from *Economic Trends*, Annual Supple-
ment 1975, p. 113. Employment data from *Economic Trends* No. 168
(February 1976) pp. 124–7. Recent data from *Economic Trends*,
various issues.

£9,000 millions per annum to over £41,000 millions per annum. As the figure shows, even at constant prices expenditure more than doubled between 1959 and 1974. Growing even faster was the public sector's borrowing requirement – the extent to which public sector income falls short of expenditure – which rose from £469 millions (less than seven per cent of expenditure) in 1959 to £6,325 millions (15 per cent of expenditure) in 1974. The borrowing requirement normally stood at about seven per cent in the late 1950s and 1960s: while it rose to 11 per cent in 1967, there was actually no deficit – indeed a surplus – in 1969 and 1970. It then rose sharply in the early 1970s, largely as a result of expenditure failing to fall in tandem with massive tax reductions.

Variations in taxation are the other principal fiscal means of altering the level of demand in the economy. In Britain taxation is mainly a matter of central government policy; while there are local property taxes and other licence fees, central government receipts amount to over 75 per cent of general government current receipts, a proportion far higher than that of the US, West Germany, France, Sweden or Italy. The most important sources of central government revenue are taxes on the incomes of individuals and corporations, taxes on expenditure (in Britain, purchase tax before 1973 and value-added tax thereafter) and social security contributions made by employees and employers. There have been other sorts of taxes in Britain: the experimental Selective Employment Tax of the 1960s was in fact a tax linked to employers' contributions – and thus to the wage bill – which was used as a transfer between sectors of the economy, principally from services to manufacturing. Governments make a wide variety of arrangements: there is great dependence on social security contributions in France and the Netherlands, but a very low personal income tax and high expenditure tax in France, and a remarkably high share borne by personal income taxation in Denmark. If one assumes that household income tax, expenditure tax, and personal social security contributions reflect the share of government receipts borne by individuals,[6] it appears that individuals in Britain bear a relatively high share of taxation: over 85 per cent, as opposed to 70–75 per cent in the US, France, or the Netherlands, though even the British figure is low in comparison with the figures of 95 per cent plus obtaining in Scandinavian countries.

The fact that a lot of taxation is personal may suggest to some that Britons are more heavily taxed than other nationals, but this comparison, because of varying tax rates and incomes, is extremely difficult to make. Perhaps the safest comparison to make is to look at general government receipts as a proportion of national income. This comparison (using gross domestic product to represent national income) can be made for a number of countries. The share of GDP taken by government current receipts rose steadily in Britain through the 1960s from about 31 per cent to 41 per cent in 1970; it then fell back with the tax cuts

---

[6] Clearly it doesn't, since some expenditure tax is borne by corporations, though as this is likely to be passed on in higher prices directly to consumers, there is a clear sense in which individuals do ultimately bear this tax as well. The data appear in *Economic Trends*, no. 277, November 1976, p. 110.

of 1971–3 to about 37 per cent, though it is probably higher again now. This appears to be a similar level to that obtaining in France and West Germany, and substantially higher than that of Japan (25 per cent), the US (29 per cent) and even Italy (32 per cent), but consistently and substantially lower than that of Sweden (50 per cent).[7]

Figure 2.6 gives a more detailed analysis of these trends in Britain covering benefits and various taxes as proportions of 'average' household income. The figure shows that from 1961 to 1975 the share of household cash income (original income plus cash benefits) provided by cash benefits rises about a third from 7.6 per cent to 10 per cent. The share taken by direct taxes doubles from 8.2 per cent to 16.4 per cent. The shares taken by contributions is more nearly

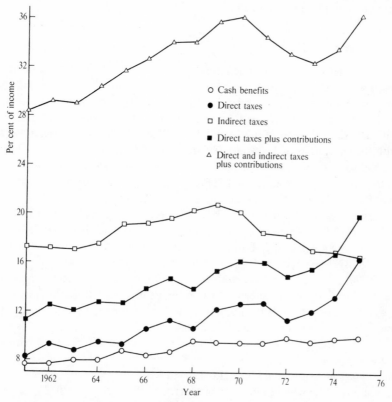

Figure 2.6. Taxes, contributions and benefits as per cent of original income plus cash benefits 1961–75

Data are from *Economic Trends*, No. **270** (January 1977), p. 107.

[7] The source is OECD, *National Accounts Statistics 1962–73*, Tables 1 and 7. Nobody can miss the correlation between the existence of a Social Democratic or Labour Government and higher rates of increase of taxation as a share of GDP (Alt and Chrystal, 1978). It may well be that the pursuit of this correlation by the Heath Government in 1970 to 1973 constituted one of Britain's more serious economic problems, since the reduction in taxation receipts was not matched by a reduction in public expenditure.

constant, rising from 3.1 per cent to 3.5 per cent, and the share taken by (local and national) indirect taxes in fact falls from 17 per cent to 16.4 per cent, though it fluctuates considerably over the period. The fact that the increases in taxation have come so largely out of direct — that is, income — tax fills in the picture provided by the other data in this section. While tax as a proportion of national income in Britain is higher than in some countries, it is similar to that of many other European countries, but the share of tax borne by individuals is relatively high, and the most visible part of this, income tax, has been increasing rapidly in recent years. If Britons consider themselves highly taxed in comparison with other nationals, this reflects the high and increasing share of personal and visible taxation rather than the share of GDP taken in taxation, where Britain occupies a more average position.

Prices and incomes policies

The third area of government economic policy consists of a variety of instruments which directly affect prices and incomes. By now most Western industrial countries have had some experience of incomes policy, and some countries like the Netherlands have had one form or another of incomes policy almost continuously since the end of the Second World War (Ulman and Flanagan, 1971). With the exceptions of 1963—5, 1970—2, and a brief period in 1974—5, Britain has had some form of incomes policy since 1961, though the first years — like earlier attempts in the 1940s and 1950s — consisted largely of governmental exhortations for restraint in wage and salary settlements.

There were two statutory policies in the decade before 1974: the Labour policy begun in 1965 and the Conservative policy begun in 1972. (Relevant government papers include Cmnd 2577, 2639, 2808, 3073, 3150, 3590, 5125, 5205, 5247, 5267 and 5444.) The main points of these policies were:

(i) The existence of a wage *guideline* or *norm*. In the 1966 freeze, the guideline for increases was 0 per cent; it had been 3½ per cent before the freeze. Under the Conservative Phase II the norm was £1 plus four per cent; under Phase III it was a choice of seven per cent or £2.25 per week.

(ii) *Exceptions* from the norm. For the sake of either efficiency or fairness, these policies have included exceptions. In 1967—8, the exceptions, for which larger wage increases could be granted, related to industries with labour shortages and to agreements to increase productivity. Phase III contained exceptions to increase settlements to eliminate 'anomalies' or compensate 'unsocial hours'.

(iii) *Early warning* or referral of wage and price increases to some body established to review them, and in some cases reject them.

(iv) Restraint on *dividends* and other profit-sharing.

(v) *Guidelines* and *exceptions* regarding price increases. Even during the Labour freeze, food was exempt from control, as were firms with less than 100 workers, and price rises were allowed to offset increased costs in imported materials, taxation, short-term changes in supply and other things. The Conservatives linked pricing to 'reasonable' profit margins, and exempted smaller firms from control.

The debate on how to run these policies, and whether or not they are effective, continues (Jones, 1973; Clegg, 1971; Brittan and Lilley, 1977). It does appear to be broadly agreed that the rate of increase of wage rates does slow during at least the early stages of control; whether this only results in a later explosion is a matter of dispute. As is so often the case, much of the argument rests on attempting to decide what would have happened in a given period if there had been *no* wage controls, and to this sort of question there is rarely a convincing answer. Nevertheless, one can conclude that between 1964 and 1974, and after June 1975, prices and incomes policies became a standard part of the government's economic management equipment, and looked like remaining that for some time to come.

In summary, slow growth, rapid inflation, and high unemployment present a picture of economic decline that practically everyone would feel. Coupled with the fact that at the end of a decade of problems and crises these economic indicators were deteriorating even further, one has as good a picture as one can get of the failure of a managed economy in Western industrial society. If ever there was a time when people should be aware of economic developments this would be it, and if ever subjective perceptions of economic well-being would have wider political effects, this would be the time. This is the context in which to place the remainder of this book, which deals in a variety of ways with the public response to the economic decline of the 1960s and 1970s.

Economic policies, perceptions, and expectations

3

Overview: the reaction to economic change

Part II is devoted to popular perceptions and expectations of economic phenomena and the investigation of the relationship between personal economic well-being and various political attitudes and activities. The ultimate aim is to investigate the effects of Britain's economic decline on political support for the two major parties, as well as on the ideological underpinnings of such partisanship. Before this, however, there is much that needs to be shown about 'psychological' economics: about the extent to which actual economic trends appear to influence economic perceptions and expectations, about the relationship between what is seen to be happening and what is expected to follow, and indeed about the process by which economic expectations are formed and the relationship between such expectations and a sense of personal well-being. Then one can begin the construction of a politics of economic decline.

There is another side to the question of the relationship between economic trends, popular economic perceptions and expectations, and support for the political parties. In the context of the theory of party competition, a vote-maximising government has an interest in the economic determinants (if they exist) of its popularity, and therefore electoral success, for two closely related reasons. If tradeoffs exist between two economic targets, both of which are valued by the electorate, and both of which affect government popularity, then there may well be some blend of these targets which is optimal with respect to government popularity. Moreover, electoral considerations may affect the timing and magnitude of particular political interventions in the economy. There is therefore (in theory at least) an interaction between economic developments, government popularity and the timing and execution of decisions in economic management. Part II also looks at this sort of interaction: at the extent to which the government manipulates the economy for its own political purposes.

This chapter sketches the relationships between the economy, people's subjective feelings of well-being, and the political system, as a foundation for the rest of Part II. It appears that, with regard to the spectrum of political concerns, people do attribute considerable *importance to economic trends*. Furthermore, they appear to perceive quite accurately that Britain's position is worsening *relative to other countries*, particularly with regard to standard of living. They *perceive economic trends accurately*, in a way which fits a model of communication rather than individual experience. Moreover, in Britain in recent years, general measures of public optimism and pessimism have come to be determined by trends in economic prosperity and depression. All this, it will be recalled from the last chapter, takes place in the context of the recent British economic experience, which was, if not unique in the Western world, at least an extreme case of what may be a widespread process.

The next chapter provides a detailed account of perceptions and expectations of inflation, widely held to be the most important of Britain's recent economic problems. Chapter 5 investigates the extent to which people can be said to have a general economic outlook (rather than expectations of personal developments) which is positive or negative, and what the origins of this outlook are. The fact that there are both a lot of partisan matters as well as economic trends and political interventions incorporated in economic outlook encourages a further look into the area of linkages between these areas. Subsequent chapters ask whether support for the government depends on evaluations of government policy and economic expectations. Can a government intervene in the economy to make itself more popular? If so, for how long does the effect last? What evidence is there of governments manipulating the economy for their own political purposes? Putting all this together, there are no grounds for arguing that inaccurate economic perceptions or the remoteness of the economy from the individual preclude the existence of an economic politics based on policy preferences and the desire for economic improvement. Rather, there is enormous scope for the political impact of economic expectations — expectations which, by and large, accurately forecast and discount the impact of economic events.

The importance of economic affairs

As Figure 3.1 shows, economic problems have been perceived as by far the most *important* facing the country in the eyes of the British public in recent years. Throughout the Macmillan Government, this was not so: foreign affairs were generally seen to be more important at first, though economic affairs came to the fore during the Lloyd 'pay pause' of 1962, and after that social problems — education, health care, housing and so on — were generally attributed most important. In the periods for which there are data, however, since 1965 there has been only one quarter in which economic problems did not receive the most mentions: this was the fourth quarter of 1970, when the Industrial Relations Act passed through Parliament and strikes temporarily became the most important problem. At all other times in the last decade economic responses have dominated, and have increased up to a point where recently they have been seen as most important by over 80 per cent of the public.

Not only has the economy come to be seen as the most important problem facing Britain, but it is increasingly the more *personal* components of economic affairs like prices which have dominated perceptions. In the early 1970s concern with prices and inflation more or less matched all other economic problems, and indeed for a short period in 1971–2 prices were seen as less important than un-

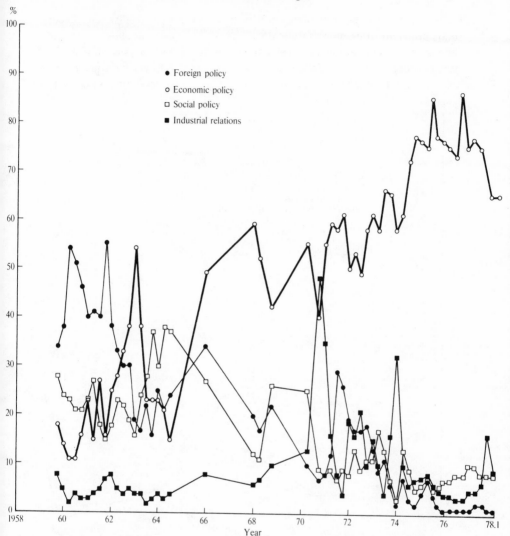

Figure 3.1. Perceptions of most important national problem by policy area 1959–78
Gallup data, averages where more than one observation per quarter.

employment (which was then rising, while the annual rise in the retail price index was seven per cent, less than in the previous year). From the fourth quarter of 1972 until nearly the end of 1977 prices constituted at least three quarters of economic responses, and sometimes as much as nine tenths.[1]

[1] In early 1978, with prices rising at an annual rate of less than 10 per cent, and unemployment still just below 6 per cent, prices nevertheless continued to be seen as the most important problem by about 30 per cent of the sample, with unemployment seen as most import-

Figure 3.2 gives better evidence of the trend towards personalisation of economic problems. It draws on responses to open-ended questions about most
important national problems, good and bad results of elections and good and bad
points about the parties. While it is not always possible to preserve comparability
across two sets of investigators, three series of questions, seven surveys and 11

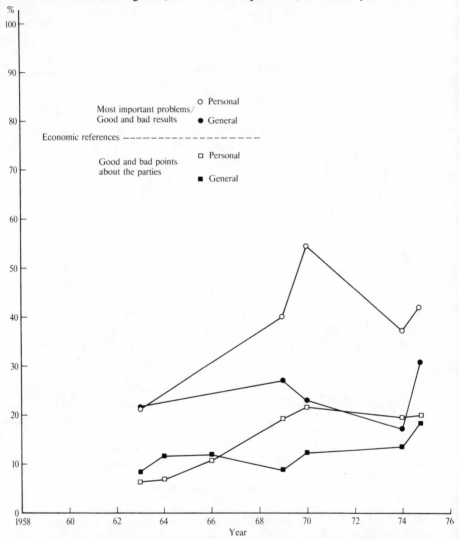

Figure 3.2. Economic references in open-ended questions 1963–74

ant by slightly fewer. Moreover, in 1974 prices were singled out most frequently by far as
the 'single most important issue when it comes to voting' (British Election Study data). It
should be noted that this is not the same as showing how important prices or other economic issues were in relation to other sorts of issues in determining the final pattern of vote
outcomes. On this more complicated problem see Budge and Farlie, 1977.

years, the breakdown employed is of sufficient generality to be fairly reliable. *General* economic responses include not just those relating to the country's prosperity, but all more specific responses relating to the soundness of a government's financial policies, level of government spending, balance of payments, trade policy, government indebtedness, and matters of unemployment. Unemployment is considered a general problem since most of the electorate have no personal experience of it, and particularly no experience of protracted unemployment. *Personal* economic responses are those dealing with things that affect everyone, or most people: in particular, prices (and more recently, subsidies) and taxes, both national and local, as well as those responses relating to prices and taxes affected by the Budget. Figure 3.2 shows that the frequency of both sorts of economic responses has increased, but the increase has been most striking among the more personal responses. The trend in general responses, indeed, is almost flat until October 1974. The frequency of more personal economic responses to the question on important problems rises from 21 per cent of the sample in 1963 to over 50 per cent by 1970, and remains over 40 per cent among results of the 1974 elections. Similar trends may be observed in the responses to questions about the good and bad points of the political parties. The lower lines on Figure 3.2 relate to both good and bad points of both major parties (four questions treated jointly as respondents could say what they liked *or* disliked about either the Labour *or* Conservative Party). Again, the trend in general responses is nearly flat (at least until October 1974)[2] while the trend in personal responses is steeply upward until 1970, and holds its level thereafter. It appears that the first Wilson Government was a time of considerable growth in the economic component of party evaluation, particularly in the more personal areas of taxation and prices rather than in the general areas of prosperity, unemployment, and the balance of payments.

Foreign comparisons

The previous section suggested that the British public have come to attribute more importance to the country's economic problems, and particularly to those with the clearest personal consequences, and moreover that this trend carries over, though perhaps less sharply, into their evaluation of the political parties. In the context of a declining economy, this should lead to decreased estimates of personal well-being, unless people believe that much the same is happening everywhere, and thus that they are not particularly adversely affected. However, not only do the British people see themselves as falling behind other countries, but they apparently (and perhaps accurately) single out the economy as the area in which the decline is taking place.

[2] Close investigation shows that the sudden increase in economic general responses in October 1974 is matched by an increase of coded responses of the greatest generality in *all* areas. This may well be due to different practices among interviewers in the amounts of information recorded or among coders.

Table 3.1 shows that between 1962 and 1972 the British saw themselves as falling behind other countries in terms of standard of living, and in particular in that part of standard of living related to money incomes rather than (perhaps) non-monetary social benefits. The first pair of columns show that the British, by majorities of 48 per cent, 38 per cent and 22 per cent respectively, see the Germans, Swedes and Dutch as better off with respect to general standard of living: the French are seen as being on a par. However, the French are clearly seen as gaining, for ten years earlier a majority of 24 per cent saw the British as better off. The Swedes have made a similar gain, and the Dutch a smaller one. Hence *large* and *increasing* proportions of the British see the people of other countries as having a better standard of living than that available in Britain.

Table 3.1. *Subjective comparisons with other European countries*

Country	Other European country's lead with respect to					
	Standard of living		Money earned		Social benefits	
	1962	1972	1962	1972	1962	1972
Germany	n.a.	48	n.a.	47	n.a.	11
Sweden	14	38	15	31	−7	8
Netherlands	14	22	15	18	−7	−8
France	−24	0	−16	4	−31	−25

Note: Cell entries represent the *net* of *British* respondents saying people in the *other* country were better off minus those saying the British people were better off. The data reflect only British views of themselves and the people of other countries.
Source: Gallup Political Index

The second pair of columns in Table 3.1 relates to money earned. What is most important about these figures is how similar they are to the first pair of columns, which could suggest how close the link between income and standard of living is seen to be in Britain. The third pair of columns relates to social benefits. In this case, the British come to a more favourable assessment of their own position: the proportion seeing the British as better off than the French is 25 per cent larger than the proportion seeing the French as better off, and even the Germans and Swedes hold very small leads in British eyes. Moreover, though the differences are small, in each case the British also see themselves as falling behind less quickly. This focus on economic matters is consistent with other recent evidence that, for instance, compared to other European countries, the British rate the running of their industry far more unfavourably than the running of their government. While, compared with other European countries, only 12 per cent believe that Britain is governed relatively badly (as opposed to relatively well or about average), 27 per cent believe British industry to be run relatively badly (British Election Study October 1974 cross-section sample). While the evidence regarding the singling out of economic failure is little better than straws in the wind, the central conclusion of this section — that the British do see themselves as behind other countries, and falling increasingly back — appears incontrovertible.

Optimism and the economy

The next problem is to show that the British people translate these perceptions of economic decline into negative feelings about their own well-being, and how this translation is made. What can be shown is that:

(i) Expectations of general betterment — optimism — are best seen as a function of expectations of general economic prosperity.

(ii) Expectations of general economic prosperity are best seen as functions of expectations of specific economic trends, in particular strikes, unemployment, and taxes.

(iii) Expectations of specific economic trends are accurate, and in a way which suggests a forecasting of future trends rather than a projection of past experience.

Each year Gallup ask a sample (at the end of the year) whether 'as far as you yourself are concerned, will (next year) be better, worse or about the same as this year?' The proportion saying 'better' minus the proportion saying 'worse' yields a general index of 'personal optimism' in Britain, which has been plotted in Figure 3.3. (See Figure 5.1, below, for comparisons with other trends.) The same sample are asked whether the next year will be a year of *prosperity* or *economic difficulties* (also in Figure 3.3), *rising* or *falling prices*, *unemployment* or *full employment*, *strikes* or *industrial peace*, *rising* or *falling taxes*, a *peaceful year* or a *troubled year*, and so on. Assume that prosperity, falling prices, full employment, industrial peace, falling taxes and a peaceful year represent the desirable ends of each choice. Let the net value of proportion saying the desirable minus proportion saying the undesirable end represent indices of expectations of specific trends. For instance, 30 per cent saying 'prosperity' and 50 per cent saying 'difficulties' gives an observation of −20 for a given year for that series. The correlations between series are shown in Table 3.2.

The series are not as highly intercorrelated as one might have expected, especially as all of them except unemployment show statistically significant downward trends (i.e. towards more pessimistic or unfavourable replies) over this period. General optimism is more closely correlated with all the economic series other than tax expectations than with peace; moreover, the closest correlation is with the trend in expectation of prosperity. The close correlation — and downward trend — of these series is evident in Figure 3.3. Indeed, it is the case that if the optimism series is regressed on the prosperity series, none of the remaining series has a significant independent effect. Moreover, no *combination* of the other series gives quite as good a prediction of the optimism series as does economic prosperity alone, which when adjusted for time effects gives the following 'best' equation[3]

[3] For each equation the unstandardised ordinary least squares (OLS) regression coefficients are presented. All coefficients presented are significant at the .05 level by a *t*-test. The un-

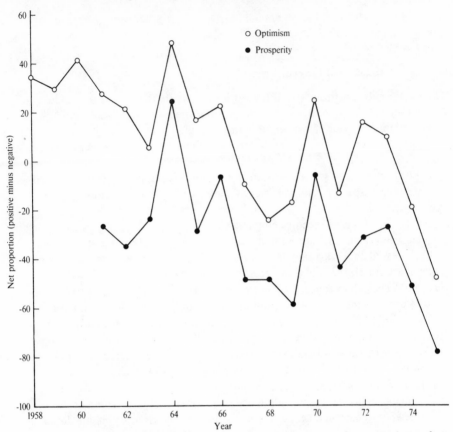

Figure 3.3. Trends in optimism about next year and expectations of national prosperity 1958–75

$$O = 44.4 + 0.83\,P - 1.27\,T$$
$$(n = 15,\, R^2 = 0.88,\, F\text{-ratio} = 43.2)$$

where O is optimism, P prosperity, and T a time trend and all coefficients statistically significant. A look at standardised coefficients (not shown) reveals that the effects of prosperity are four times as large as those of time. The significance of the time coefficient suggests that optimism has come down faster in this period than have expectations of prosperity, which were a good deal lower to begin with. Hence it appears that ((i), above) the principal component of general personal expectations is general economic expectations.

But while these other series may not contribute to optimism independent of expectations of prosperity, it is clear that some of them are very good predictors of expectations of prosperity. In fact price expectations do *not* play an independent part in determining prosperity expectations: these two series apparently

standardised coefficients allow inspection of the constant term and calculation of the expected effect of a one per cent change in any of the variables.

Table 3.2. *Correlations among series of expectations*

Series						
Employment	0.16					
Industrial peace	0.54	0.53				
Taxes	0.49	−0.19	0.18			
Prosperity	0.58	0.65	0.71	0.43		
Peace	0.58	0.33	0.74	0.24	0.65	
Optimism	0.66	0.61	0.69	0.44	0.92	0.56
	Prices	Employment	Industrial peace	Taxes	Prosperity	Peace

Note: Calculations are from data in *Gallup Political Index*.

have only a time trend in common. The other three economic series however provide jointly a very good prediction of prosperity, as follows:

$$P = 8.6 + 0.43\ FE + 0.38\ IP + 0.48\ FT$$
$$(n = 15, R^2 = 0.81, F\text{-ratio} = 15.6)$$

where P is prosperity, FE fuller employment, IP industrial peace, and FT falling taxes. In fact, the standardised coefficients (not shown) suggest that employment has the greatest impact, and strikes the smallest. Nevertheless, the joint determination of expectations of prosperity is good. It would be more in keeping with the times if the equation were summarised as suggesting that ((ii), above) expectations of economic difficulties are a weighted sum of expectations of unemployment, strikes, and taxes.

Why should people have positive or negative expectations about prices, strikes, unemployment, or taxes? There are *two* possible explanations. One would argue for the relevance of *experience*: that people's expectations of what will happen next year are a function of what has happened in the past year. There are problems with this account: in particular, low correlations have been observed between perceptions of past and projections of future economic events, even in the context of good information. Moreover, why should someone predict that because last year was a year of high unemployment that next year will be as well? Or indeed, will not be? The other explanation stresses *communication*. Some of the economic events under discussion are not entirely haphazard, and are the subject of predictions by professional economists and others. Within broad limits, these predictions are accurate, and they are communicated to the broader public at great length and in great detail by the media. Moreover politicians promulgate these forecasts, particularly when embarking on policies intended to affect these economic areas. Thus, by and large, the popular expectation series will be determined by unofficial and official forecasts prevalent at the time the popular expectations are recorded. Insofar as the official projections are roughly accurate, popular expectations will be roughly accurate.

These models can be quite simply distinguished. If the *experience* model is correct, there should be a close correlation between each expectation series and some objective measure of its economic area in the *previous* year. If the *communication* model is accurate, the stronger correlation will be with the economic indicator value in the *following* year, i.e. the year covered by the prediction, rather than the one at the end of which it is made. Table 3.3 gives the results in the form of squared correlations, or shared variances.

Table 3.3. *Expectations and economic indicators*

	Common variance with indicator in	
Series	Past year	Next year
Tax expectations and increase in total tax take	0%	49%*
Unemployment expectations and unemployment rate	7%	50%*
Strike expectations and days lost in strikes	18%	22%
Price expectations and retail price index	34%*	38%*

*$P \leqslant 0.01$ (F-test)
Note: Tax data from OECD, *National Accounts Statistics*, various. Unemployment and strikes from *Department of Employment Gazette*, various. Prices from *Economic Trends*, various. Expectations data from *Gallup Political Index.*

The evidence is strongly on the side of the communication model. In every case the strong positive correlation is with events in the subsequent year. There is no common variance between extent of change in total tax take from all sources in one year and expectations for the next; expected and actual changes have half their variance in common. That is to say, taxes go up by and large when people expect them to, rather than people expecting them to go up (or down) because they have. It is true that outlines of the Budget are often known some time in advance. However, the same pattern appears in the case of unemployment where expected changes and actual future changes go largely hand-in-hand.

The case of strike expectations is different. In this case the salient point is that strikes are not subject to modelling and prediction in the same way these other economic indicators are. There is really no reason to believe that people would predict strikes on the basis of current published predictions, since these do not exist. People are just as likely to use recent experience as a guide, or to guess wildly. And indeed the strikes series offer no distinction between the models, and no significant squared correlations appear.

The result in the case of price expectations is perplexing in that there is only a very small difference between models, results of both of which are statistically significant. Several further points can be made. One is that the difference between correlations increases, and in the direction implied by the communication model, if only the last decade is included, which is the time in which inflation came to prominence as an issue. The second is that the inflation series is quite heavily autocorrelated in this period, and therefore anything correlating with change in prices in one year probably correlates fairly closely with change in prices the previous year, as all the small observations are at one end of the series and all the large ones at the other. Moreover, it must be pointed out that expectations about prices are already almost unanimously negative by 1961, when the inflation rate is only three to four per cent. It might be that the price expectations series is really static over the last decade, and subject only to random fluctuations. Finally, it could be argued that only prices are important and personally-experienced enough to permit people to form expectations at least partly on the basis of what they perceive has been happening. Better evidence is preferable to speculation, however, and the next chapter gives a more comprehensive account of inflation expectations. For the moment, it need only be said that the price series does not really confirm — though it does nothing to contradict — the communication model of expectation formation.

However, the taxation and unemployment series do confirm the communication model strongly. Since it is unlikely that people are particularly prescient, or remarkably lucky, these figures mean that popular expectations arise out of current *predictions* about the economy, which in turn implies some degree of awareness and concern with the state of the economy in the population at large. Moreover, these specific expectations determine general expectations of prosperity, and the data suggest that feelings of well-being or optimism in Britain recently were likely to be largely economic in origin.

4

Believing what you see: inflation expectations in 1974

This chapter is devoted to the analysis of popular perceptions and expectations of price increases. Of course, there is a tradition of research which purports to show that popular perceptions of inflation are not worth investigating from the point of view of studies of public policy or voting behaviour. The perceptions are not worth investigating because popular perceptions of price rises are wildly inaccurate and idiosyncratic and because public comprehension of the term 'inflation' is low. Because of this, it is claimed, the political–economic debate on the causes and cures of inflation necessarily takes place unnoticed and misunderstood by the public. It is certainly true that the public view of causes of inflation recorded in opinion polls can frequently look unusual and ill-informed, though there are perspectives (below, Chapter 8) which make more sense of the data. Similarly, the much-cited poll showing that a majority prefer one party on prices and another on inflation (Butler and Kavanagh, 1974; Brittan, 1976) is readily explicable if as few as one fifth of one party's supporters have no comprehension of the term 'inflation', which accords well with existing data. In fact, it can readily be seen that a few none-too-heroic assumptions can render virtually either party a moderate majority on these questions.[1]

However, the question of popular inflation expectations deserves closer analysis than these inferences from scattered opinion polls. In part, the need for careful scrutiny arises from the importance attached to prices by the public and

[1] The interpretation made here is strengthened by the finding of class bias in comprehension of the term 'inflation' (Behrend, 1971b). Consider a wholly hypothetical poll, in which voting and preferences are as follows:

Prefer on inflation	Con	Votes Lab	All	Prefer on prices	Con	Votes Lab	All
Con.	38	10	48	Con.	38	5	43
Lab.	7	35	42	Lab.	7	40	47
Don't know	5	5	10	Don't know	5	5	10
	50	50	100		50	50	100

All the above table assumes is that everyone understands the term prices, all Conservatives understand 'inflation', but that ten Labour voters (one in five) do not understand the term 'inflation'. These ten, however, split their preferences 50-50 between Labour and Conservatives, though, like good partisans discussing something they understand, they all prefer Labour on the question of prices. This easily converts a Conservative majority on 'inflation' into a Labour majority on prices.

the growing attention of political analysts to the role of popular expectations in the political process. Moreover, economists have recently made popular expectations of inflation an increasingly important element in theories of inflation. Though this view is commonly associated with 'monetarist' economics, a number of schools of thought are consistent with the view that inflation itself is fuelled by widespread expectations of further inflation, particularly on the part of those responsible for making pay settlements.

Efforts have been made to ascertain the extent to which the public comprehend the term 'inflation' as well as the awareness the public display of the actual rate of inflation at any time. Much of this literature is quite old, and there is no evidence available of the effects of the rapid inflation of the mid-1970s on public awareness. A general picture can be extracted from a number of related sources (Behrend, Lynch and Davies, 1966; Behrend, Lynch, Thomas and Davies, 1967; Behrend, 1971a, 1971b, 1973; Treasure, 1972). This suggests that in 1966 substantial numbers (perhaps a third of the electorate) had little or no conception of either the meaning of the term 'inflation' or of any connection between wages and prices. This proportion had fallen by 1971 to something under a quarter of the electorate. There is evidence that in France between 1970 and 1975 public comprehension of terms like inflation increased considerably (Szmaragd, 1977). In the absence of evidence, it can only be assumed that development of public comprehension continued in Britain as well, and that the level of understanding of economic issues would now be similar to understanding of other familiar issues, with perhaps ten per cent of the electorate having little or no idea of even basic factual matters (Alt, Särlvik and Crewe, 1976b). On the question of perceiving the actual rates of increase of prices, difficulties are encountered when the public are asked to deal with percentages, and actual perceived rates of increase are generally exaggerated. There is evidence that people are familiar with price increases of some goods, at least those purchased regularly, and that people can discriminate accurately between goods whose prices have been rising relatively rapidly and relatively slowly. It is probably safe to assume that the public have enough information about price inflation so that their views cannot be regarded as meaningless or of no value. From that starting point, the next step is to move on to models of the formation of inflation expectations.

Econometric approaches to inflation expectations

What is the connection between perceptions of price changes and expectations of future price changes? Put another way, what is the process by which people form expectations of price changes? For answers, there is the work of a number of economists, largely stimulated by the increasingly common view that expectations of further inflation themselves play a role in causing inflation. Much attention has been focused on the concept of 'rational' expectations, by which is meant that 'economic agents form their expectations as if they know the process which will ultimately generate the actual outcomes in question' (Friedman,

1975). Thus, rational expectations 'are essentially the same as the predictions of the relevant economic theory' (Muth, 1961). This does not mean that to assess expectations it is necessary to know what the model is that each economic agent believes appropriate, or even assume that each person has a highly sophisticated economic model in his mind. It does require, however, that in forming expectations people should use whatever information they have efficiently.

The notion of rational expectations appears to be strictly different from another theory of expectation formation, which sees expectations as the (somehow weighted) product of recent experience. This contrast was implicit in the last sections of the previous chapter, where popular expectations of economic trends were hypothesised either to extrapolate from recent experience or to forecast the future. The predictive case was substantiated in the areas of taxation and unemployment, where people's forecasts on average accurately anticipated future developments. The case of price expectations, it will be recalled, was indeterminate between the two models.

Some recent work has tended to close the gap between these two approaches. In particular, Feige and Pearce (1976) point to a concept of 'economically rational expectations', in which they suggest that a rational agent will use an efficient scheme to employ all the predictive information contained in the past experience of inflation. Having done so, he would then ascertain that the extra benefits (in terms of predictive accuracy) from broadening the information base of expectations more than offset the extra cost of obtaining broader information. They present evidence to suggest that it might not be worth investing (time or money) acquiring knowledge of a broad range of other economic indicators which predict inflation in order to generate *cost-effective* expectations. In their terms, rational expectations are those with the greatest accuracy relative to cost; it would be irrational to devote enormous resources to finding information which generated only slightly more accurate predictions. In related work, Friedman (1975) shows that rational expectations require either the assumption of long-term equilibrium in the model employed, or they must contain some form of learning procedure. Under the assumption of agents' finite memories or incomplete specification of models, one can equate 'rational' and 'adaptive' expectation formation processes, and attention has been given to the class of adaptive models which satisfy the assumptions of theories of rational expectations (Rose, 1972; Feige and Pearce, 1976).

An *adaptive* model of expectations formation is one in which the agent periodically revises his expectations in the light of the discrepancy between his last forecast and the actual outcome since it was made. Thus for example someone who forecasts inflation monthly would make the difference between his November forecast and his October forecast be some fraction of the difference between his October forecast and the actual rate of inflation in October (after the forecast). Thus, generally, first-order adaptive price expectations for period *t* are given by

$$p_t^e = p_{t-1}^e + \lambda(p_{t-1} - p_{t-1}^e) \tag{1}$$

Extra terms (with declining weights) can be added for errors in months earlier than the previous month (Carlson and Parkin, 1973). Moreover, solving the difference equation from (1) gives a function for price expectations p_t^e in terms of a geometrically weighted moving average of past observations of price movements p_t, p_{t-1}, and so on (Muth, 1961).

Adaptive expectation formation is commonly contrasted with *extrapolative* expectations, for which the simplest formulation is that price expectations at any point are a linear function of the latest known price. This is the simple recent experience model used in the previous chapter. In this formulation, extrapolation is a special case of (1) above, in which $\lambda = 1.0$. A more sophisticated extrapolative model, which involves an element of learning, is to allow expectations to be a function both of current prices and of the rate of change of current prices (Muth, 1961), that is, to allow for the perception that at any rate of inflation, inflation may be accelerating or decelerating – given by

$$p_t^e = p_{t-1} - \delta(p_{t-1} - p_{t-2}) \tag{2}$$

This formulation differs from the process involved in (1) only by the functional form involved for lagging price movements *unless* one has independent observations of expected prices. Dissatisfaction with the view that price expectations were no more than a distributed lag or weighted moving average of past inflation has led to considerable effort being devoted toward generating independent measures of price expectations. As background to the analysis which follows, two particularly thorough papers demand review. Both these papers are distinguished by their use of survey data to generate values for inflation expectations, though they contribute interesting theoretical points as well.

The Kane–Malkiel 'return-to-normality' model

Kane and Malkiel (1976) employ data generated at three points in time by surveying a panel of investment advisers and consultants. Interviews were taken in July 1969, October 1970 and January 1972; all their evidence relates to the United States. At each point in time, respondents were asked for their forecasts of the inflation rate over a variety of periods from the next quarter or half year up to the average rate over the next ten years. The Kane–Malkiel theory is that each individual has some conception of the likely long-term rate of inflation and makes his shorter-term forecasts in terms of the discrepancy between the current observed rate of inflation and the long-term expected rate. In other words, people use current inflation as the basis of a short-term forecast, which *is* the current rate of inflation modified in the direction of long-term expectations. (The fact that individuals have a long-term expectation implies that they process information beyond that contained in past rates of inflation, and therefore suggests that the autoregressive schemes outlined above, whether extrapolative or adaptive, fall short of the demands of rational expectations models – but see Rutledge (1974) – in which people use efficiently all available information.) The Kane–Malkiel formulation is that

$$_n\Pi_{j,t} - p_t = -d(n)\,[p_t - \Pi_{j,t}^N] \qquad (3)$$

where $_n\Pi_{j,t}$ reflects individual j's forecast at time t for period n ahead, $\Pi_{j,t}^N$ is individual j's long-term 'normal' expected inflation rate at time t, p_t is the observed rate of inflation at t, and $d(n)$ reflects a weight appropriate to the particular time span n. $d(n)$ must be greater than 0 and less than or equal to 1; it also must be the case that $d'(n) > 0$, so that the longer the time span n, the greater is d, and the closer the expected inflation rate comes to the long-term rate. In fact, their formulation is readily intelligible: if inflation is currently *less* than your long-term normal expectation, your short-term expectation should be for inflation to *increase*; if inflation is currently more than normal, you should expect it to decline. The coefficient $d(n)$ simply gives the fraction by which you weight the difference between expected and normal in making a short-term forecast. For instance, if inflation is currently ten per cent per annum but you think the long-term rate is five per cent, your forecast (if $d = 0.2$) would be nine per cent.

A number of tests are presented. In particular, Kane and Malkiel present evidence that their return-to-normality model outperforms adaptive formulations of expectation formation. This result depends critically on their assumption that p_t – the observed rate of price change – is constant across all respondents, and some evidence against this assumption – and in support of adaptive models – is given below. They also investigate models combining adaptation and return-to-normality elements, and in particular attempt to assess changes in individuals' long-term forecasts. They conclude that when normal rates of inflation are revised (as for instance in the face of accelerating inflation between 1970 and 1972) the importance of error-learning increases, and that expected rates of inflation may follow observed rates very closely. This point is also supported by the experimental evidence of Schmalensee (1976), who argues that speed of adaptation increases – that is, that only the most recent observations and errors are considered – around turning points in price series, and that adaptation is slower in periods of relative price stability. However, Kane and Malkiel's central contention remains that the 'normal' rate of inflation is more than some function of past rates, and that return-to-normality elements are very important in the process of expectation formation.

The Carlson–Parkin model

Carlson and Parkin (1975) start from a monthly series of Gallup surveys in which respondents (ordinary people in this case) were asked whether over the next six months they expected prices to go up, go down, or stay about the same. They provide a method for converting the frequency distribution of these replies (from 1961 to 1973) into a set of monthly estimates of the average expected rate of inflation. Their method proceeds as follows. Some people are incapable of replying to the survey question. They are all assumed to respond 'don't know', though others may make this reply as well. Each capable individual is assumed to have his own batch of commodities to whose price changes he is sensitive, and to form a subjective probability distribution of expectations of price changes for this batch. (The probability distributions may vary among individuals and over time.) Each individual has a median price expectation; that is, a point in his subjective probability distribution of price expectations above and below which lie half of his (probability-weighted) price expectations. Moreover, there is around zero a range of price changes which are imperceptible to the individual: a percentage by which prices could rise or fall such that the individual would be unable to distinguish the change.

Given these assumptions, an individual says 'prices go up' if his median expectation is greater than the minimum perceptible rise (that is, at least half his expectations are perceptibly 'up'), 'down' if it is less than the minimum perceptible fall, and 'no change' or 'don't know' otherwise. Means of estimating the proportion incapable of answering (calculated at 2.5 per cent) and the minimum perceptible change (calculated at around 1.7 per cent) are provided. Estimates of expected inflation are then calculated by taking the proportion saying 'go up' and 'go down' and treating these as probabilities in terms of a normal distribution of expectations across the population. A unique result can be obtained by setting the average value of expectations across the entire time series equal to the actual average rate of inflation across the entire time series.[2]

Carlson and Parkin then assess a number of models of expectation formation as well, and the results are mixed. Their principal conclusion appears to be that in times of steady inflation, expectation formation is autoregressive; that is, present expectations are based simply on past expectations and there is no systematic change in expectations when the actual inflation rate is steady. Extrapolation from actual past observed inflation is not supported as an expectation-formation process by their data. In times of higher inflation, however, expectations appear to follow a second-order error-learning or adaptive process, whereby current expectations are adjusted in the light of the two most recent errors. (An adaptive process sensitive only to the last error would work as follows: if inflation were ten per cent, and your last forecast (for the present) had been five per cent, then your next forecast will be five per cent (last forecast) plus some part λ of the error (10 per cent − 5 per cent). If $\lambda = 0.5$, then your next forecast is $5 + 0.5(10 − 5) = 7.5$ per cent; if $\lambda = 1.0$, then you just expect what you see to continue.) In general their data support adaptive models of expectation formation, though they have no means of testing return-to-normality

[2] This creates difficulties when − as after 1974 − the rate of inflation shifts upward by more than the frequencies of their response alternatives can. Recall that already at the end of 1971, the annual data cited in Chapter 3 gave comparable replies showing that 88 per cent expected rising prices, and four per cent falling prices. On the Carlson−Parkin calculation, this gives an expected value of inflation of over 12 per cent, and leaves very little room for the replies to alter in response to doubled inflation rates.

models. They find that the devaluation of November 1967 sharply put up inflation expectations, but only for a few months at the most; other variables which they test have no independent effects. Inspection of their series suggests that post-election euphoria is absent, though there is a sharp one-month drop in inflation expectations at June 1970; similarly, the imposition of a wage freeze (July 1966, October 1972) appears to produce a drop in expectations of about two per cent and lasting at most two months. The adaptive scheme they defend suggests how difficult it is for popular inflation expectations to be reduced — unless inflation itself is reduced first.

The Carlson—Parkin approach has the advantage of being based on a survey question which is extremely simple for respondents to comprehend, and thus avoids generating vast amounts of unusable data. Some of the broader assumptions they make, about imperceptible changes and incapable respondents, appear quite acceptable. The normality assumption is more of a problem. Under the normality assumption it is impossible to obtain a survey result in which no one has expected prices to fall, as there is no value in the normal distribution to the left of which the probability of occurrence is zero. This contingency arose only rarely in the period they studied, and on the few occasions it arose, they could avoid it. Since their series stops in late 1973, however, it is probable that an increasing proportion of months have shown no one expecting prices to fall, and in this case the problem will not go away. There is the added problem that their estimates are very unstable when the proportion saying 'go down' is small, and their calculations make no allowance for response or transcription error creating one or two per cent 'go down' replies. They can avoid the whole problem by assuming some distribution other than the normal distribution (it only needs to have a real mean and variance), and evidence about the actual distribution of price expectations presented below will probably be useful.

In addition to the distribution problem, there is also the fact that the average expected value of inflation is tied to the true average value of inflation by *definition* rather than by observation. In this sense their results derive and defend a process of expectation formation without generating independent estimates of the actual *magnitudes* of people's expectations of price changes, which earlier work reviewed above suggested were generally exaggerated. The fact that the values of the minimal perceptible prise rise — and therefore the expected values of inflation they generate — are tied to the average actual value of inflation means that the coefficients and estimates they provide have to be recalculated more often, and are therefore less reliable, whenever inflation accelerates most rapidly. This is a great difficulty, for it is in just such a period that their estimates are most wanted.

The Kane—Malkiel study, which employed cross-sectional expectations of inflation (albeit from experts), relied on the assumption that observed inflation is the same for all individuals. The Carlson—Parkin series depends on the assumption of normally-distributed expectations, which on their methodology requires that some people more or less always expect prices to fall, which in recent years is unlikely. Moreover, the fact that their estimated values for expected inflation depend on the average value of observed inflation means that the coefficients they provide cannot be transplanted to generate new estimates from more recent surveys without rescaling the entire series. Clearly, further observations in the perceived and expected rate of inflation are going to be useful in synthesising the process-oriented econometric approaches with the direct evidence on perceptions from earlier studies.

British inflation in 1974

What did people believe the rate of inflation was in 1974, and what did they expect it to be in the future? Respondents to *both* February and October 1974 cross-section surveys were asked the following pair of questions on each occasion:
(1) Let's talk about prices for everyday goods. Let us say you spent a pound in the shops a year ago. What do you think you would have to pay to get the same goods today?
(2) And what about a year from now? What do you think you will have to pay to get those same goods in a year's time?

Responses were recorded in terms of pounds and pence. Thus for each respondent there are *four* pieces of data: *both* a perception and expectation of inflation in February, and *again* in October. Note that the observed rate of inflation is given by the response to question (1) minus one pound: thus a respondent who says that the goods would cost £1.30 today implies that inflation over the past year has been thirty pence in the pound, or 30 per cent per annum. There is an ambiguity in the responses to the second question: it is clear however that the expected increase in prices is given by the difference between replies to questions (1) and (2). To convert to an annual rate, one should divide this difference by the response to question (1) — for instance, if the respondent who said things cost £1.30 now said they would cost £1.75 in a year, his expected rate of inflation is (£1.75 − £1.30)/£1.30, or (times 100 to give a percentage) about 35 per cent. There are reasons for believing that people's replies should not be interpreted in exactly this way, but this is discussed in full in the next section.

Data on price perceptions generated this way have the advantage of allowing means and variances to be calculated directly, and also produce an extremely low rate of non-response: only *one* per cent of those asked could not give a reply to question (1), and only five per cent could or would not give a prediction. Of course, this does not necessarily mean that those who replied gave meaningful or sensible replies. In order to begin the investigation of this data by considering the accuracy and distribution of price perceptions, there is a need for a little information about the 'true' rate of inflation at the time of the survey.

The retail price index

One must assume that the retail price index published by the Department of Employment is the appropriate source for judging accuracy of individual price perceptions. This index is now periodically reweighted to reflect actual consumption patterns, is calculated and published for a variety of household compositions, and displays a high correlation with most other price series (Open University, 1975). Two further problems arise, however: one is to find a method of calculating the rate of inflation from the retail price index, and the other is to ascertain whether or not individuals are sensitive to price rises for different goods, and if so, which.

What, at any time, is the rate of inflation, even given that it is to be based on the retail price index? A fertile imagination can produce infinite possible calculations. One way is to multiply the most recent month's price increase by 12, giving an annual rate: thus if prices went up by two per cent last month, they can be said to have increased last month at an annual rate of (2 × 12) or 24 per cent. One can multiply the last quarter's increase by four to get an annual rate, or indeed, simply take (as is most commonly done) the change over the last year and divide it by the value of the index a year ago. One can also choose a weighted average scheme, whereby the current rate of inflation is taken to be the average annual rate over the past few months, with more recent months counted most heavily in the average.[3]

Depending on which calculation one makes, the annual rate of increase in the retail price index in March 1974 (when most respondents were interviewed) was 10.4 per cent (last month times 12), 18.3 per cent (last quarter times four), 13.4 per cent (last year) or 13.6 per cent (last year with declining weights). The possible ranges from these four methods of calculation are given in Table 4.1 both for the retail price index as a whole and for a variety of its components. In general, most of the extremely high and low rates shown in the table — for instance, the 45 per cent inflation rate for fuel in November and the zero per cent for tobacco in the same month — follow from taking the last month's change times twelve. Nevertheless, memories can be short, and if attention focuses naturally on more recent events, considerable variation in popular estimates of inflation can be attributed to different time horizons among individuals.

Moreover, perceptions will vary because people consider different sets of goods in estimating price changes. The question wording employed invited this, by putting the question in terms of individual spending habits. Thus anyone whose principal expenditures — which probably determine familiarity with actual price rises -- were on alcohol, tobacco, and housing in February should certainly have had a much lower perception of inflation than someone whose major

[3] One such calculation (the ratios of weights are arbitrary) used in forming Table 4.1 was

$$I = \frac{\sum\limits_{i=1}^{12} (13-i)\,[(p_{t-i+1} - p_{t-i})/p_{t-i}]}{\sum\limits_{i=1}^{12} (i)}$$

where I is the inflation rate and p_t the value of the retail price index in month t.

Table 4.1. *Price increases in March and November 1974*

		Possible range of annual rates of inflation in	
Item	Weight in retail price index	March 1974	November 1974
All goods and services	100%	10.4–18.3%	16.4–21.2%
Food	25%	12.6–20.0%	17.5–30.7%
Alcohol	7%	4.2–13.1%	6.2–19.1%
Tobacco	4%	1.8–7.9%	0.0–22.4%
Housing	12%	3.1–12.0%	7.8–16.8%
Fuel	5%	6.8–18.9%	16.2–45.5%
Clothing	9%	16.7–23.2%	12.5–19.5%
Transport	14%	4.6–28.0%	15.6–21.9%

Source: Calculated from *Department of Employment Gazette*, Table 132, May 1974, pp. 480–1, and December 1975, pp. 1342–3.

expenditure was in the area of food or clothing. Even within an area like food, rates of increase vary: in February 1974 eggs cost 62 per cent more than a year before while butter and milk cost the same as a year before. Meat and bread had increased by 30 to 40 per cent, average food prices by about half that amount (*Guardian*, 5 April 1974). People do think of different sorts of goods when discussing prices, but which goods respondents to the two surveys analysed here were considering are unknown. This, like individual time horizons, will be a source of variation in perceptions of inflation whose effects cannot be directly estimated.

Nevertheless, the data are not completely intractable. The more extreme deviations from average are in areas which are a relatively small proportion of overall expenditure. In the case of food and the general retail price index, most means of calculation converge quite well, and suggest that the overall annual rate of inflation was in the neighbourhood of 13 per cent in March 1974 and 17 per cent in November. If food alone is considered, the estimates should be about 18 per cent in each case, though there is room for a great deal of individual variation.

Perceptions of price increases

In fact the perceptions of price rises in the survey appear at first to resemble these figures very little. Actual perceptions in the February study, of the current price of goods costing one pound a year before, range from £1.05 to £5.00, though only three per cent give estimates above £2.00. In October, the perceptions of current prices (from £1.00 in October 1973) range from £1.00 to £7.00. The distribution of perceptions for February is plotted in Figure 4.1. (The figures for October would look very similar.) It is immediately clear that there is an enormous range in perceptions of inflation, and that any assertion that the rate of inflation appears the same for all subjects in a study (as in the case of Kane and Malkiel) is flying in the face of reality, at least where the general public is concerned. Several other features are readily apparent.

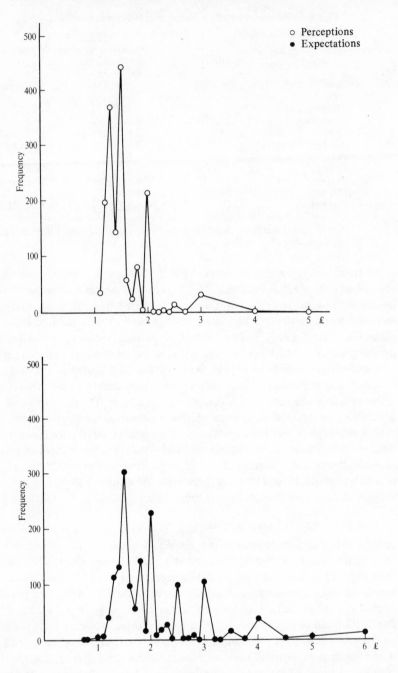

Figure 4.1. Distributions of price perceptions and expectations in February 1974

The first is that no one appears to believe that prices have fallen over the previous year. Only two respondents (*not* two per cent) in February (five in October) believed that prices had gone up in the previous year by less than 10p in the pound. Even these answers are possible, if a handful of respondents purchase only tobacco or alcohol, but this is unverifiable. On the other hand, respondents appear to have highly exaggerated perceptions of inflation. The maximum inflation rate which is readily conceivable would be reflected in responses around 50p in the pound, and there should be very few such replies. While indeed only a few give replies in excess of £2.00, on each occasion about 15 per cent of respondents said that goods costing a pound a year ago would now cost £2, and fully a quarter of respondents gave answers in excess of £1.50. Moreover, £1.50 itself is the most common single reply, given by over a quarter of respondents on each occasion. Thus, half the sample in February and October apparently believed that annual inflation was running at a rate equal to or greater than 50 per cent per annum.

The average reply in February is £1.52; in October it is £1.60 for goods costing a pound a year before. This suggests that people perceived (correctly) that inflation increased between February and October. Clearly, a number believed that inflation had lessened between February and October: as many as 23 per cent gave lower replies in October, though the difference in many cases was small. Some of this perception may have come from the effects of subsidies, which dramatically reduced the rate of inflation of prices of a number of frequently-purchased foods. Moreover, it was far more common to believe that the annual rate of inflation had remained constant (27 per cent of respondents) or increased (50 per cent).

Respondents appear to have had greatly exaggerated views of inflation, but to have, on average, perceived that inflation increased in 1974. There is another salient point. Inspection of Figure 4.1 suggests that almost all replies are given in units of 5p or 10p. In fact, the only replies which are given by at least one per cent of respondents on both occasions are £1.15, £1.20, £1.25, £1.30, £1.35, £1.40, £1.50, £1.60, £1.75, £2.00 and £3.00. Since over 90 per cent of replies on both occasions are in terms of one of these 11 amounts, these may be thought of as the 'natural' counting units of people replying to the questions. However, there are not equal intervals between the units of this counting scale: the gaps get larger as the amounts get larger. One could hypothesise that the gap between £1.60 and £1.75 was not meant to be larger than the gap between £1.20 and £1.25, in which case some transformation is needed to render the data more tractable to analysis.

Let us argue that people perceive some inflation, and that the replies they give are constrained by having to be given in units of 5p or 10p and by larger units having to be used to represent the higher inflation rates. The data can be transformed in the direction of an ordinary equal-interval counting scale by being restated as *logarithms*. That is, people perceive some percentage rate of inflation, and multiply £1.00 by ten raised to the power of that percentage rate, thus

$$\text{Reply} = £1.00 \times 10^P \quad \text{or} \quad P = \log_{10}\text{Reply} \tag{4}$$

There is no need to believe that people actually make that calculation in replying, but, rather, one should assume that it represents an approximation to the way people 'naturally' answer the inflation perception question, given that they work mainly in multiples of 10p, and do not feel that the difference between £2.00 and £2.10 is as large – in conveying the meaning of their answer – as the difference between £1.00 and £1.10.

Let us take base-10 logarithms of the February perceptions data. In this case the perceptions of inflation run from annual rates of two per cent ($\log_{10} 1.05$) to 70 per cent ($\log_{10} 5.00$). The most common reply (£1.50) becomes an estimate of an annual inflation rate of 17.6 per cent, which is more or less exactly that of the food component of the retail price index in February. The average of the logged answers is 17.2 per cent, which accords very closely to the weighted and unweighted annual increase figures for the whole of the retail price index, referred to in Table 4.1. The modal response in October is the same as in February; the mean, however, increases (after logging) to 19.1 per cent, which is again right in the middle of the estimates for the whole of the retail price index. Some replies still appear highly exaggerated, since there are still replies (though less than a dozen) placing inflation at 60, 70 or 80 per cent. However, the great majority of respondents can now be argued to be talking about perceived inflation rates of between ten per cent ($\log_{10} £1.25$) and 30 per cent ($\log_{10} £2.00$), and these are very much in keeping with the ranges discussed in the previous section for most commonly-purchased items at the time.

Thus the (logged) values appear to be distributed around an average value which approximates the annual rate of inflation in the retail price index. Now, if the determinants of price perceptions – age, sex, class, income, economic information, attention to media, purchasing habits, and so on (see below, pp. 84–88) are distributed largely independently of each other in the population, perceptions of price rises will approximate to the normal distribution expected by Carlson and Parkin. However, even casual inspection of Figure 4.1 makes it clear that there is no resemblance between the distributions of the unadjusted price perceptions and the bell-shaped curve of the normal distribution. Taking logarithms alters this considerably, especially when a certain amount of grouping is done to overcome the fact that responses cluster around a few individual values. Table 4.2 gives the distribution for the price perceptions data in February and October, adjusted to logarithmic form, and broken down into five groups. Tables 4.2a and 4.2b do obtain a result not entirely dissimilar to a normal distribution, though in each case there is evidence of a considerable asymmetry in the distribution: the distribution is skewed to the left, or contains too many observations in the category less than the one containing the mean. Moreover, in each of these cases, there are slightly fewer cases in the extreme categories, and slightly more in the middle, than one would expect if the distribution were truly normal.

Part of the problem is the presence of a few extreme replies; for instance if

Table 4.2. *Price perceptions in February and October 1974*

Range of perceptions (per cent)	Frequency	Per cent	Expectation under normal distribution
(a) February (mean perception = 17.2%, standard deviation 9%)			
Up to 5%	24	2	8
5–11%	443	27	19
12–23%	799	49	45
24–30%	298	19	19
Over 30%	54	3	8
Total	1618	100%	100%
(b) October – unadjusted (mean 19.1%, standard deviation 10%)			
Up to 5%	8	1	8
5–12%	459	28	19
13–25%	797	49	45
26–33%	267	17	19
Over 33%	87	5	8
Total	1618	100%	100%
(c) October – adjusted (mean 17.6%, standard deviation 9%)			
Up to 5%	8	1	8
5–11%	314	20	19
12–24%	867	53	45
25–31%	340	21	19
Over 31%	75	5	8
Total	1604	100%	100%

Note: The expected normal values reflect probabilities associated $\pm 0.6\sigma$, and $\pm 1.4\sigma$, where σ represents one standard deviation. For convenience and comparability, all conclusions for the remainder of this chapter, unless otherwise noted, refer to the 1,618 respondents who gave numerical answers to the price perceptions and expectations questions on *both* occasions. That is, the ten per cent of respondents with at least one reply missing are eliminated from all subsequent calculations.

the 14 observations in October of £4.00 and above are omitted (see Table 4.2*c*), the skewness goes away, but the peakedness becomes even more acute. Apparently, the data contain a handful of replies which are highly exaggerated, and which can best be eliminated. The remaining 99+ per cent, when transformed by logarithms, are approximately normally distributed around the true value of inflation, such that, with inflation at about 19 per cent, over half the population perceive it as between 12 and 24 per cent, and nearly all perceive it as between five and 30 per cent. Price perceptions are therefore 'lognormally' distributed, echoing Carlson's (1975) findings. The normality of the distribution comes from the fact that a variety of independent factors produce variation in perceptions; the exponential nature of the replies (removed by taking logarithms) is a feature of people's way of replying to the question as set. The important feature of the data, however, is the fact that the transformed responses produce an average centred on the rate of growth of the retail price index, an average which further-more moves upward with the index between February and October, emphasiz-ing the realism of popular perceptions of price rises.

Expectations of price increases

Even a casual reference back to Figure 4.1 reveals that the distribution of price expectations resembles that of perceptions closely. The distribution is highly clustered around a few values, with a very long tail containing a relatively small number of extreme observations. Since the distributions are similar, the argu-ments of the last section extend directly to expectations, and the detailed work on transforming the responses need not be repeated. As a matter of fact, the average expectation in February was £1.95 in a year, which (compared with the average of £1.52 for the current price of goods) suggests that people in February expected that inflation would abate somewhat in the following year. In October the mean price expectation for the following year was £2.25, which implies an average increase slightly greater than that contained in the present estimates of prices, whose average was £1.60. Put another way, in February 1974 people felt on average that a pound's worth of goods had put on 52p in the year to February, but would put on only another 43p in the next year; in October they felt the increase over the past year was 60p and over the next would be 65p. This does resemble a perception of accelerating inflation, though it may be unduly influ-enced by the larger number of extremely high values of expected prices in October. Indeed, 41 respondents (2.5 per cent) estimated that goods would cost £3.00 in a year, making an increase of 200 per cent over two years, and one per cent of respondents gave estimates even higher than this. At the other end of the scale, in February three respondents gave estimates below £1.00, suggesting that after two years prices would actually have fallen; in October, no one suggested this.

Of course, even in periods of rapid inflation, a few people apparently expect prices to fall, and to that extent Carlson and Parkin are borne out. Table 4.3 is constructed by subtracting perceived from expected prices for each respondent. Prices are expected to 'go down ' if the price in a year's time is *below* the present price; 'go up' if *above*; there is 'no change' if they are the *same*, and respondents saying 'don't know' to either question are included in that category.[4] The result-ing frequency distribution is remarkably close to published Gallup polls of the time, which report the results of asking people whether they expect prices to rise, fall or remain much the same. Using the published parameter estimates (Carlson and Parkin, 1975, p. 127), the expected value of inflation attaching to

---

[4] The category 'no change' in Table 4.3 would of course be larger if very small increases and declines really were treated as expectations of stability, not change. The *Gallup Political Index* reports that at the time 76 per cent expected prices to rise, 3 per cent to fall, and 14 per cent to stay the same.

Table 4.3. *Constructed categories of price movements*

Response	Percentages in	
	February	October
'Go up'	84.1	91.6
'Go down'	2.3	0.4
'No change'	7.4	1.8
'Don't know'	6.3	6.2
	100.0%	100.0%
	(*n* = 1,822)	(*n* = 1,822)

Note: Basis of construction of response categories is given in the text. All respondents in the February–October panel are included, bar eight in each case where data were not ascertained.

the constructed categories in Table 4.3 for February is 8.7 per cent per annum, while for October it is not strictly calculable, owing to the lack of people expecting prices to fall, but could be on the order of 10.9 per cent. This appears to be very much on the low side, which is attributable to a weakness in the method of calculation. When inflation has risen sharply, so has the value of the 'just perceptible price rise'. As this determines the weight they use to derive expected values of inflation, the weight is too small, and so are the resulting estimates. To get an expectation of about 15 per cent out of the February data, one would need a weight – or minimum perceptible increase – of about 2.9 per cent rather than 1.76 per cent. However, it is possible to estimate the expected rate of inflation directly from the British Election Study survey data, but in order to do this, an assumption must be made about how people actually answered the questions.

An interpretation of extrapolation

In order to treat the responses to the perception and expectation questions simultaneously, what is needed is guidance about what answers would be given by a respondent who extrapolates – who expects the same rate of inflation in the next year as in the last. If a person has perceived 20 per cent annual inflation, he should say that goods costing £1.00 a year ago now cost £1.20. In a year, if inflation continues at 20 per cent, these goods should cost £1.20 plus 20 per cent times £1.20, or £1.44. By the same logic, a person perceiving that last year's goods now cost £1.50 should expect a price in a year of £2.25, and insofar as expected rates of inflation commonly approximate perceived rates, £2.25 should be a common expectation among those believing that last year's pound's worth of goods now costs £1.50.

In fact, it is an extremely uncommon response, being made by about ten of the over 400 respondents saying that the present cost of goods was £1.50 on each occasion. On the other hand, about half these people each time said that the goods would cost £2.00 in a year's time. It is likely that these people were in fact saying that inflation would continue as it had been over the past year. This contention is not susceptible of any direct proof, though it amounts only to the claim that people are more likely to add than to multiply when answering a survey question. It is the case that of the 11 counting units enumerated in the previous section (£1.15, £1.20, etc.), in every case more people gave an expected value of future prices which would imply addition rather than multiplication. Usually the differences are quite large: in many cases (as for instance expecting £1.44) the multiplicative expectation is completely absent.

So if someone believes that goods now cost £1.50, the answer '£2.00 in a year' should denote the same rate of inflation next year as last. That is, 50p inflation next year is the same as 50p last year, even though in the next year it is only 50p in £1.50. Let E_t denote a person's price expectation looking forward a year from time t, and P_t his perception of the price of goods at time t. In this case a *constant* rate of inflation over the two years arises whenever $E_t - P_t = P_t - £1$, or by substitution where $E_t - £1 = 2(P_t - £1)$. If after two years, the amount in addition to the original £1.00 in the question is twice the extra amount after the first year, this is interpreted as the respondent's means of indicating a constant rate of inflation over two years.

The adjustment is more difficult where logarithms are to be taken, for if $E_t - £1 = 2(P_t - £1)$, it does *not* follow that $\log(E_t - £1) = 2\log(P_t - 1)$, but rather it is equal to $\log(2P_t - £1)$. In this case one takes the logarithm of $E_t - £1$, and since E_t contains two years' inflation on the original pound, divides it by two. We now require a transformation of P_t in proportion, which is given by $\frac{1}{2}\log(2P_t - 1)$. These transformations are the basis of the following analysis.

Making the adjustments discussed above,

(1) $E_t = \frac{1}{2}\log(E_t - £1)$ and

(2) $P_t = \frac{1}{2}\log(2P_t - £1)$

gives a set of values for perceived and expected inflation which are presented in Table 4.4. They give the following average values for inflation:

Perceived in February 14.4%

Expected in February 13.3%

Perceived in October 15.8%

Expected in October 16.0%

Again, the average perceptions are in line with the movements of the retail price index, though they are slightly lower than the estimates given in Table 4.2 above.[5] Expectations can be seen to lag behind perceptions in February, but to exceed them, or at least to have caught up, in October. This is particularly clear in Table 4.4 which groups perceptions into those categories most nearly giving rise to a grouped normal distribution, and then puts expectations in the same categories.

The distributions are not quite normal, since the category above the one con-

[5] They are lower because in this range of numbers, $\log(x) > \frac{1}{2}\log(2x)$, because in fact $\log(x) = \frac{1}{2}\log(x^2)$, and $x^2 > 2x$.

Table 4.4. *Distribution of transformed price perceptions and*
expectations

February Per cent range of inflation	Perception	Expectation
1–5%	2	6
6–10%	27	33
11–17%	45	39
18–26%	23	17
27%+	3	5
	100%	100%
	(n = 1,618)	(n = 1,618)

October Per cent range of inflation	Perception	Expectation
1–6%	2	3
7–11%	27	27
12–19%	43	39
20–34%	25	27
35%+	3	4
	100%	100%
	(n = 1,618)	(n = 1,618)

Note: Expectations are given by $\frac{1}{2}\log(E_t - 1)$ and perceptions by $\frac{1}{2}\log(2P_t - 1)$. The categories are determined so as to have maximum correspondence with a normal distribution, across both February and October (allowing for an upward shift in values across the eight months) and across both perceptions and expectations. Source as Table 4.3.

taining the mean is always broader than the one below it. This implies that even the lognormal distribution does not quite capture the distribution of perceptions and expectations, but it is not too bad an approximation. This in turn suggests that the Carlson–Parkin series is not based on nonsense, but could profitably be recalculated under an alternative distributional assumption. However, even more interesting is that the distribution of expectations in October is similar to that of perceptions, whereas in February, expectations were clearly lagging behind. Nearly twice as many people expected inflation of between six and ten per cent after February as expected inflation of 18 to 26 per cent: by October the proportions in the relevant categories were more or less in balance, implying that between February and October more people came to believe that rapid inflation had come to stay. At this point it is appropriate to turn to the more difficult problem of testing hypotheses of inflation expectation formation.

Deriving models of expectation formation

There are essentially two classes of model which can be tested with this data,

extrapolative and *adaptive* models. These were discussed above (see pp. 60–1).
There are no data on long-term projections to allow tests of a return-to-normality
model, and too few times of observation to allow derivation of an actual process
through time which could cast light on rationality of expectations. Recall that
an extrapolative scheme is one in which future values of inflation are forecast
solely on the basis of past observations of inflation, thus:

$$E_t = \sum_{i=0}^{n} b_i P_{t-i} \tag{5}$$

where E_t and P_t as before represent respectively expectations and perceptions of
inflation at time t. The simplest case is one where $n = 0$, so that

Model E–1 $E_t = a + bP_t$

or expectations at any time are a linear function of perceptions of inflation at
that time. (In all these models, assume for empirical estimation purposes that
there is also a stochastic error term in the equation.) In the above equation, b
will be greater than unity if people expect inflation to accelerate, equal to unity
if they expect it to continue, and less than unity otherwise. The constant a
reflects a constant adjustment made on the basis of other information. The
equation can be extended to take account of one previous observation (that in
February for the estimation of expectations in October):

Model E–2 $E_t = a + b_1 P_t + b_2 P_{t-1}$

or, with the present data, expectations are a weighted function of perceptions in
October plus perceptions in February. In this case, the sum of the two coefficients relative to unity suggests what people see as the state of inflation, and
one would in general expect b_1 to be larger than b_2, as more recent observations
of inflation ought to carry more weight. Both b_1 and b_2 ought as well to be
greater than zero. While one can place far more complicated restrictions on the
behaviour of coefficients in such a distributed-lag model, little purpose will be
served by doing so here.

An alternative model to E–2 which involves the same observations is given by

$$E_t = cP_t + d(P_t - P_{t-1}) \tag{6}$$

which allows for perception not only of the level of inflation, but also of whether
it is accelerating, constant or declining. Both c and d must be greater than zero
in this formulation; c is interpreted as before and d represents an adjustment
such that E_t is adjusted (relative to cP_t) *upwards* if $P_t > P_{t-1}$ and *downwards*
otherwise. This model can be restated by collecting terms as

Model E–3 $E_t = a + b_1 P_t + b_2 P_{t-1}$ where $b_1 = c + d$ and $b_2 = -d$.

These models are immediate (E–1), lagged (E–2), and accelerative (E–3)
extrapolative models. Empirically, both E–2 and E–3 can be distinguished from
E–1 by obtaining a (non-zero) significant estimate for the coefficient b_2. E_2 can
be distinguished from E–3 by the *sign* (plus or minus) of b_2, which should be

positive in E–2 and negative in E–3. In all cases, finding the constant term a to be significantly non-zero implies the effect of factors – information and otherwise – beyond those contained in past values of inflation.

An *adaptive* scheme is generally one in which expectations adjust in proportion to past errors, where the errors are the discrepancies between expected and subsequently observed rates of inflation. The simplest of these is a first-order adaptive or error-learning scheme, in which expectations adjust in proportion to the last recorded error; thus (see Cagan, 1956; Carlson and Parkin, 1975; Schmalensee, 1976):

$$E_t - E_{t-1} = c(P_t - E_{t-1}) \tag{7}$$

P_t represents the perceived inflation in the period since the expectation E_{t-1} was formed. Collecting terms renders the first-order adaptive scheme as

$$Model\ A-1 \quad E_t = a + b_1 P_t + b_2 E_{t-1} \text{ where } b_1 = c \text{ and } b_2 = 1 - c$$

The constant a is generally expected to be zero, or to reflect some other information, and b_1 and b_2 are expected to sum to unity. If b_1 approaches unity, the model becomes an extrapolative model, in which inflation is expected to be what it is currently seen to be, and the term relating to past expectations loses significance. A second-order adaptive scheme allows people to be sensitive to not only the last error, but the difference between the last two errors as well. This can be written

$$E_t - E_{t-1} = c(P_t - E_{t-1}) + d(P_t - E_{t-1} - (P_{t-1} - E_{t-2})) \tag{8}$$

The essence of this is that if the last error is seen to be larger than the one previous (when the result of all the brackets beyond d is positive), expectations are adjusted by c times the last error *plus* d times the growth of the error, whereas if the last error is smaller than the previous, the adjustment to expectations is proportionately smaller. If one lets $c = e + f$ and $d = -f$, then collecting terms gives

$$E_t = eP_t + (1 - e)E_{t-1} + fP_{t-1} - fE_{t-2} \tag{9}$$

with e expected to be > 0 and $f < 0$, and $f = -d$.

For estimation let t be October, and $t-1$ be February, even though these are only eight months apart and the perceptions and projections covered one year (at least each observation is within a year of each other). Even so, it appears there is no observation for E_{t-2} in the last equation, which therefore cannot be estimated on this data. But assume for a moment that E_{t-1} was formed adaptively from P_{t-1} and E_{t-2}, in the sense of model A–1 above. This assumption is made for convenience only and is strictly inappropriate, as it assumes one model in order to derive a different one. Then

$$E_{t-1} - E_{t-2} = g(P_{t-1} - E_{t-2})$$

Collecting terms

$$E_{t-2} - gE_{t-2} = E_{t-1} - gP_{t-1}$$

or $\quad E_{t-2} = \dfrac{1}{1-g} E_{t-1} - \dfrac{g}{1-g} P_{t-1}$

This can now be substituted into (9) above to give

$$E_t = eP_t + (1-e)E_{t-1} + fP_{t-1} - f \left[\frac{1}{1-g} E_{t-1} - \frac{g}{1-g} \right] P_{t-1}$$

or collecting terms

$$E_t = eP_t + \left[(1-e) - \frac{f}{1-g} \right] E_{t-1} + \left[f + \frac{fg}{1-g} \right] P_{t-1} \text{ or}$$

$$E_t = eP_t + \left[(1-e) - \frac{f}{1-g} \right] E_{t-1} + \frac{f}{1-g} P_{t-1} \tag{10}$$

which gives

$$Model\ A-2 \quad E_t = a + b_1 P_t + b_2 E_{t-1} + b_e P_{t-1} \text{ with } b_2 = 1 - b_1 - b_3$$

where the coefficients have the meaning implied by (10). This equation can be estimated from the present data.

However, the way the data were collected renders (when logarithms are *not* employed) the adaptive models slightly ambiguous. The problem is that E_t 'contains' P_t and therefore for estimation E_t should really be replaced by $E_t^* = E_t - P_t$ (see the note to Table 4.5). Should the same be done where E_{t-1} appears on the right-hand side of the equations? It can be argued either way. The argument for leaving E_{t-1} alone is that the appropriate E_{t-1} data for October should have been generated in October 1973, and thus the February estimates of expectations should contain an element of expectation for October 1973–February 1974, for which the best estimate – assuming some limited rationality – is the perception of price rises in the year to February 1974. In that sense the fact that E_{t-1} contains P_{t-1} is positively to be desired, and no adjustment should be made in model A–1. However, if someone felt that prices had risen to £2.00 by February, and would then remain fixed, it is unreasonable to treat their inflation expectations as the same as someone who feels prices rose to £1.25 by February but would go up to £2.00 over the next year. In this case, one should substitute $(E_{t-1} - P_{t-1})$ in model A–1,

$$E_t = a + b_1 P_t + b_2(E_{t-1} - P_{t-1}) \text{ or}$$

$$Model\ A-1a \quad E_t^* = a + b_1 P_t + b_2 E_{t-1} - b_2 P_{t-1} \text{ with } b_1 + b_2 = 1$$

and the necessity of the transformation can be tested by observing whether equal coefficients are obtained for E_{t-1} and P_{t-1}.

Model A–1a now contains the same terms as model A–2, though the expected restrictions on the coefficients are different. However, the same adjustment could be argued to be necessary in the case of model A–2, in which case the terms do not change but the meaning of the coefficients does. From (10) above, the last two terms become

$$\left[(1-e) - \frac{f}{1-g} \right] (E_{t-1} - P_{t-1}) + \frac{f}{1-g} P_{t-1}$$

which when grouped gives

$$E_t^* = eP_t + \left[(1-e) - \frac{f}{1-g} \right] E_{t-1} + \left[\frac{2f}{1-g} - (1-e) \right] P_{t-1} \qquad (11)$$

and gives an alternative interpretation for the coefficient of P_{t-1} in model A–2, yielding model A–2a. Model A–2a can be distinguished empirically from model A–2 by the relative magnitudes of the coefficients of the E_{t-1} and P_{t-1} terms. In model A–2a the magnitude of the P_{t-1} coefficients is larger, and in model A–2 smaller, than that of the coefficient of E_{t-1}. This follows directly from the fact that d in (8) above must be positive and f was defined as $-d$. The coefficients of either model, given some assumed value for g, can still be solved for values of e and f, which in turn give estimates of c and d in (8) above.

One final thing to note is that either formulation of model A–2 can also be interpreted as a third sort of model, combining features of A–1 and E–3 into a first-order adaptive-extrapolative model. Such a model would allow expectations to be modified both in proportion to the last error and in proportion to the perceived acceleration or deceleration of inflation:

$$E_t - E_{t-1} = c(P_t - E_{t-1}) + d(P_t - P_{t-1}) \qquad (12)$$

or   *Model AE–1* $E_t = a + b_1 P_t + b_2 E_{t-1} + b_3 P_{t-1}$

where $b_1 = (c + d)$, $b_2 = 1 - c$, and $b_3 = -d$

This formulation places no restrictions on the relative magnitudes of b_2 and b_3, but otherwise requires the same relationships as A–2 or A–2a. This extra interpretation arises solely because of the lack of an independent observation of E_{t-2}.

Estimation results

Thus, there are three extrapolative and two adaptive models to test, though the previous section reveals that the nature of the data available makes the coefficients of the adaptive models subject to a variety of interpretations. The form of the various models and the restrictions implicit on the coefficients of each model are summarised in Table 4.5 and the results of the estimations are shown in Table 4.6. Evaluation of the results takes the form of examining the goodness-of-fit to the data of the various models and comparing the derived estimates of Table 4.6 with the expected values of Table 4.5.

Significantly non-zero estimates for the constant term are obtained only in the case of the two E–1 models. This implies that, despite the good fit to the

Table 4.5. *Equations and restrictions*

Model	a	$b_1 P_t$	$b_2 E_{t-1}$	$b_3 P_{t-1}$
		Expected values of terms		
E–1	0	$b_1 > 0$	n.a.	n.a.
E–2	0	$b_1 > 0$ $b_1 > b_3$	n.a.	$b_3 > 0$
E–3	0	$b_1 > 0$ $\lvert b_1 \rvert > \lvert b_3 \rvert$	n.a.	$b_3 < 0$
A–1	0	$0 < b_1 \leqslant 1$	$0 < b_2 \leqslant 1$ $b_2 = 1 - b_1$	n.a.
A–1a	0	$0 < b_1 \leqslant 1$	$0 < b_2 \leqslant 1$ $b_2 = 1 - b_1$	$b_3 = -b_2$
A–2	0	$0 < b_1 \leqslant 1$	$0 < b_2 \leqslant 1$ $b_2 = 1 - b_1 - b_3$	$\lvert b_3 \rvert < \lvert b_2 \rvert$ $b_3 < 0$
A–2a	0	$0 < b_1 \leqslant 1$	$0 < b_2 \leqslant 1$ $b_2 = 1 - b_1 - b_3$	$\lvert b_3 \rvert > \lvert b_2 \rvert$ $b_3 < 0$
AE–1	0	$0 < b_1 \leqslant 1$	$0 < b_2 \leqslant 1$ $b_2 = 1 - b_1 - b_3$	$b_3 < 0$

Note: n.a. means not applicable, that is to say, the term is excluded from the model.

Two adjustments necessitated by the way the data were collected have to be kept in mind in interpreting the results presented in this table. The first adjustment is that where unlogged values are used, £1.00 has been subtracted from all observations of perceptions and expectations. This avoids the presence of an unnecessary constant term. Furthermore recall that the value of expectations given by the respondent already contains his perceived increase in prices, and thus at any time the real value of expectations E_t^* is given by $E_t - P_t$. This is to say that if responses were £1.50 now, £2.00 in a year, the value of perceived inflation is 50p, and the value of expected inflation is also 50p. All the models of the previous section can be written in the form $E_t^* = bP_t + \ldots$, or $E_t - P_t = bP_t + \ldots$, or most simply $E_t = (1+b)P_t + \ldots$ Bear in mind that in all the non-logarithmic estimates, the value of the coefficient of P_t has had 1.0 subtracted from it in order to be interpreted as the coefficient 'really' attaching to P_t. In the logarithmic case, taking 0.5 times the logarithm of each avoids this problem.

The second adjustment is that about one per cent of cases are missing from all the analyses. This was done to allow for 'cleaner' estimation of the actual parameters. It amounts to assuming that the model does not represent the behaviour of the one per cent of cases which it fits worst. In fact, the cases removed this way displayed expectations uncorrelated with perceptions, and consisted of a variety of idiosyncratic responses, such as '£6 now, £7 in a year' and startling declines in prices from £2 to £1.50. All equations in each set – that is, all using unlogged and all using logged values – are estimated over a common set of cases in October.

data in October, the E–1 models are inadequate (as does the significance of the E_{t-1} term), and that people clearly use some information in forming expectations other than that contained in what they perceive to be the present rate of inflation. To a large extent this information is contained in past perceptions or expectations of inflation, as the constant terms are absent from the other models. Two further

Table 4.6. *Estimation results for all models*

Model	Ordinary data Estimated values of						Logarithmic values Estimated values of					
	a	$b_1 P_t$	$b_2 E_{t-1}$	$b_3 P_{t-1}$	R^2	obs.	a	$b_1 P_t$	$b_2 E_{t-1}$	$b_3 P_{t-1}$	R^2	obs.
February E−1	0.07 (3.6)	0.69 (59.2)			0.684	1,618	0.005 (2.2)	0.88 (64.5)			0.720	1,618
October E−1	0.05 (3.1)	0.97 (88.7)			0.831	1,603	0.005 (2.8)	0.98 (93.3)			0.845	1,601
E−2, E−3	0.02 (1.0)	0.93 (78.3)		0.11 (3.7)	0.832	1,603	0.000 (0.09)	0.95 (79.3)		0.07 (5.2)	0.847	1,601
A−1	−0.002 (0.1)	0.90 (79.6)	0.10 (7.4)		0.837	1,603	−0.002 (0.8)	0.94 (82.1)	0.10 (8.3)		0.851	1,601
A−1a, A−2, A−2a, AE−1	0.01 (0.7)	0.92 (78.8)	0.16 (7.3)	−0.16 (3.4)	0.838	1,603	−0.000 (0.1)	0.94 (80.1)	0.14 (7.0)	−0.06 (2.6)	0.852	1,601

Note: All estimates are by OLS regression. Bracketed numbers under coefficients are the *t*-statistic value relating to the quotient (coefficient)/(estimated standard deviation of coefficient). Source as Table 4.3.

points should be made. In October, these other terms contribute little to the fit of the equations to the data, and, in a cost-effective sense, P_t alone in October would be the best choice as predictor. However, in February the fit of the E–1 model is substantially worse (and the coefficient of P_t substantially lower) than in October. This implies that the 'missing' terms – that is, those contained in E–2 through AE–1, for which there is no data to predict February expectations – are far more important in February, a point to remember.

Let us turn to the question of the appropriateness of models in October. In general it should be observed that the parameter estimates do not vary a great deal according to whether or not logarithms are taken. Parameter estimates were somewhat affected by the removal of the worst-fitting cases, but the increase in goodness-of-fit was considerable.

Among extrapolative models, it is clear that the distributed-lag formulation E–2 is to be preferred to the accelerative model E–3. This follows from the fact that the coefficient b_3 is estimated as significantly greater than zero. Since this coefficient is significant, E–2 is preferable to E–1, but it remains a problem that the improvement in fit is small and that the coefficients sum to more than unity, though this is not strictly inappropriate.[6] Considering E_t, P_t and P_{t-1} all to be in logarithms, a good fit to an extrapolative hypothesis is obtained (from Table 4.6) by

$$E\text{–}2 \quad E_t = 0.95P_t + 0.07P_{t-1}$$

so that people's expectations are a weighted (heavily towards more recent observations) sum of past perceptions of inflation.

Turning to adaptive models, the result depends on whether one considers the ordinary or logged data. Model A–1 gives a perfect fit to the restrictions in the case of the ordinary data: the coefficients sum to unity (unconstrained to do so), the constant term cannot be distinguished from zero at any level of confidence, and the overall fit is good. The equality of b_2 and b_3 in the case of A–2 model (last row in Table 4.6) is an important result and supports only the A–1a model, and the AE–1 model result may violate (simultaneous tests on the coefficients are required) the restriction that the coefficients should sum to unity (this also invalidates the A–1a model). Thus, with unlogged data, expectations are given by

$$A\text{–}1 \quad E_t = 0.9P_t + 0.1E_{t-1}$$

which it will be recalled can also be written as

$$(E_t - E_{t-1}) = 0.9(P_t - E_{t-1})$$

which implies that on average expectations were adjusted in October relative to

[6] If all means of the variables involved are equal, the coefficients cannot sum to more than unity, but could well sum to less, owing to missing terms further removed in time. Inclusion of the dropped extra cases (where virtually no correlation between P_t and E_t existed) would have biased b_1 downward, though the adaptive formulation is still evident even in these coefficients. Note more importantly that removing 1 per cent of cases removed over 15 per cent of the badness-of-fit.

February by nine tenths of the error observed between what one perceived inflation to be in October and what one expected it to be in February.

Where logarithms have been taken, only the formulations A–1, A–2 and AE–1 need be considered. The coefficients in the A–1 formulation sum to more than unity (1.04) and, while this is not an enormous violation, both coefficients are significantly different at the 0.05 level from values ($b_1 = 0.92, b_2 = 0.08$) which would bring them in line with this restriction. The data in the final row give an extremely good fit to an A–2 hypothesis – that is, that people adjust expectations both in proportion to the last error and in proportion to the perceived change in that error – or an AE–1 hypothesis, where people adjust expectations according to their last error and to the perception that inflation is accelerating. The coefficients do sum to 1.02 (less than the earlier error), but b_3 does not diverge significantly from -0.08, which removes the error entirely. Using this correction we obtain

$$E_t = 0.94P_t + 0.14E_{t-1} - 0.08P_{t-1}$$

which can be rewritten as

$$AE\text{–}1 \quad E_t - E_{t-1} = 0.86(P_t - E_{t-1}) + 0.08(P_t - P_{t-1}).$$

With no data for E_{t-2}, one can only write an A–2 equation conditional upon some value of g in (10) above. Letting $g = 0.5$, we obtain

$$A\text{–}2 \quad E_t - E_{t-1} = 0.90(P_t - E_{t-1}) + 0.04(P_t - E_{t-1} - (P_{t-1} - E_{t-2}))$$

in the form of (4) above. The value of d ($= 0.04$) declines if g is assumed higher. The AE–1 estimate says that people adjusted their October expectations relative to February's by 0.86 times the error between their forecast and subsequent perception of inflation plus an extra 0.08 times the movement they observed in the rate of inflation in that period. The A–2 estimate says that the adjustment was 0.9 times the last error plus an extra small correction if the error was changing – an extra correction upward if the error was increasing, downward if declining. Because of the nature of the data, there is no extra evidence on which to base a choice between these two models.

Whether a first-order or second-order adaptive model is supported by the data depends on whether or not logarithmic transformations of the data are employed. In either case the data clearly support an adaptive model, since the fits are always better (if only by a little) than those of the extrapolative models, and because the coefficients are consistently of the expected size and direction. (It should also be noted that if P_{t-1} and E_{t-1} are highly correlated, the A–1 and E–2 models converge, and one can pick the one with the cleaner estimates, in this case A–1.) Only an extrapolative model could be tested for February expectations, and this performed substantially worse than did the corresponding model for October. This is consistent with other econometric evidence which suggests that the process of adaptation speeds up when inflation accelerates, or at critical 'turning points' in the path of inflation (Kane and Malkiel, 1976; Schmalensee,

1976). Another way to describe this is to say that (since an extrapolative model is only a first-order adaptive model in which $b_1 = 1.0$) in times of accelerating inflation, extrapolation replaces error-learning adaptation as the process by which expectations are formed.

In that case one could interpret the poor fit in February as consistent with the hypothesis that the missing adaptive terms were more important, but that the visible acceleration of inflation in late 1974 led people to base their forecasts increasingly on current values of perceived inflation. In February, people may still have been seeing the increase in inflation as temporary. In terms of the original survey questions, answers of the sort 'things cost £1.50 now, £1.75 in a year', which describe an adaptive response to increasing inflation (assuming past expected values of inflation were lower) are replaced in October by responses of '£1.50 now, £2.00 in a year', which imply that the respondent simply expected the present rate of increase of prices to continue. In other words, it takes a little while for people to believe that inflation has really accelerated away from 'normal' rates of increase or decrease, but once they believe it, they expect it to continue. Inflation in February had not long since turned sharply upwards, and thus forecasts may have been based more heavily then on more distant past perceptions and expectations. This is not susceptible of proof, but it is a point of consistency between these results and other work. Moreover, if it is true that only the most recent observations count when inflation accelerates, it makes the support in the data for an adaptive hypothesis in October even more noteworthy.

This section established a rule linking inflation expectations and perceptions. In the context of survey analysis, the fact that people's expectations could be tied so tightly to their perceptions of price rises might not entirely have been expected. It also established that expectations were formed adaptively not only out of current perceptions of inflation and/or past errors in forecasting inflation. This of course implies a considerable awareness of inflation on the part of the public, which is more or less to be expected when inflation is nearly consensually the most important issue in domestic politics. Moreover, this method of forecasting should be seen in the light of earlier sections of this chapter which established that people's perceptions of price rises were broadly realistic, in the sense of reflecting relative inflation rates at different times and over different goods, and that their perceptions, by the expedient of taking logarithms, could be shown to lie in a normal distribution around a mean which was more or less equal to the true value of inflation. However, the existence of an adaptive rule linking expectations and perceptions does not clarify why some people's perceptions of price rises are higher to begin with. Purchasing habits — for which there are no available data — are one source of variation, but quite a bit can be discovered anyway.

Determinants of price expectations

There are two approaches which could be used to elicit information about other factors which influence perceptions and expectations of inflation. One approach would be to take one or another of the models tested in the previous section (say, for instance, the first-order adaptive model A−1) and see what other variables could be entered significantly into the equation. The other would be to attempt to predict the values of expected or perceived inflation directly from these other factors. The second is preferable for two reasons. First, because other variables might affect other parameters of the model in addition to the constant, one would have to employ a number of interaction terms or estimate an A−1 model disaggregated over a large number of sample sub-groups in order to determine effects, which could be tedious. Moreover, any variables which have significant constant effects by this approach are a subset of variables chosen by direct estimation. The second reason is economy: since perceptions and expectations in October are highly correlated, the second approach yields the determinants of perceptions and expectations at any point in time simultaneously. In fact, results are presented only for inflation expectations in October, but it is the case that the same variables are predictors of perceptions in October, and, with a somewhat poorer fit, of expectations in February.

By hypothesis, the determinants of inflation expectations arise in the following five areas:

(1) Political−economic *information*;

(2) General *pessimism*;

(3) Economic position and *purchasing habits*;

(4) Beliefs about the *causes* of inflation;

(5) Beliefs about the competence of political *parties*.

It will be recalled that perceptions of inflation were numerically exaggerated, especially before logarithms were taken: moreover, that insofar as foolish-seeming perceptions and expectations appeared in the data, these were almost exclusively on the high side, rather than in the form of people believing prices had fallen. Because of this, there ought to be a general association between *high* rates of expected inflation and *low* levels of information: that is, a negative relationship between the two.

The opposite sign ought to arise out of pessimism. The *more* pessimistic people are about the general state of the economy and country, the *higher* ought their expected rates of inflation to be: a *positive* relationship. On purchasing habits, it is hard to be precise, but the fact that, until the summer of 1974 at least, food and clothing were among the most-rapidly price-increasing goods should imply *high* rates of inflation seen and expected by those groups whose purchases are *most* heavily oriented to these areas. Such groups could include pensioners, women, and lower income groups, as long as too precise a prediction is not expected.

What you expect to happen to inflation may depend on what you believe causes it and therefore what can be done about it. *Low* rates of inflation ought to be expected by those who identify the cause of inflation as something which could be controlled. Similarly, expectations ought to be affected by partisanship: at a minimum, people's expectations of inflation ought to be influenced by their beliefs about the party in power, which in turn ought to be a function of their general partisanship. A large number of variables reflecting each of these groups of indicators were sequentially tested and retained in a regression equation predicting inflation expectations in October 1974: the 16 variables for which simultaneously significant coefficient estimates were obtained are listed in Table 4.7. This equation was estimated with the dependent variable both logged and unlogged; the coefficients are expressed in pence and where logged, as percentage points. Thus, in the unlogged case, one unit of newspaper quality predicts 6p less expected inflation (over two years); in the logged case, it predicts 0.54 per cent less inflation per annum.

The first relevant observation is that there is no partisan term. While October Labour voters have slightly *above-average* inflation expectations, once the other variables in the equation are taken into account, partisan variables cease to have

Table 4.7. *Determinants of inflation expectations*

| | | Coefficients of other variables with dependent variable E_t | |
| | | Unlogged (mean = £1.21) | Logged (mean = 15.9%) |
Factor	Variable		
Information	Read quality newspaper	−0.06*	−0.54*
	Attention to television news	−0.03*	−0.37**
	Often talk about politics	−0.08**	−0.62**
	Understand prices issue well	−0.12**	−0.91*
Pessimism	General political–economic pessimism	0.07**	0.58**
	Expect tougher wage controls	0.07**	0.67**
Purchasing habits	Higher income	−0.04*	−0.35*
	Accommodation owned	−0.03*	−0.27*
	Higher social class	−0.05**	−0.52*
	Male	−0.36**	−3.65**
	Increasing age	0.02*	0.27**
Causes of inflation	Blame world situation	−0.06*	−0.80**
	Blame Common Market	0.15**	1.29**
	Expect to stay in Common Market	0.06	1.03*
	Blame Government	0.17**	1.29**
	Blame trade unions	0.14**	1.19**
Constant term		£1.40**	17.5%**
	R^2	0.162	0.214
	obs.	1,603	1,601

*Significant at 0.05 level
**Significant at 0.01 level
Note: All the variables are 'dummy' variables, with the value one reflecting the characteristic described in the short title, except as noted below. Complete question texts are in the Appendix. Income is in five categories, coded 1–5; age is in deciles, and political–economic pessimism is a four-variable additive index, containing expectations of lower real income, higher unemployment, poor economic developments, and feeling that Britain is governed relatively badly. Source as Table 4.3.

any significant impact. This is true not only of voting behaviour but also of partisan-loaded variables like estimates of the Labour Government's capability in handling the issue of prices. This finding is startling testimony to the decline of 'instrumentalism' in 1974 (see Chapter 13): it is indeed one clear manifestation of the absence among 1974 Labour voters of hopes or expectations of becoming personally better off or seeing inflation dramatically reduced. Indeed, a majority of Labour voters in October 1974 felt that prices were beyond the control of the government, and this is reflected in the absence of a partisan complexion in actual expectations of price inflation.

Beyond this, however, all the observed coefficients are more or less in line with the expectations set forth above. All four indicators of political–economic information have negative coefficients, implying that lower – and therefore more realistic – perceptions and expectations of inflation come with reading a quality newspaper, paying attention to political news on television and political discussion and understanding.[7] Similarly, pessimism has the effect of increasing expected inflation. (A general additive index of pessimism is used running from zero to five with one point scored for each of expecting one's income to fall behind prices, expecting unemployment to increase, expecting the economy to become worse, feeling that Britain's government is run relatively badly, and feeling that British industry is run relatively badly. These were combined in an index since they each had independent effects of similar size and direction.) Price expectations increase by 7p (or 0.58 per cent) for each extra unit of pessimism on this scale. They also increase by a further 7p if the respondent had expected wage controls to get tougher after the February election.

Lower inflation is expected by those with, *ceteris paribus*, higher incomes, owned accommodation, and higher social class, which are assumed to relate to purchasing habits, since education has no marginal impact and other possible interpretations of higher class, like media usage, are already in the equation. The effect of sex is particularly important: the simple fact of being male takes 36p or 3.6 per cent off the value of expected inflation. This could be attributed to the low inflation rates of tobacco, alcohol, and housing (see Table 4.1) but this cannot be regarded as proven. Increased age, which probably concentrates purchasing on essentials like food and clothing, predicts a marginally higher rate of expected inflation. Under causes of inflation, it appears that those who blamed

---

[7] A further variable from this group, 'degree of interest in politics' is one of five variables which can be found to alter significantly the prediction of E_t from an A−1 or A−2 model. The other variables are sex, age, pessimism, and, marginally, trade union membership (positive coefficient) with all four variables having the same effect as shown in Table 4.7. The improvement in the R^2 attributable to all five variables jointly is about 1 per cent. Interest in politics appears to have an effect on the coefficient of P_t: the coefficient diminishes with increasing interest, implying that people of lower interest may be forming expectations more extrapolatively, and those with more interest more adaptively, or alternatively, that people with less interest adapt more slowly. Indeed, if an A−1 model is estimated within separate groups defined by degree of interest in politics, the b_2 (adaptation) coefficient is highly significant among the more interested, and insignificant among the less interested.

the government and unions particularly for inflation in February were likely to expect higher inflation after October, while those who had blamed it on the world situation saw more room for improvement. Those who blamed inflation on the Common Market also expected higher inflation, with even higher rates expected by those who said they expected Britain to stay in the Common Market. One cannot make too much of any of these effects individually, especially in view of the fact that jointly they explain only 16 per cent (unlogged) or 21 per cent (logged) of the variance in inflation expectations, but at least all the independent effects are in an intelligible direction.

It does seem incomprehensible, however, that partisanship appears to have no effect on expectations. A closer look at the data gives an alternative explanation. Consider the simplest extrapolative model for price expectations in February (the E−1 model). Among those people who voted Labour in February, the equation is

$$E_t = 0.06 + 0.55P_t \ (R^2 = 0.681)$$

while among Conservative voters it is

$$E_t = 0.06 + 0.83P_t \ (R^2 = 0.742).$$

It is immediately apparent that the P_t coefficient is substantially lower among Labour voters, implying that their expected values of inflation were considerably less than those of Conservative voters when controlling for perceptions of price rises. By October most of the difference had disappeared, with the equation for February Labour voters being

$$E_t = 0.06 + 0.91P_t \ (R^2 = 0.817)$$

while for February Conservative voters it is

$$E_t = 0.02 + 1.04P_t \ (R^2 = 0.850)$$

The coefficients have nearly converged, and some of the difference between them is absorbed in the larger constant in the Labour equation. One can conclude from this that the effect of partisanship on inflation expectations is not non-existent but ephemeral. While, perception for perception, some Labour voters must have expected substantially lower inflation after February − and had in fact perceived slightly higher inflation in the year up to February − in the absence of any significant change by October this partisan difference had all but disappeared. The ephemerality of partisan effects on inflation expectations does not mean that inflation expectations are without political consequences, however. This will be discussed in a later chapter.

5

The concept of an economic outlook

The role of economic interest in motivating political activity is generally taken for granted. It is commonly argued that political parties rise to power on the strength of their ability to increase the material welfare of their supporters. Radical political movements are argued to grow out of the economic dislocation and frustration of various sections or classes of society. The assumption that people more or less unanimously seek economic or material betterment motivates governments to pursue economic strategies based on rapid growth. The question of providing incentives to increase productivity and provide economic growth remains at the heart of much political debate. When surveys, on the contrary, provide evidence that people moderate their economic expectations in the presence of difficult economic times (Forester, 1977) the results are taken to justify front-page coverage in the newspapers. There is also evidence that people's feelings about their economic condition influence their feelings about broader aspects of polity and society. Later chapters will suggest that economic stress is related, at least in the presence of sufficient knowledge, to economic policy choices, which in turn are related to feelings about the quality of the country's government. Similar findings, at a very general level, exist for the United States (Strumpel, 1972).

Nevertheless, there are few efforts in the literature of political science devoted to measuring individual economic outlook with any rigour or precision. Opinion polls abound with a variety of questions intended to provide information about people's perceptions of levels and changes in their material state, but there is no systematic attempt to compare the results of different questions, or the same question asked at different times or in different places. This chapter is devoted to remedying that lack. It provides a background for the analytic materials of much of this volume, which discusses such central economic themes in the area of political behaviour as the role of the economy in generating public support for, and disaffection from, elected governments, and the question of instrumental voting and attachment to political parties.

The economic outlook of an individual is taken to be, at its broadest, a subjective assessment of economic well-being: an evaluative filter through which external events pass. Economic outlook is an *evaluation* of economic condition: interest centres on whether the evaluation is *positive* or *negative*. The concept of economic outlook can refer to different areas and be measured in different ways.

Many of the differences can be clarified by considering three analytic choices which have to be made in measuring the economic outlook of any individual. The first question is whether or not the evaluation is to be restricted to the existence and direction of change in the condition, or whether, independent of this, it is to be linked to a question of *aspirations*, desires or expectations. If only the direction of change is sought, the alternative evaluations are that the condition is improving, deteriorating, or unchanged; if aspirations are considered, then regardless of whether the condition is improving, the question is whether or not the individual is *satisfied* with his present state.

The second question deals with the *temporal direction* of outlook. Simply, is the evaluation one which looks backward or forward — or in the context of the last chapter, is a *perception* of the past or an *expectation* of the future being measured? Evaluations based on change or satisfaction may be sought in either temporal direction. The final question returns to a theme introduced in the Introduction: whether the economic condition refers to the *individual* or to the *country*, or, indeed, to some other collectivity. The conditions which individuals evaluate could relate to national economic activity — such as the level of unemployment, or any indicator of the general health of the economy, or to the well-being of the individual or his family such as income, material living standards, and so on.

These three dichotomous choices (evaluation–aspiration, perception–expectation, and personal–national orientations) could give rise, for any individual, to a variety of measures of economic outlook. The rest of this chapter is devoted to clarifying a number of issues. First, which of these analytic distinctions matter empirically? Are all these varieties of economic outlook simply manifestations of some single generalised economic outlook? Second, whatever emerges from the answer to the first question, what are the roles of such background characteristics as age, income, education, and indeed party affiliation in shaping economic outlook? Finally, what is the role of 'objective' economic conditions in shaping or modifying economic outlook, particularly over time?

Varieties of economic outlook

Following a largely American lead, attention to economic outlook has been focused largely on its relationship to aspects of consumer behaviour (see Heald, 1971). In consequence, there is an abundance of opinion poll material on economic outlook, some of it covering considerable periods of time. Most commonly, these questions have dealt with perceptions of personal well-being independent of aspirations. Two of the longest-running series are plotted in Figure 5.1: 'is your standard of living going up, going down, or staying the same?' and 'compared with a year ago, are you and your family better off, worse off, or about the same?' It is evident from the figure that perceptions of movements of standard of living follow widely accepted views of broad trends in the economy, moving upward to 1955, down through 1958 and up again the next year, and

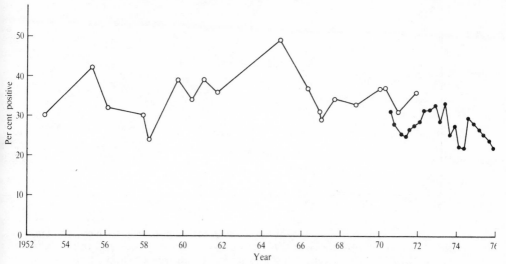

Figure 5.1. Trends in proportions replying positively to 'Is your standard of living going up, going down, or has it stayed about the same?' (Gallup, *Political Index*, various, 1953–71) and 'Do you think you and your family are better off or worse off financially than you were a year ago?' (British Market Research Bureau, quarterly averages of monthly proportions 1970–5)

reaching very high levels in 1964–5, only to drop with the disappointment of 1966 and the end of the grand economic plans of the Labour Government. There is a general upward trend in replies between 1967 and 1970, and a sharp upward movement in well-being between mid-1971 and mid-1972, and a downward trend (where there are more observations) in 1973–6.

Aspiration-independent personal economic expectation questions are also common. Two of these are plotted in Figure 5.2. The questions usually take the form of inquiring whether the respondent (or people like him, or his family) will be better off (perhaps financially) in a year's time. Intriguingly, the different wordings in this case do not provide substantially different replies, though it is clear that the studies with interviews taken just after elections (upper line) contain higher estimates of expectations than do the more occasional opinion polls. This is probably a reflection of post-election euphoria of some sort. Nevertheless, different series tell similar stories over time: all the series suggest a decline in financial expectations over the years from 1964 to 1974, with a particularly steep drop after the election of February 1974.

Aspiration-related perception indicators deal with equity ('are you getting a good deal?' as in Strumpel, 1972) or entitlement (Marsh, 1966) or satisfaction. The only British time-series data in this area are provided by Gallup, who ask intermittently whether or not people are satisfied with their standard of living or income, regardless of whether it is going up or down. The results, from about half a dozen polls conducted by Gallup between 1963 and 1973, suggest that

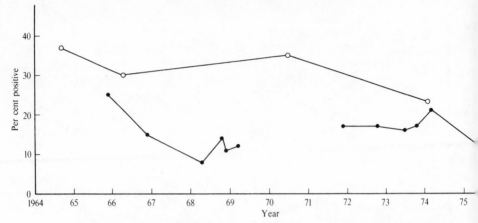

Figure 5.2. Trends in proportions replying positively to 'Now looking ahead over the next three or four years, do you think you will be better off, worse off, or will things stay about the same?' (upper line, election studies 1964–74), 'During the next year, do you think you and your family will become better off, worse off, or will things stay about the same?' (NOP *Political Bulletin*, various up to 1969), and 'And do you think people like you will be better off or worse off in a year's time?' (Gallup, *Political Index*, various since 1971)

more people are at any time satisfied with their standard of living than with their income. The proportion satisfied with standard of living varies between 56 per cent (March 1969) and 70 per cent (December 1971), while the proportion satisfied with income is never higher than 53 per cent (April 1964). The proportion who are satisfied with their standard of living is about equal to the combined proportion who see their standard of living going up or staying constant; the proportions dissatisfied and seeing a decline at any time are about the same. It is important to note that the proportions reporting themselves *satisfied* with their standard of living are the same in early 1964 and 1969, despite the difference in perceptions, revealing again the extent to which people can adjust aspirations to changed circumstances. Moreover, the difference between the proportions satisfied with living standards and income implies that people understand living standards to involve things other than money income. There are no time-series data available for personal aspiration-related expectations indicators though an example (see Forester, 1977) of such a question is how likely people feel it is that they will obtain extra money to which they feel entitled.

Far fewer questions have been asked about the national economy. The longest-running series are questions of satisfaction with national economic performance. These questions take the form of inquiring about satisfaction with the economic record of the government. A review of one such series is available elsewhere (Butler and Stokes, 1969, Ch. 18). Where perceptions and expectations of trends in the national economy are concerned, apart from the Carlson–Parkin series on inflation expectations discussed in Chapter 4, and the annual series on expectations discussed in Chapter 3, the only publicly-available data are questions contained in the monthly British Market Research Bureau Financial Expectations surveys, and these are analysed in detail below. It appears that, in contrast to the personal well-being questions, there has been little attention to and experimentation with questions about subjective judgements about the national economy.

Adaptation in economic outlook

Clearly, what the general economic outlook, or subjective evaluation of economic condition, is at any time will depend on what question is chosen to measure it. A large number of different observations happen to be available for December 1971: these show that, at the time, 70 per cent of the population were satisfied with their standard of living, 48 per cent were satisfied with the government's handling of the economy, 21 per cent thought the country was in a better state than a year previously and 28 per cent expected improvement in a year's time, 36 per cent thought their standard of living was going up, and 28 per cent thought that they and their families were better off than a year before. This variety of response is not the only problem: when one considers change across time, there are also the problems raised by the fact that economic outlook, like other subjective indicators, is dynamic, adaptive, and context-bound.

This is only to say that economic outlook changes rapidly with changing economic circumstances and changing economic aspirations. The economic dislocation of the last few years has certainly greatly increased the importance people attach to economic affairs: this is reflected both in the increase of economic themes in perceived national problems before 1974 and in the recent survey (Forester, 1977) which showed that the proportion seeing rapid economic growth as the most important political aim for the country had doubled between 1973 and 1977, while the proportion seeking economic stability had increased by a third, and all other values showed constant or shrinking proportions across the years. The same article also showed that people had lowered the material standards they felt they had achieved, would achieve, and were entitled to between 1973 and 1977 (as well as reducing their view of how good things had been in the past).[1]

People adapt to changing economic circumstances. Not only will they lower expectations in the presence of economic stress, but there is some evidence that, if growth has been steady but slow, people may not perceive that they have become better off at all. On about 30 occasions between December 1951 and August 1975, Gallup asked a sample of respondents how much income (per week) they felt a family of four needed for health and comfort. In each case

---

[1] The proportion putting economic growth first doubled from 12 to 25 per cent; economic stability increased from 29 to 38 per cent, so that mentions of either increased from 41 to 63 per cent. While 18 per cent marked their personal standard of living nine or ten out of ten in 1973, only ten per cent retrospectively gave those marks to their position 'five years ago' when asked in 1977. This implies that a means of coping with economic decline is to reduce not just expectations but also recollections of how good things used to be.

they published the arithmetic mean (average) of the replies: this value was £9.30 (£9.6s.0d) in 1951 and £50.00 in mid-1975. These averages correspond to popular *money* estimates of a satisfactory standard of living and can be transformed into real terms (constant prices, or allowing for the effects of inflation) by division by appropriate values of the retail price index in this period. A number of different means can be employed to estimate the average annual rate of growth of these popular estimates, but they converge on an estimate of growth of two per cent per annum in what people feel is the (constant) price of health and comfort.[2] The growth takes place almost entirely after 1958: people apparently believed that health and comfort cost about the *same* (in constant prices) in 1958 as in 1951. This perceived growth rate otherwise is consistently higher under Conservative administrations, and takes its lowest value after devaluation in 1967, as people apparently sharply contracted their estimates of the price of health and comfort in the presence of an economic crisis.

More important than the variations (which are always between rates of 1.6 and 2.4 per cent) is the average, real annual growth rate, two per cent. This means that, on average, the perception of ideal income for health and comfort has grown by two per cent per annum more than has the retail price index – a 'real' rate of growth nearly exactly equal to that of the real rate of growth in the economy as a whole. This in turn implies that all the real economic growth in Britain in the last quarter century (except, perhaps, before 1958, when growth was *seen* as growth, or an *increased* standard of living) has been swallowed up in the perception of what is *needed* for health and comfort. If growth is slow but steady, far from recognising widespread economic betterment, people will just incorporate the extra increments into their conception of what constitutes basic health and comfort in a standard of living.

This has a wide range of implications. It suggests a possible reason why the proportions satisfied with their standard of living are always higher than the proportions who feel themselves becoming better off. If economic growth is swallowed up in the requirements for living, people will not feel better off (after all, on average, the requirements continue to be just satisfied) but will acknowledge satisfaction with their state. Second, it suggests why only recently has economic growth grown in prominence as a political value: it isn't missed until shrinkage actually takes place, but isn't particularly valued since, perceptually,

---

[2] The most straightforward calculation is to take

$$R_t = [(I_t/I_0)/(P_t/P_0)]^{1/t}$$

where P is the retail price index, I the estimate of income, and t the number of years since the initial estimate (subscripted 0 in each case). Taking the tth root gives an annual rate of increase (compound), and the rates vary between 1.6 and 2.4 per cent, after initial estimates in 1952 and 1953 which are of the order of -2.5 per cent. One can take a large number of alternative calculations by varying what is taken to be the initial observation, or by calculating a variety of averages to begin and end the series, though this is complicated by the irregularity of intervals between samples. Taking the calculation above, if the first three intervals are not considered, the average annual rate of increase from the first point to each of the rest is 1.95 per cent.

the effects of slow growth are largely invisible. Third, it suggests that economic growth may be an unrewarding strategy for a government to pursue, for if the resulting growth is slow, people won't even notice it, and the government will get no credit for having made people (feel) better off. At least, growth may be an unrewarding strategy whenever there are attendant costs, such as increased inflation, which people then perceive and hold against the government. (It could be that the uncertainties of rapid inflation prevent people from seeing real growth as growth.) In this lack of perception of increased well-being through slow economic growth may lie the answer to the question of why being held to be the party of prosperity has for some time *not* been an electoral winner in Britain (see above, Chapter 1).

There are further reasons to believe that people do not perceive small increases in real income, even when these do occur. Since 1970, large majorities have always perceived that their income goes up from year to year, and expect it to do so. Nevertheless, whenever people have been asked, it appears that they believe that even though income goes up, prices go up faster. Only about six per cent of the electorate believed that their income had gone up by more than prices in the year to October 1974, or would go up by more than prices in the year following. Gallup asked in 1970 and early 1973, when inflation was much lower, whether over the next year people expected wages/income or prices to go up most. Less than ten per cent each time said income: 70 to 80 per cent said prices. In January 1973, only five per cent expected income to go up by more than prices in 1973, after a year in which real earnings increased on average by seven per cent. In October 1974, after a year in which *average* real earnings increased by over three per cent, only five per cent said their income had gone up by more than prices, while 41 per cent said it had stayed the same, and 51 per cent said it had fallen behind prices.

One possible interpretation of this is that while small increases in real income are imperceptible, every decrease is perceived. Thus, all the people with small increases would say 'stayed the same', while all those with any decline would say 'fallen behind', and only those with large increases in real income would actually notice. This is possible, though a preferable account might point out that for most people income increases substantially only once a year, when annual wage or salary negotiations take place and a new contract is signed, but price increases occur in some commodity more or less all the time. Let us assume that people's memories for money values only really last for three months. (Who knows?) Then the last price rise in some salient commodity will always be re-called, for it will always have occurred in the last few weeks, but for the majority of the population at any time, the last salient income increase will have passed out of memory, and income will appear to be constant (bar fluctuations due to overtime, short time, and exceptional payments) while prices will appear to have increased. One could also argue that people (in this way) discount real income gains to the extent of anticipated inflation. In any event, it appears that people's perceptions of changes in real income do not seem to recognise slow but steady growth. Thus, subjectively, perceptions of economic change as well as satisfaction with it may fail to reflect actual underlying trends over long periods, though one would expect more abrupt changes to be recognised fairly easily.

Components of economic outlook

The British Election Study of October 1974 questionnaire contained 15 items measuring aspects of economic outlook. These items are presented in Table 5.1. Questions are included which tap each of the eight possible components of economic outlook. Unfortunately, few of these questions have been asked on enough other occasions to permit time-serial or cross-national comparisons. Each of the 15 is assigned *a priori* to one of the types discussed above: included are perceptions and expectations of personal real income as well as the national economy, and such important economic indicators as inflation, unemployment and strikes. There are also questions dealing with equity, in the sense of whether people consider their income fair, and satisfaction, both with what income buys and the chance of getting ahead. There are even questions dealing with satisfaction with the parties' handling of prices, and the possibility of any government's being able to control prices. Comparisons across such diverse questions may be unrewarding, but one feature of the replies stands out: the responses to aspiration-related questions rarely imply as negative an outlook as do the rest. That is, when economic outlook is a question of satisfaction rather than observation, people are apparently much more satisfied. Only 17 per cent are dissatisfied with the things they can afford to buy, 24 per cent feel their wages are 'less than fair' and 29 per cent are dissatisfied with 'their chance of getting ahead', while over half feel their income has fallen or will fall behind prices. This is consistent with other data that suggest that the British are comparatively satisfied with their condition (Rabier, 1974) and of course with the hypothesis that popular economic expectations in Britain have become lower.

The items hardly correlate well enough with each other for there to be a single outlook ascribable to each individual. The item intercorrelations are presented in Table 5.1: correlations in excess of 0.2 are emphasised. Two items have been dropped from the matrix for simplicity: the items on wage fairness and wage movements relative to those slightly lower-paid do not have a single correlation as high as 0.1 with any other item, and therefore cannot be considered part of economic outlook at all. With regard to the remaining 13 items, the correlation matrix is at least almost entirely positive, implying that there are virtually no cases where a negative evaluation on one item *predicts* a positive evaluation on another. There are, in fact, significant cases only of positive correlation, and cases of no correlation, where an individual's reply on one question is no guide at all to his reply on another. (The only negative correlation above 0.1 in magnitude deals with perceptions of inflation and expectations of unemployment, which – at least under 'Phillips curve' approaches – one expects to find negatively correlated.) However, it must be emphasised that the overall structure of the correlation matrix is very loose, and it can hardly be said that it provides any support for speaking of individuals as if they had some unified outlook with regard to economic conditions.

On the other hand, certain conclusions can still be drawn from the data, in spite of the general lack of correlation between items. In the first place, the distinction between personal and national components of economic outlook is clearly supported. Table 5.1 is broken down according to this distinction, and it can readily be seen that almost all the higher correlations lie *within* the groups of items reflecting each component of economic outlook. Only two further considerations arise from the results. One is that inflation perceptions and expectations appear correlated more with personal than with national circumstances, relating more closely to perceptions and expectations of income rather than the national economy. The other is that two indicators, expectations of income and satisfaction with one's chances of getting ahead, appear to lie somewhere between how people feel about their personal circumstances and how they assess national political—economic trends.

The easiest way to emphasise what these items have in common with each other, and what separates them, is to factor-analyse the correlation matrix. On the assumption that each of the variables contains some part common to all of them ('economic outlook') and some unique part, the matrix can be factor-analysed, and the resulting pattern of factor loadings will identify both what the variables have in common, and how much each one is related to the common structure, or factors. The loadings are shown at the right of Table 5.1. One item, inflation perceptions, has been dropped for technical — though very good — reasons. The loadings for only two factors are shown: it is possible to interpret the results as showing up to two more factors.[3] The first two factors reflect and validate the personal—national distinction. All the variables classed as personal load on this first factor and only SG, satisfaction with chances of getting ahead (as above), also loads on the second. Similarly, all the variables classed as national load on the second factor, but not the first (except, as above, inflation expectations, which should really be considered a part of personal economic outlook). When a third factor is extracted, it contains SA and SG, the two satisfaction questions, which may be as much a reflection of the impact of like question wording as a validation of the aspiration-related/aspiration-independent distinction, though the fourth and last potentially significant factor would contain the other two aspiration-related questions dealing with the perceived and expected

[3] The correlation between perceived and expected prices is so high that it automatically defines a factor on which those two items load. Leaving both variables in produces a factor matrix which is unduly influenced by this first factor, whose orientation was defined by a single correlation coefficient. One can remember that anything said in this analysis about expected prices can also be said about perceived prices. The overall fit is poor, reflecting the low correlations: the first two factors explain only 32 per cent of the total variance. The lack of change when oblique rotation was performed confirms the validity of treating the first two factors as orthogonal. The possibility of two more factors arises both out of principal axes and alpha factoring, though the only further factor which arises in both cases is one of governmental competence: largely items *PH* and *PR*.

Table 5.1. *Varieties of economic outlook in October 1974*

Item		Type	Per cent affirming	Intercorrelations				
PI	Income has fallen behind prices	1n	51					
WH	Those with higher incomes getting further ahead	1n	31	35				
WL	Those with lower incomes are catching up	1n	47	**				
WF	Respondent's wage is less than fair	1a	24	**		Personal		
SA	Dissatisfied with what one can afford	1a	17	33	12			
EI	Expect income will fall behind prices	2n	52	70	21	19		
SG	Dissatisfied with chance of getting ahead	2a	29	20	11	19	24	
PE	British economy worse in last six months	3n	64	18	05	04	27	16
PS	More strikes in last six months	3n	49	11	01	−06	09	04
PP	Perceived highest rates of inflation	3n	*	22	04	05	12	08
PH	Best price handling either party 'not very well'	3a	33	12	03	05	12	08
EE	Expect economy to get worse	4n	38	17	04	05	25	20
EU	Expect unemployment to increase	4n	65	08	01	00	26	12
EP	Expect highest rates of inflation	4n	*	21	05	04	18	09
PR	Prices go on rising no matter what	4a	72	05	01	−05	15	08
				PI	WH	SA	EI	SG

*Variable constructed, 'negative' undefined
**All correlations less than 0.2 in magnitude
***Item eliminated from factor analysis
Note: Data source is BES, October 1974 cross-section. Full question texts are in the Appendix. Correlation coefficients are *gammas*. Responses of 'don't know' are eliminated. Number of observations varies from 1,750 to 2,295. Percentage base for negative views is

competence of any government to deal with prices. No factor separates expectations and perceptions: thus that distinction is made for analytic ease rather than predictive power. One can think of economic expectations as more largely (for any indicator) an extension of perceptions of past trends than of some

		Factor loadings 1 Personal	2 National	
		85	06	PI
		26	01	WH
		29	00	SA
		51	17	EI
		15	17	SG
		05	57	PE
		07	33	PS
		***		PP
		05	25	PH
		08	56	EE
		03	38	EU
		18	11	EP
		04	19	PR

Correlation triangle:

PE	PS	PP	PH	EE	EU	EP
32						
−01	10					
14	06	−01				
51	16	06	21			
44	24	−14	18	34		
07	13	95	03	14	−08	
14	08	10	23	22	14	18

2,365, except for *WH*, *WL*, and *WF*, where housewives are omitted and n = 1,795. Factor analysis based on Pearson correlations, number of observations as for *gamma* correlations presented. Loadings achieved by varimax rotation after principal axes solution. Variable *types* given by (by hypothesis) 1,2 = personal; 3,4 = national; 1,3 = perception; 2,4 = expectation; a = aspiration-related; n = aspiration-independent.

generalised expectation, at least in the context of cross-sectional data, though time-series data tell a somewhat different story. Nevertheless, the central conclusion of this analysis is that, at least in October 1974, people had two entirely separate economic outlooks: one dealing with their own personal circumstances, and the other dealing with the national economy.

Determinants of economic outlook

One finding which emerges repeatedly whenever questions of outlook and satisfaction are analysed is that life-cycle and material circumstances are very important determinants of attitudes in these areas: optimism is associated with youth,
higher class status, higher income, further education (with presumed career
benefits) and so on (see Campbell, 1972; Dunkelberg, 1972; Marsh, 1976). Scores
derived from the factor analysis shown above in Table 5.1 will be used to investigate the determinants of economic outlook. Factor scores are simply a weighted
sum for each individual of his scores on the variables used in the factor analysis,
where the weights are determined by (not equal to) the factor loadings, such
that most importance is given to the variable with the largest loading, and so on.
Thus, analysis of factor 1 scores will resemble analysing income perceptions with
some expectations and satisfaction added; the factor 2 scores will be largely a
matter of perceptions and expectations of the national economy, with a dose of
unemployment and strikes. Experiments with other means of constructing
indices to reflect these two components of economic outlook did not affect the
pattern of results presented below.

Table 5.2 presents the average score on each factor within a number of sub-
groups in the population. The breakdown of scores on the first factor, personal
economic outlook, shows that this component of outlook is more positive when
respondents have higher incomes, are younger, have further education, have no
recent experience of unemployment, either personally or in the family, belong
to trade unions, and are male. The outlook in families where the head of household is a skilled manual worker is positive; other workers plus non-manual
households are more negative. Scots and southerners are positive about their
personal economic outlook: the rest are not. Partisanship has mixed effects:
people who voted either Labour or Conservative − or, indeed read a partisan
newspaper − are more likely to be positive than those who did not vote or voted
for some other party or who have no partisan outlook derived from reading a
partisan newspaper. There is no evidence that having voted for the winning party
in October 1974 made Labour voters personally any more positive about their
economic condition.

Just the reverse emerges from the scores on factor 2, national economic outlook. Partisanship is practically all that counts on this factor: an enormous
difference separates the views of Labour and Conservative voters about the present and future state of the national economy, with non-voters and others in
between. A similar large difference arises between readers of partisan newspapers. On this factor, the Scots emerge as highly negative, while the rest of the
regions are less negative or are positive in outlook. Trade union members and
men are again more likely to be positive, as are the young, but the effects of
income, age and education on this component of economic outlook are far
smaller than on the personal component. Thus not only can one isolate two

Table 5.2. *Determinants of economic outlook*

| | Average score (× 1,000) | | |
Group	Factor 1 Personal	Factor 2 National	Number in group
All	14	8	2,066
Income: over £78 per week pre-tax	197	−122	196
£49–£77 pw pre-tax	141	32	427
£34–£48 pw pre-tax	118	77	460
£19–£33 pw pre-tax	−119	55	405
up to £18 per week	−183	−52	300
Age: up to 34	145	120	711
35 to 64	−1	−27	1,082
65 and over	−264	−139	273
Education: some further	116	9	801
no further	−50	−8	1,265
Household Social grade: non-manual	−28	−94	913
skilled manual	64	98	755
lower manual	−131	66	369
Unemployment: personal or family	−164	−100	208
no experience	34	3	1,858
Trade union: member	94	166	611
not member	−19	−58	1,455
Sex: male	65	102	1,075
female	−41	−93	991
Region: Scotland	80	−121	178
South/GLC	53	−12	817
rest	−26	46	1,071
October vote: Labour	41	388	737
Conservative	34	−346	611
rest	−29	−79	718
Newspaper partisanship: Labour (*Guardian, Mirror*)	31	204	534
None (*Sun*, no paper)	−41	74	713
Conservative (*Times, Express, Mail, Telegraph, Financial Times*)	55	−187	777

Note: Source as Table 5.1.

separate components of economic outlook, but there is little overlap in the social and political antecedents of each component.

Extensive analyses (using AID, described below in Chapter 9) confirm that the effects shown in Table 5.2 are largely independent of each other and cumulative: thus, the small group (four per cent of the sample) who have above-average incomes, are not married women, are aged under 34, have some further education, and come from non-manual households have a first factor score of +826, implying that they must have given a positive reply to several questions loading on this personal economic factor. At the other end of the scale, those with below-average incomes, aged over 30, with either personal or family experience of unemployment recently, have a personal outlook score of −426. None of the effects contradict Table 5.2, though the overall analyses are unstable and not especially successful in explaining personal economic outlook. There is a little evidence of small partisan effects, with Labour voters and those in rented accommodation being more positive, but these effects are confined to that part of the population which has above-average incomes, is male, and over 35. On the national side of economic outlook, the analyses confirm that if the population is split into four groups − voted Labour (+388), voted Conservative (−346), didn't vote for one of these but reads a Conservative newspaper (−230) and the rest (+10) − most of the work is done. Each of these groups can be split by sex, with men consistently 150−200 points more positive than women, and then there are a large number of residual splits by region, age and so on. The fit is much more satisfactory, with over 20 per cent of the variance in national economic outlook explained (as against ten per cent of personal outlook), almost entirely by the first four-fold split along partisan lines.

This result appears to confirm a part of the Butler−Stokes valence model discussed at the beginning of the theoretical analysis in Chapter 1, with the partisan effects confined to the national side of economic affairs, and the personal side a function of socio-economic antecedents with little electoral relevance. As such, although time- and context-bound, it is an important result, and the next two chapters will be given over to further analysis of valence models. First, however, there is some further evidence to look at about the separation of personal and national economic outlook and about the connection between changes in outlook and changes in objective economic conditions.

Economic outlook over time

There would be little point in pursuing the question of whether economic trends and the consequences of economic policies had effects on subsequent mass political behaviour if it could not be shown that these trends and policies were widely and accurately perceived and evaluated by members of the public. If no perceptual link can be established, the connection between objective economic conditions and political attitudes and behaviour remains at the level of an observed, but potentially accidental, correlation. Similarly, there would be little point in pursuing the correlation between subjective economic outlook and political attitudes and behaviour if it could be shown that economic outlook was in no way affected by broad economic changes. A further point is that, in the short term, demographic characteristics of the sort identified above as determinants of economic outlook could not fluctuate enough to produce the sort of variations in economic outlook over time shown in Figure 5.1. An account of these fluctuations results from investigating the connection between monthly movements in economic outlook and important economic indicators (see Thomas, 1975).

Time-series data on economic outlook are available in the results of a series of surveys of financial expectations conducted by the British Market Research Bureau every month since 1970. For reasons of data availability, the results are analysed between July 1970 and December 1973, more or less equivalent to the period in office of the Heath Government. This is a very short period, but data for 1974 and 1975 were published too recently to be included. Each month, the following questions are asked of a sample of about 1,000 respondents:

(1) Would you say that in this country things have generally improved or worsened in the last year?
(2) Do you think that you and your family are better or worse off financially than you were a year ago?
(3) Is your family income the same as it was a year ago, or more, or less?
(4) Do you think conditions in this country will have generally improved or worsened in a year's time?
(5) What do you think will happen next year with regard to your family income?
(6) Do you think this is a good or bad time to buy things for the home like furniture, washing machines, refrigerators, TV or things like that?
(7) Do you think unemployment in your area will increase, decrease or stay the same over the next twelve months?

Questions 1–3 deal with perceptions and 4–7 with expectations. Questions 1, 4, and 7 are 'national' and the rest 'personal'. Each question asked has five possible responses, reflecting 'a lot' of improvement or deterioration, 'a little' improvement or deterioration, or no difference at all. For the analyses which follow, each month's responses were converted into an index by subtracting negative from positive proportions, with those saying 'a lot' weighted double for intensity. Table 5.3 presents averages and intercorrelations among the various series. Expectations and perceptions of income (which peak in October 1972, just before the introduction of Phase I of incomes policy) are in nominal terms, not price-adjusted, and thus always give net positive replies, as money incomes increased steadily in these years. At the same time family well-being gives negative averages.

Perceptions of the state of the country are by far the most negative: there is not a single month in the period under study when, weighted for intensity, more felt the country had improved over the last year than felt things had become worse. The index is at its lowest in June 1971, at the end of a period of increases in both inflation and unemployment, the bailing-out of Rolls Royce and Upper Clyde Shipbuilders, the negotiations for entry into the Common Market, and the introduction of decimal currency. The highest values arise in mid-1972, just after Mr Barber's spring Budget, which stimulated the economy by over £1,000

Table 5.3. *Financial expectations data 1970–3*

Series	Index values			Index intercorrelations					
	Minimum	Maximum	Mean	Country percpn	Well-being percpn	Income percpn	Country expectn	Income expectn	Durable expectn
State of country perception	−123.7	−41.8	−80.3						
Family well-being perception	−53.3	2.1	−21.6	0.80					
Family income perception	32.0	60.1	45.3	0.46	0.66				
State of country expectation	−66.1	4.5	−33.5	0.74	0.49	0.14			
Family income expectation	25.7	48.9	38.8	0.55	0.51	0.60	0.26		
Durable goods expectation	−22.6	60.0	19.7	0.39	0.33	0.37	0.17	0.44	
Unemployment expectation	−58.4	11.5	−20.8	0.54	0.45	0.52	0.29	0.56	0.37

Note: Correlations are Pearson product–moment correlations, calculated over all observations present for each pair of variables. The number of observations underlying the correlations ranges from 35 to 41. Source is BMRB Financial Expectations data.

millions. Expectations of the state of the country are also almost never positive – indeed, are never positive again during the Heath Government after its first month in office. These expectations fall rapidly after July 1970, and reach a low point nine months later, climb again over the next year, remain steady through early 1973, and then fall to a new low as the country slid into the Miners' Strike and three-day working week at the end of 1973. The best time for durable purchases appears to have coincided with the expansionary Budget of March 1972. On the other hand, expectations about unemployment start negative and improve throughout the period.

These differences underlie the generally low level of intercorrelation between the series, and confirm that the series cannot readily be treated as a single indicator of economic outlook.[4] This contradicts work done on the American Index of Consumer Sentiment, whose five component series have been shown to be essentially unidimensional over time (Curtin, 1973). Principal component analysis of the British series reveals that no single factor is readily available which explains more than half of the total variance in the seven series, or more than three quarters of the common variance among the series. Even if perceptions and expectations are separated, the fit does not improve greatly, as witness the almost total lack of correlation between expectations about the state of the country and the other expectation series. The immediate question is whether this lack of fit is the result of random error, or of the different series responding in a meaningful way to different indicators and events. Is each component of economic outlook affected by (and only by) economic trends and political events which ought to affect that component – and does each economic trend affect only those components which logically it ought to affect?

It is possible to give a broadly affirmative answer to both parts of the question, though considerable technical difficulties have to be overcome. The approach taken was to regress each (smoothed) economic attitude series on a wide variety of economic and political indicators, chosen in accordance with survey evidence (and some inspired guesswork) about what the likely political–economic determinants of these attitudes might be. The predictive indicators chosen are listed with the estimation results in Table 5.4. Those concerned with technical estimation problems and precise definitions of variables should read the note on Table 5.4 closely. In general, the equations give reasonably good fits, and all coefficients discussed are statistically significant and have signs in accordance with expectations generated by both economic theory and common sense. Provided that the exploratory nature of the study is allowed to justify some arbitrary decisions in estimation, the results broadly confirm that each attitude series follows closely certain (different in each case) economic and political series, and the predicting series in each case are consistent with the arguments made

---

[4] Moreover, if the Carlson–Parkin expected inflation series is also included, it correlates with the other expectation series about as well as they do among themselves, viz., between 0.2 and 0.5.

above for separating personal and national economic outlook. This can best be illustrated by considering the equations of Table 5.4 one at a time.

State of the country perception

As equation 1 shows, the perceived state of the country depends on a number of factors, the fit is good, and all the signs of the coefficients are in the direction one would expect. There are large positive effects attributable to increased real personal disposable income (*rPDI*) and real industrial production (*rIIP*) and a similar negative effect attributable to short-term acceleration of inflation

Table 5.4. *Estimation results for economic outlook time series*

Equation	Dependent variable	Coefficient	Variable	t-statistic	β	r_i^2	Equation summary
1	State of country perception =	+1.15	$rPDI$	4.3	+0.70	0.65	$R^2 = 0.70(0.66$
		−689.7	$d1RPI_{t+1}$	2.3	−0.23	0.11	$DW = 1.06$
		+82.8	XR	4.4	+0.45	0.09	obs. = 42
		+298.4	$rIIP$	5.8	+0.84	0.56	$F = 16.7$
		−11.0	$(D - W)$	3.2	−0.36	0.27	
		−709.3	Constant	7.3			
2	Family well-being perception =	−3.76	$d12RPI$	6.1	−0.51	0.12	$R^2 = 0.78(0.77$
		−9.87	$(D - W)$	6.1	−0.51	0.02	$DW = 1.20$
		+1.44	$d1E$	3.2	+0.25	0.06	obs. = 39
		+10.4	Constant	2.0			$F = 42.2$
3	Family income perception =	+0.58	E	3.6	+0.26	0.09	$R^2 = 0.82(0.80$
		+4.08	B	4.9	+0.41	0.28	$DW = 1.49$
		−4.36	$(D - W)$	5.3	−0.43	0.27	obs. = 41
		+1.01	$BC1$	4.9	+0.35	0.06	$F = 41.7$
		+39.5	Constant	38.6			
4	State of country expectation =	+1.65	$rPDI$	2.3	+1.06	0.95	$R^2 = 0.68(0.6$
		−12.3	U	2.9	−0.53	0.64	$DW = 0.94$
		+67.5	XR	2.4	+0.39	0.66	obs. = 40
		−13.3	$(D - W)$	3.9	−0.50	0.89	$F = 11.5$
		−29.5	B	3.4	−1.11	0.27	
		−4.74	BR	2.5	−0.74	0.89	
		−381.9	Constant	5.5			
5	Family income expectation =	+9.01	B	12.3	+0.96	0.20	$R^2 = 0.86(0.8$
		−1.14	$BC2$	5.9	−0.42	0.08	$DW = 1.45$
		−5.19	W	5.4	−0.42	0.21	obs. = 35
		−0.45	$d2S$	3.3	−0.23	0.05	$F = 46.2$
		+39.9	Constant	4.7			
6	Durable goods expectation =	+1.17	$rPDI$	2.5	+0.63	0.88	$R^2 = 0.74(0.7$
		+16.8	B	2.2	+0.52	0.86	$DW = 1.11$
		−5.23	BR	5.6	−0.67	0.45	obs. = 40
		+18.0	J	3.6	+0.33	0.05	$F = 24.7$
		−148.4	Constant	2.1			
7	Unemployment expectation =	+2.00	T	8.4	+1.0	0.75	$R^2 = 0.87(0.8$
		+171.1	$rIIP$	2.5	+0.26	0.69	$DW = 1.15$
		−12.3	$d2U$	2.4	−0.19	0.29	obs. = 36
		−144.3	Constant	2.9			$F = 74.0$

Source as Table 5.3.

The variables are

(1) Economic series

(i) Personal
RPI Retail price index
E   Earnings index (detrended)
PDI Per capita personal disposable income

(ii) National
U   Unemployment rate
BP   Visible balance of payments
V   Vacancies
IIP Industrial production index
XR   Sterling exchange rate (dollars)
BR   Bank rate − minimum lending rate
S   Days lost in strikes (millions)
H   Housing units completed

(2) Subjective series
P   Price salience
CP   Carlson−Parkin expected inflation series

(3) Events (government policies)
D   Decimalisation (February 1971 plus
     next 6−9 months)
B   Budget (April 1972 and thereafter)
W   Phase 1 wage freeze (October 1972 plus
     next 3−6 months)
J   July 1971 reflation (4 months after
     July 1971)

(4) Cycles
T   Time trend (increase one per month)
BC1 Budget no. 1 (peak in July and August)
BC2 Budget no. 2 (peak in April)

Note: If the symbol for a variable appears alone, no transformation has been employed. One-month change in earnings would be given by $d1E$; lagged one month, it is $d1E_{t-1}$. Where no subscript is given, t is assumed. The prefix 'r' indicates adjustment to constant prices. Including the retail price index, unemployment rate, and days lost in strikes follows directly from survey responses to the question of most important problems facing the country. The balance of payments is included because of the Butler−Stokes contention that it was an important determinant of government popularity in the previous period, and the exchange rate is included as a plausible alternative to the balance of payments. Earnings are included to measure personal benefit as an alternative to a constructed monthly measure of disposable income, and the indexes of industrial production and vacancies are used to measure the level of activity and expansion of the economy. Where appropriate, each of these series was detrended (had a time trend removed) or alternatively restored to constant prices by dividing by the retail price index. The various series were also recast in dynamic terms as movements or changes over periods of one, two, three and twelve months (twelve only in the case of the retail price index, since this is how it is commonly published). A variety of time lags were tried as well, particularly with respect to unemployment, where a month to month increase may not be directly perceived but only noticed when reported a month after it has occurred. The simplest formulations of variables have always been preferred in results to facilitate replication, unless a more complex formulation *significantly* improved the result; obviously, computing time and sheer fatigue necessitate that not all combinations of all forms and variables have been investigated. Two extra series based on survey evidence are included. One is the Carlson−Parkin series of values for expected levels of inflation, discussed in Chapter 4. The other is a measure of price salience, derived from the frequency with which people responding to the Financial Expectations surveys mentioned prices as the reason for their optimism or pessimism, as the salience of prices may affect expectations independent of the actual level of prices. Events and cycles reflect the movements of the series. It does not follow except by assumption that what caused large alterations in the series after February 1971, March 1972 and October 1972 were respectively decimalisation, an enormously expansionary budget, and a wage freeze.

For each equation, the table gives the value of R^2, also corrected (in brackets) for degrees of freedom in view of the small number of observations, the F-ratio for the equation, and the Durbin−Watson statistic measuring serial correlation. All the equations have enormously (statistically) significant fits, and only a handful of coefficients are included at significance levels below 0.01, and none below 0.05. Nevertheless, in each case the t-statistic relating to each coefficient is given, as is the standardised equivalent of the coefficient, to measure (unreliably in the case of correlated independent variables) the relative impact of each variable. Tests for multicollinearity (the extent of dependence of each independent variable on all the others) are included. It is clear that multicollinearity is a problem in some cases, where the r_i^2 are high, but this would normally only increase the chance of incorrectly excluding some variable which actually has an effect, and a variety of transformations curing the multicollinearity do not indicate that any variable has been incorrectly omitted.

All the series have been smoothed before estimation by replacing each observation with the average of itself (weighted twice) and the preceding and following observations. This has the effect of reducing violent month-to-month swings in opinion. This smoothing was employed because it considerably improved the fit of the equations for the perceptions series: it does not alter the expectations series in quite the same way. but does clearly reduce the impact of survey sampling error on the results. Readers should be aware of the *ad hoc* nature of the transformation, and of the many alternative moving-average formulations which could have the same effect.

Each of the expectations series could be modelled as an expectation-formation process, in the spirit of the Carlson—Parkin argument discussed in the previous chapter. In general, where this was attempted, the results were poor: only in the case of unemployment did anything remotely resembling a learning process emerge, and even here the magnitudes of the coefficients were quite wrong. All the expectations series have first-order autoregressive elements, but the fit in most cases is poor: that is, when expectations are regressed on expectations the previous month, the fit is generally on the order of an R^2 of 0.2 or 0.3. For this reason, levels rather than monthly changes in the series are estimated. The exception is unemployment, which genuinely is an AR(1) process, and we shall have more to say about this below. More important is that many of the transformations of the independent variables — and most notably the smoothing of the perceptions and expectations series — induce autoregressive elements in the residuals from the equations. Some of these autoregressive elements are removed by the introduction of events and cycles, but where they remain in the final equation, GLS re-estimation has been employed. In general, the re-estimations do not cast any doubt on the OLS estimates reported in the table.

($dIRPI_{t+1}$). There is a large positive effect attributable to movements of the exchange rate (XR): it appears that the dollar exchange rate of sterling is a symbol to which people respond in evaluating the condition of the country. In addition, there is a significant effect attributable to two events; the introduction of decimal currency (D) appears to have had a negative effect on people's evaluations, while the introduction of a wage freeze (W) appears to have had a positive effect. These effects are consistent with independent poll evidence which shows that decimalization was held to be a major cause of inflation, but that Phase I was very popular when introduced, even if the later phases of the Conservative incomes policy were much less popular.[5] The coefficients for real personal disposable income ($rPDI$) and industrial production ($rIIP$) imply that increased personal spending potential and increased economic activity are major components of people's perceptions of the state of the country (see Chapter 3 and note that no explicit reference to economics or finance is made in the question text). Real industrial production is a measure of real economic growth, and disposable income reflects the part of growth coming home in wages and salaries: these variables, with a correction downward when the retail index shoots up sharply, play

[5] The *NOP Political Bulletin* for October 1973 indicates that when the incomes policy was introduced in November 1972, 40 per cent thought it would work and 55 per cent thought it fair; in January 1973, 33 per cent thought it would work and 44 per cent thought it fair; on 28 October 1973 (the beginning of Phase III), 20—24 per cent thought it would work and 37 per cent thought it fair.

a major part in people's perceptions of the state of the country. Once these variables are taken into account, further economic variables like unemployment, housing completions, strikes, and the balance of payments have *no* perceptible impact. If the Carlson–Parkin expected inflation values are entered (lagged one month), on the right-hand side of equation 1, about *half* the remaining variance is explained. This implies that there is indeed some further systematic portion of economic outlook (common to perceptions of the state of the country and expectations of inflation) which equation 1 has missed.

Family well-being perception

This series was shown above to be correlated with the state of the country series, and thus it is no surprise that some of the determinants are the same. Inflation (*d12RPI*, the annual rate) and the two events of decimalisation and Phase I are present, though observed inflation becomes much more important than in equation 1. This is consistent with the general argument made about separating personal and national effects: inflation, which by and large is a more 'personal' variable, is increased in importance in the context of the general level of family well-being. This argument is reinforced by the fact that the more purely national indicator, the exchange rate, drops out of the equation (that is, has no independent effect on perceived family well-being) while the monthly change in earnings enters as a predictor, albeit with a rather small impact compared to that of inflation. Indeed, any of detrended earnings, real earnings, or real personal disposable income will serve more or less as well as monthly change in detrended earnings, but always with the same size and direction of effect. The negative effect of increased inflation, and positive effect of increased earnings are in the directions one would expect. Decimalisation, which made people feel worse, and Phase I which made them feel better, have similar effects to those in equation 1, as would the inclusion of anticipated inflation (which increases the R^2 to 0.86), and the overall predictive fit is satisfactory.

Family income perception

Changes in perceived nominal income, like family well-being, vary directly with monthly movements in the (detrended) earnings index. Perceived income, however, is heavily affected by budget-related variables. In particular, there is a substantial positive effect attributable to the generous Budget of March 1972, the perceived income index being on average over 4 points higher after the Budget than before. Equally interesting is the effect of an annual cycle, with peaks around July and August. This cycle is either earnings-related, or (as labelled) a Budget-related cycle, on the assumption that it takes three or four months for the effects of Budget changes to make themselves fully felt in income. This is conjecture: there was also a reflationary 'Budget' in July 1971, and earnings appear to peak in the summer as well. All the Budgets in this period were expansionary, but the hypothesis that this is a Budget-related cycle really depends on showing a four-month lag in depressions of family income after a deflationary Budget, and there are at present no data available with which to do this. In any event, in addition to the variation attributable to earnings, and the various events of decimalisation, Phase I, and Mr Barber's Budget, perceived income moves on an annual cycle, with peaks at the height of summer, and troughs in the middle of winter, a cycle not evident in the other perception series.

State of the country expectation

Equation 4 offers the poorest fit (and worst serial correlation) of all, though even so at 0.68 the overall fit is just satisfactory. The fit, as in equation 1, may be low because this is not an explicitly economic–financial question. Personal disposable income, the exchange rate, decimalisation and the introduction of Phase I all have much the same effects as in equation 1. Unemployment provides a better fit as a general indicator of economic activity in this case than does industrial production, and the negative coefficient shows that when unemployment was higher expectations were lower. The same is true of the minimum lending rate: as interest rates rose (especially towards the end of the government) expectations dropped. Independent of this is the *negative* coefficient attaching to the variable splitting the period at the spring 1972 Budget. This variable was *positive* in the case of perceptions. After April 1972, *ceteris paribus*, people simply felt that the country was in better shape than a year before, and continued to feel that way. After April 1972, people *expected* the country to be *worse off* in a year's time, implying that the benefits that they got from the Budget were all they had expected. This stands as evidence against any hypothesis that if you give people more they simply expect even more and in favour of the view that the British at least have limited expectations of how well off the country is likely to be. This is pushing the interpretation of a single coefficient pretty far, but the fact does remain that as the economy reflated after April 1972, expectations were lower, even though they continued to respond in the usual and predictable way to other economic indicators. Much of the unexplained variance can be absorbed by the introduction of two subjective series: the Carlson–Parkin series (in the case of expectations this is becoming tautological) takes the R^2 up to 0.86, but the series on price salience also works. As the proportion mentioning prices as the cause of national improvement/deterioration increased, expectations dropped, suggesting that prices acted more as a harbinger of bad news than good. Note that half the variance of price salience is explained by the combination of actual and expected inflation. The overall interpretation is that expectations do move largely with perceptions, and therefore with the economic indicators predicting the perceived state of the country, but that expectations appear to diminish as the country is seen to get into a better state.

Family income expectation

Expectations of income in a year's time, like perceptions of income, were positively affected by the 1972 Budget, being substantially higher after April 1972. Similarly, expectations move on an annual cycle, with a peak in April and a

trough in October. Remembering that each March brought good news in the form
of an expansionary (or at least not deflationary) Budget in these years, this can
also be identified as a Budget-related cycle. Working along the general lines of a
distinction between perceptions and expectations, it appears that the effect of
an expansionary Budget on income *expectations* is *immediate*: pump money
into the economy and people immediately believe their incomes will be higher.
The impact on income *perceptions*, as above, is *slower*: the peak of perceptions
does not come until the changes actually work through over the next quarter or
so. It is also clear from the equation that people adjusted expectations of income
downward for the three months of Phase I (note that this is the opposite direction of effect from the terms of equations 1–4, where Phase I had a positive
effect), and it appears that recent increases in strikes also decrease expectations
of income. It is important to note the difference between this and the previous
equation however: whereas here even after April 1972 people expected that
their income would be higher (presumably as a result of the Budget) this was no
longer translated into the expectation that the country would be in a better
state. It is also clear that people translated the negative impact of the wage freeze
on their income into positive expectations for the country as a whole, at least for
a little while.

Durable goods expectation

People think it is a good time to buy durable goods when personal disposable income is high (or, equivalently, when earnings have increased). People certainly
thought it a better time to buy durables after the March 1972 Budget, and indeed
for a few months after the reflationary measures of July 1971. Certainly this
suggests an association at the psychological level between sensing a good time to
buy durables and the beginnings of reflationary trends, as well as increased personal liquidity. (For the connection between durable purchases and economic
upturns, see Evans, 1969.) The inclusion in the equation of the Carlson–Parkin
series would show that people think it is a bad time to buy durable goods when
they expect high rates of inflation. Most interesting is that views of desirability
of durables vary inversely with the bank rate; when interest rates are high,
people are less likely to think it a good time to buy durables. This is consistent
with the common use of credit in Britain for durable purchases. It is noteworthy
since there are few equations of the seven into which the bank rate enters. It
reflects the fact that in this period changes in bank rate (or minimum lending
rate) were still an important instrument of economic policy, and that bank rate
changes often accompany changes in hire purchase or mortgage rates.

Unemployment expectation

This series yields a simple equation. Unemployment expectations improve with
real growth, as measured by a price-deflated index of industrial production and
worsen when unemployment has recently been increasing. When unemployment
has been going up, people expect more unemployment; when growth is faster,

people expect less unemployment. However, the biggest effect is that of time: unemployment expectations improved steadily, by two points a month throughout this period. (The effect of time is somewhat smaller and the effect of unemployment change larger, after GLS re-estimation to remove autocorrelation from the equation.) It is not exactly clear why this time trend should be so evident: on the one hand, people certainly might well have expected higher unemployment at the beginning of the Heath Government, for higher unemployment was widely advertised in 1970 as a consequence of allowing inflation to continue, and there is the evidence reviewed below (Chapter 10) that people generally associate higher unemployment with the Conservative Party. On the other hand, why people should have gone on steadily hoping more and more commonly for an improvement as time went on is not clear, unless the process simply reflects the wearing away over time of the initial prejudice against the Conservative Party's willingness or ability to reduce unemployment.

Summary

The threads of this analysis can be drawn together into a number of general conclusions. First, while individual proportions may depend heavily on question wording, a variety of different measures appear to tell somewhat the same story about economic outlook over time, provided that the fundamental distinctions between perceptions and expectations, personal and national components, and presence or absence of satisfaction as a standard are not ignored. Second, at an individual level, personal economic outlook is an extension of socio-economic circumstances and life-cycle effects, while national economic outlook is largely independent of personal outlook, and appears to lie heavily along partisan lines. Finally, when time-series data are considered, good fits are obtained to a hypothesis that both personal and national perceptions and expectations are heavily influenced both by actual trends in economic indicators and by government interventions in the economy. Different areas of the economy appear to be perceived differently, and to have separable effects on the various components of economic outlook. At a minimum, one should never assume that, just because people think the country is in a better state, they also believe themselves to be better off, or that any one economic development will necessarily make them believe both of these things.

6

The economy and government support

Britain appears to have acquired the reputation of being a country in which the popularity and electoral success of governments depend largely on economic conditions. A quotation attributed to Harold Wilson sets the tone: 'the standing of a government and its ability to hold the confidence of the electorate at a General Election depend on the success of its economic policy'. Certainly the correlation between economic decline and weakening of electoral allegiance to the major parties in the period since the Second World War is too apparent to be overlooked, even if the correlation at the individual level is difficult to establish. The last decade has seen scholars and journalists alike lavish considerable attention on the question of the linkage between political behaviour and economic conditions, and economic issues have been seen by both electorate and politicians as the most important problems facing the country. In times of economic stress, as well as in election years, the fact that economic conditions influence voters becomes a conversational common-place. All the more reason, then, to ask like Stigler (1973) whether this fact is, in fact, a fact.

There are now about half a dozen studies of note about the determinants of government popularity in Britain; there is a larger and ever-growing literature on related questions in the United States. Much of it derives from Kramer's (1971) seminal contribution that the electorate judge the incumbent government by economic conditions – as reflected by relative changes in unemployment, prices, and real money incomes – and reward or punish the government according to whether or not these economic conditions are seen to be satisfactory. His conclusion is that increases in real income over the election year are associated with higher rates of support for the party which holds the Presidency at the time of the election. Kramer's choice of economic indicators has been much discussed, and other studies suggest that, of all economic variables, inflation may be most important, at least when there is considerable inflation taking place (Stigler, 1973; Arcelus and Meltzer, 1975). Recent studies also add the precaution of modelling economic effects independent of trends, either short term (for instance, personal presidential popularity) or long term (trends in party identification, represented by voter registration data) (Tufte, 1975; Bloom and Price, 1975). There is also a shorter and inconclusive literature which uses presidential opinion poll popularity as the dependent variable (Mueller, 1970; Hibbs, 1974).

In Britain, attention to these matters has been concentrated on the question of government popularity rather than election results, although much of the early work from which the later empirical studies drew inspiration dealt with the question of why incumbent governments lost by-elections. Despite superficially contradictory appearances, the British analyses produce an essentially consistent account. Government popularity is essentially a first-order autoregressive process (that is, popularity in any month is well predicted by popularity the previous month). Moreover, this process takes the form of a U-shaped trough between elections (*ceteris paribus*, popularity falls in the early months of a government and rises in the later months). Finally, economic variables explain small but significant movements of popularity around this basic cyclical pattern. No attempt will be made to contradict these findings in what follows, but, as ever, there is much more which can be said about both the estimates in the literature and the models of electoral behaviour they assume.

Estimating a popularity function for Britain

It has been a regular observation about British politics for some years that the popularity of the government (measured by voting intention in opinion polls) always falls steeply in mid-term, giving rise to some remarkable by-election defeats, only to recover to a large extent in time for the next General Election. This inter-election cycle is usually put forward as a 'great constant' of British political life, and its origins remain unclear. Figure 6.1 shows the expected shape of the cycle between elections, whether it is modelled as a parabolic curve (Miller and Mackie, 1973), or as short-term surges before and after elections, with a depreciation of popularity in between (Goodhart and Bhansali, 1970), or most efficiently as a sum of time to the nearest election plus depreciation (Frey and Schneider, 1977; see also Stimson, 1976). Superficial differences in estimation of this cycle, which is one variety of a first-order autoregressive process, should not mask the fact that all these estimates propose a broadly similar inter-election cycle.

Economic effects on government popularity are modelled as the determinants of fluctuations in popularity around this cycle. The effect of high unemployment is expected to be seen in levels of government popularity *lower* than the cycle alone would predict. Similarly, relative to cyclical levels of popularity, high rates of inflation depress, and high rates of real economic growth increase, government popularity. Attempts to link popularity to trends in the balance of payments have failed to isolate significant independent effects.[1] Relative to the predictive

---

[1] Despite the claim of Butler and Stokes (1969) discussed in Chapter 1. About the best that can be done is that if only the balance of payments, inflation and unemployment are included in the equation for government lead (or popularity) 1966–70, the resulting equation is $Lead = 30.9 + 0.006BP - 2.2I - 9.4U$; $t_{BP} = 2.9$, $R^2 = 0.45$, with the *standardised* effect of *BP smaller* than that of the other economic variables. The addition of any other economic or cycle variables (or extension of period) removes what effect is left for the balance of payments. Note also that under the different estimation procedures reported by Doreian and Hummon (1976), Chapter 4, the balance of payments is actually

(*a*) Goodhart and Bhansali (1970) model contains fall after election ('euphoria'), rise before election ('backswing') and downward trend in mid-term.

(*b*) Miller and Mackie (1973) model contains time-dependent inter-election parabolic curves whose troughs are deeper in successive periods.

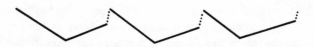

(*c*) Frey and Schneider (1977) model contains time to nearest election affected by downward inter-election time trend.

Figure 6.1. Models of inter-election cycles in government popularity (peaks in popularity coincide with elections).

power of the overall cycles, however, economic effects, though statistically significant, are small, and lack explanatory power.

The existence of a recurrent cycle forms the basis for generalisation across governments and time periods, allowing for evaluation of the popularity of individual governments against some long-term standard. Moreover, if cycles exist, and if its popularity is of any concern to the government, the government will evaluate its popularity relative to its place in the cycle. A five-point popularity deficit in mid-term is, according to the cycle hypothesis, less of a problem than a five-point deficit one year before or after an election. Moreover Miller and Mackie point out that the cycles are time-dependent, and that the decreased popularity of governments of the late 1960s relative to twenty years earlier is reflected in inter-election cycles whose troughs are deeper and longer-lasting.[2]

reduced in importance as a variable in the 1960s relative to the 1950s (or is, at least, reduced in importance relative to some other economic variables).

[2] They also show that much of the apparent impact of unemployment on popularity is spurious, owing to a *cycle* in the unemployment series. Strictly, unemployment appears to

Miller and Mackie's cyclical model covers all governments from 1948–72. However, when recent governments are considered, some difficulties arise. The Heath Government, whose popularity is plotted in Figure 6.2 along with the cycle estimates from Miller and Mackie's best-fitting equation, managed to sustain a level of popularity from October 1971 to June 1973 which was consistently higher than estimates derived from cycles observed over the previous twenty-three years would have led one to expect. In fact, over the period of the Heath Government as a whole, no clearly cyclical elements appear, although the short-term decline after an election and recovery before the next employed by Goodhart and Bhansali are clearly evident. The Heath Government was able to sustain a level of popularity in mid-term much higher than that of its predecessor, and the next Labour Government did so as well throughout much of 1975–77. In fact, the best Miller–Mackie cycle equation explains only 30 per cent of the variance in government popularity from June 1970–January 1978, less than half its explanatory power from 1948–72.

The declining fit of popularity to the cyclical model so prevalent in the earlier period (particularly 1955–70) is only one problem that merits investigation. A more serious problem is that the unprecedentedly high levels of inflation and unemployment during and after 1974 suggest that whatever magnitudes of effect might have been attributed to these economic variables in earlier years will no longer hold. It is inconceivable that the impact of one per cent of inflation in 1975 should be the same as the impact of one per cent of inflation in 1965. None of the published studies referred to above includes estimates from the last few years, but what is expected is exactly what happens: equation 1 in Table 6.1 shows that if the period 1959–77 is considered, the only terms which are well-determined are the downward trend and cycle elements within governments. Of the economic terms, only the growth rate of real income is (marginally) significant.

This is also a serious problem, for equation 1 is a replica extended three years of the equation employed by Frey and Schneider (1977), save that the present dependent variable is government popularity rather than lead. (However, all conclusions from Table 6.1 apply equally to predictions of government lead, or the difference between government and opposition popularity. See Alt and Chrystal,

contain a large number of long-term cyclical components. When detrended, the covariation between popularity and unemployment appears due largely to the presence in each series of a cyclical component apparently equal in length to a full parliamentary term. Moreover, their time-dependent cycle model explains over half the variance of unemployment in the period 1959–67. The presence of such a cycle immediately suggests the possibility of a 'political' unemployment cycle, with the unemployment rate manipulated in the interest of increasing popularity in an election year. This is taken up in the next chapter. A few problems should be pointed out as well. Fitting a cycle term (like using a lagged dependent variable) maximises the extent to which remaining variables are being forced to explain what may well be sampling error. Opinion poll results are known to contain sampling error, and this error may look larger in relation to month-to-month fluctuations than to overall levels of popularity. This raises more difficulty if some of the remaining economic variables also have long-term cyclical components, as Miller and Mackie suggest about unemployment.

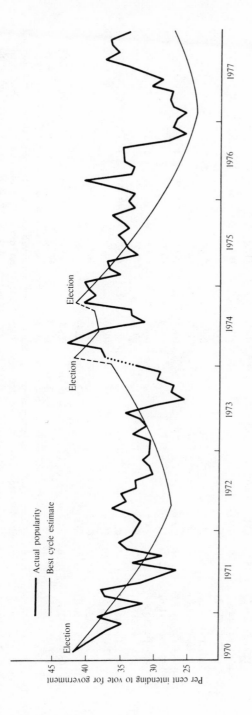

Figure 6.2. Monthly movements in government popularity (*Gallup Political Index*, unadjusted vote intention question) and best-fitting Miller–Mackie cycle estimate equation, July 1970–January 1978. The cycle equation explained over half the variance in government popularity 1948–72: it is given by *Popularity* = 42.48 − 0.113 *Last* + 1.54 *Near* − 0.0297 *Near*^{2} − 0.002738 *Time*Near* + 0.00004793 *Time*Near*^{2} where *Last* is months since last election, *Near* is months to nearest election, and *Time* is months since January 1900.

Table 6.1. *Popularity, cycles, and economic conditions*

Equation	Period	Constant	Trend	Cycle	Annual rate of inflation: Observed	Expected	Expected −Past	Unemployment rate	Growth rate of personal disposable income	R^2	F	obs.	DW	Estimation procedure
1	1959.1–1977.3	41.8 (29.5)	−0.50 (5.9)	−0.74 (3.8)	−0.11 (1.0)			−0.23 (0.4)	0.25 (1.6)	0.51	14.4	75	0.92	OLS
2	1961.1–1973.4	44.6 (24.2)	−0.59 (6.1)	−0.70 (3.3)	−0.23 (1.0)			−1.34 (1.5)	0.41 (2.1)	0.58	12.5	52	0.98	OLS
3	1961.1–1973.4	45.7 (24.8)	−0.62 (6.7)	−0.67 (3.4)		−0.56 (2.1)		−0.98 (1.2)	0.40 (2.1)	0.61	14.2	52	1.05	OLS
4	1961.1–1973.4	41.1 (11.6)	−0.31 (2.7)	−0.54 (1.3)		−0.33 (1.0)		−0.82 (0.7)	0.15 (0.7)	(0.73)	23.4	52	(2.14)	GLS ($\rho = 0.49$)
5	1961.1–1973.4	43.8 (15.5)	−0.32 (3.0)	−1.04 (3.4)		−0.74 (2.0)		−0.69 (0.5)	0.62 (2.2)	(0.79)	20.6	35	(2.07)	GLS ($\rho = 0.50$)
6	1961.1–1973.4	46.9 (11.5)	−0.77 (3.6)	−0.74 (8.6)		−0.19 (0.3)		−0.05 (0.3)	0.01 (0.3)	(0.78)	6.3	17	(1.95)	GLS ($\rho = 0.31$)
7	1959.1–1977.3	43.0 (30.4)	−0.53 (7.0)	−0.65 (3.6)			−0.45 (2.7)	−0.99 (2.4)	0.20 (1.4)	0.57	17.6	73	1.04	OLS
8	1959.1–1977.3	41.1 (19.5)	−0.36 (4.0)	−0.52 (1.8)			−0.31 (1.6)	−0.97 (1.6)	0.04 (0.2)	(0.70)	30.1	73	(2.01)	GLS ($\rho = 0.56$)

Note: Dependent variable is per cent intending to vote for government party, *Gallup Political Index*, various, averaged over quarters. Trend and cycle as in Frey and Schneider (1977). Economic data from *Economic Trends*, various. Expected inflation from Carlson and Parkin (1975). Bracketed numbers beneath coefficients are *t*-statistics. Bracketed values of R^2 and *DW* indicate that dependent variable is differenced. Expected minus past inflation substitutes actual for expected inflation where the latter is unavailable; past inflation is measured with a geometrically declining lag over two years.

1978.) To show how important the choice of period is, equation 2 repeats equation 1 for the period 1961.1–1973.4. Term by term, equation 2 says that government popularity in the Gallup poll (averaged over quarters) diminishes from a constant of 44.6 per cent by 0.59 of a percentage point each quarter, and by a further 0.7 of a percentage point for each quarter away from the nearest election, on the assumption of a four-year term in office. This gives the usual cycle of Figure 6.1. Independent of this, for each per cent annual increase in the retail price index, the Government loses 0.23 of a percentage point of its popularity, a further 1.34 percentage points for each per cent unemployed, but gains back 0.41 of a percentage point for each per cent annual growth of *real* disposable income. Note that the inclusion of a *real* income term means that inflation essentially is in the equation twice: first, the inflation rate discounts the rate of growth of nominal disposable income, and then the rate of inflation is seen to diminish popularity again.[3] Because of this, the inflation term in equation 2 can be interpreted as an *expectations* term, with the positive impact of growth of real income discounted by the extent to which inflation is expected to continue. Unless the growth rate of real income is higher than the growth of retail prices, the government derives little political benefit from the growth of money incomes.

To sustain this interpretation, equation 3 replaces the actual annual inflation rate with the values from the Carlson–Parkin expected inflation series discussed in Chapter 4, with the estimation period determined by the availability of data. The determination of the inflation term is improved without altering the other coefficients much, and the process by which expected inflation discounts past real income growth in determining government lead is clear. Even though each extra per cent annual growth of real income adds 0.4 of a per cent to government popularity, each expected per cent annual inflation costs the government 0.56 of a point (with each per cent unemployed in the workforce costing 0.98 points). However, equation 3 is plagued by technical problems, and re-estimation by generalised least squares (equation 4) shows that the apparent significance of equation 3 was greatly exaggerated by inappropriate estimation. According to equation 4, real income growth has little apparent effect on popularity, and the effects of unemployment and expected inflation, though in the expected directions, are also very weakly determined. The apparent impact of economic conditions is due to inappropriate estimation techniques. Thus when correctly estimated, independent of cycles, economic conditions appear not to matter.

What is sought is a model which can be estimated correctly, sustain the impact of economic (and particularly inflation) expectations, and be estimated over a period including the years after 1973, as well as helping give an account of the apparently non-cyclical behaviour of government popularity during the years

---

[3] The per cent annual rate of growth of real income (R) can be defined as a (linear in logarithms) function of the difference between the per cent annual growth rate of nominal or money incomes (N) and the per cent annual increase in prices, or inflation rate (I). Thus an equation like equation 1: $G = \ldots + aR - bI$ can be rewritten as $G = \ldots + a*(N–I) - b\,(I) = \ldots + a*N - (a*+b)I$ with $a* = a[100/(100 + I)]$, giving a much bigger impact to inflation.

of the Heath Government. This is an appropriate point to reintroduce the idea outlined in the first chapter, and discussed on a number of occasions below, that people have by and large the greatest motivation to pay attention to economic conditions when these conditions are deteriorating. The government may well not benefit from economic conditions when these conditions are seen to be all right, since indeed, as in the previous chapter, something like slow but steady real income growth may be taken for granted rather than seen as a credit to the government. It may be penalised when things are not all right, particularly if the electorate are more strongly motivated to notice economic conditions when these are deteriorating. Models like this for Britain are discussed by Mosley (1976a, 1976b; for criticisms, see Alt and Chrystal, 1978). In order to develop a simple version of Mosley's model, assume that members of the electorate are aware of the present rate of inflation. (Chapter 4 established that people have some idea of what the present rate of inflation is, and expectation of its future values.) Assume further that there is some average of recent experience which people see as critical. Since people's memories are not infinite, assume arbitrarily that this critical level of inflation can be represented by the average level of inflation over the last three years. When inflation has become worse than this critical standard, people are aware of it; if it is below recent experience, people pay no attention to the rate of inflation. Figure 6.3 shows how the actual inflation rate and its critical level have moved over the last two decades. Before 1960, there was only a period in 1955–56 when inflation was in crisis; since 1960, inflation has been perpetually in crisis except for periods around 1963, 1967, and 1972 (and 1978).

A straightforward extension of this argument is to hypothesise that economic conditions only affect government popularity when 'in crisis'. In other words, government popularity is diminished by inflation only when inflation is high relative to recent experience. A fall in the rate of inflation aids the government only when inflation is above satisfactory levels anyway; trends in inflation when it is below the critical standard (that is, all right in the eyes of the public) are unnoticed, and therefore do not affect the popularity of the government. Table 6.1, equations 5 and 6, give empirical estimates relating to these hypotheses.

These equations show that government popularity is determined by two entirely different processes, depending on whether inflation (expected) is in crisis (exceeding its recent trend). When it is in crisis, the effects of inflation expectations and real income growth are marked and significant: independent of cycles each per cent of expected inflation knocks 0.74 of a percentage point off government popularity but each extra per cent growth of real income puts back 0.62 of that point. The coefficient of unemployment is not significantly estimated in inflation crises, but retains the right sign. In non-crisis periods, government popularity is all cycles and trends: the economic variables have insignificant effects. The fit in both cases is excellent. This represents a good foundation for a 'satisficing' model of economic effects on government popularity. Crisis levels of inflation, relevant to recent trends, represent a perceptual threshold. Only when

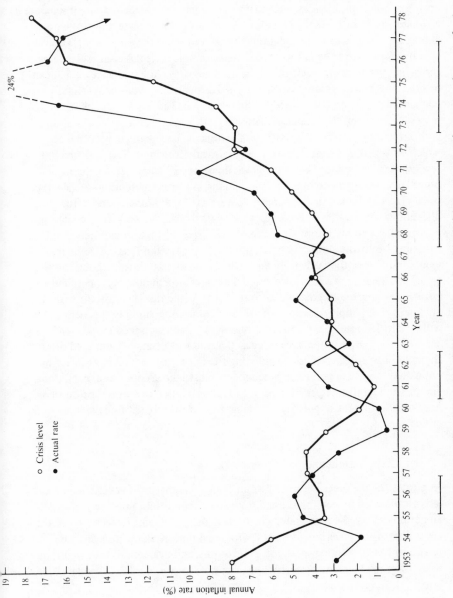

Figure 6.3. Actual annual retail price inflation rates and 'critical' (three-year moving average) rates of price inflation in Britain 1953–78. Horizontal bars denote periods when inflation exceeded its critical level.

inflation is in crisis are economic conditions perceived and brought to bear on government popularity.

One can interpret the notion of inflation crisis as a perceptual filter, such that when inflation is all right, people pay no attention to economic conditions. While this sort of interpretation makes sense in a period when inflation stays seen as the most important problem by large majorities, a better model would have separate estimates for unsatisfactory periods of each economic variable, but this would be clumsy. A more elegant formulation (though not quite the same model) is available by re-estimating equation 1 with the economic variables each replaced by the difference between itself and some average of recent experience, which can be constant, and represents satisfactory performance, or what people have become accustomed to (Hibbs, 1978). Equation 7 in Table 6.1 contains such estimates, and apparently extends equation 3 both forward and backward in time, without unduly altering the coefficient estimates. Each percentage point by which expected inflation exceeds a geometrically weighted average of the last few quarters' experience costs the government 0.45 of a percentage point of popularity, while unemployment and real income growth continue to have the usual effects.[4] Equation 7 apparently covers the longer time period without the difficulties of equation 1. However, again part of the apparent fit of equation 7 is attributable to inappropriate estimation. Corrected for autocorrelation (like equation 4 over the shorter period), inflation (expected minus past), unemployment, and indeed the cycle term are only marginally significant, though all signs are of course as expected. However, real income growth now appears to have virtually no impact on government popularity. While this is consistent with the argument that people took the growth of income for granted in this period, there will be a little more to say about this below. While this discussion must end on a somewhat tentative note, it seems clear that the sort of models outlined offer the only hope for successfully estimating the impact of economic variables on popularity over long periods. These models must take account of expectations, and of the adaptive nature of expectations, considering the impact of the economy on government popularity in the light of constantly shifting perceptions and evaluations.

Expectations and policy evaluation

Regardless of the specific form of assumptions one makes, if government popularity is affected by economic conditions, these conditions must be perceived and evaluated by the electorate, which must also have some expectation of the capability of the government to deal with economic affairs. Untangling the relationship between expectations, perceptions, and evaluations is difficult, but a first step can be made by restricting attention to competence in a single econ-

---

[4] Where expected inflation values are unavailable, current observed values have been substituted. The geometric declining lag has an initial weight set arbitrarily to 0.50. A variety of versions of equation 8 have been tried, but it must be considered still experimental.

omic area like prices over a relatively short time. One conclusion of Chapter 4 was that the differences in expectations attributable to partisanship may pass off within months, while the differences attributable to general factors like information, pessimism, purchasing habits and beliefs about inflation appear to linger. This is not to say that the effects of economic expectations on partisan matters are necessarily equally ephemeral. As a start, let us consider the question of how far people's assessment of Labour's performance in office on the issue of prices was affected by the expectations people had of inflation when Labour took over in February 1974.

Indeed, people did not have particularly high expectations of Labour's performance: less than a quarter of the electorate appeared to expect the *rate* of inflation to subside after February, and only 2½ per cent expected prices to fall, while another seven per cent appeared to expect prices to remain steady (from Table 4.3). Among February Labour voters, these last two proportions rise respectively to 3½ and 12 per cent, as against 1½ per cent and five per cent in the rest of the electorate. Thus among the rest of the electorate perhaps one in 16 and among Labour voters one in seven appeared to expect Labour to be able to freeze prices after February. This in turn does not suggest that Labour had raised people's expectations very high, but rather that one of the sources of the public's quiet reaction to the inflation of 1975 was that they so clearly expected it to happen well in advance.

It is nevertheless possible to analyse the effects of high expectations. People were asked in February how well they felt the Labour Party would have handled prices if they had been in office before February, and were given four choices of response: very well, fairly well, not very well, and not at all well. In October 1974 they were asked how well Labour had handled the issue of prices since February, with the same choice of alternatives. Few felt in February that Labour would have done very well, even among its own supporters, though it was widely felt that Labour would have done a better job than the Conservatives.[5] Interest centres on those people whose opinion of Labour's competence was *lower* in October than February, and in the extent to which this is linked to having held unrealistically high hopes in February. Because of the tendency for people to project negative feelings for all sorts of reasons onto parties not their own (Alt, Särlvik and Crewe, 1976b) the analysis is restricted to those who voted Labour in February, which is also consistent with looking only at assessment of the performance of the government.

Did Labour *disappoint* its supporters? The answer is probably yes, to some extent, and some evidence is given in Table 6.2. In general, the supporters likeliest to *lower* their *evaluation* of Labour's competence between February and October should be those who had the *highest hopes* in February and saw the least achievement in October. In Table 6.2, the 25 per cent of Labour voters expecting

[5] Only 20 per cent of Labour voters felt Labour would have done very well, but 80 per cent felt their party would have done better than the Conservatives. Only 55 per cent of Conservatives felt their party had done better than Labour would have.

Table 6.2. *Expectations, perceptions and evaluations*

Expected in February that Labour would do a	Perceived in October that Labour had done a	
	Bad job	Good job
Bad job	34% (*n* = 119)	23% (*n* = 283)
Good job	58% (*n* = 12)	16% (*n* = 118)

Note: Cell entries are the percentage of those in the cell 'disappointed' – that is, giving Labour's handling of prices a lower rating in October than in February. Total observations are 532 Labour voters in February, and the construction of 'bad job' and 'good job' are explained in the text, and are based solely on expectations and perceptions of the rate of inflation. In each case, one is (arbitrarily) defined to include three quarters of the sample. Source is BES, October 1974, panel sample.

the *lowest* rate of inflation after February are placed in the category 'expecting a good job' with the remaining 75 per cent 'expecting less'; similarly, the 25 per cent perceiving the *highest* rate of inflation before October are said to 'perceive a bad job' while the remaining 75 per cent perceive better. The proportion 25 per cent was chosen to be in keeping with the approximate proportion saying that Labour would have handled 'prices very well' in February; it is also the case that 25 per cent of February Labour voters had a lower opinion of Labour's competence on prices in October than in February. Each cell in Table 6.2 shows the proportion of people in that category who were disappointed – or had a lower opinion – in October. The rate of disappointment is low among those who *neither* expected a good job nor perceive a particularly bad job: only 23 per cent of those with neutral expectations and perceptions reduced their estimate of Labour's competence. Perceiving a bad job is associated with higher rates of disappointment, and the highest rate (58 per cent) comes as expected among those who both expected a good job *and* perceived a bad job. So in this sense there is some truth in the argument that high expectation can lead to frustration: disappointment is common among those with high hopes who see little achieved. But the proportion who fall in such a category are very *small*: this in turn suggests that by forecasting inflation more accurately, people can avoid the trap of being seduced into false hopes and then disappointed.

Table 6.2 isolates a very high rate of disappointment among a very small group. Rather than tinker with the frequencies in the cells, the same data can be presented in an alternative fashion to compare the relationship between February expectations and October perceptions among both the disappointed and the satisfied – those whose opinion of Labour's confidence was at least as high in October as in February. Let D be a variable representing disappointment and taking the value 1 if a person was disappointed (lower evaluation of Labour competence in

October) and zero if not: further let P_0 stand for (logged) perceptions of inflation in October and E_f stand for (logged) expectations in February. Creating a further 'interaction' variable by multiplying D by E_f (denoted $D*E_f$) allows direct estimation of an equation to test the hypothesis that the relationship between P_0 and E_f is different in the two groups defined by D.

One would expect that disappointment (measured by a reduced estimate of their competence) with Labour would generally be associated with higher perceived inflation in October, but that this relationship should be strongest where hopes were highest (that is, the least inflation was expected), but that if one expected considerable inflation in February, perceptions of inflation should matter less in determining the rate of disappointment. This is exactly what one finds: the least square estimates for the equation are

$$P_0 = 9.4 + 3.8D + 0.51E_f - 0.17(D*E_f)$$

with 578 observations, and $R^2 = 0.20$, and all coefficients significant well beyond the 0.05 probability level. The relationship implied by this equation is shown in Figure 6.4 wherein the upper line relates to the disappointed and the lower to the satisfied. For any level of expected inflation in February (up to about 22 per cent per annum), being disappointed comes along with higher perceived inflation in October. The difference is *biggest* among people who had expected *lowest* inflation rates and gradually disappears as expectations become more moderate. If one expected a very high rate of inflation, then level of perceived inflation no longer differentiates the disappointed from the satisfied. Though there are other sources of disappointment, it is clear that policy evaluation is linked to the perception of economic trends, and to people's expectations of economic developments and government performance. This relationship ought to be generalisable.

The economic record of the government

Butler and Stokes say that it would be surprising if the popularity of a government were not systematically tied to its economic record. Figure 6.5 gives a simple model showing what the links ought to be. Government popularity ought demonstrably to be a function of popular approval of the government's record. No other alternative is consistent with any sort of model of even minimally-informed voting and belief in the reliability of survey evidence. Even so, the existence of a strong correlation between approval of the government's record and its popularity does not establish very much.[6] Approval of the government's

---

[6] Note that even a 'rationalisation' process, whereby party preference precedes evaluation of political issues, makes this correlation appear. Because of the point raised by Miller and Mackie about differences between trends in government and opposition popularity, government popularity rather than lead is used in dealing with all series in this section. The series on vote intention is taken from the monthly Gallup question, 'If there were a General Election tomorrow, which party would you support?', where government popularity is indicated by the proportion indicating support for the governing party of the day. The

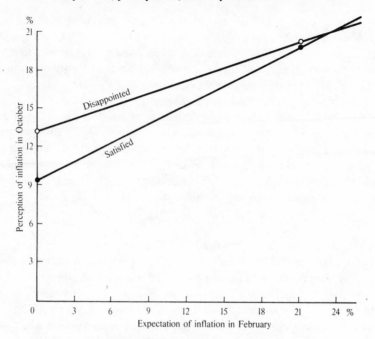

Figure 6.4. Expectations, perceptions and disappointment
Note: The equation generating the two lines is $P_t = 9.4 + 3.8D + 0.51E_{t-1} - 0.17(D^*E_{t-1})$, where D is a 'dummy' variable taking the value 1 if the individual is disappointed with Labour, and zero otherwise.
'Disappointed' implies that the respondent's evaluation of Labour's ability to handle prices was lower in October than in February.

record ought to depend at least in part on approval of the government's econ-omic record: the interesting empirical question is how closely the two are related. Similarly, the government's economic record ought to depend on actual economic developments, but only insofar as it can be shown that those move-ments are actually perceived. In other words, economic developments occur, per-haps through manipulation of a managed economy; if these developments are noticed, they may affect popular approval of the government's economic record, which in turn may affect general assessment of the government's record, which in turn may affect government popularity. Unfortunately, for no government are there simultaneous time-series data for the entire model, but parts of it can be tested on two separate occasions.

approval of the government's record is taken from the proportion indicating approval when asked 'Do you approve or disapprove of the government's record to date?'. The econ-omic record 1959–64 is taken from the monthly score obtained by the Conservatives in replies to the question of approval of the parties' handling of the issue of economic affairs. All series are taken from the *Gallup Political Index*, various issues.

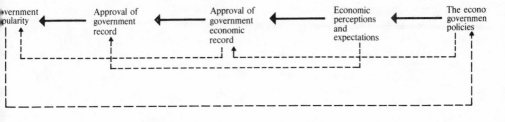

Expected significant effect
- - - - Expect <u>no</u> independent significant effect
- - - Possible effect

Figure 6.5. A model of economic effects on government popularity

One partial model, containing popularity, economic record, and economic variables, is discussed by Butler and Stokes. Some of the figures they present are inaccurate (see above, Chapter 1) though these do not appear to invalidate their argument. Their argument is that government lead in the opinion polls was closely related to the unemployment rate, and also that lead with respect to voting intention was closely related to government lead in popular approval of handling of the economy. There is unfortunately no data available to test for the intervening link of economic perceptions, but the Butler—Stokes argument can be restated in terms of the model of Figure 6.5 in three propositions: that government popularity should be closely linked to approval of the government's economic record, that the government's economic record ought to be related to movements of economic indicators, and especially, finally (from the present model, not theirs), that these economic indicators ought to have *no* effects on popularity *independent* of the effect of economic record.

This last point relates to all the steps in the model. In general, the model is strictly recursive, and furthermore, every effect in the model is expected to be a one-stage effect. Thus, what the model expects is that all effects of the economy must be channelled through the perception/expectation series before they can have an effect on the government's economic record. In other words, economic variables should have a consistent impact on economic perceptions, but *no* impact on popularity, general government record, or economic record, *independent* of economic perceptions. Similarly, economic perceptions should have *no* impact on popularity once the intervention of government economic record is taken account of. Where a term has to be omitted because of lack of data, one expects a poorer fit across the two stages compressed into one. (Note that where steps have to be omitted, significant effects are still expected across what should be two steps; there should be no significant two-step effects where the intervening variable is present.)

The three propositions from the restated Butler and Stokes hypothesis relating to 1959—64 are tested in the equations 1—3 of Table 6.3. In each case the

Table 6.3. *Government popularity, economic record, and economic trends*

Equation	Dependent variable	Constant	Economic record	Inflation rate	Unemployment rate	R^2
1	Popularity =	5.4 (1.6)	+0.56 (8.3)			0.80 (0.79)
2	Economic record =	73.9 (22.3)		−2.3 (4.5)	−9.2 (6.0)	0.78 (0.76)
3	Popularity =	−0.6 (0.1)	+0.64 (4.2)	+0.33 (0.7)	+0.68 (0.4)	0.81 (0.77)

Observations are the 19 quarters from 1960.1 − 1964.3

Equation	Dependent variable	Constant (adjusted)	Government record	Economic perceptions	Economic expectations	Other economic variables	R^2
4	Government record =	45.7 − 2.0B (11.0) (1.4)		+0.13 (2.1)	+0.02 (0.4)	insignificant	0.35 (0.30)
5	Popularity =	14.6 − 2.98B (3.0) (3.6)	+0.60 (6.2)	+0.04 (1.1)	−0.08 (2.5)	insignificant	0.68 (0.64)

Observations are the 37 months with available data, October 1970−December 1973. OLS estimation. Bracketed numbers beneath coefficients are t-statistics. R^2 values in brackets are corrected for degrees of freedom. Data on popularity and record from *Gallup Political Index*, various. Data on expectations and perceptions are from BMRB Financial Expectations Surveys. Constants in equations (4) and (5) are adjusted by a shift parameter B affecting the period after the Budget of March 1972.

result is quite satisfactory. Government popularity is a close function of economic record: the explanation of 80 per cent of the variance in the one series by the other, in view of the omnipresence of sampling error in survey results, is an excellent fit. An equally good fit is obtained when economic record is regressed on unemployment and inflation (annual rate). This confirms the model, but does little for the Butler—Stokes argument that unemployment was the variable that counted: the standardised impact of unemployment on economic record is only one-and-one-third the size of the impact of inflation, and the fit would fall from 0.78 to 0.5 if inflation were omitted. This probably shows the futility of searching for the one economic indicator which 'made all the difference'. As the previous chapter showed, there are likely at any time to be a number of trends which are salient to the electorate, and all of these should be taken into account. The third equation shows that economic trends have no impact on popularity independent of their impact on economic record (the fit is not improved, and the economic variables not only are insignificant but even take the wrong sign). In this way the importance of considering the perceptual basis of economic influence on political popularity is reinforced.

In the second case, 1970—4, there is no independent measurement of approval of the government's economic record, but a very good measure of economic perceptions from the Financial Expectations data discussed in the last chapter. The first step in the chain of effects was established in Table 5.4, which showed clearly that (with an R-squared of 0.7 to 0.8) economic trends systematically determined the movements of the perceptions and expectations series. There is no theory to guide expectations of the link between perceived economic trends and government record (missing out economic record, for which there is no data), but a common-sense approach would be to argue that approval of the government's (economic) record ought to rest largely on *perceptions* of past economic trends rather than expectations of economic trends, especially as the Gallup question seeks evaluation of the government's 'record to date'.

This argument is generally supported by the data. Equation 4 in Table 6.3 suggests strongly that government record is in large part a function of *perceptions* of the well-being of the country rather than expectations. In either case, there is a generally positive association: the higher the level of perceived (or to a lesser extent, expected) well-being, the greater is the level of approval of the government's record. This in turn suggests that in assessing the government's record − as distinct from vote intention − people are essentially backward-looking. Repeated experimentation with the economic predictor variables used in the previous chapter does not provide any evidence that the economy itself has any effect on government record independent of the perceptual link specified in Figure 6.5: no economic variable or variables have been found which, when added to the fourth equation in Table 6.3, significantly contribute to the fit.

In order to have comparable trends, Table 6.3 includes perceptions and expectations of *national* rather than personal trends to predict approval of the government's record. This is consistent with the finding of the last chapter that, insofar as economic outlook had a partisan component, it was the national rather than personal aspect of economic outlook which reflected partisanship, though this might only be a feature of the early 1970s (see Chapter 13). It should also be noted that if the fit of 0.35 for the equation between government record and economic perceptions and expectations seems low, there is of course a missing term between them. If there were a series available for *economic* record, it should fit well − though not perfectly − with the series on either side of it in the model. The two-stage fit of 0.35 should stand for two one-stage fits of 0.6 each. There is no reason to expect the government's general record to be a perfect function of its economic record, but only to be considerably affected by it.

As equation 5 shows, government popularity is heavily affected by evaluation of its record, independent of which (as expected) neither economic perceptions nor any economic trends of the sort employed in Table 5.4 have any consistent significant effects. Expectations, indeed, have a *negative* effect. Independent of how well people perceive things to be going, which directly affects their approval of the government's record, positive expectations (as in earlier sections) decrease government popularity. This could again imply that people do not expect good times to continue. It should be pointed out that the improvement in fit attributable to the expectations term is small, and that this finding runs against the model of Figure 6.5. The relationship may also arise because equation 5 is adjusted for the impact of the 1972 Budget. The negative impact of the Budget is easy to explain: the budget pushed (through the medium of a positive effect on economic perceptions) approval of the government's record up by more than popularity, so that, for the rest of the government, its popularity ran slightly *behind* approval of its record. In fact, reference back to Figure 6.2 shows that budgets have very short-term effects on popularity: four months looks about right for the duration of each of the reflationary budgets of July 1971, March 1972, and March 1973. In each case, popularity can be seen to move up for about four months, and then resume what is an overall steady decline throughout the entire period of the government. A major reflationary budget can have a great impact on perceptions of well-being; it presumably has a considerable impact on approval of the government's economic record, though the impact on approval of the government's overall record is more modest, and the impact on government popularity – furthest down the chain in Figure 6.5 – is smaller still, though there can be no doubt that it has some effect. The possibility of short-term stimulation of popularity through reflationary budgets opens up a new set of questions about the relationship between economic trends and political cycles.

A reinterpretation of the electoral cycle

Some years ago, King (1968) put forward a hypothesis accounting for governments' mid-term by-election losses in terms of short-term factors involving party identification. At the heart of his model is the suggestion that general elections are 'high stimulus' events which move people to increase their support for parties. By-elections are commonly 'low-stimulus' events, affecting people less, such that their voting is more in accord with levels and directions expected in 'normal' times. Briefly, it is the weaker identifiers who are more likely, having turned out and produced the pro-government swing at the last general election, to stay home and produce the government's mid-term losses. Whether King's account of behaviour is correct is not the present concern. What is of interest is the general model, which puts forward elections as special high-stimulus events disturbing trends in partisanship at normal times. By extension, government popularity in the opinion polls should be seen as artificially raised by general elections, in between which it gradually returns to 'normal' levels, only to be disturbed again by the next election. Thus, it is less important to explain the decline in mid-term popularity than to explain the repeated surges at election time.

The general convergence of estimates of a popularity function for Britain makes it possible to decompose the question of economic effects on government popularity into two separate problems: a long-term problem and a short-term problem. There is an upswing in popularity before every election, compensated by a downswing afterwards, which is a *short-term* phenomenon. Between every pair of elections there is also a downward time trend: this is part of a *long-term* trend. In other words, since the Second World War there has been a consistent slippage of support for governments: the time trend observed in each government's popularity is a reflection of this long-term trend.

Doubtless, the trend within governments is also partly a short-term phenomenon: Mueller (1970) argues that it reflects the slow breakup of the coalition in the electorate formed to elect a particular government, which gradually, as it stays in office, offends more and more of its supporters. If one treats the whipping-up of support at election time as a short-term disturbance of a long-term steady support level, then it could just be that that support declines slowly: whipped up quickly at election time, it does not return to a steady-state level until well after the year allowed by Goodhart and Bhansali for euphoria to wear off. Nevertheless, this account of the wearing off of support over time does not explain the fact that through the period, levels of support continuously moved lower and lower (at least until 1974), except where disturbed by elections. This is what is captured by the time-dependent cyclical model of Miller and Mackie, with its increasingly deep troughs over the years. To see why popularity should within successive governments drop lower and lower (though coming back up at election time) it is necessary to view popularity as declining in the long term; if popularity is declining in the long term, it is probable that the intra-government downward time trends in popularity stem from this long-term trend.

Clearly, elections and other events may move popularity around this long-term downward trend, though the trend, independent of these other effects, is always there, pulling popularity down. What can be said about this long-term trend? It is certainly something which affects both the major parties, which alternated in government over the period. This long-term trend is the same as the general decline in partisanship over this period in Britain, which has been extensively discussed elsewhere (Crewe, Särlvik and Alt, 1977). Turnout declined steadily from 1950 to 1970, rose a little in February and fell again in October 1974; similarly, the share of the electorate gained by the two major parties fell almost monotonically from 1951 to October 1974. These visible trends reflect the measured trends in level and strength of party identification – a measure of psychological attachment to the parties – over the last decade. While the proportion of the electorate having a party identification has not declined too sharply, the proportion having a 'very strong' identification with Labour or the Conservatives dropped from 40 per cent to 24 per cent of the electorate between 1964 and 1974. This is the same long-term trend which produces the time-dependent cycles of the Miller–Mackie model.

Trends in government popularity are a function of trends in strength of attachment to the two major parties. That is, the strength of people's psychological ties to *both* major parties has declined over the last quarter of a century. Because of this, during each successive government, support at mid-term has fallen lower, as the government's support is reduced to its strongest adherents, though support continues to be available at election time (though decreasingly). To substantiate this claim, it ought to be the case that strength of party identification displays the same 'cyclical trends' that show up in series of government popularity. There is virtually no data with which to substantiate this point, but consider Figure 6.6.

Figure 6.6 replicates part of a figure from Crewe, Särlvik and Alt (1977) with three observations added. The proportion of the electorate which identifies with one of the major parties declines between 1964 and 1974 by about five percentage points, from 81 to 76 per cent; much larger falls are recorded in the proportions having 'very' or 'fairly' strong attachments to one of the major parties. The three off-year observations — 1963, 1969 and 1975 — all fall within one year of a general election but are the only cross-sectional evidence available and thus will have to estimate strength of partisanship in 'normal' times. The proportions actually identifying with one of the major parties are relatively unchanged. Strength of partisanship, on the other hand, is greatly affected: from 29 per cent with a 'very strong' identification in 1963, the proportion rises steeply to 40 per cent of the electorate in 1964 and 1966 (election years) reporting 'very strong' identification with Labour or the Conservatives. Only 25 per cent of the electorate had a 'very strong' identification with Labour or the Conservatives in 1969, anticipating the 1974 election year level by five years. On the other hand, from 25 per cent in 1969, the proportion had sprung back to 39 per cent at the time of the 1970 election, a figure hardly changed from six years before. Again, in keeping with sharp short-term inter-election declines, the 1975 figure shows that only 17 per cent of the electorate still had a 'very strong' identification with one or another of the major parties. The same short-term disturbances are observable in the combined levels of 'very' and 'fairly' strong identifiers, although the changes are slightly more modest.

This has a number of separate implications. One is that while direction of party identification may well be a long-term component of individual political—psychological makeup, it is probable that *strength* as opposed to direction of party identification has a short-term 'cyclical' component, rising sharply at election times and falling away again after. This in turn might imply that elections are a poor time to measure strength of party identification: while direction may be unaffected, it is likely that the behaviour of very strong identifiers may be misinterpreted by the inclusion in their ranks of a number of normally weaker identifiers whose reported strength of attachment at election time exaggerates their normal level of partisanship. Indeed, the cyclical variation 1966—9 is as large as the long-term variation 1964—74. The real import of the 'cyclical' component of party identification however is that it establishes something of an identity — or at least a functional relationship — between the general level of strength of identification for the two major parties and the drift of the popularity of the government, regardless of which party is in power. The fact that strength of party identification varies with popularity in the short run suggests that it might do in the long run. The source of the time-dependency of cycles and the general downward drift of popularity between elections is the same as the downward secular trend in strength of partisanship in Britain in recent years.

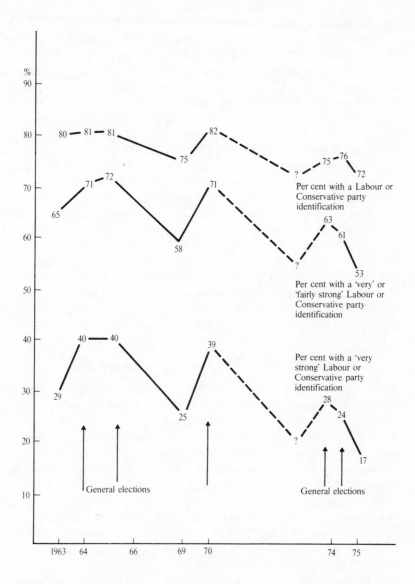

Figure 6.6. Trends and cycles in strength of partisanship 1963—75
Note: Entries are derived from the cross-section samples of 1963, 1964, 1966, 1969, and 1970 (Butler and Stokes) and February 1974, October 1974 and June 1975 (British Election Study). All samples were weighted where appropriate. Broken lines indicate hypothetical trends to missing ('?') observations.

(The discussion of Figure 6.2 also suggests that the trend may have ceased, if only for a time.)

Some of the main causes of this decline, or partisan dealignment, have been discussed elsewhere (Crewe, Särlvik and Alt, 1977; Alt, Crewe and Särlvik, 1977). It has been claimed that a balance of short-term factors, including disenchantment with economic management, among Conservatives, and the accumulation of a set of disagreements with party positions, particularly with regard to the role of unions, among Labour identifiers, lies at the heart of this partisan decline (but see Chapters 13 and 14). The trend may also have been affected by weakening of the traditional tie between class and party in Britain, though the relationship is complicated. It is certainly the case, be it cause or consequence, that electors continue to see less difference between the parties than formerly. There has also been an erosion of the perceived connection between personal economic well-being and party choice in Britain. Whatever the exact causes of the decline — and absence of evidence probably puts much certainty in this matter beyond reach — the decline in partisanship across the quarter of a century since 1950 lies at the heart of the persistent decline in government popularity reflected in increasingly exaggerated cycles between elections. As normal partisanship — and therefore mid-term popularity — has declined, however, the major parties have continued to be able to rally support at election time: this produces the apparent volatility of the electorate.

An interpretation of short-term surges in popularity

In the short term, how does the government manage to recruit the extra support observed in popularity before elections, and the increase in strength of party identification measured just after elections? Since the present subject is not techniques of campaigning, this will not be taken up in detail, but it is probably the case that appeals to traditional loyalties, threats of the doom attendant upon the election of the opposing party, and so on, have something to do with it. These things tend to occur during the campaign only, however, and sometimes, as in 1970, there is evidence of a considerable backswing in popularity before the election campaign actually begins. More relevant therefore is the question of whether there is anything 'economic' going on in the months before elections which might account for the short-term backswing cycle — the government's ability to rally support again before the next election.

In the case of the United States, Tufte (1978) has pointed out a connection between things like timing of Social Security payments and increases and the dates of elections. Moreover, he finds a general tendency for disposable income to increase before elections. Other authors have taken up the subject of the possibility of the government running the economy to its own short-term benefit, but this is the subject of the next chapter. It is important to note that most of these theoretical 'political business cycles' entail the existence of a short-term boom of some sort immediately before an election: how pronounced the boom is depends on a number of separate assumptions. Is there any sign that such a thing has taken place in Britain?

Miller and Mackie find an 'election-cycle' component in fluctuations in the unemployment rate, and indeed unemployment does decline in the latter half of a number of governments in the period under consideration. There is no real evidence of any government attempting to hold down the rate of inflation in the short-term to promote its own popularity at election time, except perhaps March–September 1974. When one considers the third variable usually included as a determinant of political popularity, personal disposable income, a slightly different picture emerges. To avoid arguments about money illusion and fiscal drag (the increase in tax revenue consequent on wage increases given a fixed tax threshold), only election-time trends in *real personal disposable* income will be considered: that is, personal income net of taxes and social security contributions, in terms of constant rather than current prices. Real personal disposable income increases throughout the whole of the period 1959–75, in line with general economic growth. The present interest is in short-term movements, and particularly in whether these tie up with the short-term movements in popularity around election times.

Consider the equation reported by Goodhart and Bhansali (1970), and summarised in Figure 6.1. The equation fits government lead to some economic variables, plus a downward time trend, plus two variables called euphoria and backswing. (Recall that euphoria describes the decline in popularity after an election and backswing its resurgence before the next election.) The argument of a decline in partisanship producing greater apparent 'volatility' in the long run implies that the coefficients of each of these variables should grow through this period. That is, the election-time decline in share of the electorate gained by the major parties – like the proportion identifying with one or the other – is smaller than the overall decline in partisanship, especially as reflected in the inter-election measures of strength of partisanship in Figure 6.6. This implies that more ground has had to be made up to restore 'normal' partisanship levels at successive elections over the last two decades. The fact that more ground has had to be made up implies that the coefficients measuring this election-time surge and decline should grow larger across the years. This can be tested directly by fitting the Goodhart–Bhansali model, not across the whole period, but within each individual government, and looking at the behaviour of the euphoria and backswing coefficients, with the expectation that they should grow in the equations relating to more recent governments.

With limited exceptions, as Table 6.4 shows, this is borne out. The coefficients attaching to 'euphoria', the post-election downswing, grow steadily, though there is (relative to trend, inflation, and unemployment) no downswing after the 1959 election. Similarly, there is no evidence of a pro-government swing over the six months before the elections of 1955 and February 1974, independent of other factors. Thus, if what is sought is an economic account of euphoria and backswing, it lies in a variable which is getting 'better' in the six months before each

Table 6.4. *Pre- and post-election trends in popularity*

	Variable	
Government	'Euphoria' (post-election)	'Backswing' (pre-election)
1951–5	0.40	0.05*
1955–9	0.56	1.4
1959–64	0.10*	2.1
1966–70	0.89	2.7
1970–4	1.0	0.10*

Note: * indicates the coefficient is *not* statistically significant at (minimally) the 0.05 level. The coefficients are derived from OLS regressions of popularity on, jointly, a time trend, 'euphoria' (which takes the value 12 in the month after an election, decreasing by one each month over the first year of a government and zero thereafter) and 'backswing' (which takes the value one six months before a general election and increases by one each month until the election). The 1964–6 government is omitted as it was too short to incorporate these variables in a regression. Popularity data from Gallup.

election and 'worse' in the year following, save that there should be no deterioration after 1959 (since 'euphoria' that year is not statistically significant), and no improvement before 1955 or February 1974 (no 'backswing').

Reasonably reliable data on real personal disposable income are available on a quarterly basis only since 1959 (thus the exclusion of 1955 from what follows); it has been converted into a per capita figure to allow for the effects of a slowly-growing population, and detrended to remove the effects of long-term growth. The series has then been recast as a difference between the current observation and the average of the previous two. In other words, each observation now reflects the level of per capita, real (constant prices) disposable (net of tax and social security) personal income relative to its average over the previous half year, approximating the sort of model discussed on page 122 above: positive when income has recently become higher and negative when it has fallen. Figure 6.7 plots trends in this variable around elections: enough observations are given to compare its behaviour with the 'cyclical' backswing and euphoria variables.

In terms of pre-election behaviour, 1974 certainly stands out from other years as the only case where immediately before an election real income was allowed to drop sharply over the previous half year; it goes without saying that the February 1974 election was also called suddenly at a time when most expected the government to continue in office without an election for another year. The general upward movement of per capita real personal disposable income is particularly marked in the months before the elections of 1966, 1970, and October 1974, and is evident also in the earlier years. Similarly, the decline in real personal disposable income after each of the elections (except 1959, when the boom continued for another year) is also clear. Using the (most reliable) income figures from 1963–71 and interpolating monthly movements, one can

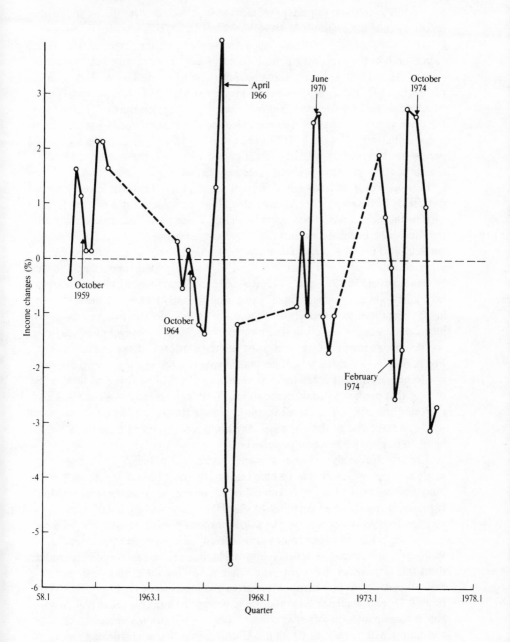

Figure 6.7. Quarterly movements in real per capita personal disposable income (detrended) around elections 1958–75
Each point reflects the difference between (annualised) growth rate of income in that quarter and the average over the two previous quarters.

restate this as follows. Consider the backswing period to cover the six months before each of the elections of 1964, 1966 and 1970 (eighteen months in all). Consider the change in personal disposable income over the three months before each month in the backswing period: that is, measure the change between January and April 1970, February and May, March and June and so on. The average per cent quarterly change for these 18 months is +1.78 per cent, a growth rate which annualises to over seven per cent. Using the same measure of change for the three sets of 12 months after each election (36 months in all) one finds an average quarterly change of −0.11 per cent in the immediate post-election period. In the remaining months of the period 1963−72, the average quarterly change is +0.79 per cent or about three per cent per annum.

In other words, before each of these elections, for a short period real personal disposable income was rising at more than double its normal rate of growth; after each of these elections, it was actually falling. These trends coincide exactly with the short-term cyclical movements observed in government popularity, and suggest that real personal disposable income movements may be a source of the repeated ability of governments (before 1974) to rally their supporters. The clearest examples are in 1966 and 1970, when the cyclical character of government popularity was at its height. Equally important, in 1974 when for the first time in 20 years there was an election without the observable backswing to the government, there was also no cyclical movement in short-term changes of per capita real disposable income. One must resist the temptation to make too much of Figure 6.7, however. Growth of personal disposable income was shown above not to be a significant predictor of government popularity. This is an illustration of how that prediction could come about, for it is short-term movements of real disposable income which match trends in popularity around election times, when the higher stimulus of the campaign may bring considerations of personal well-being to bear on government popularity.

The principal analyses of government opinion poll popularity converge to a single account, which contains a long-term and a short-term component. The long-term component is the downward trend in strength of party identification. It produces the apparent volatility of the electorate reflected in deeper inter-election troughs in popularity. The short-term component consists of a rallying of support before elections and an accentuated fall in support after elections; short-term movements in personal disposable income are a factor in these sudden short-term recoveries. More generally, when modelling the economic determinants of government popularity, more attention needs to be paid to questions of timing. There is evidence that inflation expectations and changes in real disposable income may have different effects according to both the economic climate and timing with respect to elections. All this means that sophisticated models will be required to capture economic effects on popularity, but they appear to be worth seeking and testing.

7

Political business cycles in Britain

The idea that the government might manipulate the economy for its own political ends is neither new, original, nor even particularly exciting. The example discussed in the last chapter of short-term movements in disposable income is still the most frequently argued version of manipulation (see Frey, 1978), having some journalistic currency ever since the post-election deflation of 1955 through the wage 'explosions' of 1970 and 1974. Apparently, as of this writing, expectations of a similar sort are entertained for 1978–9. It would in fact be surprising if governments did not engage in this sort of manipulation, particularly when, in the very short term, it consists mainly of *not* doing potentially unpopular things like imposing harsh incomes policies or budgets. Short pre-election spurts may not do the government of the day all that much good, and there is no evidence that they do (at least if short-term enough) the economy any particular harm, and, moreover, increasing individual real disposable income has been by near consensus one of the main purposes of government in recent times.

The idea of a political business cycle is more subtle and general than the argument that governments stimulate the economy (or allow it to stimulate itself) just before elections. The question of a political business cycle deals with longer-term questions of economic management. Part of this idea is captured in Mosley (1976a), who presents the argument that the government is basically trying to keep things 'satisfactory'. By this is meant that a government faced with, for instance, a tradeoff between unemployment and inflation will simply do nothing unless one or another of these is in 'crisis' – that is, moving outside the limits implied by recent trends – and then will attempt to move the economy back to normal. For instance, if unemployment becomes too large to be politically 'safe', the government reflates to reduce it, and then waits for the next crisis. There is certainly evidence that government fiscal decisions have followed this sort of pattern.

On the other hand, this is not showing very much – only that governments do not allow things to become intolerable. In the first place, this sort of behaviour does not produce any political *cycle*. Only repeated *overcompensation* would alternatively produce inflation and unemployment crises: a government which could control the economy could equally well allow only inflationary crises to occur, and so on. More telling is that this model is only barely *political*: there is

certainly no effort made to tie fiscal decisions to the timing or winning of elections. (For detailed comments see Alt and Chrystal, 1978.)

A more important question posed by models of political cycles is about the
extent to which management of the economy is dictated by considerations of
vote-maximisation. The more general argument is that governments take long-
term decisions and indeed calculate their entire economic policy with a view to
winning elections. In other words, what is at issue is not just the question of
small six-month spurts or short-term crises, but rather the entire long-term movement of the economy, controlled in such a way that the conditions taken to be
most favourable to the incumbent government are produced just in time for the
next election. This again would be of no great interest if nothing were lost by it.
It would be a way of making economic progress which happened to benefit the
incumbent government along with everyone else. However, the implication of
the theoretical 'political business cycle' literature is not just that governments
take decisions in accordance with their views of voters' preferences, but that this
results in extra, unnecessary cycles in economic development — or extra inflation
(Burton, 1978) — which furthermore move the economy *away* from long-term
optimal levels of development. Since this is equal to the assertion that the government consistently puts its own welfare ahead of the country's, it is certainly
worth examining the evidence.[1]

The idea of a political business cycle

There are a number of alternative sources for the theoretical basis of political
business cycles, though there are certainly points of contact between them (Nordhaus, 1975; Fair, 1975; Macrae, 1977; Lindbeck, 1976). There are always two
parts to the model of a political business cycle: a 'welfare' function which the
'government' attempts to maximise, which is a weighted sum of terms reflecting
economic conditions valued by the electorate, and an economic model or 'constraint' giving rules governing the relationships among these conditions, such that
not all combinations are possible. In the sense that the government attempts to
maximise the welfare function subject to the economic constraint, these ideas
are analogous to seeing economic management as a dynamic optimal control
problem (Chow, 1975), but in the political business cycle literature the weights
in the welfare function are (seen to be) imposed by the electorate and the purpose of the government in maximising welfare is clearly to maximise the probability of its own re-election.

---

[1] If one is prepared to believe in 'objectively' optimal economic policies, then the existence
of a 'political' business cycle rests on the government's economic policies containing
elements which are not objectively optimal, but rather are designed to benefit the government. This is equivalent to saying that to demonstrate a political business cycle, the analyst
must at least show that the government has done something other than what 'any econ-
omist' would have recommended — always assuming that such a degree of consensus existed
among various economists. Madsen (1978) develops other typologies of political business
cycles.

Macrae's formulation contains the most tractable algebra, and is therefore more straightforward to replicate in the British context. His economic constraint asserts that inflation is produced by an expectations-augmented Phillips-curve relationship:

$$I_t = aI_{t-1} - bU_t + c \tag{1}$$

where a, b, and c are all greater than zero, I_t represents inflation in year t and U_t unemployment in year t. This is a highly simplified model, implying as it does that (price) inflation in any year is a function of inflation the previous year (expected to continue) less something for each extra unit of unemployment (decreased demand). The welfare function asserts that the vote loss suffered by the government at any time will be a weighted sum of the (squared) levels of inflation and unemployment:

$$V_t = \tfrac{1}{2}qI_t^2 + \tfrac{1}{2}rU_t^2 \tag{2}$$

and that the vote loss V at the next election is the sum of the individual (periodic) vote losses suffered since the last election. If one is prepared to assume that the government wishes to maximise its plurality at the next election (or minimise its vote loss, or, as Nordhaus argues, equivalently, maximise its chance of winning the next election) and that voters consider *only* the *past* and *present* and *not* the *future* in taking voting decisions ('myopic' electorate), it follows that the government will embark on a business cycle tied to the date of the next election in running the economy.

In part, the cycle arises out of the 'Phillips-curve' relationship. The government obviously – from (2) – wants to keep unemployment and inflation down. If unemployment is reduced, more inflation results (from (1)). However, if unemployment is raised initially, lower inflation results, allowing unemployment to be reduced. This produces more inflation, but with correct timing this comes after the election and is therefore not a problem (partly because the government wants most to win the *next* election and partly because the (myopic) electorate are assumed *not* to see that this inflation *will* result from the reduction in unemployment before the election). This gives a clear cycle between elections, with unemployment pushed up (as a sort of 'investment') immediately after the election and then allowed to decline as the next election approaches. There are random shocks affecting inflation so that the government has to adjust its target annually, but it does so on the basis of the same goal – plurality-maximisation – each time. The shape – but *not* the existence – of the cycle is affected by the degree of importance attached to recent developments, and becomes more violent if the electorate are also assumed to forget all but the most recent economic events, but this extra assumption is unnecessary.

Most important of all, however, is that the values actually taken by unemployment depend not only on the parameters a, b, and c of (1) but also on the parameters q and r of (2). In other words, the choice the government makes in seeking values of unemployment and inflation which minimise vote loss depends partly on the Phillips curve the government believes exists – which determines the future rate of inflation contingent on its present choice of unemployment. It also depends on the relative weights the government believes the electorate place on unemployment and inflation: how many votes the government believes it loses for each extra per cent of unemployment or inflation. This relative weighting, or q/r ratio, can vary from country to country, and within a country from party to party and from government to government.

The question of a cycle also arises because elections occur at regular intervals. Thus, in order to keep the ultimate combination of I and U as low as possible, the government has an incentive to push unemployment up early in its term, in order to keep inflation down, and then to reduce unemployment as the election approaches, in order to optimise the combination of I and U at election time. The existence of the cycle rests on periodic elections, the assumption that the electorate are more concerned (or at least not less concerned) with the recent past than with the more distant past, and on what assumptions the government makes about some characteristics of the electorate or about its own purposes.

It is clear that if people forgot the past after a year or two – or the government believed that they did – unemployment could be pushed up very high in the early years of a government, as only the (low) values of inflation and unemployment at election time would count. More significant is what the government believes about the future. There are three possibilities. First, the government could assume the electorate to be *myopic*, that is, incapable of seeing very far ahead, and therefore attaching no inflationary expectations to low levels of unemployment at election time. This is equivalent to believing that the future is entirely discounted by the electorate: a government believing this could be assumed to be minimising its vote loss with a one-term time horizon, or, equivalently, maximising its probability of winning the *next* election.

As an alternative, the government could believe in a *strategic* electorate, capable of seeing tomorrow's inflation in today's low unemployment. Belief in a strategic electorate would moderate the 'political' aspects of the cycle, for there would be less benefit in driving unemployment down just at one particular (election) time. In other words, the strategic electorate hypothesis is equivalent to the case of a government which wants to maximise the probability of winning an election at any time – in short, a government with an indefinite time horizon. Of course, the government also has the alternative of doing nothing at all, a *naive* hypothesis in which unemployment will continue to take its own past values autoregressively, disturbed only by exogenous shocks.

There are therefore a number of parameters to estimate. The three parameters of the economic model, a, b, and c of (1), must all be estimated over a reasonably long term. Given the parameters a, b, and c, there are values of q and r from (2) which optimise the fit of observed data on unemployment and inflation to each of the myopic and strategic hypotheses. The best fit of all can be used as a test of adequacy of each of these hypotheses for a particular government. Having determined the optimal hypotheses, one can look at shifts in the values of q and r over time. Third, one can seek confirming evidence from government popularity data and economic conditions to support (by triangulation) any conclusions about shifts in the perceived relative costs of unemployment and inflation which emerge from the first exercises. Macrae concludes that in the United States the government appeared to assume myopia from 1960–8, but a strategic electorate before and after; moreover, the apparent perceived penalty for inflation was higher in 1960–4 and was lower both before and after, falling in 1968–72 to a point where the penalties for inflation and unemployment were nearly equal. The following sections repeat the estimation for Britain,[2] estimating the parameters of the economic constraint, the optimum q and r weights, and the vote loss function, as well as providing a discussion of the results.

The economic constraint

The estimation is actually done in the following manner. The first need is for estimates of the Phillips-curve parameters a, b, and c. These can be obtained by regressing the annual price inflation rate on itself lagged one period plus the current unemployment rate. Other research (Hibbs, 1977) indicates that the unemployment rate should be allowed to float upwards after the fourth quarter of 1966, so the constant term is altered by a binary variable D_{66} taking the value 1 after this quarter and zero otherwise. When this is done, the result is this equation, over quarterly data from 1947.3 to 1974.1:

$$I_t = 0.91 I_{t-1} - 0.56 U_t + 1.1 D_{66} + 1.3$$

reflecting the coefficients shown in the first row of Table 7.1.[3] While this approach to estimating the coefficients of an expectation-augmented Phillips curve may seem overly simple, the coefficients have the virtue of plausibility, are not terribly different from other published estimates (Parkin, 1974) and replicate Macrae's approach, which is the present concern. Certainly the signs are exactly as expected and the coefficients are all highly significant.

The estimates $a = 0.91$, $b = 0.56$, and $c = 1.3$ (2.4 from 1966 onwards) can be employed in evaluating Macrae's model. However, the Phillips curve was thought to be shifting in this period, and it might therefore be preferable to estimate the tradeoff faced by each government separately. Table 7.1 also gives the estimates of a, b and c derived from quarterly data, where the tradeoff faced by each government is taken to be that holding over the period of its incumbency plus that of the previous government. This is an arbitrary choice, but has the virtue of keeping moderately long periods for estimation while allowing ample

---

[2] In these estimates, it is always assumed that – in making its calculations – each incoming government expects a four-year term of office (in many countries, of course, the incumbents *know* the date of the next election) with the fifth possible year held as a sort of contingency reserve in case of unforeseen problems.

[3] Note that the coefficient of D_{66} is *positive*. This is correct since the reforms and consequent upward float of unemployment imply that a given level of unemployment would produce *more* inflation than previously, so a positive value is expected. See Hibbs (1977).

Table 7.1. *Possible tradeoff values*

| Period | Coefficient of | | |
	I_{t-1} a	U_t b	Constant c
Whole	0.91 (20.0)	0.56 (2.2)	1.3 (2.4*) (2.9)
1947–55 (1951 Government)	0.88 (9.5)	1.48 (1.5)	3.02 (1.9)
1951–9 (1966 Government)	0.86 (13.4)	0.86 (2.1)	1.65 (2.4)
1955–64 (1959 Government)	0.78 (8.6)	0.69 (2.3)	1.87 (2.8)
1959–70 (1966 Government)	0.86 (11.9)	0.41 (1.5)	1.70** (2.1)
1966–74 (1970 Government)	1.00*** (12.7)	0.31 (1.0)	0.59 (0.8)

*The value 2.4 includes the coefficient (1.1) of the dummy variable reflecting the outward float of the Phillips curve after 1966.4.

**The value 1.70 similarly includes the coefficient of the post-1966 dummy variable, which in this case is used throughout the 1966–70 government estimated.

***Unconstrained OLS produced an estimate of 1.08 for this coefficient which is not significantly different from the theoretical maximum of 1.0.

Note: Bracketed values beneath the coefficients are *t*-statistics. Unconstrained OLS regression (which is in this case not strictly appropriate) was used to generate the estimates. Data source as in Figure 2.1.

scope for the relationship to change. As the estimates show, the coefficient a attaching to I_{t-1} does not move that much until the final period, but the coefficient of U_t drops sharply and continuously, implying that the benefit of one per cent of unemployment in reduced inflation was at the end a fifth (0.31/1.48) of what it had been at the beginning. This slippage approximates to the sort of information governments could have had at their disposal (there is no certainty to be had in these matters) and so the evaluation of the model will be carried out with these separate estimates as well. It should be remembered, however, that some argue that the Phillips curve 'disappears' between 1967 and 1971 (Laidler, 1976).

The political business cycle in Britain

The next job is to estimate q/r, the relative vote loss weights which the government believe the electorate attach to each of inflation and unemployment. The reason for this will become obvious in a moment. For any given a, b and c, and for each of the myopic and strategic hypotheses that Macrae offers, there is a value of q/r which will minimise the difference between hypothetical and observed unemployment rates. What is sought is the value of q/r which, under each hypothesis, brings hypothesised and observed unemployment rates closest together. However, there is the additional problem that if a, b and c have been wrongly estimated, the value of q/r which appears optimal may also be misleading. Estimates of how variable the estimates of q/r can be are given in Alt (1978). These were calculated using the same annual unemployment and inflation data for the 1959 government (effectively 1960–4), under the assumption of a variety of tradeoff equations.

Fortunately, the precision of the estimates reported in Table 7.1 is such as to suggest that in nearly all cases the error involved is unlikely to be serious. For instance, considering figures for the 1959 government in Table 7.1, if the 'true' Phillips-curve parameters were $a = 0.7$ (not 0.78) and $b = 0.5$ (not 0.69) and $c = 2.0$ (not 1.87), which event jointly is highly improbable but not impossible, the solution of q/r would be 0.43 and not the (as it happens) 0.25 reported in Table 7.2 below. So the vote loss weight of inflation relative to unemployment would be 0.43 instead of 0.25: this in turn suggests that the estimates of q/r given below are really fairly reliable (in that 0.43 and 0.25 are not too different, relative to *potential* variability of these ratios), at least as long as the coefficients of a, b, and c are highly significant. Nevertheless, the problem is one of which anyone replicating Macrae's model should be aware.

So given a, b, and c, values of q and r can be found such that the difference between observed and hypothetical unemployment under each of the myopic and strategic hypotheses is minimised. The difference is assessed by taking the sum of squares of the difference between observed and expected unemployment for each year. The expected rate is complicated to derive, requiring a little calculus and a lot of algebra, all of which Macrae gives in his article. The procedure basically involves taking a possible q/r ratio, going back to year one of a government, looking at values of I_{t-1} and calculating optimal values of unemployment according to whether one is trying to win the next election or optimise popularity in the long run, moving forward to the next year, repeating the process, and so on until the next election year. Then iteratively note the size of the error (sum of squares between observed and expected unemployment) and try another q/r ratio, until you get to a minimum sum of squared errors.

For each government there is a q/r ratio which minimises the error sum of squares under the *myopic* hypothesis ('win the next election') and another q/r ratio which minimises the error sum of squares under the *strategic* hypothesis ('infinite time scale'). There is in fact a third *naive* comparison which can be made: $U_t = U_{t-1}$, a hypothesis of 'no change' or really no change except random error. The error sum of squares from this hypothesis can be compared to the others to see if their predictive power is any greater than the assumption that unemployment each year is just what it was the year before. For each of the five major governments since 1951, the error-minimising q/r ratios and goodness-of-fit measures are given in table 7.2; the actual yearly unemployment rates, along with the predictions of the best-fitting myopic and strategic hypotheses, are given in Figure 7.1. These are the results.

Table 7.2. *Estimated relative vote costs of inflation and unemployment (q/r ratios) in Britain*

| Years of government | Optimal q/r ratio and fit (in brackets) under | |
	Myopic hypothesis	Strategic hypothesis
1951–5	0.06 (1.05)	0.02* (0.11)
1955–9	0.20 (5.22)	0.15 (1.94)
1960–4	0.50* (0.48)	0.25* (0.08)
1966–70	0.42 (7.59)	0.16 (1.14)
1971–4	0.54* (0.64)	0.05* (0.62)

*indicates good fit (explained in text). The q/r ratios are estimated using the individual government tradeoff estimates given in Table 7.1, but similar results (Alt, 1978) are obtained with the single whole-period economic constraint.

In the first place, the myopic hypothesis never outperforms the strategic hypothesis, and only twice (1960–4 and 1971–4) outperforms the naive null hypothesis of no change. In other words, there is little evidence that any British government ever managed the unemployment rate simply with a view only to winning the next election. On the two occasions where there does appear to be some truth in this hypothesis, an even better fit (or at least as good) is obtained under the assumption that the government was trying to minimise its vote loss, but with no particular time horizon in mind. There is considerable support for the strategic hypothesis, however: in two cases (1951–5 and 1960–4) the fit is excellent. In one other case (1971–4) the fit is substantially better than that of the naive hypothesis; in 1966–70 the test is indifferent between naive and strategic, and only in one case (1955–9) can both political business cycle hypotheses be readily rejected. In other words, while there is little evidence that governments manipulate the unemployment rate for their own *short-term* ends, there is considerable evidence that governments do behave in accordance with the hypothesis that they run the economy as if faced by some vote loss function which they attempt to minimise — that is, that governments manage unemployment as if trying to maximise social welfare, without any particular time scale in mind.

The actual q/r ratios are also interesting. Bear in mind that the q/r ratio represents the government's view of the penalty in votes (or unhappiness) caused by one per cent of inflation relative to the penalty for one per cent of unemployment. The higher the q/r ratio, the more important a government feels it to be to keep inflation down relative to unemployment; the lower the ratio, the more important the government feels it to be to keep unemployment down. If one

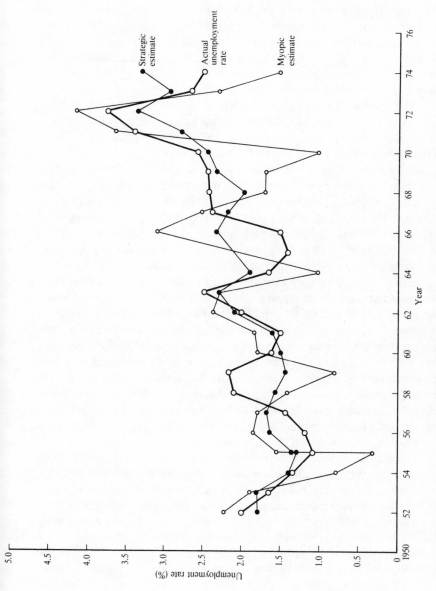

Figure 7.1. Actual course of unemployment and estimated path under each political business cycle hypothesis 1952–74

considers the data reported in Table 7.2, the best fit for 1951 is obtained if the government is seen as minimising vote loss on the assumption that inflation is very cheap relative to unemployment: the q/r ratio of 0.02 implies a penalty for inflation *one fiftieth* that for unemployment. This is exactly in accordance with the recorded perceptions of the electorate at the time: Milne and Mackenzie (1954) report great concern with unemployment and no attention at all to other economic matters. The government's perceived q/r ratio rises steadily through the 1950s: after 1959, under the strategic hypothesis, it reached 0.25, implying a perceived penalty for inflation *one quarter* that attaching to unemployment. In that sense, the model suggests the Conservative Government of 1951–64 behaved largely like a vote-maximising government (without any particular election date in mind) with regard to unemployment, but one whose behaviour was predicated on the assumption of increasing penalties attaching to inflation rather than unemployment.

The q/r ratios clearly drop for the Labour Government of 1966–70. This is to say that the Labour Government apparently predicated their behaviour on the assumption of relatively larger penalties for unemployment than had its immediate predecessor (though bear in mind that the poorer fit of the strategic hypothesis equally implies that they did not take people's preferences between unemployment and inflation into account in setting the unemployment rate). The fact that their behaviour was not based on popular preferences (or on the vote-maximising assumption of Macrae's model) could arise (as Nordhaus suggests) from their preoccupation with the balance of payments rather than the inflation–unemployment tradeoff: he suggests that this factor explains the other 'perverse' case, 1955–9. More important – since concern with other economic problems lies outside Macrae's model – is that the lower q/r ratio is consistent with the argument that left-wing governments concentrate on reducing unemployment rather than inflation, and that they do this because of the perception that their supporters (the working class) are more concerned with unemployment than inflation. There is some evidence to support this argument about left-wing government behaviour, even if the inter-class differences in attitudes toward unemployment are easily exaggerated, and it is an important point that the political business cycle model appears to reflect the same phenomenon.

The Heath Government will be considered in a moment. First, a point about the magnitude of the q/r ratios which are emerging. Macrae finds that in the United States the q/r ratio before 1964 was well in excess of unity, implying that inflation carried a heavier penalty than unemployment. Indeed in 1961–4 the apparent q/r ratio was between 3 and 4; even at the end of the period the q/r ratio had fallen no further than 0.8. This implies that the q/r ratios upon which the British government appears to act are far lower than those obtaining in the United States. Even the inflation-sensitive government of 1959–64 appears to have faced a q/r ratio in Britain of 0.25, so that inflation carried one quarter – rather than four times as in the US – the penalty of unemployment. This is consistent with the widely-held view that the British are far more sensitive to unemployment and the Americans more sensitive to inflation – indeed, this evidence supports that view – which is all the more interesting since it is not all that easy to show that such a large difference between the two countries exists (Hibbs, 1976, 1978). Nevertheless, the greater sensitivity of the British to unemployment is a well-accepted cliche – and Frey (1976) gives some evidence that suggests that in terms of opinion poll popularity the penalties for greater inflation are indeed higher in the United States than in Britain – and it is apparently a cliche upon which the governments of the two countries have acted.

It is also important to note why the myopic hypothesis has failed in the British case. Consider the first few years of Figure 7.1. While it is clear that actual unemployment does follow the expected cyclical path, the path is not nearly as exaggerated as the myopic hypothesis would imply. For example, a government following this hypothesis would have driven unemployment down to 0.3 per cent in 1955, to one per cent in 1964, and indeed to 1.4 per cent in 1974. Doubtless, some of the failure of the myopic hypothesis may derive from the impossibility of getting unemployment to respond with requisite speed – see the violent fluctuation required around 1959 – and perhaps the model should impose restrictions on the possible annual changes in unemployment.[4] More important, however, is that the model probably fails because no government in Britain has been prepared to assume that such a bribe would work, or that the electorate really would not look a day beyond the next election. Hence the better fit of the gentler oscillations implied by the strategic hypothesis: indeed, on a number of occasions government behaviour looks very much like vote-maximising – but without the extra assumption that the electorate will happily mortgage the future for the present. Indeed, all the evidence given in earlier chapters about the accuracy of popular forecasting, both of inflation and more general economic expectations, suggests that such an assumption would be foolish in the extreme.

Confirmation of relative weights

The estimates in the case of the Heath Government are a little more difficult to deal with, since the two hypotheses produce divergent results. Part of the difficulty lies in deciding which years to include in the government, since it begins just half way through 1970 and ends early in 1974. However, the results presented are typical.[5] One solution arrived at is that the Heath Government followed the myopic hypothesis on the assumption that the relative price of inflation had increased again to over 0.5: this provides a good fit. As Figure 7.1

---

[4] The results (by examination of alternative simulations) are not affected by the possibility of uncertainty about the date of the next election.

[5] If 1970 is included, the evidence goes strongly to the strategic hypothesis, as the fit of the myopic hypothesis rises to about 1.05. This however only reflects the unreality of expecting an incoming government to be able to set the unemployment rate instantly, and starting the Heath Government with 1971 is equivalent to starting the 1959–64 government (as above) with 1960.

shows, unemployment neither increased quite enough in 1971–2 nor declined enough in 1973–4 to substantiate this hypothesis. Alternatively, and with a slightly improved fit, the Heath Government behaved like a vote-maximiser with an infinite amount of time in office, and one which assumed inflation was very *cheap* ($q/r = 0.05$) relative to unemployment, given the Phillips curve they confronted (see Table 7.1). There is clearly a familiar ring to this: it is often said that the enormous reflationary measures of July 1971–April 1972 were taken in response to the increased pressure of rising unemployment (Livingstone, 1974).

This raises the question of whether it might be possible to show that, in assuming that inflation was cheap relative to unemployment, the Heath Government simply made a mistake. It is certainly the case that after the election of February 1974, prices were widely considered a very important problem, and there was widespread disaffection with the Conservative Government's handling of prices. This would be consistent with the argument that the penalty for inflation was higher in the 1970s than in earlier years. Direct confirmation of this can be sought by returning to opinion poll data and attempting to estimate the vote loss function described at the beginning of the chapter.

Recall that the government's assumed vote loss function is given by $V_t = \frac{1}{2}qI_t^2 + \frac{1}{2}rU_t^2$, where I_t is the 12-month price inflation rate, U_t the unemployment rate in per cent, and V_t is the vote loss at the time, which the government seek to minimise. V_t can be estimated by taking the difference in any period between government *popularity* in the opinion polls at that time, and their share of the poll at the time of the election. V_t can then be regressed in the usual way on I_t^2 and U_t^2: the results of this estimation are given in Table 7.3. For safety, the regressions were performed with and without allowing a constant term, and on both monthly and quarterly data: the results shown in Table 7.3 are very consistent across these choices.[6] The table gives the *ratios* of the estimates of q and r in the above equation: these can be thought of as independent empirical estimates of the q/r ratio actually *obtaining* in each of the periods discussed above, and can be compared with the government's perceived q/r ratios derived from the business cycle model, provided one is prepared to assume that all combinations of I and U lie on the welfare function, and that the q/r ratio is constant throughout each government.

The results suggest that there is a very close fit before 1970 in the q/r ratios actually obtaining in government popularity and those upon which the governments of the day appeared to base their vote-maximizing behaviour (insofar as

---

[6] For instance, if a government received a 43 per cent vote in the election, and its popularity in the polls (vote intention) stands at 30 per cent, this estimates a vote loss of 13 per cent. This vote loss is taken to increase with the squares of inflation and unemployment, where inflation is measured by 12-month change in the retail price index, and unemployment by the percentage unemployment rate published. Strictly speaking, there is no constant term in the equation, but the previous chapter's arguments about short-term stimulation of the vote at election times provides a rationale for including a constant term. The coefficient estimates are robust regardless of whether or not it is included.

Table 7.3. *Actual inflation—unemployment vote loss weights (polls)*

| | Regression and data | | | |
| | Constrained | | Unconstrained | |
Government	Monthly	Quarterly	Monthly	Quarterly
1951–5	−0.01*	−0.01*	−0.01*	−0.01*
1955–9	0.11	0.11	0.08	0.08
1959–64	0.20	0.20	0.20	0.20
1966–70	0.10	0.09	0.09	0.16
1970–4	0.44	0.73	0.53	0.56

*Wrong sign
Note: Coefficients are produced by OLS regression of popularity on I_t^2 and U_t^2. The table shows the ratio of the coefficient of I^2 to the coefficient of U^2. Both coefficients were always significant in the constrained regressions (constant term excluded) except for monthly data 1970–4; various coefficients or constraints of the unconstrained regressions were insignificant. The convergence of all four sets of estimates does help establish the trends revealed. Popularity data from *Gallup Political Index*.

their behaviour was vote-maximizing). In 1951, the estimate of q (from poll popularity regressed on inflation and unemployment squared) was negative and not significantly different from zero: in all other cases the signs are correct and almost all estimates are highly statistically significant. The 1951 estimate suggests that a vote-maximizing government should have assumed inflation was more or less free of penalty, and unemployment was all that counted in popularity: as Table 7.2 showed, this is exactly what the government of the day appeared to believe. By 1955, inflation should have appeared much more expensive, though still cheap compared to unemployment, and again this is what appeared to happen, though the fit of the business cycle model is poor. In 1959, a shrewd government would have taken account of a further rise in the price of inflation in the vote loss function (estimated at about 0.2 relative to r in the popularity estimates), and, again, this is exactly what Table 7.2 suggests the government of the day did. Now the vote loss attaching to inflation appears to have become relatively less in 1966–70, when Labour was in office, and again this is exactly – though the fit is indifferent – what their behaviour in office appeared to reflect. The trends in the estimated vote (or popularity) loss attaching to each of inflation and unemployment up to 1970 are very closely reflected in the trends in the perceived vote loss ratios deduced from fitting the political business cycle model, under the strategic hypothesis.

But not so between 1970 and 1974. Some of the estimates of the vote cost of unemployment reflected in Table 7.3 are not very statistically significant, but they all converge on suggesting an unprecedentedly *high* relative inflation cost, and confirm that 1966–70, when the q/r ratio drops, may well have been an aberration in the continuing increase in the importance of inflation. (Recall from Figure 2.1 that 1966–70 was a time when unemployment was high and rising, while inflation was, relative to its trend rate of growth 1955—65, at least until 1969—70, relatively low.) This implies that high unemployment may well alter both the 'true' q/r ratio in the electorate, and the government's perception of that ratio, but this does not alter the long-term target of minimising vote loss. Of course the perception of a drop in the q/r ratio implies that the government will choose different values for the unemployment rate — and in turn will aim at a slightly lower long-run unemployment rate and higher long-run inflation rate — but the adjustment is made within the terms of the business cycle model.

The Heath Government probably took office believing in a Phillips curve (Stewart, 1974, pp. 151—3), even if Treasury advisors 18 months later did not (Laidler, 1976). However, there is no evidence that the Heath Government did not act upon the probable increase in the electoral cost of inflation, as a statutory incomes policy was subsequently introduced. More relevant for the present discussion is the fact that unemployment was kept very low. As Figure 7.1 shows, unemployment in 1973—4 ran at about 2.5 per cent: a vote-maximising (strategic) government confronted with the 1966—74 Phillips curve (Table 7.1) and believing in a q/r ratio even as low as 0.44 (Table 7.3) would have aimed at a level of unemployment in 1974 approaching four per cent instead of the 2.3 per cent actually obtaining. In this sense, the actual behaviour of unemployment in these years approximated a *myopic* course with q/r near 0.5 (see Table 7.2) but was not pushed down as far as that hypothesis suggests (perhaps implying disbelief in the myopia of the electorate or the impossibility of pushing unemployment even lower). Alternatively, unemployment approximated the course of a 'strategic' government which mistakenly believed that inflation was relatively much cheaper and therefore kept unemployment perhaps two per cent lower than even the most generous opinion poll estimates of the q/r ratio would have indicated.

One might be tempted to say that it would have been 'politically impossible' for the Heath Government to have let unemployment rise to five per cent. The model shows (on the strategic interpretation) that the Heath Government certainly acted as if they believed it to be impossible, for this is exactly how to interpret their assumption of a q/r ratio of 0.05 (Table 7.2): the price of one per cent of unemployment is 20 times the price of one per cent inflation, and, even at 1974 prices, that looks very expensive. There is no evidence from the polls that unemployment would have been that expensive in terms of votes, though whether the price of unemployment would have increased as unemployment increased cannot really be known. It is premature to estimate the same hypothesis for the next Labour Government, when unemployment was substantially higher, but perhaps this will in time shed even more light on the problem. It cannot be *shown* (there being, as ever, no certainty on these matters) that the Heath Government assumed a strategic electorate and damaged itself by assuming that the price of unemployment (in terms of votes, assuming higher unemployment would have meant lower inflation) was higher than it really was. It is equally plausible that the costs were accurately perceived and electoral myopia assumed, in which case all the evidence given in earlier chapters about the realism of people's economic expectations may well be relevant in explaining how the election of February 1974 was lost. The simple numbers of the unemployment rates cannot tell us which of these to choose, but the political business cycle model certainly suggests entertaining one or the other conclusion.

This has been, naturally enough in view of the topic, a highly speculative chapter. The model employed is highly restrictive, allowing only a single trade-off and only two economic variables (but see Macrae, 1978), inflation and unemployment, and assuming that a highly unified government knows the tradeoff relationship and also the rates at which votes are lost for units of each economic variable. The model assumes a very quick and controlled response on the part of the economy to government decisions, and, further, is sensitive to misspecification — and indeed, to the choice of annual versus quarterly data, and so on. All this, along with the impossibility of proving, no matter how good the fit, that the government intentionally did the things the model implies, render any conclusions extremely tentative. It is also a pity that the model does not allow governments to blend long-term and short-term interests, or that myopia can only be treated as an all-or-nothing phenomenon. A model which sometimes works and sometimes does not is hard to deliver a verdict on, but some interesting findings do emerge. There was evidence that the political cost of unemployment was relatively much higher a quarter of a century ago, that in the past American governments appear to have responded to a conception of an electorate much more concerned with inflation than the British, but that the relative price of inflation appears to have increased in Britain over the years. Moreover, there were periods when movements in the unemployment rate do appear to be consistent with the 'strategic' model of a government responding to unemployment and inflation not in an *ad hoc* way, but systematically as though maximising support in the presence of perceived electoral penalties fixed for its incumbency, though without a fixed time period within which support was to be maximised. Perhaps more important, there was no evidence that any British government in the period clearly considered the electorate to be myopic — that is, believed it could 'steal' an election by mortgaging the future in the interest of an economically better present — though there are some grounds for believing this in 1970–4. Even if the model can only offer approximations of the economic policy process, however, the results it gives suggest that the model deserves extension and replication.

PART III

Popular preferences among economic policies

8

Overview: who's to blame for inflation?

This and the following chapters turn to questions of goals and questions of means. The British public have for several years quite uniformly expected prices to rise. Indeed, after 1970, rising prices or inflation came to be seen by a plurality of electors as the most important problem facing the country, a plurality which grew, apart from brief periods of concern with industrial relations and unemployment in 1971–2, into a substantial majority by the end of 1973. At the time of the election of February 1974, between 60 and 70 per cent of the electorate felt that prices were the most important problem facing the country, and about one third felt that the issue had been the 'single most important thing' on their minds when voting.

In the same period that prices came to be seen as the most important domestic issue, however, it is clear that more and more people became convinced that nothing could be done to alleviate inflation. The proportions saying that 'the present rise in prices could be stopped' in repeated surveys between 1970 and 1975 falls from about 38 per cent to 33 per cent; while there are moments of optimism in late 1971 – when the rate of increase of the retail price index slows down – and mid-1975, with the announcement and acceptance of the £6 pay limit, the trend is generally downward. In 1970, nearly 60 per cent felt that 'a government can do a lot to check rising prices'. In early 1974, only a quarter of the electorate felt that way, while the great majority felt that 'prices would go on rising fast no matter what any government tries to do'. It is against this background of increased centrality of the issue, coupled with increased pessimism about the possibility of any solution to the problem, that this investigation of popular perceptions of the causes and cures of inflation takes place.

Discussing the causes and cures of inflation is not quite the same as discussing Britain's economic problems more generally. Throughout the 1960s and 1970s there has been debate and discussion about what was wrong with the British economy. Answers proposed have covered a broad range of social and economic themes: bad industrial relations, class divisions, strikes, low productivity, low investment, mismanagement of industry, overemployment in the public or service sector, poor timing or judgement on the part of the government in fiscal or monetary measures, outdated capital stock, and too much (or indeed too little) government intervention in the economy are among reasons frequently put forward as the root of Britain's economic malaise. In this broader context, high

157

rates of inflation are both a symptom of economic trouble, and a contributory cause of flagging economic growth. In these chapters, inflation is discussed rather than broader economic issues because it is inflation which has come to be seen as the central problem and because it is an area in which people have daily personal experience with the results of government policies for economic management. There may well be subpopulations in which the effects of other aspects of governmental policy – for instance, spending cuts or unemployment – are more intensely felt, but the consequences of rapid inflation are felt everywhere, every day.

For reasons outlined in the Introduction, a period of economic decline is the ideal time to seek evidence about electors' positions with respect to economic policy. Subsequent chapters will analyse such a 'position' model, looking at the distribution of popular preferences among not only competing economic goals, like reducing unemployment or reducing inflation, but also competing economic policies for achieving one particular economic goal, the reduction of inflation. Such an enterprise rests partly on having a clear understanding of popular views of important economic relationships. In particular some information is needed on the question of how people believe inflation comes about, what can be done about it, and what the consequences are of doing or not doing something about it. Of course, the last ten years have also seen substantial shifts in the thinking of economic analysts about these matters, so the best place to begin the account is with a discussion of theories of inflation.

Theories of inflation

There is by no means consensus in macroeconomic theory today, and nowhere is this clearer than in accounts of the causes of British inflation. Both the accelerations of inflation in 1969–71 and 1973–5 have given rise to a number of explanations (Ball and Burns, 1976; Laidler, 1976; Miller, 1976; Williamson and Wood, 1976). Sometimes the problem is that little is known about the precise speed with which the consequences of policy changes are to be expected. At other times the problem is that simultaneously many things happen which some consider inflationary. In 1973, the money supply was expanding rapidly, public sector borrowing increased, many worldwide commodity prices – the case of oil being most visible – increased, domestic British wage settlements were linked by government policy to the prevailing price inflation rate, and so on. Much of the argument is which of these (if any) to treat as cause and which merely as reflection of inflation.

Of course, disagreements about inflation are not entirely new. Within the Keynesian tradition, it was and is commonly held that often the aggregate real expenditure plans of consumers, investors, and the government cannot be met by any attainable level of real output. This produces an upward pressure on prices, which is known as the inflationary gap, and is held to be the source of domestic price inflation. Within this tradition, there were two schools of thought as to the central mechanism by which inflation is triggered. One school, the 'demand-pull' school, held that an increase in the price level was caused by an emergence of excess demand at some prevailing price level, either for goods, labour or both. The other school, the 'cost-push' school, held that increases in prices were caused by the economic activities of organised groups – in particular, labour unions – who were able to push up (labour) costs either in the pursuit of some arbitrary claim on an enlarged share of the national income or in a more measured response to some earlier round of price increases, but independent of the level of excess demand. It can be readily appreciated that these schools will be more radically separated in their views as to what policy might alleviate a particular inflation than in their analysis of what factors are associated with a particular inflation, though they might diverge with regard to causal ordering among these factors. Neither school would deny that price and wage inflation could be induced by excess demand for goods and/or labour. (For more details, see, e.g., Trevithick and Mulvey, 1975.)

Events and developments in economic theory over the last ten years have tended to obscure the neat distinction drawn above. One can still find descendents of *cost-push* theories of inflation, who hold that the critical factor in fuelling inflation is the existence of powerful unions which can fix wage settlements, and have the ability to push wage rates up independent of the level of demand for labour. The cure for inflation, in the eyes of this school, is legislation to curb the power of unions and strict control over wage settlements. The excess demand school has split in two around the question of an independent effect of growth in the supply of money on inflation against excess demand principally as a fiscal problem. Both groups see budget deficits and government spending financed by borrowing as potentially inflationary. Whereas some would see growth in the supply of money as an adjustment to price rises already fiscally or otherwise caused, others would see (at least large) increases in the money supply, originating either in domestic borrowing or through international payments, as causes of inflation. People less inclined toward the latter (monetarist) views would also endorse cuts in spending as counter-inflationary, but would attach more importance to other fiscal policies like taxation to reduce personal consumption and thereby reduce excess demand (see Curwen, 1976). (It should be pointed out that with floating exchange rates, the consequences rather than the remedies of inflation change. An excess of domestic inflation over world rates produces a devalued currency rather than a reserves crisis, and the devalued currency further increases import, and therefore domestic, prices. This does not alter theories about how inflation comes about.)

There are some points of contact in all this. In particular the monetarist view emphasises the importance of expectations of inflation in people's behaviour regarding wage settlements. Price setting and wage setting behaviour combine to produce a rate of inflation which is greater when the state of excess demand is greater and when the rate at which wage and price setters expect inflation to proceed is greater (Parkin, 1974). Because of the independent role of these expectations – regardless of exactly how they are formed – any level of inflation is compatible with many different rates of unemployment, and thus there is no necessary long-run tradeoff between unemployment and inflation. That is, 'any economy which operates at its "natural" unemployment rate can inflate at any constant rate' though the rate of inflation can be accelerated by operating below the natural level of unemployment. Thus the behaviour of wage setters forms an important link between the two schools of thought.

Thus the cause of inflation appears to be held to lie principally either in the behaviour of wage setters (or, in some more particular formulations, unions) or in the activities of governments in pursuit of the managed economy, with government spending and borrowing coming increasingly to the fore as a cause of inflation. The remedies are equally controversial: while it is rare for one school of thought to see another school's remedies as in principle inflationary (but on reflation, expectations, and incomes policy see Clegg, 1971 and Laidler, 1976), there is considerable dispute about whether they actually do any good in reducing inflation. Wage and price controls are rooted in the cost-push view of inflation, but excess-demand theorists would argue that these are at best short-term policies of little avail against the upward inflationary pressure of rapidly-expanding money supply or excess demand for goods. Neither monetary nor fiscal measures are relevant, in the eyes of cost-push theorists. Monetarist measures such as cuts in spending would be too slow and their impact too imprecisely known to be appropriate as demand management techniques, unlike adjusting taxation and perhaps interest rates. The monetarist would reply that such fiscal measures could be of little avail against inflation in the context of a rapidly-expanding money supply. Finally, inducing higher rates of unemployment, the response of the Phillips curve theorist, is of no necessary value in the eyes of cost-push theories, in that the level of unemployment required to affect the behaviour of wage setters is likely to be politically untenable. Those who believe in the impact of expectations would allow each level of unemployment to be consistent with any level of inflation, though the acceleration can only be stopped by increasing unemployment, at least in the short term, to at or above its 'natural' level. While no one would argue that higher unemployment is inflationary, it is comparatively rare today to hear anyone arguing that increasing the rate of unemployment would bring down the rate of inflation. At the same time, unemployment has been allowed to go higher and higher by successive governments while ostensibly pursuing other anti-inflationary policies. In view of some of the following analysis, the relationship between inflation and unemployment needs further discussion, and this is given in the next chapter.

The main causes of inflation

If one had a roomful of economists and economic managers and asked them what was responsible for Britain's inflation rate, and how to reduce it, one would get a variety of answers. On just how varied the answers would be there is unfortunately no data, though the probability is that academic economists would give different answers from professional politicians (Brittan, 1973a). Both these groups might well give different answers from those that would be given by members of the mass public. In the case of the views of the public, there is some – though limited – data, and it is to the analysis of this data that the rest of the chapter is devoted. What the public believes are the causes of inflation has changed over the last ten years. Moreover, some evidence can be given about the relationship between partisanship and these economic attitudes, as well as what other background factors, independent of partisanship, are associated with electors' positions about who or what is to blame for inflation.

Chapter 4 noted that public comprehension of the term 'inflation' appeared to be limited. This may have changed in the decade since the studies supporting that claim were done, for it was a decade in which the problem of inflation persisted, and the question of prices and the cost of living dominated domestic political issues. Perceptions of price rises are subject to varying degress of inaccuracy, but a sense of 'realism' about economic prospects and goals can emerge, particularly among people who are educated, follow politics in the media, have some faith in the political system, and have typically large economic stakes in their lives. Because of this uncertainty over the extent of people's economic information, it is not clear how one should interpret people's judgements about the causes of inflation. People may frequently be pinning inflation onto some unpopular scapegoat rather than presenting the results of reasoned consideration about how price rises actually come about.

Moreover, blame for inflation is not the same as blame for Britain's general economic prospects. Chapter 5 showed that there are wide discrepancies between people's expectations of general economic performance and expectations of price changes. Moreover, public assessment of general governmental competence at running that remote object called 'the economy' may differ considerably from how people judge performance on that part of the economy which directly affects themselves. Furthermore, in the survey context, the view one gets of how people apportion the blame for inflation may depend very much on the alternatives they are offered. For instance, one 1967 investigation into the 'most important reason for Britain's (economic) problems' found the responses to be: 'taxes are too high' (30 per cent); 'people do not work hard enough' (30 per cent); 'trade unions have too many restrictive practices' (12 per cent); 'there are too many restrictions and controls' (eight per cent); 'the Government has not provided incentives' (seven per cent) (NOP, *Political Bulletin*, 2 June 1967). The remaining answers were split between none, don't know, and a few other responses. What the distribution would have looked like had all the choices not come from Conservative Party rhetoric is hard to judge. However, there can be no doubt that had some choices from a Labour demonology been included – mismanagement by the last government, lack of investment, and so on – they

would have attracted a substantial following. This problem of varying alternatives between polls does bedevil trend analysis, particularly at a time when economic policy was only beginning to be at the centre of public debate.

Nevertheless, Table 8.1 presents a time series of public opinion on the causes
of inflation over the decade from early 1966 to the middle of 1975. A number
of somewhat tentative conclusions can be drawn from this table, which exhausts
the available data. In the first place, (contrary to the views of contemporary com-
mentators who stress the increasing load of demands the public place on the
government) it appears that the public have become *less* likely to blame the
government for producing inflation. This is consistent with the trend mentioned
at the beginning of the chapter for people to believe increasingly that nothing
can be done about inflation. If no government's policies would be of assistance
in curing inflation, then there is no point in seeing the government as the principal cause. This is in fact exactly what people appear to be doing: the proportions seeing the government as the main cause of inflation have fallen from
about 30 per cent in the mid-1960s (when a further 17 per cent specified the previous government as the main cause) to a low of one or two per cent between
1973 and early 1975 and back up to 15 per cent in mid-1975. Some of the
decline is doubtless attributable to the inclusion of extra alternatives on the list,
but the polls of late 1967 and mid-1975 are more or less directly comparable,
and these clearly confirm the decline in blaming the government for inflation.

The extra alternatives which appear during the 1970s are of course only reflections of the political developments of those years. The persistence with which

Table 8.1. *Main causes of inflation 1966–75*

Per cent saying main cause of inflation was:	Date of survey						
	Feb. 1966	End 1967	1971–2	Oct. 1973	June 1974	Feb. 1975	Mid-1975
Trade unions/workers/ wage claims	39	34	29	14	20	19	51
Management/profits	30	10	15	–	–	–	6
World situation or world prices	–	9	17	31	32	24	28
The present government	31	30	15	6	1	2	15
The last government	–	17	4	–	–	–	–
Britain joining the EEC	–	–	–	28	24	12	–
Decimalisation	–	–	20	21	23	13	–
Price of oil	–	–	–	–	–	30	–
Total	100%	100%	100%	100%	100%	100%	100%

Note: Source for columns 1, 5, 6 and 7 is *Gallup Political Index*, various. Source for columns
2, 3, and 4 is *NOP Political Bulletin*, various. All entries have been rescaled to sum to 100 per
cent by omitting small categories of other responses and 'don't knows'.

decimalisation attracted blame for causing inflation must suggest the extent to which people, given something they dislike, then blame it for other unpleasant social phenomena. There is no evidence at all that decimalisation had more than minor inflationary consequences – certainly minor in comparison with the effects of joining the EEC or the increase in oil prices. On the other hand, there is a reflection in the figures of the extent to which inflation became a world-wide phenomenon in the early 1970s: the increasing proportions singling out world prices as the main cause of inflation accurately reflect the exposed position of Britain as an importing nation to increases in the prices of necessary raw materials and other commodities.

Finally, there is the role of trade unions and management. Management, employers, profits and the like have apparently never loomed very large in the public's view of the causes of inflation and have, if anything, declined over the decade. In the same period, there are major fluctuations in the blame attached to trade unions and wage claims. These fluctuations are largely in line with current debate among politicians. The need to curb wage increases was central to the argument for constructing the Labour Government's pay freeze and incomes policy after 1966. The official view that Britain's inflation was caused by wage increases certainly continued past the 1970 election: it should have reached a high point at about the introduction of Phase I in November 1972, but unfortunately there is no observation near this time. By one year later, with the introduction of Phase III, there was less room for blaming the unions, since so many had completed agreements within the (threshold-linked) limits of pay policy. Blame for the unions comes up a bit in the aftermath of the Miners' Strike, holds steady through the oil crisis, and then, as the effects of this wear off, reaches new highs in the period leading up to the adoption of the £6 pay limit as part of Labour's Social Contract with the unions. By 1976–7, blame probably shifted away from the unions again, after another period of wage restraint, and back onto the government, or the world situation, or perhaps somewhere else, but no published data are available. In any case, opinion on the cause of inflation did shift considerably over the decade, beginning as a choice largely between government and unions, passing through a period in which the world situation became the most important single thing, then back to a choice between unions and the world situation.

Blame for rising prices, February 1974

Clearly the next question to be answered is to what extent opinions about the causes of inflation reflect social and political cleavages, or other attitudes which reflect these cleavages. Unfortunately, there is insufficient data to pursue this analysis over time, and only the most superficial breakdowns are available in the published opinion poll data. However, an alternative data source is available. The British Election Study's February cross-section survey asked, for a number of groups or institutions, whether each was 'very much', 'somewhat', or 'not at all' to *blame* for recent rises in prices. This is a somewhat different question from the one on causes of inflation, but is the only one for which detailed background data are available, though its analysis involves accepting the difficulties of extrapolating from one question to another. Table 8.2 presents a summary of the results of this question, in the form of rankings of the eight groups, both by the entire electorate and by supporters of each of the major parties in February 1974.

Being 'very much to blame' for rising prices is not the same as being the 'main cause' of inflation. This is in part because the word 'blame' implies guilt or opprobrium not entailed by 'cause'; trade unions could be held to 'cause' inflation without the presumption that their activities are in any way wrong. On the other hand, while something could not be to blame without being *a* cause of inflation, something very much to blame need not be the *main* cause, as the higher proportions finding groups 'very much to blame' in Table 8.2 attest. While the proportions of Table 8.1 cannot therefore be accurately estimated from Table 8.2 it is nevertheless the case that what opinion poll evidence there is from the same period is consistent with the data displayed in Table 8.2, and therefore some of the conclusions about group differences in the attitudes displayed in Table 8.2 can probably be carried over — with due caution! — to the data in Table 8.1.

In Table 8.2, blame for price rises centres upon the world situation — which here must include oil prices — and Britain's membership of the EEC. If Table 8.1 is an accurate guide, blame attaching to the latter will already have been fading in this period. A comparison of the blame attaching to big business in Table 8.2, as compared with the figures concerning employers, managers and profits in Table 8.1 suggests that the evocative choice of phrasing here may have had the effect of increasing frequency of responses blaming business, though there is no real way of giving evidence for this. Not too much blame is attached to trade unions, presumably because February 1974 came at the end of a period of wage restraint, even if the campaign did centre on one union's attempt to breach the pay code. Again, blame for the outgoing government comes far down

Table 8.2. *Blame for rising prices, February 1974*

Per cent saying 'very much to blame' of:	Electorate	Labour voters*	Conservative voters*
The world situation	62	51 (3)	73 (1)
The Common Market	57	71 (1)	40 (3)
Big business	46	58 (2)	29 (4)
Trade unions	32	17 (6)	49 (2)
Shops and supermarkets	24	24 (5)	15 (6)
The Conservative government	23	44 (4)	4 (8)
Communists	20	17 (7)	25 (5)
The Labour Party	6	2 (8)	11 (7)
(base)	(2462)	(841)	(787)

*Ranks in brackets
Source: British Election Study, February 1974, cross-section.

the list: people see the Conservative Government as no more to blame than, on the one hand, shops and supermarkets, and on the other, Communists. It is also important to note that the incoming government has practically no blame at all attaching to it from its time in opposition.

Inter-party differences with respect to blame for inflation run along lines which one would expect. Conservative voters are most likely to blame the world situation for inflation, echoing the Heath Government's claim that it was powerless in the face of rapid increases in the world price of necessary commodities, of which petroleum was the leading example. The second most common object of blame among Conservative voters was the trade unions, again in line both with general trends in Conservative thought and with the outgoing government's arguments about the continuing need for an incomes policy to control wage claims. Labour voters, on the other hand, were as likely to single out the EEC for blame as Conservatives were the world situation. Even in the eyes of Labour voters, the Conservative Government comes only fourth, however, and ranks in blameworthiness behind both big business and the world situation. This relative unwillingness to blame the government is a trifle hard to understand, given that two thirds of the electorate allege that the Conservatives had handled the problem of rising prices 'not very well' or 'not at all well', and that there is near unanimity among Labour voters on this point. The key to the fact that poor handling of prices is nevertheless not really blameworthy can only be that the electorate by and large felt that no government could have done any better. As before, there was a strong trend toward such a pessimistic view of the curability of rising prices between 1970 and 1974.

This view is supported by Table 8.3, which shows that people who still believed in 1974 that a government with the right policies could significantly slow rising prices were not only far more likely to blame most of the different groups they were presented with, but also particularly likely to blame those where something might have been done. In particular, people who believe in the competence of some government are particularly unlikely to blame the world

Table 8.3. *Inevitability of price rises and blame for rising prices*

Per cent saying 'very much to blame' of:	Believe a government could be effective	Believe prices will always go on rising
Common Market	64	55
Big Business	57	42
World situation	49	67
Conservative Government	35	18
Shops and supermarkets	31	22
Trade unions	27	34
Communists	22	19
Labour Party	7	6
(base)	(632)	(1,694)

Source: British Election Study, February 1974, cross-section.

situation – the factor most outside any government's control – and are more likely to see as blameworthy the decision to join the EEC, big business, and even shops and supermarkets. These believers in governmental competence, indeed, are twice as likely as the rest to blame the outgoing government. They are also less likely to see that the trade unions are to blame for rising prices. There are two possible reasons for this, one substantive and one technical.

The substantive reason is this: 1974 began with a statutory incomes policy in force, which effectively limited very substantial numbers of trade union wage claims. Since prices continued to rise, the trade unions could not be particularly to blame for rising prices. If a government with the right policies could stop rising prices, the right policies must lie in areas other than control of the unions. On the other hand, it could just be that people who believed that a government could stop prices were typically likely to be Labour voters. Labour voters were particularly likely to blame the Conservatives and big business and less likely to blame the unions and the world situation.

There is some truth in each account. Within *both* groups of partisans, people are far less likely to blame the world, and far more likely to blame business, shop-keepers, and the Conservative Government, as well as Communists and the Labour Party, if they believe a government could stop prices rising. In the case of the EEC, it is the individual's attitude to the EEC which correlates with blame for prices, rather than the attitude toward inevitability of price rises. Independent of party choice, blaming the EEC for rising prices and wishing to see Britain leave the EEC go hand in hand. Finally, in the case of trade unions, the relation-ship is complicated: it appears that Conservatives who feel that prices could be checked are *more* likely to blame the unions for price rises, implying acceptance of the appropriateness of a statutory wages policy.[1] On the other hand, Labour voters who feel that prices could be checked are *less* likely (though the relation-ship is not statistically significant) to blame the unions, implying that the cure for inflation must lie elsewhere. These relationships, small though they may be, are consistent with party policy in February 1974.

In general, then, belief in the inevitability of rapid price rises reduces the extent to which social and political institutions are blamed for inflation, while belief in the potential effectiveness of some counter-inflation policy increases the extent of blame, at least so long as the institution in question is within the control of the government and not already under as strict control as could be expected. This relationship holds up independent of electors' partisanship, though partisanship itself has considerable effects on which groups or insti-tutions people are likely to single out for blame. No other factors emerge from

[1] Of those who wish to see Britain 'get out of the Common Market no matter what' 81 per cent feel the EEC is very much to blame for rising prices; among the rest 50 per cent feel it is very much to blame. Partisanship affects the frequency of wishing to leave the EEC, but not the extent to which those who wish to leave blame the EEC for rising prices. Among Conservatives, of those who believe prices could be checked 56 per cent feel the unions are very much to blame; of those who believe in the inevitability of price rises, 48 per cent blame the unions very much.

the data which consistently affect the pattern of which groups are blamed for rising prices.

However, there are some factors which affect the number of groups blamed for inflation, if not the pattern. On average, people blame two-and-a-half groups very much for rising prices. However, people are likely to blame about half a group *more* on average if they are *cynical* (lacking confidence in the political system), *uneducated*, and *dissatisfied* with their economic position. These three factors are associated with a desire to blame more or less everything for rising prices. Lack of confidence in the political system, lack of education, and dissatisfaction lead people to seek a scapegoat — any one — to blame for what is seen as the cause of their present discontent. While the effect in the present case is not particularly large, these factors will arise several times in the analysis which follows.

9

Realism in economic affairs

Butler and Stokes (1969) argue that the average British elector appears to favour simultaneous achievement of full employment, larger pay packets, stable prices, and a strong currency. Well, indeed, they might. Most politicians would also, if asked, be in favour of these things, and have gone on public record in support of them. What counts of course is not whether one favours all of these goals, but rather whether one thinks they can be simultaneously achieved. If the achievement of some of these goals is seen as incompatible with the achievement of others, then the choice among goals becomes the basis for one sort of position model of economic effects.

Moreover, if this perception of incompatibilities is in accordance with established economic theory, a belief in tradeoffs among competing economic goals can be seen as a characteristic of economic 'realism', as can theoretically accurate view of the causes of inflation. Unfortunately, there is extraordinarily little data available on popular beliefs about the possibility of simultaneously achieving varied economic goals. There is one data source, however, which allows a very close look at the determinants of 'realistic' views of one particular tradeoff, that held to exist between the level of unemployment and the rate of inflation. That tradeoff, often referred to as the Phillips curve, itself requires a little elucidation.

The tradeoff between unemployment and inflation

The tradeoff relationship between inflation and unemployment came to prominence in the 1960s, largely through the pioneering work of A.W. Phillips (1958). Analysing the British economy from 1861 to 1957, Phillips gave empirical evidence in support of a derived relationship in which the rate of change in money wage rates was inversely proportional to (a power of) the level of unemployment. Larger rates of increase in money wage rates were associated with lower levels of unemployment, and for every level of unemployment there could be calculated a corresponding rate of increase in money wage rates. A low level of unemployment indicates a high level of excess demand for labour. Hence, in theoretical terms, in the long run the rate of change of money wage rates can be determined by the level of excess demand for labour, as measured by the level of unemployment. In the short term, the rate of change of wage rates will oscillate around the true level for a given level of unemployment, depending on whether business is more actively bidding for labour (upturn in the business cycle) or less (downturn). Moreover, in the short term other factors like rate of growth of productivity and levels of import prices will combine with excess demand in determining the rate of inflation. Nevertheless, since in the long-term the rate of growth of productivity is steady, and the rates of increase of domestic and import prices are similar, there exists in the long run a tradeoff between wage inflation and the level of unemployment.

The Phillips curve does not imply that 'full employment' and 'steady prices' are impossible to achieve simultaneously, at least provided that 'full' employment is not taken to mean 'absolutely no unemployment'. Indeed, as economists were quick to notice, the original Phillips formulation implied that there existed a level of unemployment at which wage inflation would be nil, or, since price inflation equals wage inflation minus productivity growth, there would be some level of unemployment at which stable prices could be achieved. Given the derived Phillips relationship and assuming the level of real annual growth which Britain achieved between 1950 and 1962 (2.3 per cent per annum) it can readily be calculated that prices would be steady (i.e., wage rates rise by 2.3 per cent per annum) at an unemployment rate of 2.2 per cent.[1] This point is shown in Figure 9.1. The inverse relationship between unemployment and inflation exists

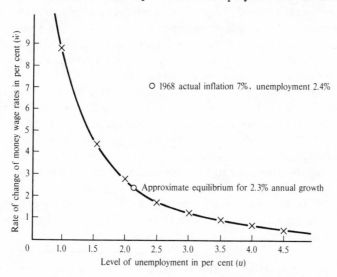

Figure 9.1. The Phillips curve: rate of change of money wage rates and level of unemployment, given by $w + 0.9 = 9.64u^{-1.39}$

[1] If unemployment were 2.2 per cent, then $9.64u^{-1.39}$ (see above, Figure 9.1) gives 3.2. If $3.2 = w + 0.9$, then $w = 2.3$. Thus an increase in wage rates of 2.3 per cent per annum could have been accommodated by growth in the period, and – in the Phillips relationships – would have been sustained by unemployment of 2.2 per cent. For most of this period the official unemployment rate in Britain was less than two per cent, 'producing' inflation.

below this level of unemployment: any effort to maintain the unemployment rate below this will produce inflation. Unemployment in Britain averaged something like 1.7 per cent in the late 1950s: at this level the Phillips relationship implies an annual price inflation rate of something like 2.5 per cent at two per cent annual growth. At that growth rate, wage inflation of 8.5 per cent or *price* inflation of 6.5 per cent is obtained at unemployment of one per cent. These points are plotted in Figure 9.1. The breakdown of the Phillips curve in the late 1960s occurred when inflation rates of up to six per cent obtained in spite of unemployment levels of up to three per cent, and both inflation and unemployment coexisted at much higher levels in the 1970s.

Nevertheless, the importance of the Phillips relation and the various theoretical attempts to maintain it lies in its implication that, barring short-term fluctuations, any protracted attempt to reduce price inflation will have the consequence of increasing unemployment, and that any attempt to obtain very low levels of unemployment will have inflationary consequences. To Phillips' original arguments, Lipsey (1960) added a sounder microeconomic-theoretical underpinning for the loop-like short-term oscillations which Phillips had described. He also provided a better-fitting equation for the long-term tradeoff relationship which included not only the level of unemployment but also the rate of change of unemployment and the rate of change of retail prices as independent determinants of wage inflation. A great deal of economic analysis in the 1960s provided sounder methodological and theoretical foundations (both demand-pull and cost-push) for the Phillips curve relationship, but the basic inverse relationship between inflation and unemployment remained central to the analysis of inflation in Britain up to 1970. It would have been consensually adhered to by academic economists if not entirely by economic policy-makers at that time. However, around 1970 it began to be observed that the Phillips curve relationship had ceased to hold. Whereas predictions of wage inflation from 1958 to 1966 based on Phillips' original equation had been generally accurate to within one or two percentage points, from 1967 to 1969 the average error level was closer to four percentage points, and after 1970 closer to ten percentage points (Prest and Coppock, 1974). What happened in this post-devaluation period was that inflation rose to unprecedentedly high levels without any corresponding decline in the level of unemployment.

Many arguments have been introduced to account for the breakdown of the Phillips curve. These include worldwide expansion of the supply of money, though particularly in the United States, from which monetary expansion was exported through a balance of payments deficit connected with the Vietnam War (Parkin, 1974), as well as exogenous shocks like the rapid rise in world commodity prices in the early 1970s. Other arguments look at disruption in the labour market, whether caused by incomes policies (Lipsey and Parkin, 1970), a change in the relationship between vacancies and unemployment (Bowers, Cheshire and Webb, 1970), differential effects at various times of labour hoarding and invisible unemployment (Taylor, 1972), inflexible tax rates pushing up money wage claims as workers attempt to maintain their levels of real wages (Jackson, Turner and Wilkinson, 1972), or union emulation of visible 'key' wage bargains (Jones, 1973). It could also be argued that devaluation increased prices after 1967, while the accompanying deflation increased unemployment. This plays a role in accounts of inflation stressing expectations. If increases in real wages are sought, and prices are increasing, then the negotiated increase in wage rates from one year to the next will include both growth attributable to productivity and to the increase in prices. This produces a larger increase in money wage rates with each passing year, insofar as each increase in money wage rates causes prices to rise in the following year by more than the workers expected at the time of bargaining. This would produce a 'family' of Phillips curve relationships for every level of unemployment and price increase (a separate curve for each level of expected inflation) or no necessary tradeoff in the long run between inflation and unemployment. In fact, in an open economy with a floating exchange rate, the result of holding inflation below its natural rate is *accelerating* rather than persistent inflation (Laidler, 1976). In general, however, these various views simply show that the question of what happened to the Phillips curve is the same as the question of what caused Britain's inflation.

Perceptions of tradeoffs in economic policy

In 1970, however, belief in the Phillips curve was widely established, and it is not until the next year that doubts appear in official circles about its validity (Stewart, 1977; Laidler, 1976). Whether or not the public believed in it is another matter. As mentioned at the beginning of the last chapter, Gallup polls occasionally inquired whether the 'present rise in prices was bound to continue or can it be stopped?' Since 1970, there has generally been a majority of around 55 per cent saying 'bound to continue' to about 35 per cent saying 'could be stopped'. When the rate of inflation slackened in late 1971 this fell to a plurality of 49–39, while when inflation was quickening, as in mid-1973 and early 1975, the majority against government efficacy widened to about 60–30. Polls have also asked whether 'the Government is or is not doing enough to control the rise in prices?'. In general, and probably largely because people could see prices continuing to rise, there has been a majority of something like 70 per cent to 20 per cent saying 'is not doing enough', though this majority does fall to about 60–30 after the election of a new government or the introduction of a pay policy. On a few occasions the polls have asked the same question about unemployment, and have obtained a similar distribution of responses implying the inability of governments to reduce unemployment.

However, showing that people are in general pessimistic about the achievement of stable prices or full employment (and even showing that they believe the government to be largely to blame for not achieving them) is not the same as showing whether people believe stable prices and full employment to be incompatible goals. Fortunately, Butler and Stokes included a question designed to tap this perception in 1969 and 1970 and some space is devoted to analysing the responses.

In 1969, their respondents were asked:

> Some people say that if you have full employment you can't keep prices steady. That is, the country can have full employment or steady prices but not both. Do you think this is true?

People reinterviewed in 1970 were asked the same question again. New respondents in 1970 were asked either the original question or a question with a somewhat different wording:

> We'd also like your opinion about handling the problems of unemployment and rising prices. Do you think that having everyone employed makes it more difficult to hold prices steady, or don't you think that having everyone employed makes it more difficult to hold prices steady? If you don't have an opinion about this, just say so.

In terms of getting at perceptions of a Phillips curve relationship between unemployment and prices, the second question, despite its extra length, is preferable. It is certainly true that having everyone employed makes it difficult to keep prices steady. On the other hand, because of the possibility of increasing productivity gains it may not be absolutely 'true' that it is impossible to have full employment (i.e. low unemployment) and steady prices. It may also be generally easier to acknowledge that something is 'difficult' than to say it is 'impossible'. Hence the second wording should produce a greater frequency of responses of 'makes it difficult' than the first wording elicits responses of 'impossible'. This is exactly what happens, as Table 9.1 shows.

Full employment and steady prices were perceived as incompatible by approximately one quarter of the British electorate. Somewhat over half saw the two goals as compatible, and the remainder professed no opinion. Between 1969 and 1970 there was a shift *away* from seeing the goals as incompatible, though this

Table 9.1. *Full employment and steady prices 1969 and 1970*

1969		1970 Original wording		1970 Revised wording		1970 combined	
Not possible to have both	22	Not possible to have both	26	Makes it more difficult	28	Realist– pessimist	27
Possible to have both	52	Possible to have both	59	Not more difficult	43	Optimist	54
Don't know	26	Don't know	15	Don't know	29	Don't know	19
	100		100		100		100
(n = 1,099)		(n = 1,301)		(n = 542)		(n = 1,843)	

Source: Butler–Stokes, 1969 and 1970 election studies.

shift takes place largely as a result of movements among people with no opinion in 1969. Of those respondents with an opinion on both questions, about two thirds profess the same view each time. There is a swing of about three percentage points towards the possibility of having both among these respondents.[2] Respondents asked the *revised* question in 1970 were even more likely to grasp the incompatibility between steady prices and low unemployment, though even so only 28 per cent did so, while 43 per cent saw no difficulty and 29 per cent professed no opinion. If the two question wordings are merged, as in the last column of Table 9.1, 27 per cent of the sample do see the incompatibility of full employment and steady prices, while 54 per cent do not. Although there are differences between responses to the two wordings — doubtless some people who said that both were *possible* would nevertheless have said that full employment made steady prices more difficult — the combined responses are retained in subsequent analyses.

The last column of Table 9.1 labelled the response alternative combining the views that full employment makes steady prices 'more difficult' or 'impossible' as 'realistic-pessimistic'. This highlights the fact that there are two analytically separate components to the perception of such a tradeoff in economic policy. Part of the response embodies sophistication or realism: an awareness of what current economic thinking indicates are the limits of macroeconomic policy. However, part of the response also embodies pessimism, insofar as saying that full employment and steady prices are not simultaneously achievable implies that one perceives limits on the efficacy of the political system, or lacks confidence in the ability of the political system to deal with pressing problems. The opposite response, 'optimism', embodies both a rejection or lack of awareness of current economic analysis, as well as a naive faith in the ability of the political system to 'produce the economic goods'.

Let us use the term 'realism' to describe the response alternative indicating perception of the tradeoff, in spite of the different aspects implied by that response. In considering the likely determinants of this attitude, the following are guiding hypotheses:

(i) The sense of realism ought to be associated with any factor reflecting a weak attachment to the two-party system, or a lack of confidence in the system.

(ii) The sense of realism ought to be associated with any factor reflecting sophistication or information about economic affairs.

(iii) The sense of realism ought to be associated with any factor reflecting centrality of economic affairs in the respondent's life.

The first hypothesis comes from the aspect of realism which implies pessimism

---

[2] Unfortunately, and quite inexplicably, respondents reinterviewed in 1970 were far more likely to say that both steady prices and full employment were possible than were respondents asked the *same* question for the *first* time in 1970. Of the 748 1969–70 panel respondents asked the originally-worded question, 23 per cent said it was true that both were impossible, 63 per cent said both were possible, and 14 per cent had no opinion. Of the 553 new respondents asked this question, 30 per cent said both were impossible, 53 per cent said both were possible, and 17 per cent had no opinion. The two groups are combined in the second column of Table 9.1.

about the ability of the political system to produce the economic goods. Weaker attachment to the major political parties, and a lack of caring about the outcome of elections are expected to be associated with a sense of limitation on the goods which the political system can produce. Similarly, if a person believes that the political system could produce full employment and steady prices, they should reveal a stronger attachment to that system.[3]

The second hypothesis follows from the fact that the realistic answer reflects awareness of current economic analysis. It is difficult to devise indicators of awareness of economic thinking, but such indicators as extent of education and media usage are reasonable surrogate measures of general awareness and sophistication (Alt, Särlvik and Crewe, 1974). Realism ought to be associated with heavier media usage and with having had some further education, as these indicate circumstances in which exposure to current economic controversies is most likely.

In the third case, the hypothesis implies that awareness follows from centrality: this is an extension of the argument that attitude formation is most likely where an issue is most central (Converse, 1970). This hypothesis can be tested with both subjective and objective measures of economic centrality. For instance, those who are best off — who have the highest incomes — ought to be the most realistic, as they have arguably the greatest stake, or the most to lose, in economic policy. Similarly, those currently employed (that is, in the labour force) are more likely to be involved in and exposed to the debate about economic policy. Group memberships have a role: those who belong to a trade union would be more likely to display the sort of sophistication inherent in perceiving tradeoffs. Subjective indicators will also be considered. In particular, holding an opinion which bears on economic centrality directly, such as perceiving that the government has an effect on personal well-being or seeing economic problems as among the most important issues facing the country, should be associated with realism about economic policy. Moreover, particularly salient economic experience, such as being unemployed, or feeling one's self to be becoming worse off, are likely to heighten the centrality of economic matters and therefore to maximise the chance of exposure to economic information and analysis, as well as to produce pessimistic views about the country's economic potential.

Attachments to the party system

Notice first in Table 9.2 that a realistic reply is most common (40 per cent) among people who voted Liberal, somewhat less common among people voting Labour, and lowest among Conservatives. Most of the movement toward opti-

---

[3] This argument simply extends the idea that the more one believes a government could produce, the more likely one is to feel that it matters who controls the government, since the expected utility from government action that the individual has is greater. A further extension is that the greater this utility potential, the more attached will the individual be to the political system which produces it. It need not be the case that the inter-party utility differential is necessarily less because the government as a whole produces less, but this seems both plausible and probable.

Table 9.2. *Economic realism and attachment to the party system*

Factor	Characteristic	Proportion giving realistic reply %	Number in group
Vote in 1970	Liberal	40	82
	Labour	35	539
	Conservative	30	548
Party identi- fication	Very or fairly strong Conservative	30	536
	Not very strong Conservative	32	82
	Liberal/none	41	214
	Not very strong Labour	39	104
	Very or fairly strong Labour	32	549
Care who wins	A good deal	32	1,045
	Not very much	34	422
Interest in campaign	A great deal	33	607
	Some	35	494
	Not much	31	382
Govern- ment can steady prices	Prices keep rising	38	602
	Could be effective	30	838

Source as Table 9.1.

mism between 1969 and 1970 took place among Conservatives; moreover, while in 1969 there was no difference between Labour and Conservative supporters, in 1970 there is a substantial difference. This suggests that a portion of the optimistic response, at least among Conservatives, may reflect a post-election euphoria over possible governmental achievements. Considering strength of partisan attachment is also revealing: the incidence of realism is greatest, just as hypothesised, among those either not identifying with either major party, or among those whose attachment is not very strong. While the differences are small in the case of Conservatives, there is a substantial difference between weak Labour identifiers and the rest. Cause and effect cannot be disentangled given the data available, but there is clearly some association between perception of limitations on achievable economic objectives and weaker attachment to the two major parties.

Further support for the first hypothesis comes from responses to the question of caring about the election outcome. Realistic responses are more common among those who profess to have 'not cared a good deal' which party won the election than among those who do care. While the difference is small, it also holds up independent of the effects of party choice, and is again larger among Labour voters. Interest in the campaign does not provide much evidence either way: while those who took a great deal of interest are indeed less likely to be realistic than are those who took only some interest, the greatest degree of optimism is found among those with the least interest in the campaign. In spite of this, the balance of evidence is consistent with the hypothesis that realism over the potential achievements of economic policy is connected with a weaker attachment to the political, or at least to the two-party, system.

Finally, there is an association between perception of trade-offs in economic policy and perceptions of the ability of the government to deal with economic problems. Independent of party allegiance, people who believe that governmental policies could be effective in checking rising prices are far *less* likely to perceive the tradeoffs inherent between full employment and steady prices. People who believe that prices are likely to go on rising no matter which party is in power are more likely (by 38 per cent to 30) to take a realistic view of tradeoffs in economic policy. It may be that there is some generalised pessimism — or realism — underlying both the sense of inability of governments to deal with inflation and their inability to provide full employment and steady prices simultaneously, but it is further evidence of the inverse relationship between economic realism and strong attachment to or confidence in the political system. Alternatively, and somewhat speculatively, realism in economic affairs — the perception that some economic goals are incompatible with others — places limits on what people expect the government to achieve. These limited expectations reduce the benefit one expects from the election of one party as opposed to another, and thus reduce the extent to which people care about elections. This lack of caring is simply a link to a more general lack of attachment to the political — and thus the party — system.

Economic information

More information, in the form of further education and broader media usage, is likely to produce greater awareness of contemporary economic analysis. Table 9.3 provides ample confirmation of this: realistic responses are far more likely

Table 9.3. *Economic realism and economic information*

Factor	Characteristic	Proportion giving realistic reply %	Number in group
Education	Academic further	44	125
	Other further, academic school	41	49
	Other further, ordinary school	38	107
	Academic school or left after minimum age	37	137
	Minimum education	30	1,077
Breadth of media usage	3–4 (highest usage)	35	700
	0–2 (lowest usage)	30	787

Source as Table 9.1.

among those with more than a minimum education (over 40 per cent against 30 per cent) than among those with minimal education. (This relationship also holds up independent of any effects of party choice.) This is confirmed by the index of breadth of media usage, which, reveals that generally higher media usage (newspapers read, campaign followed on radio and television) is associated with higher incidence of economic realism. Again, the relationship holds up independent of partisanship, and the evidence confirms the second hypothesis: greater exposure to information is associated with greater realism about economic tradeoffs. To some extent people pick up realistic economic views simply by hearing them, and education and media usage increase the probability of this happening. (Recall the argument of Chapter 3 that expectations reflect current discussion.)

Economic centrality

Anything which makes the management of the economy more salient to the individual is likely to provide a stimulus for exposure to economic analysis and therefore increase the likelihood of realistically perceiving economic tradeoffs. Moreover, since many of the experiences which make the economy most salient are negative – i.e. involve deprivation – and would therefore induce a sense of pessimism about economic potential, these experiences would also be associated with the sense of realism. Table 9.4 presents ample evidence for this claim as well. Those who are aware that governmental economic policy has an effect on their well-being are more likely to hold a realistic view of tradeoffs than are those who do not see themselves affected by governmental economic policy. Similarly, those who mention economic themes among the most important problems facing the country are slightly more likely to hold realistic views. Moreover, both people who feel they have become worse off since 1966 and those who expect to become worse off after 1970 are more likely to be realists. Most interesting is the interaction between these two factors: 41 per cent of those who feel they have become worse off and expect also to become worse off in future are realistic, against 28 per cent of those who feel they have become worse off but now expect to become better off. While this last factor is affected by party choice, and some of the others do interact oddly with partisanship, in general the conclusion is that realism is associated with subjective perceptions of economic centrality.

On the objective side, the evidence is more mixed. Those with high incomes are most likely to be realistic, consistent with the argument that the stake of a high income produces more importance attached to the economy and therefore greater incidence of realism. This relationship holds up very clearly independent of partisanship. Other effects are less clear. Belonging to a trade union produces realism, as does being currently employed, and belonging to the male sex, which may be a proxy for economic involvement, but all these only reveal any effect among Labour voters. Having been unemployed, in fact, has the opposite effect: those who have been unemployed, or who think it a special problem in their area (or indeed who profess to having been worried about unemployment) are more

Table 9.4. *Economic realism and economic centrality*

Factor	Characteristic	Proportion giving realistic reply %	Number in group
Government affects well-being	Has an effect	34	1,087
	Does not	31	422
Importance of economic problems	1 or more problems mentioned	28	432
	None mentioned	25	211
Well-being	Got worse off, will be worse	41	71
	same	34	198
	better	28	119
Income	Over £1,200 p.a.	42	334
	£850–£1,200	30	401
	£550–£850	32	265
	Up to £550	29	224
Employment status	Employed, in union	36	389
	Employed, not in union	31	557
	Not currently employed	32	527
Sex	Male	36	781
	Female	30	704
Unemployment worry	Not worried	34	1,254
	Family worry	31	251
Age	Born after 1945	38	249
	Born 1930–45	32	371
	Born 1910–30	32	530
	Born before 1910	31	333

Source as Table 9.1.

likely to be *optimistic* about the simultaneous achievement of steady prices and full employment. Age is included partly because of the relationship shown in Table 9.4 between youth and realism – a relationship which is particularly clear among Labour voters, where realism is twice as likely among those born since 1945 as among those born before 1910 – and partly because, among Conservatives, the optimists are concentrated among those born between 1930 and 1945 – i.e. those early in their careers during the Conservative era of prosperity in the 1950s. While the evidence in this section is more mixed, it is still by and large consistent with the hypothesis outlined, which accounts for realism about economic tradeoffs in terms of economic centrality, exposure to economic information, and weak attachment to the political system.

Multivariate analysis of sources of realism

The previous sections covered a number of univariate effects. However, many of the factors which are associated with economic realism might well be correlated with each other, and there is no reason to assume that people having two of these characteristics are more likely to be realists than people having each singly. Because, at least within each of the three broad groups of factors discussed above, individual characteristics are likely to be correlated with each other, and because there is no reason to assume that the effects of each factor are the same across the entire sample, a linear equation approach may be inappropriate, and it is safer to use the stepwise analysis of variance procedure known as AID.[4] Table 9.5 presents an AID analysis of realism with, as in Tables 9.2–9.4, the two question wordings merged, and 'don't knows' eliminated. The solution is constrained to provide groups larger than 60, with a minimum t-value of 1.8 (significant at the 0.05 level) before a split is made.

At the end of each branch is shown the criterion which resulted in the split, and below each one is the realism proportion for the group and (in brackets) the number in the group. The analysis begins with a 'whole sample' of 1,485 and a proportion of 33 per cent realists once 'don't knows' are eliminated. In every case, the group to the left of the split is the one with the greater incidence of realists. The first split, which can be interpreted as providing the closest correlate, or most basic background variable, is in terms of education, with the greater frequency of realists occurring among those with more than minimal education, in terms of leaving after the minimum age, attending a grammar or similar academic school, or having some form of formal further education. Within the group with more than minimal education, income provides the next division: those with larger incomes being more likely to be realists. The high-income, educated group is further split in terms of perceived ability of the government to control prices. Those who are pessimistic enough to believe that prices will continue to rise provide a group of 112 with 55 per cent realists, the highest found in the AID analysis. This results, gratifyingly, from successive splits being made in terms of three variables, one from each of the general groups outlined in previous sections. In other words, the greatest likelihood of a realistic reply arises as the interaction of three factors: low confidence in the political system,

[4] The AID analysis works in the following manner: for a sample of cases, a dependent variable and a number of categorised predictor variables are chosen. All possible dichotomous divisions of the sample in terms of each of the predictors is tried, and a 'best' split chosen. The best split is the one which maximises the variance of the dependent variable 'explained' between the two resulting groups, subject to optional constraints in terms of minimal acceptable size of the resulting groups, and minimal statistical significance of the split. Each of the resulting groups then becomes a candidate for splitting in the same way, and the procedure continues until no further splits are possible. The use of the 'between-group' sum of squares as a splitting criterion has the desirable property of devising resulting groups which are optimal in terms of (jointly) the size of each group and the difference between groups in terms of the dependent variable. The overall solution has the advantage of providing a multivariate model which is minimally constrained (and therefore maximally useful, at least in exploratory work), though it has the drawbacks of providing little information either about the magnitude of the effects of the predictor variables overall, or of the effects of variables which were 'second-best' at various stages. See Sonquist and Morgan (1964).

Table 9.5. *AID analysis of sources of optimism and realism 1970*

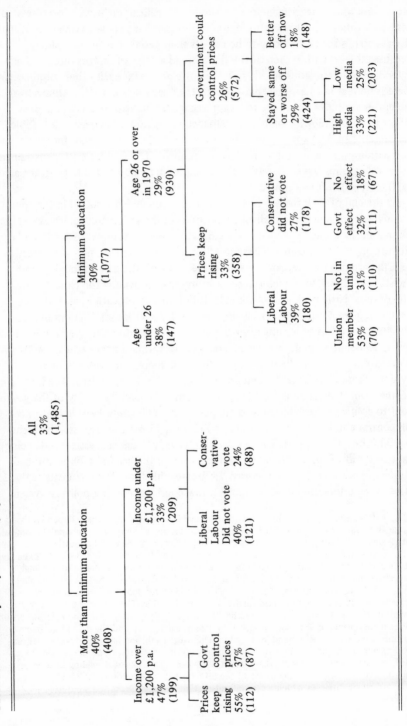

Min. group = 60   Min. *t* = 1.8   η² (explained variance) = 0.05
Source as Table 9.1.

high education or information, and high income or economic centrality. This produces a group in which 55 per cent are realists, though admittedly the group only constitutes some six per cent of the original sample. At the other extreme, the group defined by minimal education, higher age,[5] belief in the government's ability to control prices, and feeling of having become better off in recent years gives a group with 18 per cent realists. Once again, this group is defined in terms of items drawn from each of the three general factors discussed above, and all the independent effects are in the directions implied by the hypotheses outlined before. In passing, note that the same proportion (18 per cent) is reached in a group which starts out with the same definition – minimal education, lack of youth – but where lack of confidence in the government's ability to control prices is offset by the combined effects of not voting Labour or Liberal and feeling that the government has no effect on one's personal well-being.

Other groups, defined in various ways, fall in between these two extremes, and are illustrated in Table 9.5. It should be borne in mind that all the effects displayed in the table are *independent* – that is, a split takes place *after* the effects of previous splits are taken out. *Every* independent effect in Table 9.5 is in a direction consistent with the hypotheses outlined before, and with those univariate effects discussed above. This provides strong confirmation for the view that the sort of economic realism discussed above – the perception of the incompatibility of certain economic goals, along the lines of Phillips curve-based economic analysis of the 1960s – is a function jointly of estrangement from or lack of confidence in the political system, presence of economic knowledge, or at least information about current economic disputes, and presence of a sufficient stake in economic management to make the issue of managing the economy a central one for the individual. The point about realism and weak attachment to the party system or political system is not to be taken for granted. It is consistent with a general account holding partisanship to be strengthened by high expectations of political performance and weakened by 'realistic' assessments of the capacity of the political system. This argument is touched on at a number of points, and developed below in Chapter 13. It is of course not only in the area of economic policy that realism about what any government might be able to produce lessens the commitment people have to the party and political system.

---

[5] A possible interpretation of the relationship with age in Table 9.4 is that –as before– realism correlates with education, and further education is generally most common among the young. However, to many Conservatives born and raised during Depression, war and austerity, the experience of the 1950s was such as to raise greatly their expectations of what could be done by a government. This recollection of the time when both unemployment and inflation (by the standards of the 1970s) were low increases the extent of economic optimism in this particular group. Table 9.5 suggests that there is more to the relationship with age. The young are less optimistic about the potential of economic policy, even independent of their greater education. Perhaps instead it is the case that the economic difficulties of the 1960s (and 1970s) are producing people with *lower* expectations of what could be achieved than previously. It is also the case that Phillips's paper was only published in 1958: perhaps the young, with no prior view to the contrary, were more receptive to the discussion which followed its publication.

The question of the determinants of economic realism is important in its own right, for elections and the success of government policies may hang on the extent to which the 'realities' of possible economic achievements are perceived by the public. The data from 1970 suggests that these particular economic realities had not permeated very far, there being only one realist in three with an opinion, but suggest that the realities may be more widely perceived, particularly if events make the issue of economic management more central for more people. Moreover, while the empirical question of the extent of perception of economic realities is important in its own right, it will assume even more importance in the next chapter, for the sense of realism itself is a critical determinant of people's choices among alternative economic goals.

10

Inflation or unemployment: a question of goals

This chapter turns to electors' expressed preferences for reduced inflation or reduced unemployment as goals of governmental economic policy. (Let us discount for the moment the possibility that electors do not have preferences on this question, though the instability of the replies regarding this question in 1969 and 1970 suggest that these preferences may not be very firmly held.) There are two separate accounts which could be given of how electors come by preferences with regard to inflation and unemployment: one possibility is that they take cues from political influentials, and in particular from the political parties. In this case, if the parties adopt sufficiently clearly distinguished positions, one would expect the supporters of each party to cluster largely around their own party's position, much as is the case with the issue of nationalisation. The second possibility is that electors make some calculation of where their own self-interest lies — that is, some calculation of their economic return under conditions of lower unemployment or lower inflation, discounted by the perceived probability of these conditions being achieved. If either policy — reduced inflation or reduced unemployment — coincides with the 'objective' economic interests of particular social classes, then it should be possible to deduce self-interest from social position (Hibbs, 1976).

There are two extra problems raised by this second account. One is that empirically the distribution of opinions it implies could converge with that implied by the first account if the parties take positions and enough people vote their preferences on this issue. In this case it would be impossible to distinguish between the two accounts with the data which are available. The second problem is that self-interest-based accounts suffer all too easily from tautologous 'explanations': the difficulty of *showing* that someone held a view *knowing* it not to be in his own interest makes it easy to argue that the view must have been consistent with some perceived interest of his. Because of this problem, rather than try to show that all individuals calculate a preference consistent with their own interests — there isn't the data even to attempt such an account — an appropriate strategy is to see, wherever a factor exists or is perceived which should have a bearing on self-interest, whether the balance of opinions in the public moves in a direction consistent with self-interest.

In fact, electors' partisanship is not a critical determinant of the preferences between reduced inflation and reduced unemployment. Rather, what counts is economic centrality and economic realism. People prefer reduced inflation when inflation would hurt them more. Moreover, they particularly prefer reduced inflation when they perceive accurately that reducing unemployment would have inflationary consequences. The sense of economic realism discussed in the previous chapter acts as a precondition for the expression of self-interest in economic policy choices. Preferring reduced unemployment is an altruistic policy choice, since reducing unemployment will by and large serve to alleviate the suffering of others. Most important, people will be generous enough to choose reduced unemployment when they can afford to be. When they perceive that the personal costs of this choice are larger, they will prefer to see inflation reduced. While the demonstrable effects will not always be large, the general point that people are only as generous as they can afford to be will be sustained in a number of different contexts.

Partisanship, unemployment and inflation

Insofar as there is a choice between reducing unemployment and reducing inflation as goals of economic policy, one would traditionally associate the goal of reduced unemployment with the Labour Party and the goal of reduced inflation with the Conservatives. It is true that both parties were formally committed to the goal of full employment after the Second World War; it is true that both parties have recently made it clear — by their actions, if not always words — that they regard inflation as the principal priority; and it is true that Conservative candidates were particularly likely to stress their party's employment record in election addresses in 1955, 1959 and 1964. Nevertheless, in 1951 Milne and Mackenzie (1954) found Conservative candidates and electors in Bristol far more likely to mention the cost of living as an issue, and Labour candidates and electors far more likely to mention unemployment. Asked for the reasons they had for supporting a particular party, Conservatives were far more likely to mention cost of living, and Labour voters exceptionally likely to mention unemployment. Similarly, Conservative voters were far more likely to mention prices as a reason for disliking Labour in 1970 — and even in 1966 — than were Labour voters as a reason for disliking the Conservatives in 1964.[1] It has also been argued that, *ceteris paribus*, the unemployment rate is lower under Labour governments (Hibbs, 1977).

Perhaps the best evidence comes from the manifestos. In 1966, the Conservative manifesto read

---

[1] About one Labour voter in 20 in 1964 (of those with anything at all to say) who disliked the Conservative Party gave prices as a reason for doing so. This was the largest *economic* category of response in this group, though other reasons (for instance, social policy) were more common. One Conservative in ten among those giving reasons for disliking Labour mentioned prices, though taxation was a slightly more common economic response. The data are derived from the standard series of open-ended questions about the good and bad points of the political parties. See Chapter 3 for a description of these questions and responses.

Our first aim is this: to run the country's affairs efficiently and realistically so that we achieve steadier prices in the shops [*Action not Words*, p. 3].

In the same year, dealing with Labour's four central objectives, one paragraph of the Labour manifesto mentioned the exemption of high unemployment areas from public expenditure cuts, and the next began 'To maintain full employment . . . ' (*Time for Decision*, p. 5). Of course, the Conservative manifesto does subsequently mention 'better job prospects' and the Labour manifesto includes the need to attack the rising cost of living, but the difference in priorities is clear. The same difference is evident in 1970. The Conservative manifesto, though mentioning both unemployment and inflation as Labour failures, says 'In implementing all our policies, the need to curb inflation will come first . . . ' while the Labour manifesto mentions 'secure and rising employment' before there is any mention of inflation. Thus both according to electors' perceptions and parties' public pronouncements, in 1970 one would expect a desire to see unemployment reduced associated with the Labour Party and a desire to curb inflation associated with the Conservatives.

Such is not the case. There is unfortunately no data available on public perceptions of party positions with regard to this issue. As Table 10.1 shows, however, there is hardly any difference at all between the distribution of opinions within each of the major parties. When Butler and Stokes asked

Suppose it were true, that you couldn't keep unemployment down and keep prices steady, which of the two would you rather have?

or

Suppose the government had to choose between keeping everyone in employment and holding prices steady, which do you think it should choose?

48 per cent chose reduction of unemployment, 40 per cent chose steady prices,

Table 10.1. *Partisanship and economic policy preferences 1970*

		Vote in 1970	
Preference	All	Voted Conservative	Voted Labour
Keep unemployment down	48	47	49
Keep prices steady	40	42	40
No opinion	12	11	11
	100%	100%	100%
(base)	(1,843)	(663)	(662)

Note: Responses describing preferences are merged from two question wordings described in the text. Source is Butler–Stokes 1970 election study.

and 12 per cent had no opinion. There is no difference in response distributions to the two versions of the question, and the distribution of opinion is more or less the same in 1969, though there are very large but counterbalancing shifts of opinion between 1969 and 1970.[2] Among Conservatives, 47 per cent chose reduced unemployment and 42 per cent steady prices; among Labour voters, 49 per cent preferred reduced unemployment and 40 per cent steady prices. The difference between the parties is in the direction expected, but is very small indeed. Among only those people able to choose one alternative or the other, the proportions preferring reduced unemployment are 55 per cent among Labour voters and 53 per cent among Conservatives.

Part of the reason for this absence of fit with party positions may lie in the fact that the choice between unemployment and steady prices cannot easily be integrated into the broader patterns of economic policy cleavage between the parties. It does not, for instance, involve the choice between economic intervention and laissez-faire, or, if preferable, between planned and market economies. It is also only loosely linked to the question of growth versus restraint, identified in Robertson (1975) as dimensions of inter-party cleavage. Nevertheless, as Table 10.2 suggests, there may be a role for partisan perceptions. If economic policy preferences are considered within groups based on direction and strength of expressed party identification, the following emerges: among very strong or fairly strong Conservatives, 48 per cent express a preference for steady prices. Among very or fairly strong Labour identifiers the proportion preferring steady prices is 42 per cent. This difference is a little more substantial than that observed between groups of voters. Steady price preference among those with a Liberal or no identification is tidily half-way between these two, at 45 per cent. However, the lowest proportion preferring steady prices comes, not among Labour identifiers, but among those who see themselves as 'not very strong' Conservatives: 40 per cent. Similarly, the highest preference for steady prices comes among those who describe themselves as 'not very strong' Labour: 55 per cent. The association is between weak partisanship and the holding of an opinion which is contrary to that held by the majority of a party's supporters, or indeed

[2] Only about half of those interviewed on both occasions held the same view at each time, though this proportion rises to 62 per cent of those with an expressed preference each time. There are no differences between groups of partisans with respect to either amount or direction of change between 1969 and 1970, and there are no differences attributable to question wordings in 1970. However, it clearly does matter how the choice is phrased. A Gallup poll in April 1975 asked 'which should the Government give greater attention to – trying to curb inflation or trying to reduce unemployment?' and found that people opted for curbing inflation by 61 per cent to 33 per cent. An NOP poll in February 1975 asked 'if to solve our economic problems we had to choose between a cut in living standards and a slight rise in unemployment which would you prefer?' found that people opted for the cut in living standards by 66 per cent to 13 per cent. The Gallup poll question had previously been asked in October 1962 and obtained replies of 53 per cent to 27 per cent in favour of curbing inflation. The principal difference between 1962 and 1975 appears to lie in the reduction of the proportion with no opinion from 20 per cent to seven per cent, which can be taken to imply that the subject matter – that is, the choice between inflation and unemployment – had become more familiar over the years.

Table 10.2. *Party identification and preference for steady prices 1970*

Party identification	Proportion preferring steady prices	Number in group
Very strong or fairly strong Conservatives	48%	(573)
Not very strong Conservatives	40%	(94)
Liberal or no identification	45%	(184)
Not very strong Labour	55%	(118)
Very strong or fairly strong Labour	42%	(604)

Note: Proportions are those who 'preferred steady prices' to 'unemployment down'. People responding 'closer to one party or other' classified with 'not very strong' identifiers. Source as Table 10.1.

contrary to something perceived as being part of the ideology or policies of one's preferred political party, an effect which has been noted elsewhere (Alt, Särlvik and Crewe, 1976b). Clearly, there may be other attitudes with greater swaying power, but the link is suggestive. Even if it were true that these weak identifiers did perceive themselves to be out of step with the bulk of their parties' supporters, or their ideas, it is nevertheless more striking how small a role partisanship appears to play in guiding preferences between reduced inflation and reduced unemployment. An alternative account is needed.

Self-interest, unemployment, and inflation

One way to seek the effects of self-interest on economic policy preferences is to look at the advantages accruing to different social and economic groups from particular policies. If, for instance, periods of steady prices favour expansion of corporate profits rather than wages and salaries, and periods of rapid inflation improve wages and salaries relative to profits (see the literature reviewed in Hibbs, 1976), then a preference for reduced inflation is in the economic interest of those most concerned with profits, by implication those in the highest social positions and with the highest incomes. A preference for reduced unemployment (and high inflation) is consistent with the economic interests of the working- and lower middle-class, who suffer most from unemployment and gain most from inflation. The Hibbs study, however (Hibbs, 1976), shows a mild relationship between class and opinion. Members of the working class are more likely to find unemployment a particularly important problem, and members of the highest professional and managerial social grade are slightly more likely to prefer reduced inflation to reduced unemployment. In fact, however, because this social grade is numerically small, in general members of the middle class are slightly more likely than working-class electors to prefer unemployment reduced. This absence of class polarisation in opinion is reflected in the absence of partisan differences noted above. However, it is still possible to build a model in which self-interest plays a role in this choice, and to argue that a preference for reduced inflation follows from self-interest, as opposed to altruism, and is particularly likely when it is clear that the individual recognises the *costs* to himself involved in choosing to alleviate unemployment.

Most people agree that unemployment is a bad thing. The only direct evidence is a Gallup poll (*Gallup Political Index*, February 1972), asking 'is unemployment a bad thing or can it be justified?' It found only 20 per cent saying it could be justified. Nevertheless, very few people suffer the effects of unemployment, severe though these effects may be. About 17 per cent acknowledged in 1970 that they or someone in their family had 'been worried' about losing a job in the last year. (Butler and Stokes data.) In October 1967 (*Gallup Political Index*), 27 per cent of the adult population recalled 'some experience' of unemployment, though only ten per cent remembered having been out of work for as much as three months. This is *not* to say that the psychological and economic effects of the experience of being out of work can be discounted for those who have had the experience, but rather that this actual experience is not widespread in the population. Therefore, looking at a *national sample*, when people calculate the effect of increased unemployment on themselves, *on the whole* it must be the basis of a possibly large deprivation multiplied by a fairly small probability of being affected. There are unfortunately no data with which to measure the deprivation.[3] There are of course people for whom the probability of being affected is large, but it should be remembered that even if unemployment rose to ten per cent of the workforce, the odds would still be substantially in favour of being in work, and not even at risk of unemployment. Therefore, if, as in the last section, about half the population would prefer to see unemployment reduced, it must be the case that many of them are making an *altruistic* choice: expressing a preference for a policy which would alleviate suffering in *others* rather than themselves.

People will tend to make such a choice only if they feel they can *afford* to. McKean (1976) points out that the greater an individual's wealth or well-being, the more altruistic or generous he can afford to be. 'People may be generous when things go well but may revert to savagery when things get tough.' Inflation probably affects everyone, though it affects some more than others. Therefore, unlike the unemployment case, when people opt for reduced inflation they are

---

[3] The deprivation is clearly larger than the simple difference between normal pay and compensation, but estimating money (or any other) equivalents for the psychological cost of unemployment would be difficult. Most of the work on the personal costs of unemployment is impressionistic though suggestive. See, for instance, Marsden and Duff (1975) or Hill, Harrison, Sargeant and Talbot (1973).

certain of feeling the benefit — or certain of feeling the cost if inflation increases — though it may well be that the benefit or cost is quite small. The greater the perceived cost, the *less* likely are people to make the *altruistic* choice of alleviating unemployment, and the more likely they are to choose reducing inflation.

This division is exaggeratedly simplified to maintain the possibility of analysis. In fact, one could argue that some preferences for reduced inflation follow from altruistic motives. An example would be a preference to reduce inflation to alleviate the suffering of those on fixed incomes, especially pensioners. On the other hand, those who feel that way are probably extending self-interest to encompass that of a slightly extended family, or are welfare-oriented ideologues, in which case they would be equally likely to endorse alleviating the suffering of the unemployed, and no pronounced tendencies would appear in the data. More problematic are those who would claim to endorse reduced inflation 'for the good of the country', and thereby appear altruistic. Such beliefs are not likely to persist if they came in conflict with self-interest. Those who believe in alleviating inflation for the good of the country presumably expect to benefit themselves from the prosperity which would follow from general economic improvement.

It is also possible to argue that low unemployment symbolises 'good times', and thus self-interest indicates a preference for reduced unemployment. If this were true, however, both steady prices and low unemployment would provide small benefits to all, and the choice between them would become idiosyncratic. Furthermore, the Introduction pointed to some evidence that the public differentiate between parties' competence at handling 'employment' and 'prosperity', and the trend analysis in Chapter 5 underlined this. However, the possibility that both reduced inflation and reduced unemployment offer everyone small and uncertain benefits might help explain the instability of preferences between 1969 and 1970.

How much can be said about the determinants of this choice? There is a considerable lack of theory and research in this area, but a few hypotheses can be suggested. A preference for *reduced unemployment* will be associated with:

1. the experience of unemployment
2. being a member of the workforce, and particularly belonging to a trade union
3. feeling oneself better off
4. having a middle, as opposed to particularly high or low income
5. not perceiving the personal costs of inflation.

The background for these hypotheses is as follows: Hypothesis 1 follows from the argument that being unemployed makes one more aware of the costs involved, and may make one consider more likely the possibility of being unemployed again. Hypothesis 2 is derived in this way: unless one is in the workforce, the consequences of increased unemployment are unlikely to be large. Awareness of the risks of unemployment may also be heightened by trade union membership, as may altruistic feelings of solidarity, but more important is the security enjoyed by union members of their relatively greater ability, given their collective strength, to secure wage increases to withstand the effects of price inflation. Thus, feeling a responsibility for other workers and being cushioned from the effects of inflation make union members likely supporters of reducing unemployment.

The last three hypotheses all go together. Hypothesis 3 reiterates the point made above that those who feel better off, whatever this means, are more likely to feel they can afford any small inflationary costs to themselves involved in alleviating suffering in others. Generosity and altruism increase with well-being. An objective measure of the same phenomenon is given by hypothesis 4. Remarkably little is known about the redistributive effects of inflation, though some more work has been done recently. In general the conclusions appear to be that inflation transfers resources from those who are in credit to those who are in debt, from those whose income depends on profits to those who earn wages, and in particular that inflation hits those whose incomes are fixed or administered rather than negotiable. In terms of distribution of incomes, this appears to imply that middle to middle-high income groups benefit from inflation at the expense of the less well-off and at the expense of those with the highest incomes, at least around 1970 (Curwen, 1976). Hence hypothesis 4, that those with middle-high incomes, who appear most cushioned from inflation, will be most prepared to make the altruistic choice of alleviating unemployment. It would be desirable to be able to show (like Hibbs, 1978) that high rates of inflation make people inflation-averse, but this requires data replicated over time.

Hypothesis 5 is particularly important. Two quite separate effects are involved in not perceiving the costs of inflation. One is minor: there are those who, pre-occupied with other things, are less concerned with economic effects on their lives. This would be captured by a correlation between low economic centrality, as defined before, and preferring reduced unemployment. The important effect is this: people who do not see the link between government policy and their own well-being are particularly unlikely to endorse reduced inflation. Put another way, the precondition for expressing self-interest through choosing reduced inflation as a goal is *perceiving the cost* of reducing unemployment in the form of increased inflation. Those who are economic *realists* in the sense of the previous chapter should be far *less* likely to opt for reduced *unemployment*, for it is they who see that reduced unemployment means more inflation, and therefore greater personal cost. Those who are *optimistic* enough to believe that they are not hurting themselves — i.e., who do not see increased inflation as a cost of reduced unemployment — should be far *more* likely to choose a policy of reduced unemployment. Moreover, the difference between the preferences of realists and optimists should be particularly clear among those who feel that the government could be effective in controlling prices. If, on the contrary, prices are going to rise anyway, even a realist might as well say the generous thing and choose reduced unemployment.

As Table 10.3 shows, all the univariate effects are in the direction hypothesised, even though many of the effects are small. The proportions preferring reduced unemployment are higher (62 per cent) among the six per cent of the

Table 10.3. *Preferences for reduced unemployment 1970*

Characteristic	Proportion preferring reduced unemployment	Number in group
	%	
Worried about unemployment	62	154
Not worried	54	1,627
Currently employed, in union	58	402
Currently employed, not union	53	600
Not currently employed	52	610
Better off now	57	469
Same as 2–3 years ago	54	721
Worse off now	51	437
Income up to £950	52	562
Income £950–1,450	58	423
Income over £1,450	53	325
No economic problems	60	222
One mentioned	54	278
Two or more mentioned	49	156
Government affects well-being	54	1,165
Does not	54	462
Prices keep rising	56	670
Government could be effective	52	888
Optimist	59	918
Realist	45	444

Source as Table 10.1.

population reporting personal worry about losing a job than in the rest (54 per cent). (It is essential to keep those reporting worry about unemployment somewhere else in the family (not themselves) separate as they are no more likely than the rest of the population to choose reduced unemployment.) The proportions choosing reduced unemployment are higher (58 per cent) among the unionised employed than among non-union employed (53 per cent) and than among those not currently in the workforce (52 per cent). People feeling they have become better off in the last few years are more likely (57 per cent) to prefer reduced unemployment than those who have stayed the same (54 per cent) or those feeling worse off (51 per cent). Similarly, those who ought to be best insulated against the effects of inflation — those in the middle to higher end of the income distribution — are more likely to support reduced unemployment than are those lower down the income ladder or at the top. Most striking, however, are the effects of perceptions of the importance of economic problems and the possibility of containing inflation. Sixty per cent of those who do not mention economic problems as among the most important support reduced unemployment; the proportion is 54 per cent of those mentioning one economic problem, and sinks to 49 per cent among those mentioning two or more economic problems.

While the perception that governmental economic policy affects the individual fails to correlate at all, those who believe the government could deal effectively with rising prices are less likely to opt for reduced unemployment than are those who think prices would go on rising anyway.

The biggest discriminator by far, however, is the sense of realism discussed in the last chapter. Those who do *not* see any tradeoff involved – i.e. those who do not believe that a policy to reduce unemployment would have inflationary consequences – are almost three to two (59 per cent) in favour of reduced unemployment. Of those realists who see the tradeoff, 45 per cent are for reduced unemployment: that is, realists are six to five for reduced *inflation*.[4] People are much less likely to be altruistic if they realise the cost to themselves of their choice. In fact, the division between the policy preferences of realists and optimists is so great that it seems appropriate to describe the sense of realism as a precondition for the expression of self-interest in policy choices. In any case, a preference for reduced inflation is certainly more likely if people perceive the inflationary consequences of reducing unemployment. It is also more likely if economic problems are more pressing, if people feel the government could be effective against inflation, if people are not cushioned against the effects of inflation, or do not feel they have been getting better off.

Multivariate analyses

Unfortunately, many of the determinants identified in the previous section are themselves sources of realism, as discussed in the last chapter. It is therefore appropriate to reinvestigate the hypotheses to see whether the relationships displayed in Table 10.3 hold up independent of the division between optimists and realists. Table 10.4 presents proportions expressing a preference for unemployment by categories of the other variables reviewed in the previous section, controlling for the optimism–realism distinction. (It is worth pointing out in advance that practically all the first-order effects shown in Table 10.3 hold up independent of partisanship; it is not necessary to include a table to make this point.)

Many of the first-order effects do hold up independent of the optimism–realism division as well, although the table displays a number of different inter-

---

[4] Bear in mind that (insofar as it ever did) the Phillips curve relationship did exist in 1970, at least as a more or less unchallenged piece of economic orthodoxy. It is interesting to note that the one significant factor in the change of opinion on the preference question between 1969 and 1970 is a swing toward preferring reduced inflation among *realists*. In the 1969–70 panel, while the overall balance of preferences in favour of reduced unemployment remains more or less the same, there is a pronounced shift from 47 per cent to 42 per cent in favour of reducing unemployment to 41 to 50 *against* among realists, among whom in compensation there are fewer in 1970 than in 1969. This change is in turn compensated for by the fact that those defined as realists by the revised 1970 wording of the perception question are even more strongly (54–35) in favour of reduced inflation, reflecting the extra clarity of the definition of the tradeoff in this question. It is not clear what caused the shift toward optimism in the panel, particularly as this causes a significant difference between panel and non-panel respondents asked the same question in 1970.

Table 10.4. *Preferences for reduced unemployment, by realism–optimism 1970*

Characteristic	Proportion of realists preferring reduced unemployment %	Number	Proportion of optimists preferring reduced unemployment %	Number
Worried about unemployment	42	39	71	93
Not worried	46	405	58	825
Currently employed, in union	44	124	65	231
Currently employed, not union	46	160	56	357
Not currently employed	45	157	57	321
Better off now	48	128	60	276
Same as 2–3 years ago	45	200	59	407
Worse off now	42	116	58	235
Income up to £950	47	142	58	316
Income £950–£1,450	47	106	60	261
Income over £1,450	46	125	57	174
No economic problems	47	52	59	159
One or more mentioned	41	109	59	280
Government affects well-being	44	329	60	664
Does not	51	115	55	254
Prices keep rising	49	203	59	353
Government could be effective	41	229	58	537
Conservative 1970	40	148	57	353
Liberal 1970	66	29	64	45
Labour 1970	47	172	61	322

Source as Table 10.1.

actions. The tendency to prefer reduced unemployment among those worried about unemployment is restricted to optimists. Those who are personally worried about unemployment but perceive the inflationary cost of a policy of reduced unemployment are no more likely (indeed, perhaps less) than other realists to prefer reduced unemployment. This can be interpreted also as showing that in the presence of the economic stimulus of personal concern over unemployment or the fact of being on a fixed income, economic realism predicts a large difference (a minority of 42 per cent among realists against a majority of 71 per cent among optimists) in the likelihood of preferring a policy of reduced unemployment. The difference between realists and optimists is smaller among those not worried by unemployment. (For another finding, in a different context, of the inflation-aversiveness of those most at risk to unemployment, see Hibbs, 1978.)

Similarly, there is not too much difference in the likelihood of preference for reduced unemployment between optimists and realists who do *not* believe the government affects their well-being. If one does think the government has an effect, then it really does matter whether or not one is a realist about the inflationary costs of reducing unemployment (44 per cent prefer reduced unemployment) or an optimist (60 per cent). On the other hand, if one is an optimist, it does not appear to matter how serious a problem the economy is, but if one is a realist it does: if one knows there are costs, then the more pressing the economic problems, the more likely one is to support reduced inflation. The same holds for governmental effectiveness: only if one is a realist does the belief that the government could be effective in steadying prices make one more likely to support reduced inflation. Other effects appear to take place principally among optimists: income and union membership are examples. The union case particularly implies that it is solidaristic feelings, coupled with economic optimism, that lead to support for reducing unemployment. On the other hand, the effect of personal well-being appears among both realists and optimists: regardless of the perception of tradeoffs, personally feeling better off is likely to incline one toward a more altruistic policy choice. The clearest conclusion to be drawn from Table 10.4, however, is that, even though most of the other effects do hold up independent of realism–optimism, and in the direction hypothesised, it is in the division between realists and optimists – between those who do and do not perceive the existence of tradeoffs in economic policy – that the strongest distinction between preferences for full employment or steady prices lies.[5]

If one attempts to look at joint effects of the variables discussed in Table 10.4 by combining them into four-way or even higher-way tables, small cell frequencies rapidly come to preclude the finding of significant effects, and many of the variables appear to have inconsistent effects. One way to summarise the joint effects is to place them in a linear model predicting preference for unemployment: the 'best' available model isolates independent *positive* (increasing probability of preferring reduced unemployment) effects for trade union membership, income of £950 to £1,450 per annum, and personal worry about unemployment, and independent *negative* effects attributable to Conservative partisanship and, by far the largest effect, a sense of realism.[6] Again all these independent effects are in

---

[5] Class differences in economic policy preferences are dwarfed by the difference introduced by awareness of tradeoffs in economic policy. There is indeed a slight tendency for more middle-class electors to be economic realists, though this too is almost entirely a function of class bias in the distribution of further education. In short, economic knowledge produces economic realism; economic knowledge *is* more common among those with further education, but, once education is controlled for, *not* particularly more common in one class or another. Once economic realism is controlled for, the class differences in policy preferences are insignificant.

[6] The equation is:

$$P_u = 58 - 14R - 4C + 8U + 4I + 3T, \text{ where}$$

P_u is the proportion preferring unemployment reduced (per cent)
R indicates that the respondent is a realist
C respondent voted Conservative
U worry about unemployment in the family
I income between £950 and £1,450 per annum
T respondent is a trade union member

the directions hypothesised: that is, recognition of the costs of reducing unemployment is likely to diminish preference for it, while insulation from its
costs, solidaristic feelings, or personal concern with unemployment are likely to
increase preference for full employment policies. The size of the effects is such
as to imply that the effect of realism is cancelled by the joint effects of trade
union membership, medium high income, and personal concern with unemployment.

The weakness of the linear model lies not only in its poor overall fit, but also
in the fact that there is no reason to assume that the predictor variables have
similar effects across the entire sample. Moreover, practically no one is simultaneously worried about unemployment, in a trade union, and in the medium-
high income group: hence the joint effect of these three variables, even though it
is large enough to offset that of realism, does not occur in practice. For this
reason it seems preferable to employ the more unconstrained analysis used in
the case of the determinants of realism to look at independent effects determining preference for reduced unemployment. The results of the wholly-interactive,
AID analysis are given in Table 10.5. As before, no split is made which is not significant at the 0.05 level, and no group is formed containing less than 50 members. The overall variance explained is disappointing, but predictive success in
many cases is good, and the effects are all in the directions expected. The smallest proportion preferring reduced unemployment, 38 per cent, are in the group
of 173 (almost ten per cent of the original sample) who are economic realists,
believe the government could be effective in steadying prices, and believe that
the government's economic policies have an effect on their own well-being. At
the other extreme are those optimists who are personally concerned about unemployment: as before, 71 per cent opt for governmental policies to reduce it.
In the middle, with equal and approximately average probabilities of supporting
reduced unemployment, are those realists who are not Conservative and do not
believe that the government could steady prices (partisanship counts only when
realism is offset by pessimism about the possibility of reducing inflation) and
those optimists who are not personally worried about the prospects of unemployment and who are at least likely to be cushioned against inflation, having
either the highest or lowest incomes. Nevertheless, in spite of the overall poor fit
of the model, the results are consistent with the central argument of this section:
that an altruistic policy choice for reducing unemployment is always more likely
to be made by those who feel themselves most able to afford it, and in particular
by those who do not believe that a policy which reduced unemployment will of
necessity have inflationary consequences.

Altruistic policy choices: further evidence

The previous section interpreted a preference for reduced unemployment as a

Only the coefficients of R and U are significant at the 0.05 level (t-test), though the others
border on significance at this level, and signs are as expected.

Table 10.5. *Preferences for reduced unemployment, AID analysis*

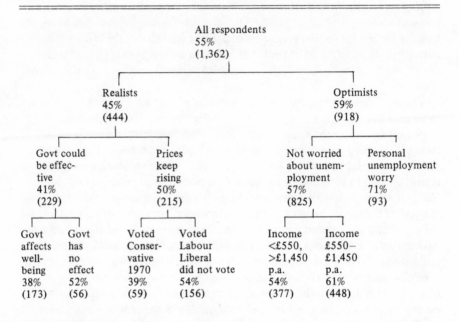

η^2 (explained variance) = 0.04

Note: Group characteristic (e.g. 55%) is proportion preferring reduced unemployment. Sizes of groups are in brackets. Minimum group size is 50. Minimum *t*-value for a split is 1.8. Source as Table 10.1.

policy goal as altruistic: that is, as reflecting a preference for alleviating someone else's suffering. This interpretation arose because the number of people who preferred reduced unemployment was far greater than the proportions who were worried about becoming unemployed or who had ever had any experience of unemployment. This altruistic preference could also be called *generous*: it is held by those who feel they can best afford it, whether through ignorance of or insulation from the inflationary costs of such a preference. The analysis of the determinants of preference for reduced unemployment showed that this preference was *less* common among people who *more* clearly perceived the personal *costs* of such a preference. Confidence in this interpretation will be strengthened if it can be shown that the preference for reduced unemployment is correlated with other altruistic attitudes.

Butler and Stokes also asked their respondents

> If the government had a choice between reducing taxes and spending more on social services, which should it do?

The self-interest versus altruism conflict implied by that question is broadly the same as in the unemployment–inflation question, for, in sum, far more people are likely to benefit from a reduction in taxes (even though the benefit may be small) than from an increase in services, and, therefore, those who prefer increased services are more likely to be expressing a preference for a policy to benefit others. There are three important differences between the questions, however. One is that a far larger proportion of the population do benefit from social services than are likely to be unemployed, and in that case the proportion of pro-service replies which derive directly from perceived personal benefit is larger than is the corresponding proportion of pro-full-employment replies. The second is that the issue of social services is contentious: only half the electorate would endorse spending more on pensions or services, while a far larger proportion would agree that unemployment was a bad, indeed unjustifiable, thing. It hardly makes sense to inquire of those who believe the government should spend less on services whether it should (also) reduce taxes – the odds are 13 to one in favour of reduced taxes among those who independently assert that the government should spend less on services, and over five to one among those who feel that spending should remain the same. Only among those who feel that more should be spent on pensions (three to one for reduced taxes over increased services) or more on social services generally (equal proportions) do the proportions begin to be capable of analysis.

The third difference follows from the above: the question of the value of social services is deeply integrated into the British party system. Whether one feels that Conservative attitudes are defined by less spending on services, fewer areas covered by services, or by selectivity rather than universality of benefits, there can be no doubt that the Conservative Party is clearly identified with a position less in favour of social services, and Labour with the opposite (Alt, Särlvik and Crewe, 1976b). Partisanship will therefore be much more closely linked with preferences between taxes and services than with the choice between unemployment and inflation.

Unfortunately, there are no data corresponding to the question of perception of the reality of tradeoffs: no measure of whether or not respondents believed that services could be increased without raising taxes. Clearly, people who believe there is no personal cost involved in increasing services would be far more likely to support increasing them. Table 10.6 presents the results showing the effect of a preference for increased services rather than reduced taxes. The table shows that there is indeed a relationship. Independent of the effects of partisanship and attitude to services, people who would prefer unemployment reduced rather than inflation would also prefer services increased rather than taxes cut. As predicted, the effects are largely confined to those who would be prepared to see at least some increase in services. When people would prefer to see the same or less spending on services, even the combination of fairly or very strong Labour partisanship *and* the altruistic preference for reduction of unemployment does not increase the proportion preferring services to reduced taxation beyond 24 per cent. Among those prepared to see at least some extra spending on services, partisanship has a major effect in increasing the proportion preferring more services

Table 10.6. *Preference for increased services over reduced taxation*

Preference for spending on services is:	Proportion preferring services %	Partisanship is:	Proportion preferring services %	Economic policy preference is for reduced:	Proportion preferring services %	(base)
All 30 (1,491)						
Spend more on services/more on pensions only	44 (752)	Fairly or very strong Labour	56 (351)	Unemployment	61	(205)
				Inflation	48	(146)
		None, not very strong Labour	42 (158)	Unemployment	48	(88)
				Inflation	36	(70)
		Conservative	29 (243)	Unemployment	31	(124)
				Inflation	28	(119)
Spend same or less on services	16 (739)	Fairly or very strong Labour	24 (209)	Unemployment	25	(114)
				Inflation	23	(95)
		None, not very strong Labour	15 (167)	Unemployment	19	(75)
				Inflation	11	(92)
		Conservative	11 (363)	Unemployment	12	(194)
				Inflation	10	(169)

Note: Per cent entries are the proportions preferring more services rather than reduced taxes. Numbers in brackets give the group size in which the proportion was calculated. Partisanship is defined as in Table 10.2. Source as Table 10.1.

to less taxes from 29 per cent among Conservatives to 56 per cent in favour among fairly or very strong Labour identifiers. In fact, the data underlying the table show that 'not very strong' Labour identifiers are identical to non-identifiers and different from stronger Labour identifiers with regard to this altruistic question as well as the other. This is suggestive, but far better indicators would be needed to show that perceived self-interest at odds with party goals lay beneath weaker identification with Labour. More important, at each level of partisanship on this side of the spending dispute, the likelihood of preferring *more services* to less tax is *higher* among those who prefer to see *unemployment* reduced rather than inflation. In some cases indeed the effects are quite large, from 48 per cent to 61 per cent favouring services among stronger Labour identifiers. This correlation between preferring services at the price of higher taxes on the one hand with less unemployment at the price of greater inflation on the other, independent of attitudes to services and partisanship, strengthens the central argument of this chapter, that preferring reduced unemployment is a generous, altruistic policy choice, and is far less likely to occur when the costs of such a choice are higher, and when they are clearly perceived.

Economic policy and attachment to the party system

It is time to draw together the strands of the last two chapters. Before the joint upward surge in the 1970s of both unemployment and inflation, it was generally held to be the case that a tradeoff existed between two possible goals of macroeconomic policy: reducing inflation and reducing unemployment. While the necessity of this tradeoff would have been commonly perceived by politicians and economists, it was visible only to about one third of the electorate. In the electorate the perception of this tradeoff was linked to information or education, to the centrality of economic affairs for the individual, and to having looser ties to the parties, which can be interpreted as having less faith in the ability of the political system to produce all possible economic goods. This sense of economic realism, or the accurate perception of the incompatibility of two desirable economic goals, was itself closely linked to electors' positions with regard to a major issue of economic policy: whether the government's priority should be the alleviation of inflation or unemployment. Positions with regard to unemployment and inflation were affected by the centrality of economic affairs and by individuals' economic circumstances. Exposure to and perception of the costs of choosing one alternative greatly reduced the likelihood of its being chosen. In particular, the altruistic choice of reducing unemployment was far less common among those who perceived the inflationary costs of such a choice. The accurate perception of these costs is a precondition for the expression of self-interest in the choice among macroeconomic policy goals.

Moreover, Gallup polls in 1975 suggest that substantial majorities (approaching two thirds of those with an opinion) chose reduced inflation rather than reduced unemployment. While in terms of Table 10.5 this is similar to the average elector having become a realist who believes the government's economic policies (if effective) affect his well-being, it is far more likely that the high inflation rates of 1974–5 contributed substantially to making people more inflation-averse, while the reduction of inflation (with high unemployment) in 1978 should make people more unemployment-averse. Hibbs (1978) shows that these effects arise among the American electorate.

With economic problems generally perceived to be the most important, it would be surprising not to find that economic attitudes and assessment of the economic capabilities of the political parties became increasingly important in determining more general evaluation of and attachment to the political system. Chapter 3 discussed the extent to which economic expectations were bound up with general optimism and pessimism. One would expect years of economic failure to loosen people's ties to the political parties and the political system. In this vein, it has been argued after the elections of 1974 that the failure of *both* parties to deal with inflation was a source of weakened attachment to the two major parties (Crewe, Alt and Särlvik, 1976). In particular, as Table 10.7 shows, the probability of a person's not caring very much which party won the election of February 1974 increases greatly as perceived ability of the parties to deal with inflation declines. Regardless of partisanship, if at least one (either) of the major parties was seen to be able to handle prices very well, only 8 per cent didn't care very much who won; 21 per cent didn't care who won if the best a party could so would be 'fairly well'. If neither party could do better than 'not very well' at handling prices, 39 per cent didn't care very much who won; if the best was 'not at all well', 45 per cent didn't care about the election.

This effect was already visible in 1970. As Table 10.7 also shows, in 1970,

Table 10.7. *Inflation and concern with election outcomes*

	Proportion *not* caring a great deal who won %	Number
(a) 1974		
Best handling of prices was:		
Very well	8	121
Fairly well	21	667
Not very well	39	240
Not at all well	45	62
(b) 1970		Number
Preference and party:		
Reduce unemployment – Conservative	12	304
Reduce inflation – Conservative	16	275
Reduce unemployment – Labour	26	325
Reduce inflation – Labour	34	263

Source: BES February 1974 panel sample; Butler–Stokes 1970 cross-section sample.

independent of party, the probability of not caring very much which party won was higher among those who would prefer inflation controlled rather than unemployment reduced, both among Conservative and Labour voters. The effect attributable to economic policy position is similar within each party. If the effect were true only in the case of Labour voters, it could be argued that the failure of the Labour Government to deal with inflation had disillusioned its supporters. But Conservatives as well who felt inflation was the more urgent goal were more likely to care less who won. This means that they as well did not hold out much hope for their party putting inflation before unemployment if the choice arose. This is a little evidence, as early as 1970, for the failure of both parties to deal with inflation producing a sense of disillusionment with the capacity of the political system. This effect was to be much more marked four years on, when views about the desirability of different policies for controlling inflation were closely associated with views of how well the country was governed. In the 1970s, assessment of economic policies became increasingly central in the general evaluation of parties and the British political system.

11

Controlling inflation: a question of means

Given the extraordinary importance apparently attached to controlling inflation by successive British governments since the late 1960s, and given the importance attached by the public to control of prices, it is striking how little information has been collected on the preferences of the public for different means of dealing with inflation. Opinion polls have asked whether people approved of the policies of the government of the day, and survey inquiries have been made into whether or not people approved of incomes policies, or felt that they were necessary. On the other hand, there have been no enquiries in the last ten years into what people felt could be done about inflation, or, given a number of things which could be done about it, which they would find most appropriate or most desirable.

In part, this lack of attention on the part of the research community to public reaction to what was consensually the most important problem of the decade probably reflects the continuing tradition of assuming that people are either ignorant of the policy choices, or, if not ignorant, have no clear preference among them, or at least none which are not directly cued by the party of their choice. People's perceptions of price rises seem to be greatly exaggerated, if not incomprehensible. Furthermore, it is unlikely that even today a great number of people would have much to say if asked what they themselves could do to help fight inflation. Some of the answers expected ten years ago — work harder, buy British and so on — have fallen by the wayside as Britain's inflationary problem has grown. Nor do the occasional occurrences of epidemic wage claim 'free-for-alls' prove that the public are unaware of the inflationary consequences of their actions, or indeed that they are irrational for accepting these inflationary consequences. There is nothing rational about a person's voluntary abstention from a large wage claim if others are making large claims, and one's abstention has no effect on whether or not others will also abstain.[1] Indeed, it is precisely the diffi-

[1] As in so many cases of collective behaviour, it is the question of obtaining guarantees about the behaviour of others which is critical. If no one wage claim involves a large enough sector of the workforce to materially affect the overall rate of inflation, and much the same rate of inflation will ensue regardless of the actions of any one worker or union, then one only becomes worse off by abstaining from a wage claim (through the effects of inflation attendant on others' not abstaining) unless somehow sufficient guarantees are obtained of the abstention of all others. Hence the importance given in early 1975 to obtaining promises from the largest unions first, for the abstention of these did actually promise a reduced

culty of getting great numbers simultaneously to agree to abstain — and to convince themselves that others will not renege on the bargain — that has led in the past to statutory income policies. The Labour Government's attempts in 1975 and 1976 to secure union approval in advance for 'voluntary' wage restraint policies are an alternative means around the problem, but it should be recognised that they stand as testimony not to mass irrationality, but to the rationality of not restraining wage claims in the absence of sufficient guarantees about the conduct of others.

In any event, there appears to be no compelling reason to assume that the public are ignorant, unaware, or uninterested in the problem of curing inflation. Furthermore, in so far as economic realism or sophistication was related to, among other things, centrality of economic affairs in people's lives, the increased centrality of economic affairs may well have increased the general level of sophistication in economic matters in the electorate well beyond its 1970 levels. In this case, the failure to find out more about people's perceptions of inflation and its cures in the early 1970s can only be regretted as an opportunity lost.

In an effort to redress the loss, respondents to the British Election Study October 1974 cross-section survey were given the following list of things they 'might have to put up with in order to curb rising prices':

1. More taxation
2. More unemployment
3. Strict wage controls
4. Less money for schools, roads, and many other things.

Respondents were then asked which of these, in order to tackle rising prices, they would be 'least willing to accept', which was 'second-worst', and which they would be 'most willing to accept'. A full set of answers gives a rank ordering for the four alternatives which is directly interpretable as a preference ordering among alternative counter-inflation policies, and from this rank ordering all pairwise preferences among alternatives can be deduced.[2]

Two comments on the question are in order at this point. First, there are other alternatives which could have been included. Items like 'harder work' or 'increased productivity' on the one hand, and 'floating exchange rates' on the other had dropped out of public discourse sufficiently to be excluded: it would have been too dangerous to mix the contemporary debate with more remote items from the past. 'Higher interest rates' were excluded in part because other alternatives from the same approach to inflation were present, and because to those who save, or at least do not borrow, these would look an attraction, rather

inflation rate if others went along. Previous incomes policies had employed legal sanctions to guarantee compliance.

[2] The ranking is obtained since with four alternatives the knowledge of which is worst (ranked fourth), next-worst (third) and best (first) leaves by force only one alternative unmentioned, which must be ranked second. One deduces pairwise preferences by equating 'ranked higher than' with 'is preferred to'. A difficulty of this 'order $k-1$ of k' procedure is that in this case it may lead to the least familiar object being left unmentioned and thus too often imputedly ranked second.

than a sacrifice.[3] In fact, the strength of the list as presented to respondents is that it contains an alternative from each major approach to counter-inflation policy: more taxation represents the Keynesian fiscal approach, more unemployment is the response of the short-term Phillips curve, wage control is the policy of those who believe trade unions cause inflation, and cuts in spending represents the centrepiece of the monetarist approach.

The other point about the question is a limitation. There is no telling, given only this question, whether people's preferences were based on a belief that a particular policy would work, or whether they felt that they themselves would come out best under a particular policy. Someone who paid little tax might well favour more taxation, even if they did not feel it to be the most effective means of controlling inflation. Or people might endorse higher taxation for ideological reasons — believing it to redistribute incomes — even if they themselves would also have to pay more tax as a consequence. Moreover, views on this question are bound to be tied up with perceptions of what a government — and in particular a Labour government — was likely to do. There is just no direct evidence available of people's perception of whether the parties had particular positions in October 1974 with regard to these alternatives, though it is possible to elicit some indirect evidence from other questions.

Partisanship and counter-inflation policy preferences

Table 11.1 breaks down people's responses to the question of alternative policies for controlling inflation, giving responses classified by vote in October 1974.[4] Partisanship is *a priori* the likeliest general guide to attitudes, and a basic attribute of which any other explanatory characteristics must be shown to be independent. Unfortunately, there are no hard data on perceptions of the parties' positions or capabilities with respect to these policies. While individuals' policy preferences cannot be linked with perceptions and evaluations of the political parties, a few connections can be made between individuals' policy preferences, issue importance, and evaluation of the parties.

As Table 11.1 shows, by October 1974, electors of all persuasions were convinced of the desirability of wage controls: two thirds of all electors found strict

[3] Both Britain's lagging rate of growth of productivity and floating exchange rate continue to be problems for the economy. In 1974, however, they were not much under discussion, as the rapid fall of the pound through $2 two years later was not foreseen, and the question of price increases occurring through rapid, unwanted devaluation of the currency affecting imports had not really been raised. Moreover, even though floating exchange rates came under discussion as a 'cause' of inflation in late 1976, it is not really clear what the related policy alternative that would curb inflation would be, or how it would be phrased in the question. Similarly, it is hard to state a policy alternative relating to increased productivity which is equivalent to the four alternatives employed: compulsory longer hours of work without extra pay has never been seriously proposed or considered.

[4] Note that complete rank-orders were obtained from over 90 per cent of respondents, suggesting again that these matters are no less familiar to the electorate than other political issues (Alt, Särlvik and Crewe, 1976b). The preference orders deducible from the rankings are analysed in a later section.

Table 11.1. *Partisanship and best and worst counter-inflation policies 1974*

Policy	Least acceptable policies			Policy	Most acceptable policies		
	All	Conservative voters	Labour voters		All	Conservative voters	Labour voters
Strict wage controls	8	7	8	Strict wage controls	65	74	58
Cuts in spending	13	11	13	Cuts in spending	18	15	18
More taxation	34	44	24	More taxation	14	8	22
More unemployment	45	38	55	More unemployment	3	3	2
Total	100%	100%	100%		100%	100%	100%
(base)	(2,263)	(680)	(789)		(2,229)	(676)	(777)

Source: British Election Study, October 1974, cross-section survey.

wage controls the policy they were most prepared to accept, a proportion which rises to three fifths among Labour voters. The preponderant willingness to accept wages policies is in accordance with other evidence about the acceptability of incomes policies: as early as 1970, three quarters of the electorate – independent of party – were prepared to agree that some control over wages and salaries was necessary for the health of the economy, a proportion which, if anything, had grown by 1974 (Fosh and Jackson, 1974). On the other hand, there is considerable evidence that the Conservative incomes policy became less popular during 1973 (NOP *Political Bulletin*, various), perhaps because inflation was seen to continue, and as many as one elector in three in February 1974 either wished or expected wage controls to ease off in the following months. Indeed, there was widespread sentiment in October 1974 that voluntary wage agreements were the most effective means of limiting wage settlements: this view was shared by a small majority of Conservatives, but by more than four out of five Labour voters. Nevertheless, despite the absence of any great enthusiasm for strict wage controls, almost no one considered them the worst alternative, and to most electors they appeared to be the alternative which would hurt the least.

The great debate over spending cuts in 1976 was not forecast in the minds of the electorate in 1974: less money for schools and roads, among other things, attracted little attention, either positive or negative. Eighteen per cent of electors found cuts in spending the most attractive policy and 13 per cent the least, with inter-party differences not too marked. In fact, more taxation is slightly more likely to be the most attractive alternative among Labour voters: this preference for preserving government spending at the cost of higher taxation might reflect the same partisan attitude discussed previously (Chapter 10). While 22 per cent of Labour voters see higher taxation as the most acceptable counter-inflation policy, only eight per cent of Conservatives do: this difference is mirrored on the other side, with 44 per cent of Conservatives but only 24 per cent of Labour voters, picking out higher taxation as the *worst* policy. Indeed, among Conservatives, more taxation is the single most unpopular alternative, while among Labour voters it runs a very distant second to unemployment. Among all electors, however, higher unemployment is the most unpopular policy, a view which is held by a majority of Labour voters, and a substantial minority (38 per cent) of Conservatives. Practically no one is prepared to say that higher unemployment would be the most acceptable policy.

So, to sum up, unemployment and taxation are the most unpopular alternatives, and wage controls the most popular, though large differences exist between different groups of partisans. In particular, Labour voters are about as likely to find taxation the most acceptable alternative as the least acceptable, while Conservatives are far more likely to find it the least acceptable. Both sides are far more likely to find unemployment the least acceptable, and wage controls the most acceptable policy. More important, for Labour voters unemployment is by far the worst alternative, while among Conservatives taxation is more commonly seen as the least acceptable policy.

However, taking the electorate as a whole, it is easy to show that a collective preference order existed among these policy alternatives, with strict wage controls most preferred, followed by cuts in spending, increased taxation, and more unemployment last. Since a majority find wage controls most acceptable, they are clearly preferred to any other alternative. Large majorities rank cuts in spending higher than unemployment (by 78–22) and taxation (by 63–37), and a majority (60–40) prefer more taxation to more unemployment. For a counter-inflation policy, other things being equal, it is plain that majority rule after the October election – or a government which wished to claim majority support – would have selected first wage controls, then cuts in spending, then increased taxation, and finally increased unemployment. Each step along this order would carry majority support, at least so long as what was already done did not affect preferences among remaining alternatives.

This is not quite the same as saying that the Labour Government should have introduced strict wage controls sooner after taking office in March 1974. Wage controls one year sooner *might* not have had that large an impact on British inflation, and this in turn might have proved counter-productive for extending controls in the future. Moreover, slim majorities of Labour's own supporters both preferred and expected wage controls to ease off after the February election. More important, the data do not answer the question of how much extra inflation people would have accepted in return for not having strict wage controls, or indeed even the extent to which people acknowledged that that was the choice before them. On the other hand, it does appear that it might have been an error of judgement for the Labour Party to commit itself so explicitly against wage controls: even among the Labour Party's own voters, wage controls are an easy winner against all other policy alternatives. In its first year, the Labour Government probably exaggerated the hostility to wage controls, at least in the eyes of the mass public.[5]

The perception of issue importance

There is a little evidence that the perception of acceptability of policies which might reduce inflation is carried over into broader areas of perceptions of the importance of economic issues and the positions of the political parties. In particular, as Table 11.2 illustrates, finding a policy unacceptable as a means of dealing with inflation is linked with the perceived importance of that policy as an issue in its own right. People who would find taxation the least acceptable policy are more likely to regard taxation as the most important issue than are people who would find taxation most acceptable, regardless of party affiliation:

[5] This might simply illustrate the gap between the political opinions of influentials like union leaders and their followers in the rank and file, a gap which appeared to open (in the opposite direction) in the spring of 1977. Whether to be guided by the clearly audible advice of influentials or the (less clearly known) attitudes of the mass of supporters is a problem for the government at a number of times.

Table 11.2. *Counter-inflation policies and importance of issues*

	Per cent finding policy issue most important of those who	
Policy	Regard policy as least acceptable	Regard policy as most acceptable
Taxation	10%	7%
Unemployment	15%	11%
Wage controls	21%	15%
Spending*	56%	46%

*Question is not the standard issue probe, but reflects the proportion finding it 'very important that the Government should put more money into the National Health Service'.
Source as Table 11.1.

the same is true of unemployment, wage controls, and government spending, though the question in this last case is not quite a perfect replication of the others. The same relationship does not arise among those who see a policy as most acceptable. This implies that a component at least of the importance of an issue for electors is that they would prefer it *not* to be done. It is likely that importance of an issue is a precondition for the expression of diverse partisan preferences on that issue (Alt, Särlvik and Crewe, 1976b). This suggests that part of an elector's positive evaluation of a party for its economic policies might rest on the belief that it was unlikely to do something the elector found highly undesirable, rather than that the party was most likely to do whatever the elector found least undesirable. This view of negative priorities for dealing with inflation is in keeping with the finding above that the greatest party differences exist where the question is of whether taxation or unemployment is the *least* acceptable counter-inflation policy.

It is likely, given the views of their supporters, that electors also have perceptions of the parties with respect to these policies, and that these perceptions would link the Labour Party with low unemployment and the Conservative Party with low taxation. There is some evidence from the past that the Conservatives are seen as the party most likely to reduce taxation, though these perceptions could be heavily coloured by immediate historical circumstances.[6] There is no direct evidence of these perceptions, but there is a relationship which is only interpretable if one assumes that such perceptions exist. This relationship is summarised in Table 11.3.

What the table shows is this: *Conservatives* who feel that more taxation is the

[6] In reply to the Butler–Stokes 1970 question of which party would be more likely to reduce taxes, 60 per cent said the Conservatives and 10 per cent Labour. These responses may have been affected by short-term considerations relating to Conservative promises to reduce taxes in 1966 and 1970, in which year taxation played an unusually large role in themes associated with the images of the parties.

Table 11.3. *Party positions on economic issues*

(a) Taxation

| | Per cent of voters preferring their *own* party on issue of those who find | |
| | More taxation | More taxation |
Vote in *February*	least acceptable	most acceptable
Conservative	73%	61%
	(231)	(39)
Labour	41%	57%
	(139)	(119)

(b) Unemployment

| | Per cent of voters preferring their *own* party on issue of those who find | |
| | More unemployment | More unemployment |
Vote in *October*	least acceptable	not least acceptable
Conservative	14%	18%
	(255)	(425)
Labour	31%	24%
	(434)	(355)

Source: BES, February and October 1974, cross-section samples.

worst policy are *more* likely to assess their party positively at handling taxation than are those Conservatives who consider taxation the best policy. That is, they are more likely to assert that the Conservative Party is better than Labour at dealing with taxation. *Labour* voters who believe that more taxation is the *worst* are *less* likely to prefer their party when it comes to matters of taxation, than are those Labour voters who consider taxation the best policy. For these differences to make sense, it must be the case that Labour is identified with more taxation — making it more popular with those, regardless of party, who endorse more taxation — and the Conservatives with less taxation, such that those who dislike taxation most are more likely to prefer the Conservatives. Exactly the opposite is the case for unemployment. Where people are most hostile to increased unemployment, Conservatives are less likely to prefer the Conservative Party's handling of the issue, and Labour voters more likely to prefer the Labour Party's handling of the issue. This difference is consistent with the assumption that the Labour Party is seen to stand for relatively less, and the Conservative Party for more, unemployment.

No such differences in preference can be found for wage controls, and there are no data available which allows such a test for spending. Nevertheless, such differences in mass perceptions of the parties are consistent with evidence from past surveys, and certainly suggest that perceptions of party policy line up with individual policy preferences of different groups of partisans. One can probably assume, therefore, that the analysis of these policy preferences at the mass level is not an empty exercise, for hostility to a policy alternative is linked not only to extra importance being attached to the issue, but also to a view of a one-dimensional party system which, with respect to counter-inflation policy, sees the Conservative Party as tied to a position involving less taxation and more un-employment, and the Labour Party to a position embodying the opposite.

A unidimensional issue?

An earlier chapter reviewed Downs' (1957) argument that, if a campaign is fought on a truly unidimensional issue continuum, a competitive party seeking to maxi-mise votes should move to the centre of that continuum, or more precisely, adopt the position of the median voter. More generally, this should be the strategy of any candidate seeking to maximise his advantage or support with respect to any single issue. From this point of view, it would be very interesting to know if the alternative policies for fighting inflation which we are discussing meet the criteria for unidimensionality. In a trivial sense, one can always declare the alternatives unidimensional, but the more important question is whether unidimensionality can be deduced from the perceptions and attitudes of the electorate.[7] The answer to this question provides information both about the extent to which the elector-ate share a common perceptual basis for looking at an important political issue, as well as about the nature and possibility of party competition on issues.

Unidimensionality and single-peakedness

A set of alternatives, and preferences over those alternatives, are unidimensional if, for some ordering of the alternatives, all individuals have preference functions which are single-peaked (Niemi and Weisberg, 1974). The essence of a single-peaked preference function is that there is a single point at which the individual's utility is maximised (his ideal point, reflecting the alternative from which the individual derives most benefit), on both sides of which utility declines mono-tonically as the alternatives become more remote. Figure 11.1 shows a hypo-thetical ordering of the four counter-inflation alternatives, with the individual preference orders of two electors, A and B. A has a single-peaked preference function: his preference order is $WUST$, and as the figure shows, his preference curve turns only once, from upward to downward, at W. B, with preference order $TSUW$ does not have a single-peaked curve: it must turn downward twice, at (or to the left of) U and at (or to the right of) T, and there is no single point to both

---

[7] In the context of Chapter 1, this is investigating the possibility of counter-inflation policies conforming to Downs's (1957) analysis of issues, save that his notion of the left—right dimension will be replaced by one to be abstracted from the counter-inflation policy alter-natives. This does not reflect on Downs's more general argument about the movement of parties when *all* issues can be simultaneously reduced to a single dimension, the notion which Stokes (1966) criticised as an oversimplification. On the other hand, this does follow Stokes's argument that the most appropriate criterion for determining the dimen-sionality of the space underlying these alternatives is the perceptions of the electorate, though it does not appear that the question of counter-inflation policy was as remote or ill-understood as he claims the notion of left—right to be (Butler and Stokes, 1969).

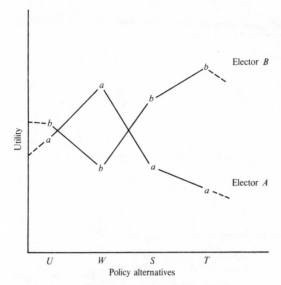

Figure 11.1. Preference function examples

sides of which *B*'s utility monotonically declines. Because of this, the ordering *U–W–S–T* shown in Figure 8.1 cannot be considered to be a unidimensional order bridging the preferences of *A* and *B*. Because of this, one cannot locate *B*'s 'ideal' point, nor can one identify a single point where the joint utilities of *A* and *B* are maximised. Furthermore, unless all preferences are single-peaked, one cannot use distance along the axis of policy alternatives to determine relative preferences for candidates who take up positions along the axis; nor can one derive implications about the position a candidate should adopt to maximise support. On the other hand, if an ordering for the alternatives can be found which renders all individual preference orders single-peaked then a great deal of other information can be obtained. Unidimensionality implies the possibility of aggregation of individual preferences into a collective choice, avoiding paradoxes attaching to intransitivities (Arrow, 1951). Relative preferences for candidates at different points on the continuum can be derived from individuals' ideal points, and strategies for candidates can be suggested.

The meaning of possible scales

As important as the existence of a unidimensional scale underlying these policy alternatives is the interpretation of that scale. This interpretation is a somewhat arbitrary business, but insofar as people appear to sort these alternatives into some intelligible order, the ordering criterion they choose reflects the meaning they attach to the issue. In terms of the four counter-inflation policy alternatives, Figure 11.2 shows three possible qualitative orderings, each of which has a different interpretation. Perhaps the easiest way to interpret these dimensions is by

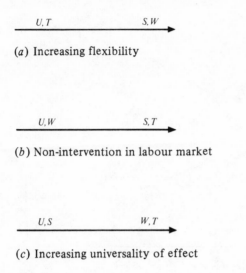

(*a*) Increasing flexibility

(*b*) Non-intervention in labour market

(*c*) Increasing universality of effect

Figure 11.2. Possible pairings for dimensions

dividing the four alternatives into two pairs, and seeing what each pair has in common, which is not shared by the other pair. If the pairings were unemployment and taxation as opposed to spending cuts and wage controls (Figure 11.2a), it would be difficult to interpret the scale. There is a sense in which spending cuts and wage controls are the more flexible policies: certainly more discretion can be used in applying them to different groups. Taxation and unemployment are the more market-oriented, traditional policies. Were this joint scale to be found, it would suggest that electors looked upon the policy alternatives for fighting inflation much as a policy analyst or economic historian might. It would therefore be surprising were this scale or any like it to emerge as the best-fitting joint scale.

Figure 11.2(b) suggests a more probable alternative: the difference between pairs is that particularly more unemployment but also wage controls imply interference with the labour market as the solution to inflation, while spending and taxing do not. Put one way, it reflects the difference between two schools of thought about inflation: the descendants of the cost-push school being found closer to U and W and the descendants of demand-pull theory lying closer to S and T. A sharper line is drawn if the difference is seen to lie in whether or not counter-inflation policy requires a defence of workers' rights and interests: in this case one would expect to find trade unionists and those closest to the unions furthest from the U, W end, and those hostile to unions and workers at that end. Were this scale to emerge, it would imply that the battle over counter-inflation policy was fought by groups which stood for workers' rights and for control of workers: this is one plausible interpretation of inter-party conflict in Britain.

Indeed, defence of workers was the initial reason for the establishment of the Labour Party, and continues to be an important part of its policy, as witness the repeal of the 1971 Industrial Relations Act.

An equally plausible alternative is given in Figure 11.2(c). Here the dimension has to do with universality of impact, or slightly more remotely, egalitarianism or defence of the underprivileged. Most electors pay taxes; if direct taxation is increased, taxpayers pay more and a new class of taxpayer is probably created. If indirect taxation is increased, goods and services cost more. In either case there is an immediate impact on a very large number of people. Wage controls are similar, but both less general and less immediate. Money which is taken away by wage controls is not money one ever had, more people and more sorts of income lie outside a wages policy, and there are more ways to evade its consequences than there are with increased taxation. In all these ways, wage controls are less universal in their impact than is increased taxation. Cuts in spending (this is an unsubstantiated argument) are less universal, at least because they feel less universal. One can always hope that what is cut will affect someone else: particularly if people perceive cuts in spending to mean cuts in welfare benefits, many would assume their impact to fall elsewhere. As argued in a previous chapter, more unemployment is the least universal of all: only a quarter of the population ever experience it, and the rest presumably hope that if unemployment goes up, it isn't their jobs which are lost. In this case evaluation of counter-inflation policies rests upon whether the individual believes that whatever is done should affect everyone (if one believes that, one lies at the T, W end) or at least should not affect only the unemployed or those who benefit most from government spending.

The latter two alternatives are the probable ones. In one case, evaluation of a counter-inflation policy depends on whether some sacrifice of workers' rights or interests is involved, or whether the policy's impact is through interference with the labour market. In the other case, the choice will arise depending on whether the policy is universal in effect, or at least not oriented against the interests of socially-dependent groups. Both of these are plausible interpretations of ideological cleavages in the British party system. Which arises most commonly?

The dominant *J*-scale

The 'dominant *J*-scale' is the joint ordering which best fits the individual rank orders ('*I*-scales'). Finding a dominant *J*-scale from the others is often called unfolding (Coombs, 1964) and a variety of solutions are available for finding the dominant *J*-scale from a group of *I*-scales.[8] A solution along the lines out-

---

[8] Unfolding is used to find a unidimensional ordering, as well as 'metric' information about the distances between objects, from individual preference orders. The method works as follows. Assume that any individual and each alternative or stimulus over which he has a preference function can be located as a point on a common dimension called a *J*-scale (for joint scale). The individual is located at his ideal point, where his utility is maximised. Each individual's preference ordering from most to least preferred corresponds to the rank

lined in the work of Coombs and Lingoes (1975) holds that the dominant *J*-scale is the one which fits the largest number of *I*-scales. It happens in this case that alternative solutions would isolate the same joint scale in any case. Since there must be a perfect two-dimensional solution for four choices, multidimensional solutions offer little improvement on the basic data, and are not pursued.

In fact, with only four stimulus points, finding the dominant *J*-scale is quite straightforward. All the most common *I*-scales begin with *W*age controls (most preferred), but three of them – *WSUT* (that is, wage controls preferred to spending cuts to unemployment to taxation) (n = 402), *WSTU* (n = 396), *WTSU* (n = 268) – are far more common than the rest. All *I*-scales from a common *J*-scale must end in only two of the points, and these two define the endpoints of the *J*-scale. It is evident that what is required is the *J*-scale which contains the three most common *I*-scales, and ends in *T* and *U*, since these are the most unpopular alternatives, and are the endpoints of the three *I*-scales. This *J*-scale, with its *I*-scales, is shown in Figure 11.3 and is interpreted in the next section.

This dominant joint scale has a number of desirable properties. The number of cases whose individual preference orders it accounts for is 1,349, 65 per cent of the total, substantially more than the next best scale. The metric implication, that *T* is further from *W* than *S* is from *U*, follows from the choice of *WSUT* (n = 402) over *SWTU* (n = 93), which again gives a clear decision. Not only does this scale contain the three most common *I*-scales, but it also contains the most common *I*-scale beginning with *T* (*TWSU*, n = 87), *S* (*SWUT*, n = 94), and even *U* (*USWT*, n = 20). Thus – and this did not have to happen – the dominant *J*-scale contains the most common *I*-scale beginning with each possible item. Moreover, there are only two *I*-scales having a relative frequency greater than five per cent of the admissible sample which are not accounted for by the dominant *J*-scale.

How good is the fit really? This is hard to say, for it is difficult to define the sampling properties of these scales and to provide a realistic null hypothesis against which to assess the goodness of fit. Coombs (1964) suggests that, when error is present, one ordinarily obtains a best-fitting *J*-scale which accounts for about 72 per cent of cases. Another recent study reported a dominant scale satisfying 77 per cent of *I*-scales, better than the current 65 per cent (Särlvik, 1976). On the other hand, that study reported a far higher rate of excluded data, and the 57 per cent of the present total sample contained in the dominant *J*-scale compares well enough with the 60 per cent accounted for in that study, where the objects being ranked were political parties. Different methods of data collection make it impossible to compare with Coombs's examples. Probably one must

order of absolute distances of the stimulus points to the individual's ideal point, with the nearest stimulus being most preferred. Any *J*-scale gives rise to $_mC_2 + 1$ *I*-scales ($_mC_2$ denoting the number of combinations of *m* things taken 2 at a time). However, as there are *m'* (*m* factorial) possible orders of *m* things, there will characteristically be an excess of observed *I*-scales over those possible to fit to one *J*-scale. The dominant *J*-scale is the one which fits those *I*-scales observed most frequently, which also determine the relative distances between points on the *J*-scale (called 'metric implications').

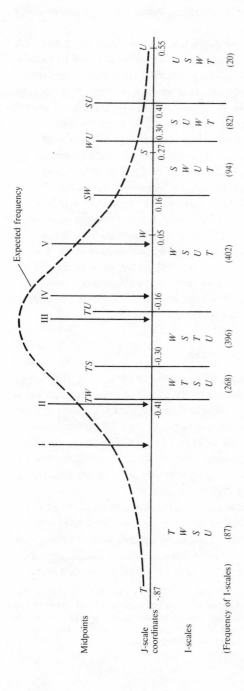

Figure 11.3 The dominant *J*-scale, its *I*-scales, and the positions of various groups

Group: I. Britain governed relatively well, same/more social services, great deal of interest, prices not very important (scale value = −0.430, n = 26)

II. Britain governed relatively well, same/more social services, some further education (scale value = −0.302, n = 11)

III. Average Labour voter (scale value = −0.196, n = 543)

IV. Average Conservative voter (scale value = −0.098, n = 439)

V. Britain not governed well, cut back social services, middle-class, private sector, expect economy will get worse (scale value = −0.026, n = 76).

conclude that the fit is not really very good, though it is not particularly bad. Nevertheless, unless one is prepared to exclude very large amounts of data as random response errors, the assumption that counter-inflation policies form a unidimensional continuum over which electors' preferences are distributed is *not* really justified.

One reason that the dominant *J*-scale might not account for more cases could arise if there were a number of fairly common *I*-scales which could all be fitted to another *J*-scale, but none of which fit the dominant *J*-scale. In this case there would simply be an electorate with two different bases of perception. Such, however, is not the case; there is no *J*-scale which contains all the next most frequently occurring *I*-scales outside the dominant *J*-scale. In fact, the next best *J*-scale is $T-S-W-U$, but contains the reverse metric implication from the dominant *J*-scale. This *J*-scale contains a number of *I*-scales also found in the dominant *J*-scale and accounts for 1,144 cases, or 55 per cent of the eligible total. Moreover, these two best *J*-scales between them account for over 80 per cent of *I*-scales, and at that level one can discount other scales as idiosyncratic. Indeed, the only two *I*-scales of any frequency which do not follow from one of these two *J*-scales are *WTUS* ($n = 139$) and *WUTS* ($n = 64$). These are very similar: both display hostility to spending cuts, and the groups which have these views are typically young, educated, drawn from top social grades, work in the public sector, and vote Liberal.[9] There is not a great deal to say about the second *J*-scale, but it has one interesting property, which, in conjunction with the interpretation of the dominant *J*-scale, merits discussion.

Economic policy and the party system

The dominant *J*-scale may not contain enough *I*-scales to allow the evaluation of counter-inflation policies as unidimensional in the minds of the electorate, but it is clear that the most common dimension underlying evaluation of these policies is the question of universality or welfarist ideology. That is, the dominant *J*-scale is of the type described in the discussion of Figure 11.2(c). This in turn implies that, insofar as counter-inflation policies are integrated into a wider frame of reference, they are evaluated as a sub-group of welfare policy, rather than the industrial relations policy described in Figure 11.2(b).

The best evidence for this is to show that the attitudes contained in the *I*-scales from which the dominant *J*-scale can be unfolded correlate better with some other measure of welfare ideology or universalism than with anything else. The likeliest candidate for such a test comes from a question on social services and benefits, on which respondents were asked to say whether they felt social

[9] A similar analysis is developed in the next chapter. The idiosyncracy of these scales is that spending cuts are seen as worst, rather than merely bad. The next chapter shows that those who would suffer directly from unemployment and spending cuts (in this case civil servants in non-manual social grades) are particularly likely to find these alternatives undesirable ways of fighting inflation. They are, however, more likely to place unemployment last than spending cuts.

services and benefits should be cut back, stay as they are, or whether there should be more social services and benefits. It is true that a response of 'cut back' is as likely to mean that less should be spent or fewer areas covered as it is to mean that benefits should be available to fewer people, but it is the closest question available.

Table 11.4 shows the proportion of respondents at each I-scale position of the dominant J-scale saying that social services should be cut back. The proportion is smallest at the T end of the scale, indicating that a high preference for more taxation to fight inflation is associated with a preference *not* to see social services cut back. From a low of 21 per cent at that end of the scale, the proportions wishing to see social services and benefits cut back rise steadily through 30 and 40 per cent to a high of 65 per cent at the other end of the scale. At this end, those most in favour of increased unemployment to fight inflation are also most in favour of reducing social services. Note that this interpretation is strengthened by the fact that the proportion wanting benefits cut back is *not* highest where cuts in spending are most preferred: it would be if the question of cutbacks were seen only in spending terms. Moreover, this ordering holds up very well independent of partisanship: at the T end of the scale, 23 per cent of Conservatives and 19 per cent of Labour voters want benefits cut back; these proportions rise to 70 and 50 per cent respectively at the other end of the scale. This provides strong confirmation for this interpretation of the scale: again, it appears that evaluation of counter-inflation policy is most closely tied to evaluation of welfare policy, and particularly with that aspect of welfare policy which relates to whether benefits are selective or available to all.

Not only does the dominant J-scale show this relationship with welfare benefits independent of partisanship, but in fact the scale itself does not correlate all that well with partisanship. As Table 11.5 shows, the proportions at each scale who vote Conservative do not change across most of the J-scale. There are fewest Conservatives in the small group at the 'more taxation best' end of the scale, and the largest proportion of Conservatives at the other end, but in between the proportion is relatively constant, and certainly does not increase or decrease monotonically as one proceeds along the J-scale.

Table 11.4. *Counter-inflation policies and social service attitudes*

I-scale	Proportion wanting benefits cut back	(base)
TWSU	21%	87
WTSU	28%	268
WSTU	39%	396
WSUT	44%	402
SWUT	47%	94
SUWT	51%	82
USWT	65%	20

Source as Table 11.1.

Table 11.5. *Partisanship and economic scales*

I-scale	Dominant scale Per cent voting Conservative	(base)	I-scale	Second scale Per cent voting Conservative	(base)
TWSU	15	87	TSWU	11	75
WTSU	30	268	STWU	17	48
WSTU	30	396	SWTU	20	93
WSUT	40	402	WSTU	30	396
SWUT	31	94	WSUT	40	402
SUWT	32	82	WUST	49	121
USWT	50	20	UWST	78	9

Source as Table 11.1.

This implies that there is a weak correlation between position on the dominant J-scale and partisanship. Table 11.5 illustrates how much stronger the correlation is between partisanship and the second J-scale: the spread of proportions voting Conservative is greater, and the increase in Conservative proportion as one moves from the taxation end to the unemployment end is smoothly monotonic. Insofar as this second J-scale represents economic policy as a question of industrial relations, with evaluations depending on the extent to which the policy implies intervention in the labour market, it is clear that this aspect of policy is tied much more closely to partisanship in the electorate.

How is this to be interpreted? Figure 11.4 gives a spatial representation of these points. It allows two dimensions for the representation of the counter-inflation policy alternatives, since the perceptual data did not really satisfy the specification of unidimensionality. The four policy alternatives are given arbitrary coordinates, though the metric implications of the J-scales are satisfied. Since by inspection the dominant and second-best J-scales are correlated (they contain some of the same I-scales) they are represented in the usual way as a pair of line segments with an angle of less than 90° between them. The scale position of each alternative is given by its projection on each line segment, and the J-scale is defined by the order of these projections. Thus the dominant J-scale is $T_1.W_1S_1U_1$ (where the '.' indicates the greater distance) and the second scale is $T_2S_2W_2.U_2$. The U_1 end represents the region of greatest desire to see welfare benefits curtailed; the U_2 end represents greatest willingness to see counter-inflation policy take the form of interference with the labour market. The T_1 and T_2 ends represent the opposites. The cleavages of party system in Britain represent both these dimensions, and so partisanship can be represented by another line segment lying *between* the two J-scales: in this case it will be moderately correlated with both of them. The fact that the correlation is better with the second J-scale implies that the line representing the party system should be drawn closer to the line representing the second J-scale, as has been done in Figure 11.4. Thus, insofar as evaluation of counter-inflation policy is linked with

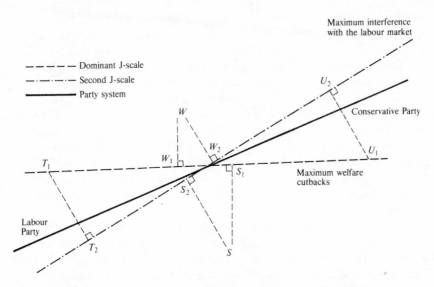

Figure 11.4. Counter-inflation policies and the party system
T More taxation the best policy (located at T_1 for convenience)
W Strict wage controls the best policy
S Spending cuts the best policy
U More unemployment the best policy (located at U_1)

other ideological attitudes, most commonly the link is with welfare policy, but insofar as there is a dimension underlying evaluation of counter-inflation policy which is closest to the general line of cleavage between the two main parties in Britain, it is the aspect of economic policy which is related to industrial relations. The aspect of counter-inflation policy choice which best reflects the party system is its industrial relations aspect: the aspect which the most people employ in evaluating counter-inflation policy is how the policy bears on general questions of social welfare and universality of effect.

The economic politics of 1974

The position of the famous 'median voter' on the dominant *J*-scale of Figure 11.3 — that elector whose position a vote-maximising competitive party would adopt — is just closer to taxation than unemployment, and therefore lies within the region of the preference order *W–S–T–U*. Because governments are not restricted to using only one policy to fight inflation, it is not easy to impute clear preference orders to the political parties to describe which position they could in fact be said to have taken up. The situation is probably more clear in the case of the Conservative Party, which in the February election had stood for the position *W–S–U–T*, just to the right of the centre. By October 1974, their manifesto read 'rigorously control public spending and the money supply and there must be restraint in prices and incomes'. This suggests a shift towards the $S-W-U-T$ area, and foreshadows the general trend in Conservative arguments even more to the right of Figure 11.3 which followed in 1975–77. Even if the shift towards spending cuts as their preferred counter-inflation policy was in the October manifesto, however, it is not clear that the message was received quickly by Conservative followers. Indeed, one interpretation of the lack of fit between partisanship and the dominant counter-inflation scale is the absence of Conservative support in the area of strongest preference for spending cuts. Were one able to reconstruct Table 11.5 in 1977, on the assumption that partisans do pick up at least some of their ideas from party rhetoric, one would expect the *SWUT* and *SUWT* categories of the dominant scale to be both more numerous and more Conservative, in response to change in the position of the Conservative Party after February 1974.

In February 1974, the Conservative Party made wage controls a question of industrial relations (in the sense of Figure 11.4) and thereby made counter-inflation policy a question of industrial relations or workers' rights. The Labour Party position adopted in response, stressing the Social Contract and voluntarism in wage constraint, is difficult to place in terms of the dominant scale. In terms of the second scale (see Table 11.5), Labour adopted a position well to the left, either at *SWTU* or *STWU*. Labour's October manifesto stressed that the party had 'stopped printing money to finance unnecessary expenditure', and also that *VAT* had been cut, implying a readiness to cut expenditure rather than increase taxation. Of course, in the summer of 1975, by adopting a long-term policy of wage controls, the Labour Government moved back onto the dominant scale, and has occupied positions WTSU or WSTU ever since. In that way, Labour has come, three years after the October election, to the position of the median voter at the time they were elected. Whether the median position is still there is not known, as shifts in party positions can have altered public opinion. More important is that in 1974, the political parties appear not to have 'seen' or competed with each other over counter-inflation policies along the lines or dimensions used by the electorate. Some of the lack of fit to individual preferences of the dominant joint scale of universalism in effect may in turn reflect the choice of the parties – the Conservative Party in particular – to treat counter-inflation policy as a question of industrial relations, introducing different dimensions into popular appraisal of economic policy.

12

The determinants of economic policy choice

The interpretation of the dominant scale in the last chapter — increasing universally in effect — linked the predominant popular interpretation of counter-inflation policy to questions of social welfare. An earlier chapter gave an account of other economic policy preferences — for the government to reduce inflation rather than unemployment — in similar terms. The determinants of individual electors' positions on this dominant policy scale should therefore relate closely to the determinants of opinions about the desirability of social services. Partisanship will play a role, though the previous chapter makes it clear that partisanship will by no means tell the whole story. Other factors like ideology and a spirit of generosity controlled by changes in personal economic position relate to attitudes about social services and benefits. Moreover, the dominant J-scale did not fit nearly all cases, and this necessitates an initially more general discussion of the background of attitudes towards counter-inflation policies. The expectation is that

1. Economic policy preferences of a 'left-wing' sort — for instance, acceptance of taxation — ought to correlate with other left-wing policy preferences, notably the desire to extend social welfare or improve the condition of the underprivileged. The argument can also be extended to other left-wing attitudes like endorsement of nationalisation of industry.

2. Social leftism, however — the desire to defend the interests of minorities and extend welfare — will be tempered by economic centrality and personal economic deterioration. In particular taxation, which has the most immediate economic effects, will be opposed by those who perceive imminent deterioration in their economic condition.

3. Preference for those policies which Britain has had — taxation and wage controls — should be related to any measure reflecting confidence in or close personal ties to the political system, such as interest in politics or a favourable assessment of Britain's government.

Each of the next three sections present a detailed argument supporting one hypothesised effect, and gives an example of a relationship bearing out the hypothesis. The next part of the chapter retains the arguments of the first part, but gives multivariate analyses of pairwise choices, as well as the scale positions of the dominant (welfarist) J-scale isolated in the last chapter.

Economic and other policy attitudes

Given the centrality of economic policy in contemporary British politics, one would expect attitudes towards alternative economic policies to come to be associated in meaningful patterns in the mass public. However, even casual examination of a correlation matrix among related attitudinal measures makes it apparent that attitudes must be treated either as multidimensional or as containing large random components. Nevertheless, this does not mean that significant associations do not arise, at least where the objects of the attitudes in question are sufficiently familiar and central to the public and sufficiently linked to give rise to realistic expectations of association. Given the evidence linking lower taxation with the Conservative Party, it is realistic to inquire whether hostility to taxation is associated, independent of party, with other attitudes of a 'right-wing' nature. Table 12.1 shows that this is so in at least two instances: a desire for less nationalisation, and a desire to see social services curtailed. These two desires are themselves moderately correlated with each other, though with enough slippage to make it worth treating them as *separate* sorts of 'right-wing' attitudes.[1]

Table 12.1. *Partisanship, taxation and policy attitudes*

Vote in October	More taxation would be	
	Least acceptable	Most acceptable
(*a*) Nationalisation: per cent wanting some nationalised industries to become private companies		
Conservative	42% (292)	31% (51)
Labour	6% (162)	2% (159)
(*b*) Social services: per cent wanting social services cut back		
Conservative	61% (295)	50% (50)
Labour	26% (186)	19% (168)

Source as Table 11.1.

[1] For instance, of those wishing to see social services cut back, 39 per cent want less nationalisation, against 19 per cent wanting less nationalisation in the rest of the sample. There is clearly a relationship between these two sorts of 'right-wing' attitudes, but it is not so close as to make one wish to describe them as the same. It is possible that the average inter-correlation with carefully standardised and well-chosen items might reach the level of 0.4 or even 0.5, but this still seems low given the extraordinary closeness of the items involved. The problem of multidimensionality is vexed, particularly because the presence of error in the data may lead to an appearance of multidimensionality which is in fact exaggerated. There are some ways of determining the 'true' dimensionality of data in the presence of error: see Spence and Graef (1974).

In both cases, independent of party, hostility toward taxation as a counter-inflation policy is closely tied up with 'right-wing' views, whether these lie in the area of economic intervention or social welfare. Thus, favouring denationalisation of industry is 11 percentage points (42 to 31) more common among Conservatives hostile to taxation, and similar relationships hold in the other cases. While the associations are not particularly large, related attitudes show similar relationships, and it appears that attitudes toward alternative economic policies are becoming integrated with broader socio-economic attitudes.

Economic well-being and economic policy attitudes

Chapter 10 discussed the relationship between personal economic well-being and expressions of self-interest and altruism in political attitudes. Counter-inflation policy gives a further instance of the same argument. Unemployment, as argued before, does not affect everyone: in fact, it affects at most a substantial minority, and even among all these the effects may not be severe. Taxation, on the other hand, now affects nearly everyone. Strictly, it affects everyone who buys anything, in one indirect way or another, but even when only income tax is considered, most adults either pay tax or might have to if taxation were increased. Therefore, the judgement that unemployment is an *unacceptable* policy is essentially altruistic, since few making the judgement can expect with any probability to benefit were it accepted. Hostility to taxation can be seen as essentially self-interested, since those disliking taxation would themselves benefit. The people most likely to make an altruistic judgement are those who can afford it, and they in turn will be those who are cushioned from economic stress and hardship, or those who do not see the relevance of economic policy for their economic interests.

The most relevant measure of economic stress in the current economic climate is the experience of one's income falling behind prices. Those who have been falling behind should be much less likely to accept taxation, and those who have been at least keeping up would be more likely to accept taxation, and more likely to be hostile toward increased unemployment. Table 12.2 shows that the data bear out this hypothesis quite well. Of course, as Table 11.1 suggested, partisanship is a powerful pull. Regardless of economic outlook, Labour voters are substantially more likely to find unemployment the least acceptable policy. Nevertheless, within both groups of partisans, the differences attributable to economic well-being are large. Conservatives who have been falling behind are more likely by 50 per cent to 31 per cent to find more taxation the most unacceptable policy. Among Labour voters, a majority of less than two-to-one (51 to 28) against more unemployment among those falling behind becomes a majority of three-to-one (59 to 20) among those keeping up. While economic distress is not a precondition for hostility to taxation – and economic insulation not a precondition for hostility to unemployment – it is clear that a strong relationship exists. Economic stress produces responses of less generosity, and is

Table 12.2. *Partisanship, economic well-being, and counter-inflation policies*

	Conservative voters		Labour voters	
Least acceptable policy would be	Income fell behind	Income kept up or up by more	Income fell behind	Income kept up or up by more
More taxation	50	39	28	20
More unemployment	31	45	51	59
Other	19	16	21	21
Total	100%	100%	100%	100%
(base)	(351)	(317)	(376)	(392)

Source as Table 11.1.

closely linked with partisanship in determining people's preferences among counter-inflation policies. As argued before, hostility toward unemployment is often an attitude of the economically comfortable.

System evaluation and economic policy attitudes

Chapter 3 showed that in Britain in recent years, people's expectations about whether times were good or bad were very closely linked, or practically determined by, their expectations about the future course and state of the British economy. Just as people may judge the state of their economic system by its inflation rate, people's views on counter-inflation policies are likely to affect and be affected by their more general ties to and assessment of the political system. Where successive governments have done what people want to see done about inflation, popular overall evaluation of the political system becomes more positive. Where the government have not done what people want — or have done what they do not want — people become more negative. Correspondingly, when a counter-inflation policy has failed, negative feelings about the political system produce negative feelings about the policy.

The British economy continued to inflate through 1974, and indeed inflation was recognised as a serious problem for years before. Therefore, it can be argued that any counter-inflation policies used by governments in the years before 1974 would generally be seen to have *failed* to cure inflation. Therefore, it ought to be the case that whatever policies a person felt were *desirable* would be associated with *positive* judgements about the running of the country *if* those policies were actually *used* in Britain. Unfortunately, there are no data about what Britain's counter-inflation policies were perceived as being, but it seems safe to say that everyone was aware that wage controls had been used, on and off, for nearly a decade, without too much success, but that there were other countries which did not have wage controls.[2] A first hypothesis is that, independent of partisanship,

[2] There is on the other hand an NOP poll which suggests that in early 1975 while an overwhelming majority of men had heard of the Social Contract, among women only half

liking wage controls ought to be associated with the view that Britain is governed *well*. Taxation is not quite so clear. The British probably consider themselves heavily taxed, and many cite heavy taxation as a reason for Britain's poor economic performance. On the other hand, there are many European countries with higher rates of indirect taxes, particularly value added tax, and some with higher rates of direct income tax. On the other hand, some visible countries like the United States have much lower rates of income tax. Furthermore, as before, there is evidence that the public link the Labour Party with higher taxation. In this case, after October 1974, it ought to be the case that *liking taxation* as a policy for curbing inflation would be associated with the view that Britain was relatively *well*-governed. The reverse ought to be true with cuts in spending, not because spending was never cut: particularly in the late 1960s spending was curbed on a number of occasions as part of the government's deflationary measures. On the other hand, in the 1970s government indebtedness, the balance of payments deficit, and the money supply in general all grew rapidly, and it is unlikely that anyone in 1974 would have held the view that a major feature of British anti-inflationary policy had been continuing cutbacks in government spending. Therefore, *support* for *cuts* in spending ought to be associated with the view that Britain is relatively *badly* governed. The same ought to be true of unemployment, given that British governments have repeatedly denied that they were using more unemployment as a cure for inflation. On the other hand, unemployment has risen rapidly in Britain (even relative to other countries) and it might be that people believe that high unemployment has become a characteristic of the British situation in times of economic difficulty. Even so, unemployment is lower in Britain than in, say, the United States, and so it ought to be the case that *wanting more unemployment* as a cure for inflation would lead people (in the absence of more unemployment) to believe that Britain was *badly* governed.

Table 12.3 suggests that these expectations are fairly well borne out. If it were replicated within groups of partisans, it would show that the average level of seeing Britain as governed well was a few percentage points higher on the Labour side (of course, since their party was governing) and that all the relationships were larger on the Labour side, but, regardless of party, the relationships are in the same direction. While 44 per cent of those who would find more taxation the most acceptable means of dealing with inflation regard Britain as governed relatively well, only 27 per cent do so of those who see taxation as the worst alternative. (The respective proportions are 52 per cent and 31 per cent among Labour voters.) Similarly, 33 per cent of those most in favour of wage controls, but only 27 per cent of those most against them, regard Britain as well governed.

claimed to have heard of it (*NOP Political Bulletin*, April 1975). The lack of familiarity with a specific term does not indicate that people were generally unaware that wage freezes and controls had existed. The NOP study also shows that many people who claimed to have heard of the Social Contract did not know what it meant. This echoes earlier findings: for instance, that in 1969 while most people claimed to have heard of the phrase 'productivity agreement' very few had any real grasp of what one was. On this point see Behrend (1971a).

Table 12.3. *Counter-inflation policies and system evaluation*

	Per cent who feel that Britain is governed relatively well of those believing policy to be	
Policy	Least acceptable	Most acceptable
More taxation	27% (745)	44% (312)
Strict wage controls	27% (167)	33% (1,405)
More unemployment	40% (981)	39% (57)
Cuts in spending	37% (291)	28% (380)

Source as Table 11.1.

The experience of wage controls and taxation, combined with their perceived undesirability as counter-inflationary policies, appears to have made them a factor in the most general assessment people make of the quality of their government. The same is also true of cuts in spending: because these appear to have been avoided, those who want spending cuts least are *more* likely to regard Britain as well-governed. Only in the case of unemployment does no relationship appear: this could be affected both by the small numbers who regard inflation as the most desirable policy and by the possibility that many people regard Britain as a country where high unemployment has been and continues to be tried as a counter-inflation policy. Indeed, the magnitude of some of the relationships suggests the importance people attach to the policy areas involved in fighting inflation and is a further reflection of the extent to which judgements of inflation and economic policy have come to be central to contemporary British politics.

Counter-inflation policy preferences

The three previous sections have presented supporting evidence for three central hypotheses about the determinants of counter-inflation policy preferences in the public. In each case, numerous other examples of essentially the same relationship could have been given. Conservative voters who believe the government should reduce poverty are far more hostile to spending cuts, and far more receptive to taxation than other Conservatives. Among Labour voters, those expecting the economy to get worse, or expecting high rates of inflation are substantially more hostile to taxation and wage controls, and more receptive to unemployment and spending cuts, than are their more optimistic fellows. The hostility of the self-employed to taxation and more spending is marked.[3] While in the case

[3] As a theme in the imagery of the parties, the question of promoting initiative as opposed to laziness (as a consequence of welfare policies) is raised by about eight per cent of

of system evaluation the status of cause and effect is much less clear, the analysis of general feelings about the running of the country can be extended to other related areas like interest in politics and dissatisfaction with contemporary standards and values.

There is an extra problem involved in dealing with the complicated choices among alternative means of dealing with inflation. An advantage of the preceding analysis is simplicity: the disadvantage is that it fails to take account of the trade-offs inherent in these policy choices. Principally, it fails to take account of the fact that what makes a person warm toward wage controls relative to, say, unemployment, may make him cool toward wage controls relative to taxation. Strictly, electors' preferences between all possible pairs of alternatives should be analysed, but this would be space-consuming, and an analysis of positions on the dominant joint scale contains most of the same information. To explain why someone is closer to the taxation end of the scale than the unemployment end is similar to explaining a preference for taxation. The approach is less good for explaining preferences for one alternative over another close to it on the scale.

As a check on this, the analysis of pairwise preferences was carried out. Fortunately, it does not add a great deal to the analysis of scale positions, and most of the effects are in the expected direction. Some interesting findings do emerge: for instance, those with any further education are substantially more likely to prefer taxation to spending cuts, and among the educated, the preference for taxation is even more marked among those working in the public sector, who presumably perceive accurately that serious spending cuts must reduce public employment. (This 'instrumental' hostility to spending cuts arises frequently.) Most of the effects are nevertheless reflections of the general arguments put forward in the preceding sections. Table 12.4 summarises an AID analysis of positions on the dominant J-scale. One must extrapolate from this analysis to what might have been the case had the dominant scale been found to underlie the attitudes of the whole sample. Scale positions are given metric values according to the method of Abelson and Tukey (1970), which guarantees a maximum correlation in the presence of error with the 'real' scale values. Thus, the alternative 'more taxation' gets a value of -0.870, wage controls 0.050, spending cuts 0.270, and unemployment 0.550. These coordinates preserve the metric implication that the distance $\overline{TW}$ should be greater than $\overline{SU}$. Midpoints can be calculated directly from the location of individual alternatives: thus the TW midpoint is $(-0.87 + 0.05)/2$ or -0.410. The midpoints are shown in Figure 11.3. Then, each rank ordering of preferences can be given a value equal to the middle of the

respondents. This is similar to the frequency with which a specific policy like taxation is raised, though of course far less common than the raising of all economic matters. (The eight per cent includes both major parties and both positive and negative feelings.) The theme is brought up predominantly by people with a Conservative or Liberal party identification, who are themselves actively engaged in a career (aged 30 to 55). In this group something like 17 per cent mention the theme of initiative; if one isolates further within this group those who are self-employed, the frequency of occurrence rises to 23 per cent. The question of spending promoting lack of initiative appears to be a feature of considerable importance in the party imagery of the actively self-employed.

Table 12.4. AID analysis of dominant J-scale positions for counter-inflation policy attitudes

For wage controls and taxation ←------

For spending cuts and unemployment ------→

Whole sample
−0.136
(1,349)

- Britain governed relatively well
  −0.200
  (449)

  - More/same social services
    −0.238
    (274)
    - Further education
      −0.302
      (112)
      → Economy will get worse* ------→
    - No further education
      −0.194
      (162)

  - Cut back social services
    −0.141
    (175)
    → Income has fallen behind* ------→

- Britain governed average/worse
  −0.103
  (900)

  - More/same social services
    −0.137
    (535)
    - Further education
      −0.203
      (202)
      → expect low inflation or trade union member or Labour voter* ------→
    - No further education
      −0.097
      (333)
      - Income has kept up
        −0.139
        (142)
      - Income fell behind
        −0.067
        (191)

  - Cut back social services
    −0.054
    (365)
    - Working class (C2/D)
      −0.088
      (164)
    - Middle class (A/B/C1a/C1b)
      −0.026
      (201)
      → Private sector* ------→
        → Economy will get worse* ------→

η^2 (explained variance) = 0.13
*Split significant, group size <100.
Source as Table 11.1.

region containing it. Thus, for the ordering *WTSU*, one arrives at the value half-way between *TW* and *TS*, or $(-0.410 + -0.310)/2$ or -0.355. These final scale values (corresponding to *I*-scales, preference orders, or ideal points on the dominant *J*-scale for each respondent) are used to calculate average values for sub-groups of the sample.

The tree of Table 12.4 itself is quite straightforward. The average value for the whole sample (1,349 cases fitting the dominant *J*-scale) is -0.136, just to the right (more unemployment) of the *TU* midpoint in Figure 11.3. Every split that results in a group with a more positive mean indicates increased receptivity toward unemployment: more negative means indicate increased receptivity to taxation. In fact, the first split is according to how well people feel Britain is governed: those who feel it to be governed relatively well have a scale value of -0.200 (to the left of the *TU* midpoint) and the rest have a scale value of -0.103, to the right of the *TU* midpoint. Being receptive to taxation and wage controls as remedies for inflation goes hand-in-hand with general approval of Britain's government: these are, as before, the remedies which were actually in use at the time. Within the group who feel the country is governed relatively well, the next split is according to beliefs about the desirability of extended social services: those who feel that services should at least stay as they are, or grow, lie even closer to the increased taxation end of the scale. Within this group, those with some further education are even more pro-taxation, and in fact lie to the left of the *TS* midpoint, so that their average preference order is *WTSU* (see Figure 11.3). This system-approving, pro-welfare, highly-educated group can be further split, according to optimism about the future of Britain's economy, though the resulting groups are numerically small. In keeping with the general drift of the argument that economic well-being increases generosity or altruism, notice that the impact of economic pessimism at this point is to render people more receptive to increased unemployment, and more hostile to taxation. Both lack of further education and desire to cut back social services increase hostility to taxation and receptivity to increased unemployment and cuts in spending: those who feel Britain is governed well but are opposed to social services and benefits at even their present level have an average counter-inflation policy scale position which is typical of that of the population as a whole. In this group again a further split can be made according to views of personal economic well-being: while the resulting groups are small, the effect is again the one expected, namely, that economic stress increases opposition to taxation.

In the case of this analysis – and this is quite fortuitous, given the nature of the AID procedure – the other half of the tree is remarkably similar, and many of the effects appear quite symmetric. Among those who feel that Britain's government is at best average, the split is according to attitude toward social services, again with pro-welfare people more receptive to increased taxation. Among the group which is more in favour of social services, the next split is again according to further education, and both the resulting groups can be further split according to personal economic perception. All these splits are in the direction expected. Among those opposed to social services, the next split is according to social class of the household, with those in middle-class households being most opposed to taxation. Within this system-negative, anti-welfare, middle-class group, there is a further group consisting of those in the private sector (those in the public sector being more hostile to unemployment and spending cuts) with pessimistic expectations about the economy which is the most 'right-wing' of all: this group, amounting to about six per cent of the eligible sample, is the most receptive to cuts in spending and unemployment, and the most hostile to taxation of any group of any real size isolated by the analysis.

The AID analysis can be summarised as follows. The first split — indicating the closest correlate of scale positions — is according to a general measure of approval of the political system, which in the present context is taken to be heavily influenced by recent experience of counter-inflation policies. That is, people who are warm toward taxation and wage controls as remedies for in-flation are also warm toward the governing of Britain since, in terms of counter-inflation policy up to 1974, the governing of Britain consisted of wage controls and taxation. Regardless of one's views on that question, the next split is accord-ing to an ideological view of social services and benefits, which is interpreted as reflecting a question of universality. Those who favour extensive social services and benefits are also most in favour of those counter-inflation policies — wage controls and taxation — which are most universal in applicability. Once these splits are made, the next divisions are in terms of education and social class, and the final divisions are in terms of economic perceptions: economic stress appears to play a role, though a small one, in the analysis of attitudes toward counter-inflation policies.

Figure 11.3 gives a graphical representation of these results by locating various groups on the dominant J-scale. The most 'right-wing' group identified in Table 12.4 is shown, comprising the six per cent of the electorate whose preferences fit the dominant 'welfarist' J-scale, who are negative toward the quality of British government, in favour of reducing social services, middle class, not employed in the public sector, and pessimistic about the future of the British economy. This group is located squarely in the middle of the preference order $WSUT$, indicating that while they are prepared to see wage controls first, they see spending cuts as next best, then unemployment, and increased taxation worst of all. Because the attitudes to the right of this group were relatively uncommon, at least in late 1974, there isn't a group of any size that actually has an average scale position with spending cuts first. Of course, the prominence given to spending cuts in inter-party debate in and after 1976 may well have altered this.

The eight per cent or so of the eligible sample shown at the extreme left of Table 12.4 is also represented here: their average scale value of -0.302 puts them just to the left of the TS midpoint and therefore implies an average preference order of $WTSU$. In fact, a number of variables can be employed to isolate groups even further to the left, once warmth toward the British government and support for the welfare state are established: further education combines with economic confidence and faith in voluntary wage policies (non-intervention in the labour market again) to produce attitudes even more in favour of increased taxation and hostile toward increased unemployment. The most 'left-wing' group of all, however, amounting to just under two per cent of the eligible sample, are those who believe Britain is governed well, support social services, have 'a great deal' of interest in politics, and consider the issue of prices to be 'not very important'. This group have an average scale value of -0.430, placing their average position well into the area of the J-scale which folds to a preference order of *TWSU*.

Clearly – this follows from Table 11.5 – any group at this end of the J-scale will be largely composed of Labour voters, just as any group very far to the other end will be more largely Conservative. Nevertheless, this scale does not maximise the correlation with partisanship, and indeed it is made clear in Figure 11.3 that the average Labour and Conservative voters are not located all that far apart with respect to this joint scale. Unfortunately, there are no data to allow us to compare the positions of these groups of voters with their perceptions of the positions of the parties, though Table 11.3 does suggest that what limited data there are imply a difference between parties similar to the difference between their supporters. However, the importance of this analysis is that it establishes an attitudinal underpinning for electors' different choices with respect to counter-inflation policy. In so doing, it establishes the basis for a position model of economic management as a political issue, by showing that very different counter-inflation policy preferences are themselves linked to broader concerns about politics, and could serve as the basis for an evaluation of the political parties' capabilities with respect to macroeconomic policy.

Summary and conclusions

This chapter concluded the investigation into a possible position model of economic effects by showing that an important attitude toward economic policy – preference among competing alternative policies to curb inflation – was closely linked, not only with partisanship, but also with other relevant attitudes. Of particular importance were attitudes which could be described as relating to two sorts of 'left–right' dimensions: support for government intervention in the economy and industry, and support for more social services and benefits. It also showed that preferences were closely related to people's own economic position and their perception of that economic position: the correlation between employment in the public sector and hostility toward cuts in government spending and increased unemployment, and between perceived economic deterioration and hostility to increased taxation are good examples of this. Moreover, it showed that perceptions of economic policy carried over into appraisal of the general political system: those who approved of taxation and wage controls were more likely to have closer ties to the political system and to express more confidence in it, perhaps because taxation and wage controls were seen as an important part of the governing of Britain which they were evaluating positively.

While, through the AID analysis of positions on the dominant *J*-scale isolated in the previous chapter, the attitudinal basis of counter-inflation policy preferences could be made clear, the relationship between partisanship and these preferences was not large. This in turn arises because there are really two alternative perceptual orderings employed by the electorate when it comes to counter-inflation policy. One is counter-inflation policy as it relates to industrial relations and the question of the power and rights of unions and workers. The other is counter-inflation as an instance of the general issue of social welfare benefits and universality in application of policy. The party system, at least as it bears on counter-inflation policy, is a compromise between these two orderings, and thus the attitudinal discriminants discussed are much more powerful than partisanship alone.

Unfortunately, the one thing which it is impossible to do is tie together economic trends, preferences among alternative counter-inflation policies, perceptions of government policy, and voting behaviour, for there are no data enabling models to be tested. This critical test of a position model of economic effects — which would show that general evaluations of economic performance are based on differing views about questions of economic goals and the means to achieve them — must await replication of these questions with data on voting subsequent to at least one point at which preferences were known. Nevertheless, the number of relationships described, which link system appraisal, personal economic well-being, and general ideological attitudes to specific preferences for counter-inflation policies, make it clear that the attitudinal basis for such a position model of economic effects does exist.

PART IV

The politics of economic decline

13

The decline of instrumental voting

In Britain, there has long been known to be a connection between personal economic condition and partisan political considerations. Independent of social class, support for the incumbent party was regularly higher among those believing that they had become better off during its time in office (Butler and Stokes, 1969). Similarly, the swing toward Labour in 1966, for instance, was highest among those who felt that the Labour years since 1964 had seen an upward reversal of their previously deteriorating personal economic condition. Moreover, Butler and Stokes show that the appropriate partisan beliefs exist about the likely effects of the election of one or another party on people's personal fortunes. That is, most people appear to believe that the election of one party would aid them economically while the election of the other would (relatively) harm them, though a substantial minority — 40 per cent in 1966 — believe that there will be no change in their economic condition regardless of which party forms the government. It is also the case that there is considerable partisan bias in the reporting of changes in personal economic condition, which reduces some of the correlation between perceived change of condition and vote defection to a tautology.[1]

Similarly, American survey research has established the existence of some connection between economic outlook and voting. The authors of *The American Voter* (Campbell et al., 1960) note a small but significant correlation between economic outlook and vote for President in 1956, even independent of other partisan predispositions. The ambiguity in their results comes from the fact that in this case economic outlook is itself heavily correlated with partisan predispositions, as the data are from a post-election survey, and their measure of economic outlook is heavily weighted toward expectations, including expectations of general 'good times' for the country. Thus, since their Republican identifiers are predominantly optimistic (and Democratic identifiers pessimistic) the correlation amounts to showing that Republican identifiers who have more pessimistic expectations are somewhat more likely to have stayed home on election day than are the more optimistic Republicans. More recent research emphasises their point.

[1] Because class differences in perceptions of economic well-being are small compared to inter-party differences (before 1974), there is always the usual risk (in explanatory terms) that saying that one is worse off is simply a form of abuse directed at an incumbent party one has decided to desert for other reasons.

According to this model, American electors appear to respond to perceived changes in the overall direction of the economy in cases where their congressional vote is at variance with their traditional party loyalty (Ben-Gera, 1977). Why it is changes in the national rather than the personal economy which predict voting 'defection' is not entirely clear, though the explanation with the greatest mileage in it is probably that American electors are particularly prone to see changes in their own personal economic condition as resulting from causes other than national politics (Katona, Strumpel and Zahn, 1971).

In spite of the avowed importance of economic problems in the eyes of the electorate, and in spite of all the evidence about the connection between the economy and political behaviour presented in earlier chapters, there is a paradoxical sense in which the election of February 1974 meant *less* to the electorate on economic grounds than any of the three elections preceding it. Throughout the 1960s it was clear that, among other reasons for having attachments to one party or another, substantial portions of the electorate felt that their personal economic fortunes were intimately tied up with the incumbency of one or the other of the major parties. In 1974, however, economic expectations appeared to have unprecedentedly little to do with partisanship: in particular Labour voters appear to have supported their party without much hope of immediate personal betterment, and Conservative voters as well were less likely to believe that a change of government would mean a change of personal economic fortunes. Moreover, there was little evidence of partisan differences in expectations of inflation in 1974 (Chapter 4).

This and the next chapter return to the level of the individual elector. Part II was concerned largely with relationships at some aggregate level, with the perceptual processes linking movements in the national economy with broad swings of public opinion. These chapters are less concerned with the effects of economic trends. Instead, they look at the relationships between partisanship, political attitudes and beliefs, and individual perceptions and expectations of economic improvement and decline. In doing so, they return to many points raised in earlier chapters, including the general discussion of 'instrumental' voting raised in Chapter 1, the connection between economic condition and the social welfare aspect of political ideology discussed in Chapter 11, and the difficult question of locating the impact of partisanship on economic expectations mentioned in Chapter 5.

This chapter develops two related themes. It begins by recalling the evidence about an 'instrumental' aspect of voting, the evidence recording a link between people's choice of a party and their beliefs about its effect on their personal well-being. The evidence is brought forward to 1974, and the effects of incumbency and popular beliefs about the effectiveness of the government on this instrumental attachment to parties are discussed. Since the evidence points to a dramatic *decline* in instrumental voting between 1966 and 1974, the second part of the chapter will deal with the role of economic conditions in sustaining partisanship. In particular, it reveals sharp falls in the partisan attachment of those supporters of the incumbent government whose initial hopes for economic improvement were not fulfilled, as compared with those partisans whose hopes were either fulfilled or even exceeded. Because of the evidence that between 1966 and 1970 Labour partisanship weakened appreciably more among those whose high hopes for becoming better off in 1966 had not been fulfilled by 1970, the next chapter continues this theme with an investigation of the dynamics of partisan dealignment. This investigation points to the role of individual economic deterioration in producing ideological or attitudinal shifts of considerable importance for British electoral politics and the maintenance of a two-party system.

The rise and fall of instrumental voting 1964—74

The question of instrumental voting arises out of the tradition of rational choice theory in electoral studies. In a recent and stimulating study, Harrop (1977) establishes a distinction between 'affective' and 'instrumental' attachment to parties in an attempt to contrast the strength of the two forms of attachment in modern British electoral behaviour. His approach is to label as 'instrumental' the belief that a particular party will be best at dealing with the problem seen (unprompted) by the individual as most important among those facing the country at the time. Thus, if an elector believes that unemployment is the most important problem facing the country, and that Labour is best at dealing with unemployment, he is said to have an instrumental attachment to the Labour Party. (Instrumental attachment is in fact summed over up to three problems mentioned.) For the 'affective' orientation, described as the 'valence of an elector's feelings . . . the extent to which he likes or dislikes the party', Harrop proposes using the difference between 'thermometer' rankings given to each of the major parties. Thus, having asked survey respondents to give each party a score out of 100 reflecting how 'warm' they felt about the party, the difference between scores for the major parties is taken to reflect the balance of affect or liking that the elector has for the parties.

Harrop then employs the 1969 and 1970 levels of these two measures (and changes in each between 1969 and 1970) to predict both turnout and voting choice and change in those years. In general his results show that the importance of the affective orientation is greater than that of the instrumental orientation. In particular, increased probability of turnout is predicted by increased difference between the parties in affective, but not instrumental, terms. Similarly, where there is a disagreement between the implications of the two orientations (that is, an elector affectively favours one party and instrumentally favours the other) the affective orientation is the better predictor of ultimate voting choice. These conclusions are well confirmed by the data, and Harrop takes them to support the 'psychological' approach of the Michigan school against the 'rational choice' approaches of Downs and others.

There is no real quarrel with Harrop's specific conclusions, or with the methods he employs to reach them. There may be some doubt, however, about whether his conclusions have the broader theoretical significance he assigns them: whether, in fact, he has tested the relative strengths of the 'Michigan' and 'rational' approaches. Consider first the measure of instrumental orientation. The term implies that the party is seen as an 'instrument' of attaining some end. Downs and his followers measure this instrumental value of the parties in terms of differential utility flows to the individual under alternative possible governments. Utility does not mean money, or money-substitutable commodities: peace and war have distinct values which fit the framework of this approach. To this extent Harrop's approach of looking at parties' perceived abilities in dealing with what people identify as the most important problem does provide an approximation of utility flows. Most of the things identified as most important problems in 1969 – cost of living, taxes, housing, pensions, strikes – sound like the sort of policies which have a direct effect on how well off the respondent can expect to be under one or another of the parties.

On the other hand, there is a sense in which the format of asking for spontaneous identification of the most important problem may discourage reference directly to utility flows. If asked for the most important problem facing the country, 'how well off I am' is an improbable answer. In 1974, 'raising everybody's standard of living' came up far more often as a prompted choice for the most important aim of government (29 per cent) than did all references to standard of living in open-ended questions about good and bad points of the parties or results of the election (on average, about seven per cent).[2] To start from an open-ended question about the country's problems forces people to think in *policy* terms of those things which affect their well-being, and may result in many cases in missing – owing to the difficulty of the task – the simple answer to the question of under which party the respondent believes he would be better off. In this connection, it is important to note the enormous partisan bias in response to the open-ended question Harrop uses: *more than twice* as many respondents have a pro-Conservative instrumental orientation (on Harrop's criteria) as pro-Labour, though in terms of vote the electorate was more or less split between the two parties.

The explanation of this is that large numbers of Labour voters are instrumentally 'neutral', as they simply did not reply to the open-ended question about important problems. This could, of course, only emphasise Harrop's point about the lack of importance of the instrumental orientation, or it could reflect an inter-party difference (in that the instrumental orientation is more important to Conservatives, while Labour voters have a different orientation), or it could be a reflection of something special about the 1970 election, or it could simply be

---

[2] In the closed-ended question, people were asked which of six things – promotion of private enterprise, maintaining individual liberty, maintaining law and order, greater equality, protecting the weakest and worst-off, or raising everyone's standard of living – was the most important fundamental aim of any government. The open-ended questions are those shown in Figure 3.2.

response bias owing to the difficulty of the initial question. The cure, discussed below, is to measure instrumentalism (as a more precise reflection of utility flows anyway) by using replies to the question of under which party the respondent feels or expects to be better off.

It is also by no means clear that Harrop's affective orientation measure is a good proxy for what it claims to represent. *The American Voter* argument about the importance of a sense of *identification* with parties (or a sense of belonging) is broader than the question of simply whether people like a party. The authors of *The American Voter* repeatedly stress the importance of policy attitude components in the eventual electoral decision as well as the maintenance of partisan identification, and are at pains to point out the *separate* cognitive and affective aspects of these matters. The question they raise is of the importance of policy-related attitudes *compared* to the evaluation of candidates, group references, domestic and foreign issues, and the parties' records.

Harrop's question is not quite the same. His measure of affect is a summary measure, equivalent (as he says) to asking which party people like better. As such, it can be treated as a weighted (individually) sum of *all* affective components of electoral decision. Harrop's test is then to ask which is the best predictor of vote of *overall* relative liking of the parties or *policy-related* liking of the parties. (In terms of *The American Voter* presentation, it is like asking whether two of the six components of electoral decision are better predictors of vote than are all six taken together. For a discussion of this general problem see Budge and Farlie, 1977, especially Chapter 10.) With regard to thermometer ratings, it has been shown elsewhere that (at least in 1974) *major* party supporters almost never (within the margin of sampling error) give the highest score on this sort of question to some party other than the one for which they vote (Alt, Crewe and Särlvik, 1977). This confirms the choice of thermometer rankings as a measure of which party is liked best. It has also been suggested that, in terms of a wide variety of possible sources of relative evaluation of the parties, style and performance are two general organising principles of evaluation. That is, the things people like and dislike about political parties range from the extremely stylistic – how they speak and dress, whether they appear arrogant – to questions of precise policy-related performance in office (Alt, Särlvik and Crewe, 1976a).

It may well be that aspects of style are, at least at times, as or more important than policies in determining vote choice. This may have been the question Harrop meant to test, for it is one way of asking whether instrumental or non-instrumental orientations are more important in electoral choice. That would have been a good question, though difficult to answer in terms of available evidence. To parallel his approach on instrumentalism, he would have had to elicit the most important *non-policy* aspect of politics, and then ascertain which party was seen as better, and then compare the magnitudes of effects derived in this way with those derived from the handling of important problems. With Harrop's approach, instrumental reasons for liking a party could *at most exhaust* the reasons for liking a party, in which case the two measures proposed by Harrop would, barring measurement error, perform equally well. The fact that the instrumental measure performs less well only reflects the fact that there are indeed some other reasons for choosing a party than the manifest policy content of its past or expected times in office.

On the other hand, Harrop's paper raises a number of interesting questions which can be further looked into. Timeless questions of the instrumental value of voting sometimes appear to imply that this value does not change. Instead of asking whether instrumental attachments are more or less important than some other forms of attachment to parties, it is worth seeing whether there is any reason to believe that instrumental attachments have become more or less important over time.

In the most purely 'instrumental' system, people would see the political parties solely as instruments of their own well-being. If benefits really were distributed along lines of party support, the supporters of the government would all become better off and expect to continue becoming better off if the government remained in power, while supporters of the opposition would become worse off, and would expect that to continue were the government to remain in office. If an election were held, and the government for some reason were defeated and the other party took over, then the electorate would be distributed as in Table 13.1. All supporters of the previous government would now have negative expectations, but positive perceptions of the past, while the opposite would be true of all supporters of the new government.

There is an air of unreality about Table 13.1. Clearly, benefits are not distributed along partisan — or even class — lines with sufficient differentiation to guarantee the deprivation of all of one group and the assistance of all of another, even if there are differences between groups under the incumbency of one or another party. Similarly, there is sufficient scope for many to become better or worse off through their own efforts, regardless of which party is in power. Nevertheless, Table 13.1 presents the opportunity for estimating the instrumental value of voting for one party or the other at various times, for one can see whether there

Table 13.1. *Change of government in a purely instrumental electoral system*

Perception of past well-being is	Expectation of well-being in future is	
	Better off	Worse off
Better off		All supporters of the *previous* government
Worse off	All supporters of the *new* government	

is any tendency at all for the electorate to align itself along these lines, and, if so, how pronounced the tendency is.

One can take as a measure of the *instrumental gap* between the parties at any time the proportions of the electorate behaving as if politics were in reality like the suggestion made in Table 13.1. For instance, consider 1966, when Labour were re-elected after a short period in office. If Britain were a purely instrumental system, all 1966 Labour voters would say they had become better off and would expect to become still better off; all Conservatives would say the opposite. Now of course a number of people don't see their prosperity as changing, and similarly not everyone votes for one of these two parties, but among those meeting both the criteria for this notion of instrumental voting, the distribution is as shown in Table 13.2. Clearly, there is something in the idea of an instrumental gap between parties: Conservatives are by about two to one more likely to say they have and expect to become worse off than better off, while for Labour the opposite is true, save that for expectations the odds rise to about four to one. One can arrive at an estimate of the instrumental gap between the parties by adding together the frequencies in Table 13.2 *consistent* with an instrumental party politics and subtracting the frequencies *inconsistent* with it (and get a ratio by dividing by the total number involved), thus:

$$GAP = \frac{211 - 118 + 193 - 107 + 281 - 71 + 187 - 89}{211 + 118 + 193 + 107 + 281 + 71 + 187 + 89} = \frac{487}{1,257} = 0.39.$$

This estimate of an instrumental gap is a system-level characteristic; it would take the value 1.0 if everyone had the appropriate instrumental attitudes, 0.0 if there were no differences between groups of partisans in their perceptions and expectations of well-being, and negative if partisans actually tended to believe that the other party would make them better off.[3]

Table 13.2. *Instrumentalism in Britain 1966*

	Vote in 1966 was:	
	Labour	Conservative
Perception of past well-being is		
Better off	211	107
Worse off	118	193
Expectation of future well-being is		
Better off	281	89
Worse off	71	187

Source: Figures are unweighted frequency counts from the Butler–Stokes 1966 cross-section sample.

[3] Using this expression for a divisor gives a range of −1 to +1 most readily. Strictly, the divisor could also be all major party voters, or all voters, or the whole electorate, in which case all values of the instrumental gap will be reduced by the frequency of replies of per-

Now while the value of the instrumental gap between parties does not say anything directly about the relative importance of instrumental motivations in voting, it does say something about the impact of considerations of well-being on the electorate as a whole. In other words, when the gap is small, people must see that economic well-being is little affected by which of the two parties takes office; when the gap is large, considerations of well-being appear to produce larger partisan divisions in the electorate. Insofar as considerations of well-being measure the general sense of instrumental attachments, the gap between parties measures the fluctuation over time of the extent of an instrumental electoral politics.

As Table 13.3 shows, the extent of that fluctuation over time is considerable. The instrumental gap between the major parties in 1964, the first election for which this calculation can be made, is 0.27. It rises, as above, to 0.39 in 1966, a level not reached since or likely to be reached again soon. In 1970 the instrumental gap drops back to 0.29, and in February 1974 it falls to a new low of 0.22. Absence of strictly comparable question formats bedevil further trend analysis at this time, but it is probable that the instrumental gap fell further still in October 1974. Since the instrumental gap as defined here is one means of measuring the instrumental value of voting for one major party or the other, it is clear that this instrumental value, taken across the electorate, was more or less halved between 1966 and 1974.

Table 13.3. *The instrumental gap in Britain 1964–74*

Election	Conservative and Labour voters	Conservative and Labour voters, expectations only	New incumbents' supporters, expectations and perceptions	New incumbents' supporters, expectations only
1964	0.27	0.37	0.46	0.77
1966	0.39	0.50	0.44	0.60
1970	0.29	0.32	0.42	0.65
February 1974 (panel)	0.22	0.30	0.12	0.29
February 1974	0.07*			
October 1974	0.05*			

*Cross-section sample data, questions not comparable.
Note: 'Incumbents' means the newly-incumbent party after an election.

sonal well-being remaining the same, people voting Liberal or not voting, and so on. One could, by dividing by the largest defensible divisor, reduce the instrumental gap in 1966 to something more on the order of 0.15, but this would leave the trend analysis unaffected. For comparative analysis with other countries, some different standardisation might be desirable.

The remaining columns of table 13.3 tell an interesting story about what happened over a decade to the instrumental value of voting in Britain. The second column of the table shows that 'instrumentalism' is greater when only *expectations* are considered: the instrumental gap between the expectations of partisans reaches a high of 0.5 in 1966 and falls to 0.3 in 1974. In fact, the absence of partisan bias in perceptions of well-being under the previous administration is marked both in 1964 and 1974: in neither case were voters for the newly-incumbent Labour Party especially likely to feel that they had become worse off under the previous Conservative Government, and indeed in February 1974 as many Labour voters felt they had become better off as worse off. The instrumental gap was reduced further in 1964 by the positive *expectations* of Conservative voters, and this was the case among Labour voters in 1970 as well. The enormous growth of pessimism about personal economic well-being among Conservatives after the 1966 election (compared with 1964) is at the root of the increased 'instrumentalism' of that election.

Perhaps because of a political focus on growth, instrumentalism up to 1970 is greater among supporters of the party which has won the election: this only shows that supporters of the winning party are relatively more likely to believe that their party's victory will make them better off than are supporters of the losers to believe that they will now become worse off. Indeed, the instrumentalism of the new incumbents' supporters holds at a fairly steady level until 1970, and then drops remarkably among Labour voters in 1974. This is in complete contrast to the recent past: it appears that Labour supporters in 1974 had little instrumental reason for supporting their party. In other words, when looking at the connection between personal well-being (even solely in terms of expectations, as in the final column of Table 13.3) and vote, Labour's supporters in February 1974 were unprecedentedly unlikely to believe that their personal well-being was particularly affected by the change of government. For the first time in a decade, a party was elected whose supporters neither felt particularly badly off under the previous administration (though they opposed it), nor expected particularly strongly to become better off under their own new administration.

To see how this came about, consider Table 13.4, which shows values of the 'instrumental gap' in 1970 and 1974, calculated within groups separated by their beliefs about the economic effectiveness of the government. If one leaves aside the question of different groups of partisans for a moment, Table 13.4 shows that in both 1970 and 1974, those who believed that a government could affect rising prices in some way were more 'instrumental' in their orientation: that is, more likely to see their personal well-being as linked to their choice of party. The differences are modest: 0.32 against 0.24 in 1970 and 0.22 against 0.18 in 1974. The differences are consistent with the common sense view that if you believe prices to be within the control of the government, it is more likely that you will believe that the party forming the government is relevant to how well off you are. Recall in this context the evidence in Chapter 5 that over time between 1970 and 1974, the proportions saying they felt better off were consider-

Table 13.4. *Instrumentalism and government competence*

Election	Voted Conservative Government is:		Voted Labour Government is:		Combined Government is:	
	Effective	Not effective	Effective	Not effective	Effective	Not effective
1970	0.45 (497)	0.35 (204)	0.11 (307)	0.17 (298)	0.32 (804)	0.24 (502)
February 1974	0.14 (51)	0.28 (391)	0.25 (173)	0.02 (260)	0.22 (224)	0.18 (651)

Note: Source for 1970 is the Butler–Stokes 1970 cross-section survey, for 1974 it is the British Election Study February panel sample. Numbers in brackets are the divisors in the calculation of the instrumental gap. That is, each decimal value is the instrumental gap (calculated from the formula in the text) for the sub-group defined by the column heading, in which sub-group there are the number of people shown in brackets.

ably affected by the actual rate of inflation. Since there appears to be this connection between the general level of well-being and inflation, it is not surprising that those who link vote to well-being are more common among those who believe the government could control prices.

However, this effect is confined to supporters of the incoming (newly-incumbent) government, the Conservatives in 1970 and Labour in 1974. In each case, instrumentalism is substantially higher among those believing the government can affect prices ('gaps' of 0.45 against 0.35 in 1970, 0.25 against 0.02 in 1974). Note particularly that while those who do *not* believe the government can control prices are a small *minority* of Conservatives in 1970, they form the great *majority* of Labour voters in 1974. In this group, accounting for 60 per cent of Labour voters in 1974, the instrumental gap is 0.02, which is equivalent to no instrumentalism at all. In short, among those February Labour voters who did not believe the government could control prices, there was simply no connection between personal economic well-being, past or future, and party choice. If one feels no government could control prices, one's economic well-being, at least as regards prices, does not depend on which party forms the government.

There is one other feature of Table 13.4 which deserves comment. Among supporters of the newly-elected government, instrumentalism was stronger among those believing the government could control prices. Among supporters of the losing party, instrumentalism was *weaker* among those believing the government can be *effective*. The most probable interpretation of this paradox is that those supporters of the losing party who believe that a government can affect prices may well believe this of the new government, even though they did not support it. The effect of this is that, insofar as well-being is affected by inflation, if you believe that the new government might be effective in controlling inflation (even though you didn't vote for them) you will be less likely to assume that you will become worse off now that they are in office, and therefore the instrumental gap calculated among people like you will be smaller. Unfortunately, it is not possible to give independent evidence for this interpretation, and so it must remain a plausible speculation.[4]

Instrumentalism and partisanship

This measure of instrumentalism is close to the original sense of utility flow or how well off people are and expect to be. When instrumentalism is measured this way, it can be seen to be a dynamic characteristic of an electoral system. Thus, at a minimum, any assessment of the extent of instrumental voting, or of the relative importance of instrumental and non-instrumental sources of attachment to political parties, should be carefully restricted to appropriately time-bound contexts. There was a steep decline in the instrumental value of party choice between 1966 and 1974, and furthermore there was a link between instrumentalism and belief in the effectiveness of the political system. Chapter 6 discussed the decline in strength of partisanship in the period 1964–74. Since these two trends have a superficially obvious relationship to each other, it is worth seeing whether people's personal economic expectations and perceptions are related in any meaningful way to strength of partisanship.

Instrumentalism as measured in the previous section has always been strongest among the strongest partisans.[5] This is no surprise: if there is anything which partisans do, the odds are that the strongest partisans will appear to do it most. Thus, in 1964, only very strong Conservatives expected to become worse off once Labour had been elected; after February 1974, while many Labour supporters did expect to become better off, the tendency was clearest among the strongest identifiers. Even so, among this group the odds of expecting to be better rather than worse off were a little over two to one, while in 1964 among the same group the odds were nearer ten to one. Over the decade both the number of strong partisans and their instrumental attachment to their party declined.

[4] The competence question is phrased 'prices will go on rising fast no matter what *any* government tries to do', but even so it is likely that people responding negatively after an election will probably be thinking largely of the competence of the present government. Even among other voters, the estimate of Labour's competence at dealing with prices was higher among those who also believed that prices were within the control of some government: 30 per cent of those February Conservatives and Liberals agreeing with the previous question (that the government was incapable) said that Labour would handle prices at least fairly well, while 41 per cent of those believing in some government effectiveness said Labour would handle prices at least fairly well.

[5] Partisanship is measured by the response to, 'Generally speaking, do you think of yourself as Conservative, Labour, Liberal or what?' (If no party given) 'Do you think of yourself as a little closer to one of the parties? Which?' followed, where a party is mentioned, by 'Would you call yourself a very strong (party mentioned), fairly strong, or not very strong?'. For instance, among those identifying themselves as 'very strong' Labour in 1964, the 'instrumental gap' is 0.59, in comparison to the 0.46 recorded in Table 13.3 for all 1964 Labour voters, and in February it is 0.20 as against 0.12 for all Labour voters. In terms of the previous analysis, this suggests again the link between retaining a strong partisanship and continuing to believe in the competence (even if limited) of the political system.

But what was the connection between the two declines? At a minimum, one would expect strong partisanship to be *sustained* by *both* high expectations of doing better and a clear perception of having done better while the party one identified with was in power. Equally, one would expect a high rate of partisan decline among those with unfulfilled expectations of their party; this should be particularly clear where people initially expected to become better off when their party was elected and subsequently acknowledged having become worse off while it was in power. The effects in the other possible cases are more difficult to anticipate, though it ought to be the case that, among those believing they have become worse off while their party was in power, partisan dealignment is less common among those who expected to become worse off anyway.

Table 13.5 explores these matters, and gives some support to these hypotheses. Two periods are included: Labour incumbency 1966–70 and the Conservative Government 1970–4. Partisan decline or dealignment is measured by considering identifiers for the incumbent party at the beginning of the government, and taking the proportion who at the end of the government identified with their party *less* strongly, or identified with another party, or had no party identification (similar figures for weakening of 'very strong' identifiers are presented in Crewe, Särlvik and Alt, 1977). Each cell in Table 13.5 gives the pro-

Table 13.5. *Weakening of partisanship 1966–70 and 1970–4*

(a) 1966–70: Per cent of 1966 Labour identifiers weakening in partisanship by 1970

1966 expectation of well-being was	1970 perception of well-being		
	Better off	Same	Worse off
Better off	25% (73)	36% (88)	53% (48)
Other	34% (109)	40% (173)	43% (112)

(b) 1970–4: Per cent of 1970 Conservative identifiers weakening in partisanship by 1974

1970 expectation of well-being was	1974 perception of well-being		
	Better off	Same	Worse off
Better off	37% (78)	51% (69)	45% (23)
Other	47% (62)	53% (118)	43% (54)

Note: Sources are (a) Butler–Stokes 1966–70 panel and (b) British Election Study February 1974 panel survey. Numbers in brackets are total cell frequencies; that is, the number of identifiers of the appropriate party initially of whom the proportion shown in the cell subsequently weakened.

portion thus weakening within the *joint* distribution of their initial expectations and final perceptions of personal economic well-being.

Thus the upper left-hand cell of Table 13.5(*a*) shows that of those 1966 Labour identifiers who expected to become better off and who also in 1970 said that they had become better off, 25 per cent 'weakened' in their partisanship over the four years (that is, ceased to identify with Labour, or identified with it less strongly than in 1966). (Note that panel rather than recall data is used, so there is no retrospective bias in the initial expectations or partisanship.) This figure of 25 per cent is far lower than the overall weakening rate of 39 per cent among 1966 Labour identifiers, and is consistent with the expectation that partisanship is sustained by fulfilled high expectations. Similarly, in 1966–70, the *highest* rate of partisan weakening among Labour identifiers was among those with initially high but unfulfilled expectations: it is a small group, but the weakening rate of 53 per cent is the highest in the table. Among those who felt that they had become worse off, the weakening rate was lower among those with lower initial expectations, and indeed, provided that initial expectations were low enough, the effect of perceiving that one has done well or badly ceases to have much effect on the rate of partisan decline. (Of course, over all partisans, the effect of perceiving oneself to be worse off is clear.) Similar effects are generally detectable among Conservative identifiers between 1970 and 1974, though (partly through lack of numbers) there is no confirmation of the impact of initially low expectations on the weakening of those who feel they have done badly. Nevertheless, the point about high expectations and perceptions sustaining partisanship holds again in the later period.[6] Here, however, despite the small cell frequencies, it is less clear that simply perceiving oneself to have become worse off is actually associated with partisan weakening: the highest rates of partisan decline are among those who feel their condition unchanged.

There is therefore reason to believe that this sort of instrumental disappointment is at least a component of partisan weakening, and as such is part of the background of the general trend toward partisan decline and dealignment over the last decade. The process is not infinite: in particular, once initial expectations are as low as in 1974, it may well turn out to be the case that the effect

[6] The general sense of this discussion is confirmed if the responses to another question are considered. Butler and Stokes also asked in 1970 whether people felt they were better or worse off with the Labour Government. Of former Labour identifiers saying they were worse off with Labour, 75 per cent weakened, regardless of initial expectations; of those saying it had made no difference, about 35 per cent weakened. Of those saying better off, 23 per cent of those expecting to become better off in 1966 weakened (just like Table 13.5*a*) but of those with initially negative expectations, only 15 per cent who subsequently said they were better off with Labour weakened in their identification. One might argue that this alternative question pulled too hard for exactly this pattern of replies, but the difference in defection rates of those with negative expectations might be significant: of those with negative expectations who subsequently weakened in their Labour support, the view that Labour was irrelevant to their subsequent improvement must have predominated. Among those who felt they owed their improvement to Labour, weakening was indeed very uncommon where their progress exceeded their expectations.

just described simply can no longer be detected. Nevertheless, there is a connection between perceived economic decline and a weakening of attachment to particular political parties, when that party has been in power. Moreover, this effect appears to have been more marked in the late 1960s when Labour was in power than in the early 1970s under the Conservatives, in spite of the fact that initial expectations of each government were about equally high. It could be chance, but it is also worth asking whether there might be some reason for this apparent asymmetry of effect between the political parties — why indeed Labour identifiers more than Conservatives might defect from their party when its time in office coincides with a period of economic decline.

14

Ideology and economic outlook

If there were some reason that economic decline, or unfulfilled economic expectations, affected different groups of partisans differently, it would be reasonable to expect it to lie in the attitudinal or ideological structure which sustains or accompanies a party identification. Ultimately, the argument of this section will recall the point repeatedly established in Part III, that economic decline appears to make people less generous in their policy preferences. Because this generosity or altruism is involved in some — but not all — questions underlying the British two-party system, the effect of economic decline will be to alter some of these attitudes, particularly, as we shall see, those dealing with questions of social welfare. This is a long story, and is best taken in steps.

There are three fundamental hypotheses covering the expected effect of economic decline on partisan attitudes and behaviour. One is the instrumental argument just covered, that decline turns supporters of the incumbent party against it, whatever their social origins. The second is the notion of 'status polarisation', proposed by Converse (1958) and taken up subsequently by Butler and Stokes. The central idea is straightforward: if one has two parties, each of which predominantly derives its support from a different social class, then in hard times the class polarisation of the electorate will increase, at least insofar as the electorate will tend to divide into two increasingly class-biased party blocs. In times of prosperity, people will be more inclined to forget social differences, and the class mix of each party's supporters will increase. (Refer back to Chapter 1 for a discussion of many points surrounding this model.) The model does assume that economic benefits are not entirely class-related: if people only became better off when their 'own' party were in power and worse off under the 'other' party, there would be no incentive ever to change parties, and the class bias would remain. In other words, the model assumes that the party in power can use good times to entice away supporters of the other side; in hard times, with no benefits flowing, people should turn to the party of their own class. The model rests to a degree on people turning, in times of stress, to their 'trusted' or 'natural' party. A relevant example of this is the continuing support for Labour (even when the incumbents) in areas of high unemployment (Miller, 1977).

The alternative expectation of the effects of economic decline is not exactly contradictory, but takes a somewhat different line. Instead of economic decline hardening the lines of partisanship in the electorate, it tends to turn people toward extremist groups previously outside the recognised electoral arena. This sort of account is occasionally put forward in connection with the growth of Nazism or Poujadism, and more recently evidence has been put forward to suggest that the *perception* of personal economic decline lay at the heart of the increase in support for the extreme-right German NDP in the late 1960s (Lipset, 1960; Liepelt, 1967; Brunner, 1970). Even though evidence for this is slight, the argument does periodically come up, and has for instance recently been mentioned in newspaper leaders in connection with the growth of support for the National Front in Britain. In general, this hypothesis has in fact been put forward in the context of right-wing rather than left-wing extremism, though the general formulation encompasses either. It appears to be the case that (so runs this hypothesis) right-wing extremism is a response among those whose past expectations for improvement are not fulfilled, whose personal economic condition is worsening, but who see the social remedy not in the redistributive policies of socialism but in the extension of control over lawless elements (or just minority groups) whose existence threatens the traditional production of economic benefit.

The common ground of these latter two approaches to the question of the political effects of economic decline is that each anticipates a move toward extremism, though in the first case the move is toward the extremes of each of two existing parties and in the second toward some new alternative outside the existing parties. It does not require too much imagination to argue further that either account could be upheld in different circumstances, and that what determines which direction events take is whether, with class-based parties, the critical political questions of the day are seen in terms of class interests or not.

Evidence is lacking over a sufficient span of time to test directly hypotheses of the effects of general economic decline on mass political behaviour. However, the hypotheses can be extended in two ways to see whether the basis of such accounts can be established. Instead of attempting to measure national economic hard times, one can move to the individual psychological level and investigate the effects of *perceived* personal economic decline. Secondly, one can look for the effects among the policy attitudes or ideologies of partisans.

In this chapter the term ideology is used loosely to describe a structured set of attitudes toward possible government policies. Possible policy areas cover a very broad range of subjects, and some areas are far more central than others to the package of ideas that parties project to their supporters. Blocs of partisan identifiers (at least in part because of that) have shared attitudes to a greater or lesser extent on different policy questions, and similarly often the principal division of opinion on some policies is not along party-political lines. Attitudes to immigrants and immigration are a case in point where at times there is no particularly large inter-party division of opinion, and indeed considerable unclarity about which of the political parties is more favourably disposed toward immigrants (Fox, 1975). It is hard to see this reflecting anything other than the general lack of centrality of the issue in electoral politics, as well as years of ambiguous statements by the parties about their positions on the issue. On the more basic issues underlying the two-party system (nationalisation, social services) as well as more central issues in recent years (the Common Market), there is a clearer inter-party division of opinion, as well as much more clarity about the relative positions of the parties. (Alt, Särlvik and Crewe, 1976b.)

There is a somewhat chicken-and-egg quality about the question of whether the ideology or the party identification came first. Clearly, strong partisans are most likely to share at least a good many of the most central of their party's policy ideas, and they are more likely to be guided by their partisanship into ignoring (by misperception or attaching little importance to them) conflicts between party policy and their own political ideas. Weaker identifiers are more likely to admit policy preferences at variance with the (accurately-perceived) position of their party, though whether the extra receptiveness to alien ideas came before or after the weaker partisanship is beyond available data to test (see Alt, Särlvik and Crewe, 1976b; Crewe, Särlvik and Alt, 1977). However, this section seeks to elucidate the effects of economic decline, and this is not beyond the data.

The determinants and dimensions of political attitudes

For the purposes of this chapter economic decline is loosely defined, at the individual level, as the perception of having become economically worse off recently, and expecting this to continue. This is the personal side of economic outlook described in Chapter 5. The expectation of its effects on political attitudes or ideology, involving the two possibilities discussed earlier in this chapter, is as follows:

(1) Where a policy issue or ideological component is *essentially partisan* in nature, the effect of economic decline is to move otherwise similar blocs of partisans ideologically further apart. In other words, hard times make partisans ideologically more partisan.

(2) Where an ideological component is *not* essentially partisan, economic decline makes people more rigidly attached to the status quo, more intolerant, less permissive, more oriented toward social control of deviants, and so on.

This hypothesis can be tested with cross-sectional data from the October 1974 post-election survey, in which a series of questions was asked to elicit from respondents their views of which of a number of policy areas most needed further government action, and which they felt had already been carried far enough or too far (texts are in the Appendix). The ideological structure is recovered by factor-analysing the correlations among reponses to these items. The solution is conceptually efficient, but readers should recall that the number of factors, and the order in which they are extracted, depends on the inclusion and exclusion of items in the list presented to respondents at least at much as on anything happening in the 'real world'.

Certainly the factor structure obtained is familiar, and related versions have been discussed extensively by Eysenck (1963) and Brittan (1973b) among others. Three factors are readily identifiable as the common dimensions contained in differing amounts by the individual items. The first two of these factors are plotted in Figure 14.1 and the loadings of various individual items on each factor (where these loadings are large enough to merit discussion) are given in Table 14.1 along with some summary statistics.

The first factor is the familiar *socio-economic radicalism* factor; the single item most composed of this factor is the necessity for redistributing wealth, followed at some distance by establishing comprehensive schools, the need to control land and to give workers more say in running their place of work, as well as the need to spend more to alleviate poverty, provide greater welfare benefits, and finally, move to promote modern teaching methods. (These exhaust the items with loadings greater than 0.3 on this factor.) This is clearly also the two-party factor among these items, as shown in Figure 14.1 by the location of each group of party identifiers according to the mean score on this factor within the group.

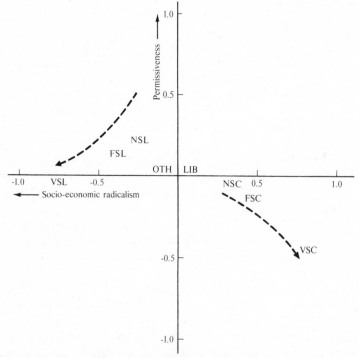

Figure 14.1. Ideology and economic outlook.
Groups of partisan identifiers are plotted according to mean factor scores within groups (first two factors only). The groups correspond to *V*ery, *F*airly, and *N*ot very *S*trong *L*abour and *C*onservative, *LIB*eral, and *OTH*ers. All data relate to October 1974. − − − − − → represents the expected effect of economic deterioration.

Table 14.1. *Ideological factors in 1974*

Item	Loading	
Factor 1. Socio-economic radicalism:		
For redistribution of wealth	−0.71	Eigenvalue 3.0
For establishing comprehensive schools	−0.51	
For state control of land	−0.48	Root mean square
For giving workers more say	−0.46	correlation 0.26
For spending more to reduce poverty	−0.44	
For more welfare benefits	−0.39	
For promoting modern teaching methods	−0.35	
Factor 2. Permissiveness:		
Against right to show nudity and sex	−0.70	Eigenvalue 1.4
Against abortion on the NHS	−0.51	
For respect for authority	−0.46	Root mean square
For curbing activities of Communists	−0.35	correlation 0.25
For tough measures to prevent crime	−0.33	
Factor 3. Racial nationalism:		
For repatriation of immigrants	+0.73	
Against further equality for coloured people	+0.62	Eigenvalue 1.0
Against spending more on aid to poorer countries	+0.40	Root mean square correlation 0.35

Note: Data are from the British Election Study October 1974 cross-section survey. Pairwise deletion of missing values was employed, but there are at least 1,900 cases underlying each coefficient in the original correlation matrix. Signs of loadings match axes are drawn in Figure 14.1. The factor analysis is varimax rotated from a principal axes solution.

Thus, very strong Conservatives have an average first-factor score of 0.8 and very strong Labour identifiers of nearly −0.7 (unit standard deviations) with other groups of identifiers ranged in between. The equation of this socio-economic radicalism with the *two-party* system is supported by the fact that Liberal identifiers occupy a place more or less central on this dimension.

Note that the first dimension is first *not* because the items loading on it have the highest average level of intercorrelation among themselves, but because, while they are moderately intercorrelated, there are a lot of appropriate items in the set presented to respondents. In fact the average level of intercorrelation (root mean square) among the items loading at a level above 0.3 on the first factor is 0.26: not very high, though higher than that among the less-related items discussed by Butler and Stokes (1969, Chapter 9). On the other hand the fact that there were many such items in the set reflects the extent to which contemporary political issues are structured along party-political lines rather than bad judgement in selecting items for inclusion. Any item on which people can be divided largely according to party identification will correlate with this dimension. The variable whose groups are plotted in the figure, strength and direction of party identification, would itself load at about |0.7| on this factor if it were included in the correlation matrix to be factored.[1]

The second factor is less partisan in nature, and is a social *permissiveness* factor. People at the permissive end are likely to believe in allowing pornography and abortion, while people at the non-permissive end are not. Similarly, non-permissive people are likely to feel that respect for authority has declined too far, that the activities of Communists should be curbed, and that there is a need for tougher action to combat crime. The intercorrelations among items on this factor are about the same as for the first factor, and a look at Figure 14.1 confirms that the position of the average partisan of each party is not too far apart. Indeed, the negative scores of each group of very strong identifiers should alert readers to the possibility that this is an age-related factor, with the old being less permissive. Indeed this is so: those under 35 have an average score on this factor of +0.44 while those over 55 have an average score of −0.45. This is a much greater difference than that between the most extremely opposite subgroups of partisans on this factor.

The third factor (not plotted) is *racial nationalism*: it deals with feelings about immigrants and the relative priority of foreign affairs. At the nationalist end are those seeking repatriation of immigrants, opposed to further moves toward race equality, and against further spending on foreign aid (though not necessarily other sorts of spending). This is again not a major-party partisan factor, but the most anti-nationalist group are Liberal identifiers (the score is −0.16), a group whose stress on civic egalitarianism has been noted elsewhere (Alt, Crewe and Särlvik, 1977). The most nationalist partisans are predictably very strong Conservatives (+0.22), but the inter-party variation is very small compared even with the second factor, let alone the first. Positions on this factor are less socially explicable than were the first two, but more on this in a moment.

The hypothesised effects of economic decline are shown with arrows in Figure 14.1. Since the second and third factors are not partisan in nature, the second hypothesis above applies to the effect of economic decline on these attitudes. Economic decline, as before, ought to make people less permissive, and more oriented toward the need for control, especially of deviants, and thus the arrows point downwards. Similarly, economic decline ought to make people more nationalistic in the sense of the third factor, that is, more suspicious and resentful of immigrants, less inclined to approve of spending money on foreign countries instead of at home. On the first factor, however, which is partisan, economic decline should simply separate the partisan blocs more. If Figure 14.1 were redrawn reflecting the scores of only those whose personal economic situations were deteriorating, one would expect the blocs of partisans to the left and

---

[1] Because of the tendency of differently-worded sets of questions to cluster separately, independent of content, introducing other questions into the factor analysis has been avoided. Factor scores have unit standard deviations. Strength and direction of party identification were defined in Chapter 13, note 5.

right to be further apart, as well as all groups to be moved further down the page, and of course, more toward the racial-nationalist end of the third factor as well.

However, before testing this, recall from Chapter 5 that economic decline — which is only the negative direction of personal economic outlook — is itself a correlate of such variables as age, education, income, and social class. Therefore, before looking at the effects of economic decline on ideology, it is necessary to remove the effects of these other variables. One can omit social class, since it will have no effect independent of an eight-fold party identification scale, which in turn is treated as a predictor variable, along with age (in deciles), education, and income. These predictors are defined in the Appendix. These do in fact exhaust the main socio-political determinants of these attitudes, even though the purpose here is not to analyse all determinants of these ideological factors. The results are shown in Table 14.2.

In terms of the socio-economic radicalism factor, all these variables are significant predictors, though (in standardised terms) strength and direction of party

Table 14.2. *Determinants of ideological positions*

Variable	Coefficient	t-statistic	Standardised coefficient
Factor 1. Socio-economic radicalism (− means radical) =			
Strength and direction of identification	−0.18	31.0	−0.53
Age in deciles	+0.05	6.5	+0.12
Education	+0.08	7.5	+0.13
Income	+0.02	1.9	+0.03
(Constant)	+0.40		
$R^2 = 0.35$ obs. = 2,294 F-ratio = 305.7			
Factor 2. Permissiveness (+ means permissive) =			
Strength and direction of identification	+0.03	5.0	+0.09
Age in deciles	−0.17	23.3	−0.45
Education	+0.04	3.4	+0.07
Income	+0.04	2.8	+0.05
(Constant)	+0.43		
$R^2 = 0.25$ obs. = 2,294 F-ratio = 188.9			
Factor 3. Nationalism (+ means nationalistic) =			
Strength and direction of identification	−0.04	6.1	−0.13
Age in deciles	+0.03	3.8	+0.08
Education	−0.15	11.7	−0.25
Income	+0.02	1.2	+0.02
(Constant)	+0.34		
$R^2 = 0.09$ obs. = 2,294 F-ratio = 53.5			

Note: Data are from the British Election Study October cross-section survey. Note that the high ends of the scales are Labour identification, old, educated most, and highest income for the explanatory variables and conservatism, permissiveness and nationalism on the factors. Thus the coefficient of −0.18 for identification in equation 1 shows that conservatism decreases (radicalism increases) at the Labour end; in equation 2 the old are least permissive, and so on.

identification has an effect over twice the size of the other three predictors together. Independent of partisanship, however, older, better-educated and higher-income people all tend to be less radical, and the four predictors together statistically explain over a third of the variance in individual first-factor scores. The fit on the second factor is not as good, though a quarter of the variance is explained, in this case largely by age, which has over twice the impact of the other variables together. Increased age appears to go closely with less permissiveness, but independent of this is a tendency for Labour identifiers to be slightly more permissive, as are those with greater education and higher incomes, though these effects are small. On the third factor, it is education which counts most: the greater the extent of education in the individual, the less likely are the racial-nationalist ideas contained in the third factor. Independent of this, these nationalist ideas are less common among Labour identifiers and the young. Income is not a significant predictor. So the ideological space described by the three factors is also a sort of social space, describing ideas that vary principally with party identification on the first factor, age on the second, and education on the third.

The effects of economic decline can now be analysed, and are documented in Table 14.3. This table presents mean scores on each factor, broken down by economic outlook and within categories (as a control) of the principal demographic predictor of each factor, taken from the equations in Table 14.2. (In fact, this analysis could be presented by breaking down the residuals from each

Table 14.3. *Average ideological scores and economic outlook*

Group	Economic outlook			
	Gains	(base)	Deterioration	(base)
Factor 1. Socio-economic radicalism				
Very strong Conservatives	0.74	(49)	0.84	(115)
Fairly strong Conservatives	0.43	(116)	0.53	(197)
Not very strong Conservatives	0.42	(52)	0.41	(79)
Not very strong Labour	−0.22	(35)	−0.33	(113)
Fairly strong Labour	−0.39	(157)	−0.45	(186)
Very strong Labour	−0.73	(101)	−0.68	(162)
Factor 2. Permissiveness				
Age up to 34	0.45	(248)	0.43	(312)
Age 35–64	−0.08	(320)	−0.14	(549)
Age 65 and over	−0.48	(83)	−0.55	(218)
Factor 3. Nationalism				
Academic further education	−0.49	(60)	−0.36	(101)
Other extra education	−0.11	(307)	0.00	(456)
Minimum education	−0.09	(281)	0.22	(530)

Note: Data are from the British Election Study October cross-section sample. 'Gains' indicates that income has at least kept up with prices since February, and is expected to continue at least to keep up. 'Deterioration' indicates that income has fallen behind prices since February, and is now expected to do no more than keep up. Numbers in brackets give the frequency over which the mean scores were calculated.

equation by economic outlook categories. This approach might be more difficult
to interpret in some cases, but does in fact give results hardly distinguishable
from those presented below.) Economic outlook is determined by a classification
of perceptions and expectations: 'gains' describes those whose income has gone
up relative to prices and is expected to go up or stay the same, or has stayed the
same or gone down but is expected to go up by more than prices. 'Deterioration'
means that income has stayed the same as prices and will now fall behind, or has
fallen behind and will now stay the same or continue to fall. In short, gains are
positive expectations regardless of the past, or a good past expected to be maintained; decline means past decline expected to continue or worsen further.

Table 14.3 contains considerable confirmation of the two hypotheses, though
not quite as neatly as might be liked. On the first 'socio-economic radicalism'
factor, decline does appear to strengthen partisanship to some extent. Those very
strong Conservatives whose economic position is felt to deteriorate are more
Conservative (0.84 to 0.74) than their (subjectively) economically better-off
fellows; the same size and direction of effect are observable among fairly strong
Conservatives. Not very strong Conservatives do not vary in their views according
to economic outlook. On the Labour side, the two groups of less strong identifiers act in accordance with the idea of status polarisation: in each case the
worse-off have the attitudes of stronger partisans. Not so among the strongest
identifiers with the Labour Party: here those who feel worse off are *less* radical
than their better-off counterparts. This contradicts the status polarisation argument in its extended form, and needs elucidation (presented in the next section).

The other hypothesis, that where a policy was not particularly partisan economic decline ought to predict a preference for control of deviants, and so on, is
broadly confirmed. In the case of the second factor, permissiveness, it is the case
that those feeling economic deterioration are less permissive, controlling for age,
but the differences in general are not large. On some individual items the differences are more impressive: the tendency of the young who feel badly off to
support tough measures to control crime is especially noteworthy. On the third
factor the differences are more substantial: independent of extent of education,
economic decline is consistently associated with hostility towards immigrants,
race equality and foreign aid. The effect is not quite so large as that of education
itself, but is nevertheless impressive.[2] One may get an impression of the size of

---

[2] Among those under 30 who feel economic deterioration, the proportion opposing moves
to go easier on people who break the law is 27 per cent, while among the younger more
optimistic it is 20 per cent. This bears some relationship to the suggestion by Harrop and
Zimmerman (1977) that National Front support is common among working-class younger
people with minimal education. Bear in mind (Chapter 5) that minimal education and
lower social grade predict negative economic outlook, and that among the young (where
economic outlook is so much more positive among the higher-income educated) the contrast between economic opportunities might provoke extreme responses, and there is a
clear symmetry between these two sets of findings. This also may illuminate the renewed
concern of the electorate with immigration as an issue after a period of economic decline.
If one takes the residuals from equation 3 in Table 14.2 and calculates the mean residual
within economic outlook groups, it is −0.13 among those showing gains and +0.33

the effect from proportions: 32 per cent of those feeling economic decline think that moves for race equality have gone too far, as against 21 per cent of those feeling gains; 40 per cent of those in declining economic positions wish to see immigrants repatriated, as against under 30 per cent of those feeling better off. Both these effects hold up independent of education, and indeed, other socio-political effects.

Economic decline, generosity, and ideology

This nearly locates the ideological effects of economic decline. Clearly, on the less partisan attitudes of permissiveness and nationalism, economic decline predicts the taking up of 'hard-line' attitudes, opposing immigrants and favouring various sorts of social control. On the partisan aspects of ideology, economic decline does appear to predict hardening of the partisan lines again, except among the strongest Labour supporters. Part III of this volume repeatedly noted a tendency for one form or another of economic stress to be associated with less generosity or altruism in economic policy attitudes, whether this took the form of favouring curbing inflation rather than unemployment, or favouring increased unemployment or spending cuts over taxation to fight inflation. These points are entirely consistent with each other.

The partisan division of attitudes or ideologies contains a number of separate themes, on all of which attitudes will be correlated around party lines, though the correlations will be of varying strength.[3] Some aspects of this partisan division include nationalisation of industry, the question of the rights of workers and the power of trade unions, and indeed social services and the provision of welfare benefits. Only this last aspect involves the notion of generosity or altruism discussed earlier. On questions of spending on social services, people are supporting an idea which is altruistic; they are supporting a benefit which will largely go to others. The same is true of supporting a reduction of unemployment, as long as one is not personally threatened with the loss of one's job. But it is the Labour Party only which must convince its supporters (if they need convincing) to endorse these altruistic measures, and it has been the contention throughout this volume that it must make people feel better off in order to make them feel able to afford altruistic policies. This is more or less what is at the heart of the weaker partisan ideology of those very strong Labour identifiers who feel themselves becoming economically worse off. In other words, economic decline poses a dilemma for strong Labour supporters. On the one hand, economic

(nationalistic) among those showing deterioration. The corresponding residual averages on the second factor are +0.11 (gains) and −0.07 (deterioration), making the same point about anti-permissiveness among the psychologically worse off. Alternatively, one could insert dummy variables representing 'gains' and 'deterioration' into equations 2 and 3, with significant results in each case.

[3] For a large amount of empirical work along these lines, see Budge, Crewe and Farlie (1976), especially Chapters 7–13. None of the studies there includes consideration of the role of economic health as a precondition for some sorts of ideological conflict.

decline should make them stronger partisans. On the other, it should also make them less generous and therefore less able to support Labour Party policies concerned with social welfare.

Two published pieces of evidence support this contention. First, it is only among strong Labour identifiers that there is any large measure of support for more spending on social services: in the weaker groups of Labour identifiers, less than 40 per cent endorse extended social services (1974), while among very strong Labour identifiers a majority of 55 per cent feel more social services are needed (Alt, Särlvik and Crewe, 1976b). Thus it is only in this group of strong partisans that economic decline could show a substantial effect in moving people away from a pro-welfare attitude and thereby weaken the attraction of the Labour Party. Second, it has been shown that support for the Labour principle of extended social services increased appreciably more among *young, middle-class* Labour supporters than the rest of the party's support (Crewe, Särlvik and Alt, 1977). Recall from Chapter 5 that being young and middle class virtually defined a positive economic outlook in 1974. Numbers are insufficient in available data to disentangle two such correlated effects, but the general implication – that it is among those feeling best off that extending social services has its greatest support – is reinforced. An extra straw in the wind would be to recall that in 1964 support for extended social services was higher (within the span of election surveys in this country) than it has ever been since (Crewe, Särlvik and Alt, 1977) and a quick reference back to Figure 5.1 above will show that economic outlook, both perceptions and expectations, has also never again been as high, and Figure 3.1 shows that it was also the last time that social problems were seen as most important.

It is possible, though within limits, to show the process at work through panel data. The argument is that economic decline, particularly among Labour supporters, works to shift people away from a pro-welfare position, and in that respect may weaken the partisanship of strong Labour identifiers. Weaker Labour identifiers are less likely to believe in extended social services: their support for Labour rests on other aspects of socio-economic radicalism, and they are thus immune to this effect. To support this, it is necessary to show two things: first, that economic decline has this effect on the welfare attitudes of Labour identifiers, and second, that it does not have the same effects on other aspects of socio-economic radicalism underlying a Labour identification. The evidence is in Table 14.4; the cell frequencies are *very* small, but the evidence is exactly as it ought to be.

Voters are split between those identifying with the Labour Party in 1964 and the rest of the electorate; they are also split according to the fate of their 1964 economic expectations of the Labour Government in comparison with their perceptions of recent well-being six years later. In this second split, those who 'gain' felt that they had become better off, regardless of initial expectations, or stayed the same having expected to become worse off; those 'deteriorate' who have done worse than they expected. This gives four groups by party and economic outlook,

Table 14.4. *Ideological defections 1964–70*

1964 Party was	1964–70 economic position	
	Gained	Deteriorated
(a) Per cent ceasing to favour more spending on social services		
Labour	19% (69/79)	50% (62/64)
All other	28% (32/45)	35% (108/150)
(b) Per cent ceasing to favour more nationalisation of industry		
Labour	32% (47/86)	39% (38/54)
All other	*	*
(c) Per cent ceasing to sympathise with strikers		
Labour	28% (46/80)	13% (23/51)
All other	43% (21/57)	10% (34/119)

*Too few initially in favour of nationalisation to compute conversion rate.
Note: Data are from the Butler–Stokes 1964–70 panel study. 'Gains' implies that respondent saw self as better off under Labour, or at least better than originally expected, 'deterioration' implies perception of doing worse than expected. Bracketed numbers indicate the proportion initially agreeing with the proposition defining the table; the numerator of this ratio is the base for calculating conversion rates in each cell.

and each group defines a cell in each of the tables. Within each cell are given the proportions shifting to the 'right' from an initially 'left' position on the issue over the six years.

Take the cell at the upper right-hand corner of Table 14.4(a). In 1964, 62 of the 64 Labour supporters who were subsequently disappointed economically supported spending more on social services; by 1970 31 of these 62, or 50 per cent, had moved to a position of feeling that enough or too much was being spent on social services. (The extra response provided in 1970, 'spend more on pensions', is grouped with the response 'same'.) Among those who had done all right – done well, or better than expected – the comparable rate of moving 'right' was only 19 per cent, far lower. Among the rest of the electorate, there is a much smaller effect in the same direction. Twenty-eight per cent of those becoming better off shift to the 'right' (less in favour of spending) while 35 per cent of those becoming worse off shift to the right. Moreover, by 1970, among those whose economic position had deteriorated, the likelihood of supporting more social service spending was the same, regardless of position on this issue six years before. In other words, the proportions supporting more social services are the same in 1970 in both cells of the right-hand column. The gap between groups of partisans has grown, but only in the left-hand column, where all feel better off, or better than they thought they would.

To this extent, within the ranks of Labour supporters, support for social service spending dropped most sharply among those disappointed in their personal economic hopes for the new government. To show that this is a particular effect which reduces people's inclination toward social generosity, it is necessary to show that the same trends are not evident among changes in other partisan attitudes of the sort to be found in or near the socio-economic radicalism factor. This is indeed what the rest of Table 14.4 shows. Even though initial support for nationalisation in the rest of the electorate is too infrequent to allow comparison of rates of change, it is evident that the gap is much smaller within the Labour Party, and that frustrated expectations do not appear to have had nearly the same differential effect in this case. In the case of sympathy for strikers, in fact, the trend goes the other way: among 1974 Labour identifiers, it is those who did better than expected who are the more likely to abandon their position of automatic sympathy for labour in industrial disputes. Those who have become worse off are more likely to retain their partisan views.

Implications

Not long ago, it was often thought that the increasing affluence of many of Britain's workers might weaken their traditional allegiance to the Labour Party (see Goldthorpe et al., 1968). What has just been shown is that in a limited sense it is the opposite which was true: the affluence was required to make people feel well enough off to continue supporting the 'altruistic' social reform policies of their preferred party. As Labour supporters' initially high expectations of further economic improvement wore off in the 1960s, so too went their support for extending the welfare state, a principal point in Labour Party ideology. The weakening of this ideological connection accompanies the weakening of Labour party identification so much more common among those feeling themselves to have become worse off in the later 1960s. Because of this, the odd situation exists that in personal 'hard times' strong Conservatives become even stronger Conservatives, while on the Labour side those with the strongest identification run into the dilemma of lessened support for social welfare policies and thus for the party itself.

Nevertheless, partisanship itself appears to weaken dramatically among a party's identifiers if it fails to provide economic benefits up to its supporters' initial expectations. This instrumental weakening of partisanship is at least as important an effect as any tendency of people to harden their attitudinal support for a party owing to the greater stress placed on them by hard times. The analysis in this chapter does suggest an asymmetry between the parties in the effect of hard times. Because of the limitation placed on strength of Labour support by the need to accept extended welfare policies, it appears that Labour can never gain as much from hard times under the Conservatives as the Conservatives can from Labour's economic failures: at least that is the direction in which the evidence, fragmentary as it is, points. Of course, the asymmetry does exist in other directions: generosity will spread among Conservatives as well when they begin to feel well enough off, and this may weaken the attachment of the strongest to their (predominantly anti-welfare) party. It is worth pointing out in this context the enormous reversal of opinion on social services among Conservative identifiers between 1964 and 1966:[4] from a small minority of 32 per cent against further spending in 1964 to a majority of 56 per cent against it 18 months later (Crewe, Särlvik and Alt, 1977). This change accompanied the sudden decline in economic expectations discussed in the last chapter from the relative optimism of 1964 to the instrumental pessimism of 1966. This implies that, for ideological reasons, there are limits to the benefits the Conservatives can reap by providing good times for their supporters. On the other hand, this is the sort of problem which in modern Britain most political parties would welcome.

[4] It is also worth recalling that in 1964 problems of social policy were seen as the most important facing the country (see Figure 3.1), something else which has not recurred since. One could also suggest that the psychological affluence of that time is a precondition for predominance in politics of such questions.

15

Expectations and economic contradictions

One of the more fashionable intellectual topics of the mid 1970s was the growing 'ungovernability' of Britain. A number of different arguments were put forward to sustain the view that Britain was becoming increasingly difficult, if not impossible, to govern. Some of the arguments, for instance the policy conflicts likely to arise out of an increasingly complex set of government institutions (Rose, 1977), are clearly important. Other variations, particularly those seeking to show an incompatibility between the governability of the country and popular expectations that the government would provide a good and increasingly better life, may be less so.

A detailed version of this argument, with particular reference to the economy and economic expectations, was recently put forward by Samuel Brittan (1976). His argument covers a wide range, and some of it, dealing with the disruption and inefficiency generated by political conflict among coercive groups, is not relevant to the present discussion. The claims which are relevant are as follows:

    (i) The public are not familiar with economic theory or with the debate underlying economic policy choices.

    (ii) Competitive party politics produces party leaders who believe that they can substantially alter the status quo, and induces all politicians to promise more than they can produce.

    (iii) Much of public policy does not affect individual experience, and therefore individual opinions are unduly subject to the 'non-rational' influence of advertising in the sense of political promises.

    (iv) Information costs are such that the average elector does not have any incentive to obtain detailed knowledge of the facts and arguments of political issues.

    (v) Because of (i) through (iv), individual expectations are not subject to a 'budget constraint' as are personal expenditures: no personal experience induces people to limit their expectations of governmental output, and indeed competitive party politics increases these expectations.

Point (i) raises enormous questions, and nearly the whole of this book has been devoted to examining it. It is certainly not a point to be taken for granted. Since (as Brittan acknowledges) personal finances are one area where personal experience is relevant, point (iii) merits investigation, as does point (iv) and consequently (v).

One can restate Brittan's argument more succinctly, in order to isolate some critical points at which empirical evidence can be brought to bear, and to restrict it to the present context:

(i) Politicians promise to solve economic problems which they cannot actually solve.

(ii) The electorate believe them.

(iii) Consequently, people have exaggerated economic expectations.

Brittan argues that because politicians inevitably promise to solve insoluble problems, the resulting popular expectations produce a 'contradiction' or inherent source of stress, tension, disruption, or some such, in democratic politics, which, allied with other problems, leads to its decline and downfall. Brittan does acknowledge that there are times when politicians resort to exhortations to sacrifice rather than promising growth, but does not believe that the gap between expectations and performance is self-correcting. Moreover, he also acknowledges that external events like Depressions can reduce expectations (citing Runciman, 1966) but again does not regard this as sufficient to reduce what appears to be an irresistible tendency towards increasingly unfulfillable economic expectations.

In fact, it is probably Brittan's fears rather than popular economic expectations which are most exaggerated. This is so for two quite separate reasons. One is that the public treat politicians' claims with far more scepticism that Brittan allows. He himself acknowledges a poll in which a majority felt less than confident that the political parties could solve Britain's problems. More to the point is that only ten to 15 per cent of the electorate believe that politicians of either major party 'very much' keep their promises. Indeed, only 30 per cent of Labour voters in October 1974 believed that the Labour Party 'very much' kept its promises; only 25 per cent of Conservative voters believed that the Conservative Party 'very much' kept its promises. Large majorities all round believe that politicians 'somewhat' keep their promises, so what exists is not widespread cynicism, but rather realistic public assessment of political promises. Politicians do keep some of their promises — else they would stand no chance of re-election — and the public believe that politicians keep some of their promises.

The second is that people's expectations are also more realistic than Brittan allows. It is possible to provide voluminous evidence on this point, touching on increasing comprehension of the meaning and causes of inflation, realistic perceptions and expectations of the rate of inflation, accurate monitoring of other economic trends, the tendency for the popular sense of well-being to move closely with changes in the country's economy, and the probability that expectations of improvement were finite, and declined rather than increased as things actually got better. Minute proportions of Conservatives in February 1974 believed that their party had handled prices 'very well', and only one Labour voter in five believed that had their party been in power it would have done 'very well'. The same realism emerges from the survey of opinions after the October election. While by and large voters for a party believe it would handle prices better than the other party, there is no evidence of unduly optimistic expectations of a quick solution to the problem of rising prices. Similarly, Mr Heath's promise-that-never-was to reduce prices 'at a stroke' was greeted with disbelief and hung around for years as a taunt at politicians' promise-vending (Butler and Kavanagh, 1974). Finally, there is the additional evidence that in October 1974 less than one voter in four, regardless of party, went so far as to *disagree* with the proposition that 'prices would go on rising fast no matter what any government tries to do'. Not only did people not believe that some party would cure rising prices, but in fact they regarded it as a problem beyond the capacity of any government in Britain.

In part, the problem is that Brittan confuses desires, demands, and expectations. The evidence he gives for unrealistic expectations rests for instance on some data showing that people feel entitled to a higher standard of living than they have, on average by about 20 per cent of their present income. That is, two thirds of a sample of respondents felt in late 1973 that they were entitled to a standard of living higher than what they had, and that on average the extra amount they wanted was 20 per cent of their current income. But that is a *desire*. If it is articulated as a legitimate claim on public resources, it becomes a *demand*. Even so, it may not be an irrational demand, for rationality in these circumstances depends on what everyone else is doing. If everyone else is going to demand 20 per cent, only a fool would not, and a rational person would moderate his demands (though not his desires) only if guarantees were forthcoming about the behaviour of others. Even something which is a demand need not be an *expectation*, and there is no analytic connection between the two. Demands are put forward in a bargaining situation, and are subsequently modified in the light of strategic developments: only a victorious army puts forward demands which it *expects* to be complied with in full. Even if a majority desired an increased standard of living in 1973, and possibly were demanding it, there is no evidence that they expected it: other survey results show that a derisory *five* per cent of the electorate *expected* their income to go up by more than prices in 1974, and a majority expected their income to fall behind prices. There are some problems with this datum, which has been discussed in the more general context of economic outlook and expectations, but even so it stands as a salutary reminder of the gap between what people *want* and what they *expect*.

This does not dispose of Brittan's argument altogether, nor is it meant to. The point he raises about politicians being induced to promise what they cannot provide is a valuable insight even if the consequence does not appear to be widespread belief in the impossible, but rather widespread belief that politicians do not keep all their promises. More important is the observation that the public evaluate policies and politicians' achievements at least partly in terms of their initial expectations. There was evidence for this in a number of places, though the effects have often been small. Unfulfilled expectations of personal economic improvement appear to be part of the underlying source of increasing partisan dealignment in Britain (Chapter 14); similarly, dissatisfaction with the Labour Government's handling of prices was linked to initially high expectations of their performance in February 1974 (Chapter 6). People who do not expect a government to stop rising prices are going to be less frustrated and disappointed with continuing price rises than are those who do expect the problem to be solved. This popular adaptiveness leads to a situation in which the electorate can take virtually any economic development calmly.

Expectations and the quiet reaction to inflation, 1974—6

The inflation rate soared to 25 per cent in 1975, and the rate of unemployment gradually climbed to its 1976—7 peak of six per cent of the workforce. It is true that there was not in addition a sharp decline in real disposable income, which nevertheless remained below end-1974 levels two years later. Even so, given the social dislocation frequently expected in situations of rapid economic decline like that experienced after 1974, it would have been reasonable to expect a certain amount of discontent, protest, or unrest among the British public. Yet the reaction to the rapid inflation of 1974 and 1975 was very calm, and far indeed from the doom-laden predictions some journalists made in 1974 of chaos and the breakdown of democracy in Britain (Jay, 1974). There were a few protest marches in 1975, principally concerned with the increase in unemployment, but these were generally small affairs. A cynic might shrug and wonder aloud what else was to be expected, and indeed it might be unrealistic to expect the sort of demonstrations and boycotts attending the (much lower) American inflation rates of the same period to occur in Britain. Nevertheless, the decade from 1964 to 1974 witnessed — even in Britain — large anti-Vietnam demonstrations, student protest on a previously unprecedented scale, and massive — and sometimes not quite legal — resistance to the Conservative Industrial Relations Act on the part of militant trade unionists. In the context of this unconventional political activism, it does seem reasonable to inquire why the rapid inflation and economic dislocation of 1974 and 1975 did not provoke more protest. How do people take 25 per cent annual inflation so calmly? Five different accounts of this lack of protest spring to mind. They deal respectively with *insulation*, *culture*, *integration*, *legitimacy*, and *expectations*. Each of them will be discussed in turn, but only expectations has much mileage in it: reaction to rapid inflation was calm because the inflation had long since been expected, and discounted.

The first alternative, *insulation*, means that economic decline did not lead to protest because people were somehow insulated personally from the effects of the economic situation. People would be insulated from the effects of economic deterioration if their sense of optimism, or well-being — whatever it is that leads people, when they have enough of it, not to engage in political protest — were not clearly tied to economic trends, or were not a matter of economic condition. It need not be: there are times when concern with war and peace, for instance, might replace concern with the state of the economy as people's principal concern. This is not the case in modern Britain, however: trends in personal optimism and other general indicators of well-being are in recent Britain heavily economic in nature and closely tied to trends in the country's economy (see Chapters

3 and 5). Moreover, there is no evidence that people really have any alternative source of pride or reward with which to compensate for the sense of economic loss.[1]

There are further ways in which difficult economic times such as those experienced in Britain in recent years might nevertheless *not* be translated into general unhappiness, pessimism, or sense of lower personal well-being. One is through a *lack of importance* attributed to economic developments. This could come about if people do not perceive that adverse economic trends affect their well-being, or if the economic component of individual well-being is small, or only important below some minimal threshold, or if those economic trends which have the most prominence or are judged to be the most important are not seen in personal terms, or at least not widely so. Much of the evidence of Part II argues against this however: in Britain, the personal aspects of the economy (like prices) continue to be seen as the most important problems facing the country and trends in perceived personal well-being fluctuate with trends in prices and earnings.

Another way in which economic difficulties might not affect personal well-being is through *lack of comparative judgements*. Subjective well-being requires comparisons; it may well be that people assume that those economic trends which are occurring in Britain are matched everywhere else. Certainly leading politicians have on occasion encouraged people to believe this. Moreover, the belief that what was happening to one was happening to all could insulate personal well-being from economic trends, whether the comparative judgements were accurate or not. There is not much evidence available on this point, but such as there is (see Chapter 3) suggested that, like other economic perceptions, a general sense of realism surrounded the assessments people made of their condition relative to that of other countries, and there is no reason to believe that people are unaware of the uniqueness of their country's economic position.

The impact of economic events could be tempered through *lack of knowledge*. Governments have manipulated the calculation of the retail price index to make the economic situation appear less unfavourable.[2] Less deliberate, but perhaps as important, particularly in the light of comparative judgements, are methods of calculation which differ between countries. Britons may have consoled themselves

---

[1] There is just a hint contained in Table 3.1 above that the British consider themselves well off relative to other nationals in respect of social benefits available. The evidence is fragmentary, and in fact really implies only that the British see themselves as 'not worse off' than others, and not falling behind as quickly as is the case with cash incomes. Similarly, the decline in the importance attached to foreign affairs (see Figure 3.1) also suggests that this area is no longer available as a source of sustenance in the face of economic difficulties.

[2] On the manipulation of the retail price index, consult Open University (1975). The British government was able to manipulate the retail price index during the Second World War by subsidising a number of commodities, so limited was the coverage of the index. The result was to make the index increase slowly (by half a per cent per annum between 1941 and 1946) to facilitate control of wage negotiations: in fact, commodity prices as measured by other sources probably increased by more like 20 per cent in those years. The broader coverage of the index after 1947 probably prevents such manipulation now.

for years with the argument that at least unemployment wasn't too bad compared to some other countries, while in fact the differences were largely attributable to methods of counting (Chapter 2). Even if this sort of situation is uncommon, it should be remembered that the seriousness of the economic situation
– and the likelihood of it affecting people's sense of well-being – may well
depend on how indicators are defined, and how much people know about them.

Nevertheless, it seems quite clear that the economic events of 1974 to 1976
were clearly perceived and probably well understood by the public, and that in
no way did ignorance or lack of standards of reference insulate people from the
effect of economic changes. In this case, one must seek elsewhere for the basis of
the lack of protest in these years. One argument could cite Britain's well-behaved
political *culture*: that is, one could argue, for example, that the British simply
are unlikely to engage in this sort of activity. On the other hand, at least some of
the British were engaged in precisely these sorts of protest activities in the previous decade. In support of the cultural argument stand the findings that the
British do generally have a low psychological potential for protest. The exceptions are confined largely to the young, who are nevertheless the best off and
most optimistic. Older people, while more pessimistic and frequently worse off,
are nevertheless more satisfied with what they have (Marsh, 1977), and remain
of course more strongly psychologically attached to the party system. It does
seem to be relevant that those with the greatest potential for protest also happen
to be those most optimistic and therefore most insulated from the economic
difficulties of the period. On the other hand, it should be borne in mind that protest potential is really only an attitude toward some unconventional form of political activity, and does not exhaust the possible paths of impact of dissatisfaction
and pessimism.

A different line of argument would stress the importance of the *integration* of
possible protest groups – especially the unions – into the planning process.
According to this reasoning, there was no protest because the groups most likely
to lead it were partly responsible through consultation and prior agreement for
the counter-inflation policies the government put forward. Again, there is certainly something in this argument, particularly after 1975 when the advance
agreement of the Trades Union Congress to the various incomes policies was
obtained. It could also be argued that in 1974 the unions made their protest
against inflation not by demonstrating but by securing for their members the
largest possible wage settlements. Similarly, the protest against economic decline
one would have expected from the unemployed was cushioned by the higher level
of benefits obtainable.[3] While the lack of protest from organised groups is important, it should nevertheless be remembered that there was also a lack of protest at
the mass level, and one should be careful about assuming that people take their
political cues exclusively from organised groups. This is particularly true at a time

---

[3] This argument has certainly been put forward to explain the calm acceptance of even
quicker increases in unemployment in West Germany. See Whitney (1976).

when, as shown in Chapter 3, the personalisation of economic effects is a dominant trend in economic perceptions.

Yet another argument is that people do not protest against the activities of the government in allowing large price increases because in some way the government retains a *legitimacy* (or popular confidence) gained in earlier periods of prosperity or some other manifestation of competence. This legitimacy then carries over in times of low output and protects the government of the day against more extreme protests. Two points stand against this argument. One is that there is some evidence of a large decline in support for the two parties in this period, indicating that the legitimacy of government did slip over the years. The other is that the argument implies that direct measures of expectations of competence on the part of the government should hold firm, or even increase as people continue to expect things to get better. In fact, there is evidence in this period of a substantial decline in popular expectations of governmental economic achievements.

Even if the last argument is not satisfactory — and it might do better if used to explain events of a decade earlier — it does raise the important point that protest is not independent of *expectations*: that there is no point raising your voice about government policy if you do not think the government can do (or could have done) anything. In this case, the fourth argument takes the form that protest does not occur at least partly because of a 'revolution of declining expectations': that is, that realistic expectations sufficiently discount future deterioration which might otherwise have appeared catastrophic, and thus ameliorate the impact of consequent dissatisfaction. Perhaps it was the analytic expectation that there should have been a strong reaction to the inflation of 1974 and 1975 that was exaggerated, and the inflation didn't hurt as much as one would otherwise have expected because people by and large expected it and no longer believed the government could do anything about it.

Two separate factors are involved here. One is that people's expectations of actual economic trends are realistic. Evidence for this was given in both Chapter 3, dealing with a variety of economic areas, and Chapter 4, dealing with inflation in particular. It is a commonplace that the psychological impact of or distress caused by an otherwise catastrophic event — for instance, a death in the family — is lessened by advance knowledge or expectation of the event. By extension it could be argued that the impact of rapidly-rising inflation rates — or any economic difficulties — will be less if people already expect them, and that this expectation reduces the potential the events have for provoking popular protest. It is beyond the scope of this work to prove that such a psychological process actually occurs, but all the fragments of evidence discussed above about lower dissatisfaction in the presence of (unfulfilled) lower initial expectations makes it at least a highly plausible conjecture.

The second relevant point is that people no longer expect the government to provide the goods. The fact that people do not believe that any government could stop prices rising rapidly has been referred to repeatedly. Moreover, people by 1974 had increasingly ceased to identify their own personal well-being with changes in incumbency: in this sense the instrumental value of voting had declined. Also relevant is the tendency noted in Chapter 8 away from blaming the government for inflation, or seeing government policies as a cause, a tendency which was generally in line with the economic thinking of the time. Moreover, much the same appears to be the case with unemployment: through 1976 people were more likely to blame the trade unions, world economic problems, or lack of desire to work among the unemployed than the government for the high rates of unemployment (*Gallup Political Index*, various).

In large measure, then, the story of the mid 1970s is the story of a politics of declining expectations. People attached a great deal of importance to economic problems, people saw clearly the developments that were taking place, and people expected developments in advance and thus were able to discount the impact of the worst of them. However, in unprecedented numbers, people also ceased to expect the election of their party to make them better off, largely because they also ceased to expect it to be able to do very much about what they identified as the principal economic problems of the time. The result of this — as well as perhaps some of the other factors discussed above — was not a politics of protest, but a politics of quiet disillusion, a politics in which lack of involvement or indifference to organised party politics was the most important feature.

The consequences of further economic decline

For the past few years, Britain's economic condition has included high rates of inflation, high rates of unemployment, and slow growth or no growth at all. The political consequence of this has been a growth of what Rose (1977) calls 'citizen indifference'. As he puts it, the question is not whether the country will be governed, but how; part of the answer, when the government ceases to be able to produce the goods people would like, is that people will simply become indifferent towards the government, uninvolved in its activities, and heedless of the many claims it might make upon them. A specific consequence of this is that, for instance, it becomes harder to secure popular acquiescence in continued incomes policies. This need not be because incomes policies are particularly unpopular: polls have long suggested that majorities of people are prepared to accept, and indeed welcome, incomes policies, at least until they demonstrably cease to work. Chapter 11 showed that wage controls received an overwhelming vote of preference in 1974 as a remedy for inflation, at least when compared to taxation, unemployment, and spending cuts. The problem is that if the government ceases to produce the goods, then people will cease in turn to believe that it has any special claim upon their activities, and then no one will be inclined to take any risks in complying with an incomes policy.

Another consequence of continuing decline is likely to be an extension of the trends discussed in the area of economic policy choices. It does not appear that questions of reducing unemployment or inflation are particularly class-based policy issues: any evidence of an association between social class and for instance the perceived importance of unemployment as a problem is slight. This could mean that actual experience of unemployment is not distributed in as class-biased a manner as it used to be. Even in the absence of direct evidence on this point, it is clear that the classes are not as polarised in their attitudes towards unemployment as was the case even 20 years ago.

This appears to be because, of the twin economic problems of inflation and unemployment, inflation affects more or less everyone, and is more or less universally disliked, whereas unemployment, although no one really approves of it, does not appear to attract much sympathy beyond the relatively small group actually threatened by unemployment. Thus, in late 1976, with the number of unemployed approaching 1.5 million, only about 17 per cent of the electorate (*Gallup Political Index*) believed unemployment to be the most important problem facing the country. Of course this 17 per cent was a great increase on the two or three per cent who felt unemployment to be the most important problem a few years before, when the unemployment rate as well stood at between two and three per cent. Even so 17 per cent is enormously less than the 50 to 80 per cent who have voted for prices as the most important problem over the last few years. Only in early 1978, with unemployment at six per cent and annual price rises in single figures, do the two proportions *approach* equality. The limits of the importance people are likely to attach to unemployment are shown by the fact that, with unemployment approaching six per cent in late 1976, only a quarter of the population felt any personal risk of losing their jobs, a figure similar to the proportion of the population who at any time have actually experienced unemployment.

The tendency for people to attach less importance to the problem of unemployment (relative to inflation) is probably a reflection of two trends discussed throughout this analysis. In the first place, people's attitudes toward reducing unemployment were clearly coloured by their knowledge of the economic consequences of reducing unemployment. This was shown to be true in 1970, when the relationship between inflation and unemployment was much less familiar. It has probably become increasingly true that people acknowledge the inflationary consequences of any serious attempt to reduce unemployment, and therefore attach less importance to the policy goal of reducing unemployment. Second, there is the point that a preference for reduced unemployment is generous or altruistic. Even the higher unemployment rates of the late 1970s do not appear to be producing anything like majorities worried about actual personal unemployment. Thus, were a majority in favour of reducing unemployment at whatever other cost to emerge, it would still be an altruistic majority, and personal economic decline inhibits this sort of altruism.

The reduction of unemployment is the economic end of general policies for maintaining and extending the welfare state. The frustrated personal economic expectations which reduced Labour identifiers' support for social service spending in the 1960s probably also reduced the commitment of the same people to the alleviation of unemployment. (Recall in this context the link between the inflation—unemployment and taxation—spending tradeoffs in Chapter 10, as well as the analysis of the decline of this part of partisan ideology in Chapter 14.) Insofar as the economic decline of the country continues to produce the perception of personal economic deterioration, it can only continue to erode support for generous social policies.

It appears that people have to feel well off before they can be persuaded to be generous towards others in their social outlook. Evidence of the continuing decline in this sort of generosity comes from some recent opinion polls: support for cutting unemployment benefits as a means of reducing public expenditure far outstripped cutting food subsidies, industrial subsidies, or road or defence expenditure (Marplan poll in the *Sun*, October 1976). In a similar vein, evidence from a comparative survey in a number of European countries suggested that the British were far more likely than others to believe that laziness and lack of will power cause poverty (*Guardian*, 21 July 1977). These are straws in the wind, but they are symptomatic of the sorts of attitude which continuing economic decline is likely to make more common.

The decline of instrumentalism and the general weakening of attachment to both major parties are likely to overcome any advantage either party might derive from the ideological consequences of economic deterioration. In this respect, one can expect to see a continuing drift towards the sort of extremes discussed in the last chapter: the tendency toward less permissiveness and more racial intolerance observed among those who felt worst off should continue to be evident. This need not mean that parties reflecting these views will necessarily expand rapidly, though, for two reasons.

First, all these tendencies are based on subjective measures of personal economic decline. Thus, expectations come to occupy a critical place in the chain of events. Chapter 5 suggested that people were capable of internalising slow but steady growth into their notions of what was required for comfort; in the same way people may internalise some degree of decline in living standards, and after some initial shocks, base their feelings about how well off they are on a lower level of expectations. In this way, a slow economic decline could continue without necessarily increasing the number of people who consistently feel that they are becoming worse off. If memories are short enough, brief upswings will also produce improvements in subjective economic outlook. Second, the growth of a fringe party, as distinct from a growth in support for some of its ideas, requires that people believe it has some solutions to offer. Even if there is growing hostility toward immigrants as a consequence of economic decline, Britain is probably a long way from the point where any substantial numbers believe that repatriation of immigrants is actually a solution to Britain's economic problems. Were the sort of anti-permissiveness and racism bred by economic deterioration to come to be seen as a *cure* for Britain's economic ills, the story could be quite different. In this context it is important to compare the growth of support for the Scottish National Party, whose supporters were extremely negative in economic outlook as far as the British government is concerned (see Chapter 5), but who probably believed, in terms of their greater personal optimism, that the SNP actually had a solution to the principal economic problem they faced.

At least outside Scotland, however, it is more probable that the politics of indifference will continue to grow. This would not be unique to England: the United States, where people clearly do not see their personal fortunes tied up with the party currently in power, is an example of a two-party system which continues to exist at much lower levels of involvement than has been the case in Britain. Rather than the chaos and unrest which many have predicted, elections with decreasing turnout and weaker attachment to the various political parties would seem to be the order of the day. It has been suggested that free collective bargaining, steady prices, full employment, and government by consent are incompatible with each other (Jay, 1974). Far from the breakdown of democracy which was predicted as a consequence, it seems more likely, looking back over the last few years, that the commitment to full employment will be redefined consensually to keep unemployment down to a million, and that inflation at rates of around ten per cent per annum may be seen as reflecting relative stability. Uncertainty about perceptual time horizons — or length of popular memory — makes it difficult to know how quickly or for how long such stable interludes would be evaluated positively. Moreover, such figures provide no good grounds for believing that one's well-being is particularly tied in the long term to any particular party, so the parties will continue to alternate in government, re-elected from time to time with decreasing enthusiasm on the part of their supporters. Such a politics of 'throwing the rascals out' may not seem an especially appealing prospect, but it is by no means incompatible with the survival of Britain's political institutions.

Appendix

This Appendix contains the complete question texts of survey questions analysed in the foregoing chapters. Each closed-ended question is presented in such a way that readers can determine what the response alternatives presented to respondents were. For each question, a description is also given of the source from which the question was taken. Questions from 'Gallup' were taken from the *Gallup Political Index*; from 'NOP' indicates that the source was the NOP *Political Bulletin* (latterly *Political and Social Report*). 'BMRB' denotes the British Market Research Bureau's monthly Financial Expectations Survey. Many questions were drawn from the national surveys conducted between 1963 and 1970 by David Butler and Donald Stokes. These surveys were:

BS63, 1963 pre-election questionnaire, $n = 2,009$.
BS64, 1964 post-election questionnaire, $n = 1,769$.
BS66, 1966 post-election questionnaire, $n = 1,874$.
BS69, 1969 pre-election questionnaire, $n = 1,114$.
BS70, 1970 post-election questionnaire, $n = 1,107$ (panel) or $1,843$ (cross–section).

The largest single source of questions are the three surveys carried out by the British Election Study at the University of Essex in 1974. These are:

BES74a, post-February election panel, $n = 1,096$.
BES74b, post-February election cross-section, $n = 2,462$.
BES74c, post-October election questionnaire, $n = 1,830$ (panel) or $2,365$ (cross-section)

In addition, for each question reference is made to all tables and figures in which the question appears, or in the analysis of which the question was used. More detailed information about the questions can sometimes be had by referring to the text describing the table in which the question appears.

I Economic outlook

	Source	In tables
(1) Would you say that in this country things have generally improved or worsened in the last year?	BMRB	5.3, 5.4, 6.3
(2) Do you think you and your family are better or worse off financially than you were a year ago?	BMRB	5.3, 5.4, Fig. 5.1
(3) Is your family income the same as it was a year ago, or more, or less?	BMRB	5.3, 5.4
(4) Do you think conditions in this country will have generally improved or worsened in a year's time?	BMRB	5.3, 5.4, 6.3

	Source	In tables

(5) What do you think will happen next year with regard to your family income? — BMRB — 5.3, 5.4

(6) Do you think this is a good or bad time to buy big things for the home like furniture, washing machines, refrigerators, TV, or things like that? — BMRB — 5.3, 5.4

(7) Do you think unemployment in your area will increase, decrease or stay the same over the next twelve months? — BMRB — 5.3, 5.4

(8) Let's talk about *prices* for everyday goods. Let us say you spent a pound in the shops *a year ago*. What do you think you would have to pay to get the *same* goods today? — BES74b,c — 4.2, 4.4, 4.6, 4.7, 5.1, 5.2, 6.2, 12.4, (Figs.) 4.1, 6.4

(9) And what about a year from now? What do you think you *will* have to pay to get those *same* goods in a year's time? — BES74b,c — 4.3, 4.6, 4.7, 5.1, 5.2, 6.2, 12.4, (Figs.) 4.1, 6.4

(10) Looking back over the last six months, would you say that the state of Britain's economy has stayed about the same, got better, or got worse? — BES74c — 4.4, 5.1, 5.2, 12.4

(11) And what do you think will be the state of Britain's economy in the next few years — will it stay about the same, get better, or get worse? — BES74c — 4.7, 5.1, 5.2, 12.4

(12) Looking back over the *last six months*, do you think the number of *strikes* and industrial disputes has gone up, gone down, or stayed about the same? — BES74c — 5.1, 5.2

(13) How about you? Compared with two or three years ago, are you and your family better off now, worse off now, or have you stayed about the same? (See Note 1.) — BS63,64, 66,70, BES74a — 9.4, 9.5, 10.3, 10.4, 13.2–13.5

(14) Now looking ahead over the next year or two, do you think that you will be better off, worse off, or will you stay about the same? (See Note 1.) — BS63,64, 66,70, BES74a — 9.4, 13.2–13.5

(15) And do you think that *unemployment* over the next year will go up, go down, or stay about the same? — BES74c — 4.7, 5.1, 5.2, 12.4

(16) Looking ahead to next year, do you think your income will *fall behind* prices, *keep up with* prices, or *go up by more* than prices do? — BES74c — 4.7, 5.1, 5.2, 12.4, 13.2

(17) Looking back over the last year or so, do you think that your income has *fallen behind* prices, kept up with prices or has gone *up by more* than prices? — BES74c — 5.1, 5.2, 12.2, 12.4, 13.2

(18) Here is a card with three boxes (*point to box A*). Box A stands for the kind of jobs which are usually paid *a bit more* than yours (your husband's) (*point to box B*). Box B stands for jobs which are usually paid *about the same* as yours (your husband's) (*point to box C*). Box C stands

	Source	*In tables*

for jobs which are usually paid *a bit less* than
yours (your husband's).
Let's think first about Box A and Box B — that
is, jobs usually paid a bit more than yours (your
husband's) and jobs usually paid about the same
as yours (your husband's). Over the last few years,
do you feel these boxes have come closer
together, or moved further apart, or stayed about
the same?
Now let's think about Box B and Box C — that
is, jobs usually paid about the same as yours
(your husband's) and jobs usually paid a bit less
than yours (your husband's). Over the last few
years, do you feel that these boxes have come
closer together, moved further apart, or stayed
about the same?   BES74c   5.1, 5.2
(19) We would like to ask some questions about
people's salaries and wages. First, think about
the average level of pay for people in your
(your husband's) *kind* of job. Would you say the
pay for your (your husband's) kind of job is
just about fair, a bit less than fair, or much less
than fair?   BES74c   5.1
(20) Now let's take wage controls. Do you think
that in the next year or so *legal control on wages*
will stay about the same, get tougher, or ease
off?   BES74b   4.7

II Political issues and opinions

A Economic policy questions

(1) Which of these is the main cause of the
present rise in prices? (Which one item has been
the most important cause of rising prices and   Gallup
inflation?)   (NOP)   8.1
(2) How much would you say the last Con-
servative Government was to blame for rising
prices — very much to blame, somewhat, or
not at all?   BES74b   4.7, 8.2, 8.3
And how much is big business to blame?
And the Labour Party?
The Common Market?
Communists?
The Trade Unions?
The World Situation?
Shops and Supermarkets?
(3) People have put forward different ideas for
tackling rising prices. Many times these ideas
mean giving something up. This card shows some
of the things we might have to put up with in
order to curb rising prices.

	Source	*In tables*

More taxation
More unemployment
Strict wage control
Less money for schools, roads and many other
things.
In order to tackle rising prices, which of these
would you be *least* willing to accept?

And which of these do you feel is second-
worst?

Now which of these would you be *most* willing
to accept in order to tackle rising prices?

	Source	*In tables*
(top question block)	BES74c	11.1–11.5, 12.1–12.4, (Figs.) 11.1– 11.4

(4) How important to you when you were
deciding about voting was the issue of rising
prices (taxation) (unemployment) – the most
important single thing, fairly important, or
not very important? — BES74b,c — 11.2, 12.4

(5) Suppose it were true, that you couldn't
keep unemployment down and keep prices
steady, which of the two would you rather
have? — BS69,70 — 10.1–10.7

(6) Suppose the government had to choose
between keeping everyone in employment and
holding prices steady, which do you think it
should choose? — BS70 — 10.1–10.7

B Assessment of competence or satisfaction

(7) How well do you think the last *Conserva-tive* Government handled the problem of rising
prices – very well, fairly well, not very well, or
not at all well? — BES74a,b — 5.1, 10.7, 12.4

(8) If the *Labour* Party had been in power at
the time how well do you think *they* would have
handled the problem of rising prices – very well,
fairly well, not very well, or not at all well? — BES74a,b — 5.1, 6.2, 10.7, 12.4, Fig. 6.4

(9) Some people say that prices will go on
rising *fast* no matter what *any* Government tries
to do. Would you say you agree or disagree? — BES74a, b,c — 5.1, 5.2, 8.3, 13.4

(10) Could you tell me the one which best
describes how you feel about the things you
can afford to have? (from very happy – happy
– satisfied – mixed feelings – not satisfied –
unhappy – very unhappy). — BES74b,c — 5.1, 5.2, 12.4

. . . and the standards and values of today's
society? — BES74b,c — 12.4

. . . and chances of getting ahead in Britain? — BES74b,c — 5.1, 5.2

(11) Do you think the recent Election campaign
generally gave the people the *facts* about the
problems facing the country? — BES74b,c

(12) Now we would like you to think about
how well the Conservative and Labour Parties
handle matters of taxation. Which of these
statements do you agree with?

	Source	In tables
The *Conservative* Party is *much* better		
The *Conservative* Party is *somewhat* better		
There is no real difference between the parties		
The *Labour* Party is *somewhat* better		
The *Labour* Party is *much* better	BES74b	11.3

(13) Now, using one of the statements on this same card, could you say which describes how you feel the parties handle the problem of unemployment? — BES74c — 11.3

(14) Which party do you think can best handle the problem of (unemployment) (prices and the cost of living) (maintaining prosperity)? (See Note 2.) — Gallup, various — 1.4

(15) Did the Labour Government make you better off, or worse off, or didn't it make much difference? — BS70 — 1.5

(16) Speaking more generally, how satisfied were you with the Labour Government's handling of Britain's economic affairs? — BS66,69, 70 — 1.5

(17) Some people say that if you have full employment you can't keep prices steady. That is, the country can have full employment or steady prices but not both. Do you think this is true? — BS69,70 — 9.1–9.5, 10.3–10.5

(18) We'd also like your opinion about handling the problems of unemployment and rising prices. Do you think that having everyone employed makes it more difficult to hold prices steady, or don't you think that having everyone employed makes it more difficult to hold prices steady? If you don't have an opinion on this, just say so. — BS70 — 9.1–9.5, 10.3–10.5

(19) Some people say that prices will go on rising no matter who's in power. Others think that the government can do a lot to check rising prices. Which do you think? — BS70 — 9.2, 9.5, 10.3, 10.4, 10.5, 13.4

(20) We are also interested in how well off people are these days. Do you think that what the Government does makes any difference to how well off you are? — BS63,66, 69,70 — 9.4, 9.5, 10.3–10.5

(21) Are you satisfied or dissatisfied with the Government's handling of the balance of payments? — NOP

(22) Do you approve or disapprove of the Government's record to date? — Gallup — 6.3

(23) How strongly to you approve or disapprove of the Government's handling of economic affairs? — Gallup — 6.3

(24) Is a person in (Sweden) (Germany) (Netherlands) (France) better off or worse off with respect to (the money he earns) (benefits like sickness pay, unemployment pay, health

	Source	*In tables*
service, pensions) (general standard of living)?	Gallup	3.3

(25) Which of these do you think is likely to be true of 19*??* (next year)? It will be a year of:
    rising prices or falling prices
    full employment or rising unemployment
    strikes and industrial disputes or industrial
        peace?
    taxes will rise or taxes will fall?
    economic prosperity or economic difficulty?

	Source	*In tables*
peaceful year or troubled year?	Gallup	3.2, 3.3, Fig. 3.3

(26) As far as you yourself are concerned, will
19*??* (next year) be better, worse, or about the

	Source	*In tables*
same as this year?	Gallup	Fig. 3.3

(27) Compared with other European countries,
do you feel that Britain is relatively well-
governed, relatively badly-governed, or is it

	Source	*In tables*
about average?	BES74c	4.7, 12.3, 12.4

(28) Compared with other European countries,
do you feel that British industry and commerce
is relatively well-run, relatively bad-run, or is it

	Source	*In tables*
about average?	BES74c	12.4

C Other policy questions

(29) Now we would like to ask what you think
about social services and benefits. Which of
these statements do you feel comes closest to
your own views?
    Social services and benefits have gone much
        too far and should be *cut back a lot*
    Social services and benefits have gone some-
        what too far and should be *cut back a bit*
    Social services and benefits should stay
        much as they are

	Source	*In tables*
More Social services and benefits are needed	BES74b,c	11.4, 12.1, 12.4

(30) There has been a lot of talk recently about
nationalisation, that is, the government owning
and running industries like steel and electricity.
Which of these statements comes closest to
what you yourself feel should be done? If you
haven't a view on this, just say so.
A lot more industries should be nationalised.
Only a *few more* industries should be nationalised.
No more industries should be nationalised but

	Source	*In tables*
industries that are now nationalised should	BES74a,	
stay nationalised	b,c	
Some of the industries that are now nationalised	BS63,64,	
should become *private companies*	66,70	12.1, 12.4, 14.4
(31) When you hear about a strike, are your sym-	BS64,66,	
pathies generally for or against the strikers?	69,70	14.4

(32) Do you feel that the government should
spend more on pensions and social services or

	Source	In tables
do you feel that spending for social services should stay about as it is now? (See Note 3.)	BS64,66, 69,70, BES74a	10.6, 14.4
(33) If the government had the choice between reducing taxes and spending more on social services, which should it do?	BS63,64, 69,70	10.6
(34) Now, using one of the answers on this card, what is your view about putting more money into the health service?	BES74c	11.2, 14.1– 14.3, Fig. 14.1

1. *Very important* that it *should* be done
2. *Fairly important* that it *should* be done
3. It doesn't matter either way
4. *Fairly important* that it *should not* be done
5. *Very important* that it *should not* be done

	Source	In tables
Establishing comprehensive schools in place of grammar schools throughout the country?	BES74c	14.1–14.3, Fig. 14.1
Sending coloured immigrants back to their own country?	BES74c	12.4, 14.1– 14.3, Fig. 14.1
Increasing state control of land for building?	BES74c	14.1–14.3, Fig. 14.1
Giving more aid to poorer countries in Africa and Asia?	BES74c	14.1–14.3, Fig. 14.1
Taking tougher measures to prevent crime?	BES74c	14.1–14.3, Fig. 14.1
Getting rid of pollution like dirt in the air and rivers?	BES74c	14.1–14.3, Fig. 14.1
Giving workers more say in the running of the place where they work?	BES74c	14.1–14.3, Fig. 14.1
Taking tougher measures to prevent Communist influence in Britain?	BES74c	14.1–14.3, Fig. 14.1
Spending more money to get rid of poverty in Britain?	BES74c	12.4, 14.1– 14.3, Fig. 14.1
Redistributing income and wealth in favour of ordinary working people?	BES74c	14.1–14.3, Fig. 14.1
Shifting power from London to the regions and local authorities?	BES74c	14.1–14.3, Fig. 14.1
More efforts to protect the countryside and our finest buildings?	BES74c	14.1–14.3, Fig. 14.1
(35) Now I would like to talk about trade unions and big business in this country. Do you think that the *trade unions* have *too much power* or not?	BS63,64, 66,69,70, BES74a,c	12.4
(36) Do you think that *big business* has *too much power* in this country or not?	BS63,64, 66,69,70 BES74a,c	12.4
(37) There has been a lot of talk about how to keep *wage increases* within *reasonable* and *fair* limits. Some think that a *voluntary* agreement between the government and the trade unions is the *most effective* way to do this. Would you agree or disagree?	BES74c	12.4

	Source	*In tables*

(38) Now, using one of the answers on this card,
how do you feel about attempts to ensure   14.1–14.3,
equality for women?   BES74c   Fig. 14.1
    Gone too far
    Gone a little too far
    Is about right
    Not quite far enough
    Not gone nearly far enough

And how do you feel about moves to go easier   14.1–14.3,
on people who break the law?   BES74c   Fig. 14.1

Next, how do you feel about the *right to show*   14.1–14.3,
nudity and sex in films and magazines?   BES74c   Fig. 14.1

How do you feel about people showing less   14.1–14.3,
respect for authority?   BES74c   Fig. 14.1

And how do you feel about recent attempts
to ensure equality for coloured people in   14.1–14.3,
Britain?   BES74c   Fig. 14.1

Next, how do you feel about the police being   14.1–14.3,
firm when they handle demonstrations, sit-
ins, and things like that?   BES74c   Fig. 14.1

How do you feel about the change of modern
methods in teaching children at school now-   14.1–14.3,
adays?   BES74c   Fig. 14.1

And how do you feel about the availability of   14.1–14.3,
abortion on the National Health Service?   BES74c   Fig. 14.1

How do you feel about the welfare benefits   14.1–14.3,
that are available to people today?   BES74c   Fig. 14.1

Finally, how do you feel about the reduction   14.1–14.3,
of Britain's military strength?   BES74c   Fig. 14.1

(39) What do you yourself feel are the most
important problems the government should do   BS63,   5.4, 10.3, 10.4,
something about? (See Note 4.)   69,70   Fig. 3.2

(40) What would you say is the most urgent
problem facing the country at the present time?   Gallup   Fig. 3.1

(41) Now that you know the outcome of the
election, what are the (good) (bad) things that
you think will happen as a result of the elec-
tion? (See Note 5.)   BES74b,c   Fig. 3.2

III Political and social background

A Partisan

(1) If a general election were held tomorrow,
for which party would you vote?/If there were
a general election tomorrow, which party   6.1, 6.3, 6.4,
would you support?   Gallup   7.3, Fig. 6.2

(2) Is there anything in particular that you
(like) (dislike) about the (Conservative)
(Labour) (Liberal) Party? (See Note 5.)   All   1.3, Fig. 3.2

(3) *Generally speaking*, do you think of

	Source	*In tables*
yourself as Conservative, Labour, Liberal (Scotland: Scottish Nationalist; Wales: Plaid Cymru), or what?	All	9.2, 10.2, 10.6, 13.5, 14.2, 14.3, (Figs.) 6.6, 14.1

If 'None' or 'Don't know' 'Refused'
Do you generally think of yourself as a little *closer* to one of the parties than the others? Which party?
Else
How strongly (party chosen) do you generally feel – very strongly, fairly strongly, or not very strongly?

(4) Which party did you vote for?	BS64,66, 70, BES74a, b,c	5.2, 8.2, 9.2, 9.5, 10.1, 10.4, 10.5, 10.7, 11.1, 11.3, 11.5, 12.2, 12.4, 13.4
(5) Would you say that you cared a great deal which party won the election or that you didn't care very much which party won?	All	9.2, 10.7
(6) Generally speaking, how much interest did you have in the recent election campaign: a good deal, some or not much?	BS64, 66,70, BES74a	9.2
(7) How much interest would you say you take in politics – a great deal, not much, or none at all?	BS63,69, BES74b,c	12.4
(8) How often would you say you talk about politics – often, sometimes, or only rarely?	BES74b,c	4.7, 12.4
(9) On some issues people feel that they understand the problems that are involved, while on others they tend to feel that they don't really understand what the problems are. How well would you say you understand the problems of rising prices – very well, fairly well or not very well?	BES74b,c	4.7, 12.4

B Occupational and personal

(10) Employment status, combining Current working Temporary unemployment Permanent unemployment or retirement	All	9.3, 10.3, 10.4
(11) Sex	All	4.7, 5.2, 9.4, 12.4
(12) Union membership, coded Respondent in union Other member of family in union No member	All	5.2, 9.4, 9.5, 10.3, 10.4, 12.4
(13) Income of family (See Note 6)	All	4.7, 5.2, 9.4, 9.5, 10.3–10.5, 12.4, 14.2
(14) Are/were you self-employed or did/do you work for someone else?	BES74a, b,c	12.4

	Source	In tables
(15) Head of household social grade (See Note 7)	All	4.7, 5.2
(16) Have *you* been unemployed or had great difficulty in getting a job in the last year or so?	BES74a, b,c	5.2, 12.4
(17) Has *anyone else in your family* been unemployed or had great difficulty getting a job in the last year or so?	BES74a, b,c	5.2, 12.4
(18) People talk about unemployment. Have you or anyone in your immediate family been worried about losing their job in the last year or so?	BS69,70	9.4, 10.3– 10.5, 13.2
(19) Do you work for a private firm or for a public organisation like the civil service, local government, or a nationalised industry?	BES74c	12.4
(20) Can you tell me whether this home is owned or rented?	All	4.7
(21) Region Scotland Wales North Midlands GLC South	All	5.2
(22) Year of birth	All	4.7, 5.2, 9.4, 9.5, 12.4, 14.2, 14.3
(23) Education, combined from various questions into: Academic further Other further, from academic school Other further, from ordinary school No further, but either attended academic school or left after minimum age Minimal education	All	5.2, 9.3, 9.5, 12.4, 14.2, 14.3
(24) Do you read a morning newspaper regularly?	All	4.7, 5.2
(25) How closely do you usually follow programmes about *politics* on *television* – very closely, fairly closely or just once in a while?	BES74a, b,c	4.7

Appendix notes

1 For alternate wordings from other sources, see Chapter 5, Figures 5.1 and 5.2.
2 The wording of these questions changes occasionally. Since 1969 'maintaining prosperity' has been replaced by 'the present economic situation'. 'Prices and the cost of living' before 1965 read 'keeping prices down'; in 1969 it once read 'preventing the cost of living from rising' and once 'controlling prices and incomes'. Before 1969 'unemployment' read 'full employment' and sometimes also 'full-time working'.
3 In 1970 the sample was split and some were asked two questions, one dealing with 'pensions' and the other with 'other social services'.
4 The detailed codes for this open-ended question are given in the ICPSR codebook for *Study of Political Change in Britain 1963–70*, vol. II, note 9.

5 For 1970 and before, the detailed codes are in *Study of Political Change in Britain*, vol. II, note 2. For 1974, both party likes and dislikes and election codes may be found in J. Spence, 'The British Election Study of October 1974 Methodological Report' (London: SCPR, 1975).
6 These data are normally collected by asking the respondent to estimate household income from personal knowledge. In 1974, respondents were given the choice of answering in weekly or monthly terms and stating whether their answers were pre-tax or post-tax. The division of households into three to five broad categories is fairly reliable; finer gradations are more risky.
7 Social grade is usually measured in six categories — upper and lower professional/managerial, skilled/supervisory non-manual, lower non-manual, skilled manual, and unskilled manual — plus a residual category.

References

Abelson, R. & Tukey, J. 1970. 'Efficient conversion of non-metric information into metric information'. In Tufte, 1970.

Abrams, M. 1973. 'Subjective social indicators'. *Social Trends.* 4, 35–50.

Abrams, M., Hinden, R. & Rose, R. 1960. *Must Labour Lose?* Harmondsworth: Penguin.

Almond, G. & Verba, S. 1965. *The Civic Culture.* Boston: Little, Brown.

Alt, J., 1978. 'Political business cycles in Britain, 1951–74'. Presented to the European Consortium for Political Research, Grenoble.

Alt, J. & Chrystal, A. 1978. 'Endogenous government behaviour'. Presented to the Conference on the Politics of Inflation, Unemployment and Growth. Stanford.

Alt, J., Crewe, I. & Särlvik, B. 1977. 'Angels in plastic: the Liberal surge in 1974'. *Political Studies.* 25, 343–68.

Alt, J., Särlvik, B. & Crewe, I. 1974. 'Issue positions, party identification, and party preferences'. Presented to the American Political Science Association.

1976a. 'Individual differences scaling and group attitude structures: British party imagery in 1974'. *Quality and Quantity.* 10, 297–320.

1976b. 'Partisanship and policy choice'. *British Journal of Political Science.* 6, 273–81.

Apter, D. (ed.) 1964. *Ideology and Discontent.* New York: Free Press.

Arcelus, F. & Meltzer, A. 1975. 'The effect of aggregate economic variables on congressional elections'. *American Political Science Review.* 69, 1232–9.

Arrow, K. 1951. *Social Choice and Individual Values.* New York: Wiley.

Atkinson, A. 1975. *The Economics of Inequality.* Oxford: Clarendon Press.

Axford, B. & Brier, A. 1976. 'Interpretations of the British crisis'. Presented at the Political Studies Association, Nottingham.

Bacon, R. & Eltis, W. 1976. *Britain's Economic Problem: Too Few Producers.* London: Macmillan.

Bain, A. 1970. *The Control of the Money Supply.* Harmondsworth: Penguin. Second edn 1976.

Ball, R. & Burns, T. 1976. 'The inflationary mechanism in the UK economy'. *American Economic Review.* 66, 467–84.

Barry, B. 1965. *Political Argument.* London: Routledge & Kegan Paul.

Barry, E. 1965. *Nationalisation in British Politics.* London: Cape.

Beckerman, W. (ed.) 1972. *The Labour Government's Economic Record 1964–1970.* London: Duckworth.

Beer, S. 1965. *British Politics in the Collectivist Age.* New York: Knopf.

Behrend, H. 1971a. 'What does the word "inflation" mean to you?' *Industrial Relations Journal.* 2, 35–45.

1971b. *Frames of reference for judging incomes.* Report to the Social Science Research Council.

1973. 'Attitudes to Price Increases and Pay Claims'. London: National Economic Development Office.

Behrend, H., Lynch, H. & Davies, J. 1966. *A National Survey of Attitudes to Inflation and Incomes Policy*. London: Edutext.

Behrend, H., Lynch, H., Thomas, H. & Davies, J. 1967. *Incomes Policy and the Individual*. London: Oliver & Boyd.

Ben-Gera, M. 1977. 'Short-term economic changes and individual voting behaviour'. Presented to the Canadian Political Science Association.

Blackaby, F. (ed.) 1978. *British Economic Policy 1960–74*. Cambridge: Cambridge University Press.

Bloom, H. & Price, H. 1975. 'Voter response to short-run economic conditions'. *American Political Science Review*. **69**, 1240–54.

Bowers, J., Cheshire, P. & Webb, A. 1970. 'The change in the relationship between unemployment and earnings increases: a review of some possible explanations'. *National Institute Economic Review*. **54**, 44–63.

Brittan, S. 1971. *Steering the Economy*. Harmondsworth: Penguin.

1973a. *Is There an Economic Consensus?* London: Macmillan.

1973b. *Capitalism and the Permissive Society*. London: Macmillan.

1976. 'The economic contradictions of democracy'. *British Journal of Political Science*. **6**, 129–60.

Brittan, S. & Lilley, P. 1977. *The Delusion of Incomes Policy*. London: Temple Smith.

Brunner, R. 1970. 'Data analysis, process analysis, and system change'. Presented to the American Political Science Association, Los Angeles.

Budge, I., Crewe, I. & Farlie, D. (eds.) 1976. *Party Identification and Beyond*. London: Wiley.

Budge, I. & Farlie, D. 1977. *Voting and Party Competition*. London: Wiley.

Burton, J. 1978. 'The demand for inflation in democracy'. Presented to the European Consortium for Political Research, Grenoble.

Butler, D. & Kavanagh, D. 1974. *The British General Election of February 1974*. London: Macmillan.

Butler, D. & Stokes, D. 1969. *Political Change in Britain*. London: Macmillan. Second edn 1975.

Cagan, P. 1956. 'The monetary dynamics of inflation'. In Friedman, 1956.

Campbell, A. 1972. 'Aspiration, satisfaction, and fulfilment'. In Campbell and Converse, 1972.

Campbell, A. & Converse, P. 1972. *The Human Meaning of Social Change*. New York: Russell Sage.

Campbell, A., Converse, P., Miller, W. & Stokes, D. 1960. *The American Voter*. New York: Wiley.

1966. *Elections and the Political Order*. New York: Wiley.

Carlson, J. 1975. 'Are price expectations normally distributed?' *Journal of the American Statistical Association*. **70**, 748–54.

Carlson, J. & Parkin, M. 1975. 'Inflation Expectations'. *Economica*. **42**, 123–38. Extended mimeo 73-05, 1973.

Chow, G. 1975. *Analysis and Control of Dynamic Economic Systems*. New York: Wiley.

Clegg, H. 1971. *How to Run an Incomes Policy and Why we Made Such a Mess of the Last One*. London: Heinemann.

Converse, P. 1958. 'The shifting role of class in political attitudes and behaviour'. In Macoby, Newcomb & Hartley, 1958.

1964. 'The nature of belief systems in mass publics'. In Apter, 1964.

1970. 'Attitudes and non-attitudes: continuation of a dialogue'. In Tufte, 1970.

Cook, C. & Ramsden, J. (eds.) 1973. *By-Elections in British Politics*. London: Macmillan.

Coombs, C. 1964. *A Theory of Data*. New York: Wiley.

Coombs, C. & Lingoes, J. 1975. 'Unidimensional unfolding in the presence of error: the dominant and the stochastic J-scale'. University of Michigan, mimeo MMPP 1975-1.

Costner, H. (ed.) *Sociological Methodology 1973–1974*. San Francisco: Jossey-Bass.

Crewe, I., Alt, J. & Särlvik, B. 1976. 'The erosion of partisanship in Britain 1964–75'. Presented to the Political Studies Association.

Crewe, I., Särlvik, B. & Alt, J. 1977. 'Partisan dealignment in Britain 1964–74'. *British Journal of Political Science*. **7**, 129–90.

Curtin, R. 1973. 'Index construction: an appraisal of the index of consumer sentiment'. In Mandell et al., 1973.

Curwen, P. 1976. *Inflation*. London: Macmillan.

Cutright, P. 1963. 'National political development: measurement and analysis'. *American Sociological Review*. **28**, 253–64.

Denison, E. 1967. *Why Growth Rates Differ*. Washington: Brookings.

Doreian, P. & Hummon, N. 1976. *Modelling Social Processes*. New York: Elsevier.

Dornbusch, R. 1976. 'The theory of flexible exchange rate regimes and macro-economic policy'. *Scandinavian Journal of Economics*. **78**, 255–75.

Downs, A. 1957. *An Economic Theory of Democracy*. New York: Harper & Row.

Dunkelberg, W. 1972. 'The impact of consumer attitudes on behavior: a cross-section study'. In Strumpel, Morgan & Zahn, 1972.

Evans, M. 1969. *Macroeconomic Activity: Theory Forecasting and Control*. New York: Harper & Row.

Eysenck, H. 1963. *The Psychology of Politics*. London: Routledge & Kegan Paul.

Fair, R. 1975. 'On controlling the economy to win elections'. New Haven: Cowles Foundation Discussion Paper 397.

Feige, E. & Pearce, D. 1976. 'Economically rational expectations: are innovations in the rate of inflation independent of innovations in measures of monetary and fiscal policy?' *Journal of Political Economy*. **84**, 499–522.

Forester, T. 1977. 'Do the British sincerely want to be rich?' *New Society*. **30**, 158–61.

Fosh, P. & Jackson, D. 1974. 'Pay policy and inflation: what Britain thinks'. *New Society*. **27**, 311–17.

Fox, A. 1975. 'Attitudes to immigration: a comparison of data from the 1970 and 1974 general election surveys'. *Journal of the Community Relations Commission*. **4**, 1–12.

Frey, B. 1976. 'Politico-economic models and cycles'. Konstanz Discussion Paper 83.

1978. 'The political business cycle: theory and evidence'. Presented to the Institute of Economic Affairs, London.

Frey, B. & Schneider, F. 1977. 'A politico-economic model of the United Kingdom'. Zurich, mimeo 7707.

Friedman, B. 1975. 'Rational expectations are really adaptive after all'. Harvard, mimeo.

Friedman, M. (ed.) 1956. *Studies in the Quantity Theory of Money*. Chicago: University of Chicago Press.

1968. 'The role of monetary policy'. *American Economic Review*. **58**, 1–17.

Goldthorpe, J., Lockwood, D., Bechhofer, F. & Platt, J. 1968. *The Affluent Worker: Political Attitudes and Behaviour*. Cambridge: Cambridge University Press.

Goodhart, C. & Bhansali, R. 1970. 'Political economy'. *Political Studies.* **18**, 43—106.

Harrop, M. 1977. 'Beliefs, feelings, and votes: the British case'. *British Journal of Political Science.* **7**, 301—20.

Harrop, M. & Zimmerman, G. 1977. 'The anatomy of the National Front'. University of Essex, mimeo.

Heald, G. 1971. 'Consumer confidence and its effect on expenditure for the British economy'. *Journal of the Market Research Society.* **13**, 224—37.

Heller, R. 1976. *The Naked Investor.* London: Weidenfeld.

Hibbs, D. 1974. 'Problems of statistical estimation and causal inference in time-series regression models'. In Costner, 1974.

1976. *Economic Interest and the Politics of Macroeconomic Policy.* Cambridge: MIT Center for International Studies.

1977. 'Political parties and macroeconomic policy'. *American Political Science Review.* **71**, 1467—87.

1978. 'The mass public and macroeconomic policy: the dynamics of public opinion toward unemployment and inflation'. Stanford, mimeo.

Hill, M., Harrison, R., Sargeant, A. & Talbot, V. 1973. *Men Out of Work.* Cambridge: Cambridge University Press.

Hirsch, F. and Goldthorpe, J. (eds.) 1978. *The Political Economy of Inflation.* London: Martin Robertson.

Jackson, D., Turner, H. & Wilkinson, F. 1972. *Do Trade Unions Cause Inflation?* Cambridge: Cambridge University Press.

Jay, P. 1973. 'How public spending defies the axe'. *The Times.* 19 December 1973, 19.

1974. 'Inflation, full employment and the threat to democracy'. *The Times.* 1 July 1974.

Jones, A. 1973. *The New Inflation.* Harmondsworth: Penguin.

Kane, E. & Malkiel, B. 1976. 'Autoregressive and nonautoregressive elements in cross-section forecasts of inflation'. *Econometrica.* **44**, 1—16.

Katona, G. 1975. *Psychological Economics.* New York: Elsevier.

Katona, G., Strumpel, B. & Zahn, E. 1971. *Aspirations and Affluence.* New York: McGraw-Hill.

King, A. 1968. 'Why all governments lose by-elections'. *New Society.* **21**, 413—15.

Kramer, G. 1971. 'Short-term fluctuations in US voting behavior 1896—1964'. *American Political Science Review.* **65**, 131—43.

Laidler, D. 1976. 'Inflation in Britain: a monetarist perspective'. *American Economic Review.* **66**, 485—500.

Liepelt, K. 1967. 'Anhänger der Neuen Rechtspartei'. *Politische Vierteljahresschrift.* **8**, 237—71.

Lindbeck, A. 1976. 'Stabilization policy in open economies with endogenous politicians'. *American Economic Review Papers and Proceedings.* **66**, 1—19.

Lipset, S. 1960. *Political Man.* Garden City: Doubleday.

Lipsey, R. 1960. 'The relation between unemployment and the rate of change of money wage rates in the United Kingdom 1861—1957: a further analysis'. *Economica.* **27**, 1—31.

Lipsey, R. & Parkin, M. 1970. 'Incomes policy: a re-appraisal'. *Economica.* **37**, 115—38.

Livingstone, J. 1974. *The British Economy in Theory and Practice.* London: Macmillan.

Maccoby, E., Newcomb, T. & Hartley, E. (eds.) 1958. *Readings in Social Psychology.* New York: Holt Rinehart & Winston.

McKean, R. 1976. 'Ethical codes and the invisible hand'. Presented to the International Political Science Association, Edinburgh.

Macrae, D. 1977. 'A political model of the business cycle'. *Journal of Political Economy.* 85, 239–64.

1978. 'The aggregate demand policy cycle'. Presented to the Conference on the Politics of Inflation, Unemployment and Growth, Stanford.

Madsen, H. 1978. 'Electoral outcomes and macroeconomic policies'. Presented to the European Consortium for Political Research, Grenoble.

Mandell, L., Katona, G., Morgan, J. & Schmiedeskamp, J. (eds.) 1973. *Surveys of Consumers 1971–72.* Ann Arbor: Institute for Social Research.

Marsden, D. & Duff, E. 1975. *Workless.* Harmondsworth: Penguin.

Marsh, A. 1976. 'The decline of deference'. Presented to the Political Studies Association, Nottingham.

1977. *Protest and Political Consciousness.* London: Sage.

Miller, M. 1976. 'Can a rise in import prices be inflationary and deflationary? Economists and UK inflation 1973–74'. *American Economic Review.* 66, 501–19.

Miller, W. 1977. *Electoral Dynamics.* London: Macmillan.

Miller, W. & Mackie, M. 1973. 'The electoral cycle and the asymmetry of Government and Opposition popularity: an alternative model of the relationship between economic conditions and political popularity'. *Political Studies.* 21, 263–79.

Milne, R. & Mackenzie, H. 1954. *Straight Fight.* London: Hansard Society.

Morrison, R. 1973. *Expectations and Inflation.* London: Lexington.

Mosley, P. 1976a. 'Towards a satisficing theory of economic policy'. *Economic Journal.* 86, 59–72.

1976b. 'Images of the floating voter, or, "the political business cycle" revisited'. University of Bath, mimeo.

Mueller, J. 1970. 'Presidential popularity from Truman to Johnson'. *American Political Science Review.* 64, 18–34.

Muth, J. 1961. 'Rational expectations and the theory of price movements'. *Econometrica.* 29, 315–35.

Myers, R. 1975. 'International comparisons of unemployment'. *The Banker.* 1257–62.

Niemi, R. & Weisberg, H. 1974. 'Single-peakedness and Guttman scales: concept and measurement'. *Public Choice.* 20, 33–45.

Nordhaus, W. 1975. 'The political business cycle'. *Review of Economic Studies.* 42, 169–90.

Oakeshott, M. 1973. 'Towards an economic theory of by-elections since the war'. In Cook & Ramsden, 1973.

OECD. 1973. *National Accounts Statistics 1962–73.*

Okun, A. 1975. *Equality and Efficiency: The Big Trade-Off.* Washington: Brookings.

Open University. 1975. *Statistical Sources Unit 11: Inflation.* Milton Keynes: Open University Press.

Parkin, M. 1970. 'Incomes policy: some further results on the determination of the rate of change of money wages'. *Economica.* 37, 386–401.

1974. 'The causes of inflation: recent contributions and current controversies'. University of Manchester, mimeo 7405.

1975. 'The politics of inflation'. *Government and Opposition.* 10, 189–202.

Parkin, M. & Sumner, M. (eds.) 1972. *Incomes Policy and Inflation.* Manchester: Manchester University Press.

Phillips, A. 1958. 'The relation between unemployment and the rate of change of money wage rates in the United Kingdom 1861–1957'. *Economica.* **25**, 283–99.

Prest, A. & Coppock, D. (eds.) 1974. *The U.K. Economy: A Manual of Applied Economics.* London: Weidenfeld.

Rabier, J.-R. 1974. *Satisfaction et Insatisfaction quant aux Conditions de Vie dans les Pays Membres de la Communauté Européenne.* Brussels: Commission of the European Community.

Robertson, D. 1975. 'A Theory of Party Competition'. London: Wiley.

Robbins, Lord et al. 1972. *Inflation: Economy and Society.* London: Institute of Economic Affairs.

Rose, D. 1972. 'A general error-learning model of expectation formation'. Presented to the Econometric Society, Budapest.

Rose, R. 1977. 'Governing and ungovernability: a sceptical inquiry'. University of Strathclyde, mimeo.

Rose, R. (ed.) 1974. *Electoral Behaviour: A Comparative Handbook.* New York: Free Press.

Rose, R. and Peters, G. 1978. *Can Government Go Bankrupt?* New York: Basic Books.

Runciman, W. 1966. *Relative Deprivation and Social Justice.* London: Routledge & Kegan Paul.

Rutledge, J. 1974. *A Monetarist Model of Inflationary Expectations.* Lexington: Lexington Books.

Särlvik, B. 1976. 'Mapping the party space: distances, evaluations and ideological prespectives'. Presented at the International Political Science Association, Edinburgh.

Schmalensee, R. 1976. 'An experimental study of expectation formation'. *Econometrica.* **44**, 17–41.

Shapiro, H. 1972. 'The index of consumer sentiment and economic forecasting: a reappraisal'. In Strumpel, Morgan & Zahn, 1972.

Sonquist, J. & Morgan, J. 1964. *The Detection of Interaction Effects.* Ann Arbor: University of Michigan Survey Research Center.

Sorrentino, C. 1972. 'Unemployment in the nine industrialised countries'. *Monthly Labor Review.* **95**, 29–33.

Spence, I., & Graef, J. 1974. 'The determination of the underlying dimensionality of an empirically obtained matrix of proximities'. *Multivariate Behavioral Research.* **9**, 331–41.

Stewart, M. 1972. 'The distribution of income'. In Beckerman (1972).

1977. *The Jekyll and Hyde Years.* London: Dent.

Stigler, G. 1973. 'General economic conditions and national elections'. *American Economic Review Papers and Proceedings.* **63**, 160–7.

Stimson, J. 1976. 'Public Support for American presidents: a cyclical model'. *Public Opinion Quarterly.* **40**, 1–21.

Stokes, D. 1966. 'Spatial models of party competition'. In Campbell et al., 1966.

Strumpel, B. 1972. 'Economic dislocation and societal discontent'. Presented to the American Sociological Association.

Strumpel, B., Morgan, J. & Zahn, E. (eds.) 1972. *Human Behavior in Economic Affairs.* New York: Elsevier.

Szmaragd, J., 1977. 'L'information économique des Français a travers les sondages d'opinion'. *Bulletin de l'Economie et des Finances.* **79**, 23–8.

Taylor, J. 1972. 'Incomes Policy, the Structure of Unemployment, and the Phillips curve'. In Parkin and Sumner, 1972.

Thomas, R. 1975. 'The effect of averaging components on the predictability of the index of consumer sentiment'. *Review of Economics and Statistics.* **57**, 84–91.

Treasure, J. 1972. 'Public opinion and knowledge'. In Robbins, 1972.

Trevithick, J. & Mulvey, C. 1975. *The Economics of Inflation.* London: Martin Robertson.

Tufte, E. 1975. 'Determinants of the outcomes of midterm Congressional elections'. *American Political Science Review.* **69**, 812–26.

1978. *The Political Control of the Economy.* Princeton: Princeton University Press.

Tufte, E. (ed.) 1970. *The Quantitative Analysis of Social Problems.* Reading, Mass.: Addison-Wesley.

Ulman, L. & Flanagan, R. 1971. *Wage Restraint: A Study of Incomes Policies in Western Europe.* Berkeley: University of California Press.

White, R. 1976. 'Slumpflation. The consumer response'. In *Consumer Change in the Mid-70s.* London: J. Walter Thompson

Whitney, C. 1976. 'West Germany's unemployed prove no rebels'. *International Herald Tribune.* 1 March.

Williamson, J. & Wood, G. 1976. 'The British inflation: indigenous or imported?' *American Economic Review.* **66**, 520–31.

Index